BIOGRAPHICAL ACCOUNT OF INDIAN ANTHROPOLOGISTS

About the Editors

Prof. P. C. Joshi (B.Sc. (Hons.), M.Sc., M.Phil., Ph.D. in Medical Anthropology , Delhi University) is the former Pro Vice-Chancellor and officiating Vice Chancellor of the University of Delhi. He has been the Head of the Department in Anthropology in the University of Delhi. He served as head of the Department of Anthropology in various institutions like HNB Garhwal University and Institute of Human Behaviour and Allied Sciences. He has organized fifteen Conferences included one in the University of Hue, Vietnam in the year 2010. He is the current president of the Society for Indian Medical Anthropology, Mysore and specializes in the fields of Medical Anthropology, Himalayan Anthropology, Antibiotic Resistance and Qualitative Research Methods. He has supervised around 30 Ph.D. and around 25 M.Phil. students.

Prof. Prasanna K. Nayak taught anthropology at Utkal University, Bhubaneswar, Odisha, India, for about 36 years and superannuated in June 2011 as professor and head of the Department of Anthropology. He served as director of the Scheduled Castes and Scheduled Tribes Research and Training Institute (SCSTRI) of the government of Odisha on deputation from 2000 to 2005, and established the Museum of Tribal Arts and Crafts in that institute. Post retirement (2012–2015), he became the chairman of the Nabakrushna Choudhury Centre for Development Studies (NKCDS), an Indian Council of Social Science Research (ICSSR)-sponsored interdisciplinary research institute in Bhubaneswar. He was an Alexander von Humboldt fellow at the Free University of Berlin and Baden Wuertemberg fellow at the University of Heidelberg. He also conducted and guided field researches in tribal areas of Odisha and published several articles based on intensive fieldwork in tribal Odisha. His books include *Blood, Women and Territory: An Analysis of Clan Feuds of the Dongria Kondhs* (1989) and *From Bondage to Rural Enterprise: A Situational Analysis and Participatory Strategies with the Bondo Highlanders* (2003).

BIOGRAPHICAL ACCOUNT OF INDIAN ANTHROPOLOGISTS

Edited by

P. C. Joshi

Prasanna K. Nayak

CONCEPT PUBLISHING COMPANY PVT. LTD.
NEW DELHI - 110 059

ISBN: 978-93-5594-168-8

First Published 2023

Published and Printed by

Concept
Since 1974

Concept Publishing Company Pvt. Ltd.
A/15-16, Commercial Block, Mohan Garden
New Delhi-110059 (India)
T : +91-11-41101460
E: publishing@conceptpub.com, W: www.conceptpub.com

Cataloging in Publication—Courtesy: D.K. Agencies (P) Ltd. <docinfo@dkagencies.com>

Biographical account of Indian anthropologists / edited by P.C. Joshi, Prasanna K. Nayak.
pages cm
Includes bibliographical references and index.
ISBN 9789355941688

1. Anthropologists—India—Biography. 2. Anthropology—India—History. I. Joshi, P. C., 1956- editor. II. Nayak, Prasanna Kumar, editor.

LCC GN20.B56 2023 | DDC 301.092254 23

Preface

The idea to compile biographies of Indian Anthropologists germinated in a casual meeting with Professor Prasanna Kumar Nayak on one of my visits to Bhubaneswar. Professor Nayak started talking about L.K. Mahapatra and his commitment and dedication to the cause of anthropology discipline. Gradually our discussion expanded to mention role played by stalwarts like L.P. Vidyarthi, D.N. Majumdar, N.K. Bose, S.C. Roy, K.P. Chattopadhyay and many other anthropologists who have devoted their life for the cause of anthropology. Both of us came to an agreement in our discussion that many of Indian Anthropologists who have made great contribution to the subject-matter of anthropology have remained unsung and obscure. There is acute shortage of comprehensive account on their life and works. It was decided there and then that both of us will identify notable Indian anthropologists and contact appropriate authors to write on various aspects of personal, social and professional dimensions of these anthropologists. We brainstormed and prepared a tentative list of prominent anthropologists of India and also tried to identify probable writers for them. A structure for the write up was prepared to facilitate uniformity in the content. The word limit for the write-up was also decided.

The structure of the write-up included information on Early Life consisting of education, family background, decision to take anthropology as a subject. This personal information was sought to familiarize readers to the circumstances leading to becoming of an anthropologist in India as anthropology is not a commonly known subject of study. Information was then asked on the early career which included doctoral work, influential teachers, major fieldworks and early career. The next section consisted of exploration of seminal contributions to the discipline of anthropology and its sub-branch reflected through research papers, books, talks, reports and awards. The administrative and institutional building efforts were then required to comprehend creative and constructive contributions of these stalwarts. Many of them are well known for going beyond the confines of teaching and research by playing an unfathomable part in establishing anthropology in India. Many anthropologists have crossed over the disciplinary boundary of anthropology and have meaningfully contributed to the enrichment of other disciplines as well. For anthropology as a holistic science of human, it is quite natural. The contribution of anthropologist beyond anthropology was therefore, included in the write-up by the authors. International collaborations were also closely examined as recorded in the biographical information. Finally, current or post-retirement activities were focused upon along with notable students of the anthropologists.

We initially wanted to include fifty anthropologists in this book but many important personalities are not finally part of the biographies because authors defaulted. We have therefore missed out on S.C. Dube, B.K. Roy Burman, S.C. Tiwari, I.J.S. Bansal, B.R.K. Shukla, S.S. Sarkar, R.K. Mutatkar, Makhan Jha, T.N. Pundit, A.C. Bhagwati and B.M. Das. No one can undermine the enriching and enduring contribution that these anthropologists have made in expanding the horizons of anthropology besides opening up new vistas and mentoring generations of anthropologists. Each one of the above is an institution in himself/herself. These and many more worthy anthropologists are needed to be covered and written about in the days to come. We were particularly not able to have a fair representation from the North-east part of India which have contributed very significantly to the subject matter of Indian anthropology.

India being an immensely diverse country presents the best academic and research opportunity for doing anthropology. While it has taken a long time to come out of the colonial ascendancy, it is maturing enough to subject Indian situation, challenges and opportunities to indigenously evolved theoretical framework. In general, Indian anthropologists have been diffident about the subject and seekers of anthropology in India. However, anthropology has now come of age and it can now swagger beaming with new found confidence in contributing originally to the great subject keeping in mind the great civilizational heritage and rich tradition of literature and scholarship which will guide the new anthropological theories routed in Indian philosophical traditions.

P. C. Joshi
Prasanna K. Nayak

Acknowledgements

We dedicate this book to the legend of Indian anthropology Professor Vinay Kumar Srivastava, Former Professor and Head of the Department of Anthropology; former Principal of Hindu College and Director of Anthropological Survey of India and Dr. Indrani Chattopadhyaya former Associate Professor of Archaeological Anthropology in University of Delhi, both of whom we lost while this book was being prepared. Dr. Chattopadhyaya contributed a chapter on the notable prehistorian of India Professor V. N. Misra and Professor Srivastava contributed three chapters in the book. In fact, Professor Srivastava was very closely associated with this project and helped not only by contributing chapters but also advised on the possible authors for biographies. He came to our rescue when we were not able to find a suitable person to write on Gopala Sarana in Lucknow. He volunteered to accomplish this task and came out with excellent biographical portrayal on the scholar.

We are thankful to Aditya Nayak for going through the biographical sketches and suggesting changes, where necessary. Thanks are due to Prof. Jatindra Kumar Nayak for his comments and helpful suggestions. Dr.Manas Ranjan Kar and Dr.Rajkishor Mahana compiling the biographical information that was needed for Professor Nayak.

We are grateful to all the authors who have put in hard work to write the chapters and some of them have gone to the extent of interacting with the acquaintances of the scholars covered in the book. Professor Abhijit Guha has been especially helpful in agreeing to write on three stalwarts. He, along with Professor Abhik Ghosh have been quite sensitive to the past of Indian anthropology and have to their credit many scholarly expositions of historical importance.

P. C. Joshi
Prasanna K. Nayak

Contents

List of Contributors

Abhijit Guha – ICSSR Senior Fellow, Institute of Development Studies, Kolkata. *Email:* abhijitguhavuanthro@rediffmail.com

Abhik Ghosh – Professor, Department of Anthropology, Panjab University, Chandigarh. *Email:* abhikg@gmail.com

Arbind Sinha – Director (Former), Mudra Institute of Communication, Ahmedabad. *Email:* arbind21@gmail.com

B.V. Sharma – Professor, Department of Anthropology, Central University of Hyderabad, Hyderabad, Telangana. *Email:* sharmabhallamudi@gmail.com

Dipak K. Midya – Professor, Department of Anthropology, Vidyasagar University, Midnapur, W.B. *Email:* dkmidya@gmail.com

Indrani Chattopadhyaya – Passed away in 2020. Associate Professor (Former), Department of Anthropology, University of Delhi, Delhi.
Email: indrani.hello@gmail.com

Kishor K. Basa – Vice Chancellor, Sriram Chandra Bhanja Deo University, Baripada, Odisha. *Email:* kishorkbasa58@gmail.com

Keya Pandey – Head, Department of Anthropology, Lucknow University, Lucknow. *Email:* keyapandey9@gmail.com

M.K. Singh – Professor, Department of Anthropology, University of Delhi, Delhi. *Email:* mksinghanthro@rediffmail.com

Manas Ranjan Kar – Monitoring and Evaluation Specialist, Finance Department, Government of Odisha. *Email:* manasranjan.kar@gmail.com

Nadeem Hasnain – Professor and Head (Former), Department of Anthropology, Lucknow University, Lucknow.
Email: nadeemhasnain@gmail.com

N. Sudhakar Rao – Professor (Former), Department of Anthropology, Hyderabad University, Hyderabad, Telangana. *Email:* nsrss@uohyd.ernet.in

Nabakumar Duary – Research Associate (Cultural), Anthropological Survey of India, Kolkata. *Email:* nabakumarduary@gmail.com

P. Venkatarao – Senior Professor, Department of Anthropology, Central University of Hyderabad, Telangana. *Email:* pvrao2000@gmail.com

Prashant Khattri – Assistant Professor, Department of Anthropology, Allahabad University, Allahabad. *Email:* Prashant_khattri2002@yahoo.co.in

R.K. Mutatkar – Chairperson (Former), Department of Anthropology, Savitribai Phule Pune University, Pune. *Email:* rkmutatkar@gmail.com

R.P. Mitra – Professor, Department of Anthropology, University of Delhi, Delhi. *Email:* rpmitra@gmail.com

R.R. Prasad – Director (Former), NIRD & PR, Hyderabad, Telangana. *Email:* rrprasad21@gmail.com

Rajkishor Mahana – Assistant Professor, Khallikote University, Behrampur, Odisha. *Email:* rkmahana@gmail.com

Rajan Gaur – Professor (Former), Department of Anthropology, Panjab University, Chandigarh. *Email:* rajan_gaur7@yahoo.com

Ranjana Ray – Professor (Former), Department of Anthropology, Culcutta University, Kolkata. *Email:* prof.ranjana.ray@gmail.com

Ravinder Singh – Associate Professor, Department of Medical Anthropology, IHBAS, Delhi. *Email:* medicalanthropology.ihbas@gmail.com

Rukshana Zaman – Assistant Professor, Department of Anthropology, IGNOU, New Delhi. *Email:* rukshanazaman@ignou.ac.in

S. Sumathi – Professor and Head (Former), Department of Anthropology, Madra University, Chennai. *Email:* sumathirajesh2004@yahoo.co.in

Sekh Rahim Mondal – Chair Professor (Former), Sociology and Anthropology, Center for Himalayan Studies, NB University, Siliguri.

Email: rahimanthronbu@yahoo.co.in

Subhadra Mitra Channa – Professor (Former) Department of Anthropology, University of Delhi, Delhi. *Email:* channa.subhadra@gmail.com

Sukant K. Chaudhury – Professor Department of Sociology, Lucknow University, Lucknow. *Email:* sukantkchaudhury@gmail.com

Sumahan Bandhopadhyay – Professor, Department of Anthropology, Vidyasagar University, Midnapore, West Bengal. *Email:* sumahan.b@gmail.com

Tilak Bagchi – Assistant Keeper (Former), Anthropological Survey of India, WR, Udaipur. *Email:* tilak_bagchi@yahoo.com

V.S. Sahay – Professor and Head (Former), Department of Anthropology, Allahabad University, Allahabad, U.P. *Email:* vijoysahay@gmail.com

Vinay Kumar Srivastava – Passed away in 2020. Director (Former), Anthropological Survey of India, Kolkata. *Email:* vks/@yahoo.com

Vineetha Menon – Professor and Head (Former), Department of Anthropology, Kannur University, Kannur, Kerala. *Email:* vineetha@gmail.com

Virendra Pratap Yadav – Assistant Professor, Department of Anthropology, MGIHU, Wardha. *Email:* virupy@gmail.com

Introduction

P.C. Joshi and *Prasqnna K. Nayak*

Anthropology, as the science of the human, has a unique place among academic subjects. At the meeting point of various subjects, a bridge between art, science, humanities and the economy, it looks at humans from a holistic perspective. Anthropologists are also a very peculiar class of scholars, ever looking for the extraordinary in the ordinary and mundane. The anthropological perspective *per se* champions cultural relativism, bottom-up viewpoints and experiential versions of reality. However, while the above remarks may reflect the universal characteristics of anthropology as an academic discipline, anthropology has also been shaped by the political and historical antecedents of the countries in which it is being practiced today. For example, for British anthropology, other cultures were a major source of the discipline's developent, but for Americans the 'others' were at close quarters, in North America itself, while for the British they were distant 'others', like Indians. Likewise, Indian anthropology is shaped by the circumstances that prevailed in nineteenth-century India. Indian anthropology is certainly a product of colonial efforts to understand Indian culture and society through an agenda of justifying the Empire's hegemonic structure. The study of customs, traditions, rituals and customary laws was undertaken so that the British could rule the country better, and anthropology, particularly ethnographic monographs, were used as British administrators' reference books.

Thus, the early ethnographies were written with a particular framework in mind, even those by Indian authors. By the beginning of twentieth century, Indian anthropologists had started writing on various themes, with Roy Bahadur Sarat Chandra Roy starting a journal (*Man in India*) exclusively to document anthropological writing on India, mostly by Indians. Well before this, in 1886, the Journal of the Anthropological Society of Bombay started publishing articles to capture the "physical, intellectual and moral development of man of the Indian Empire", as stated in the preamble to the Society's rules. This journal, which continued till 1936, published many articles, brilliant research papers and resource-rich monographs written by Indians. After India's first Department of Anthropology was launched at Calcutta University in 1921, many new departments were established to train students in the art and science of anthropology. Many other Indian anthropology students were trained in Europe and America. Interestingly, those Indian anthropology departments that came under American influence see what they do as cultural anthropology, while departments influenced by the British prefer to focus on social anthropology. Anthropology was an elitist specialization in its formative stages. The Indian scholars who first pursued anthropology were rich Parsees, well-known lawyers, Rai Bahadurs and other title-holders. The phenomenon of commoners doing anthropology only emerged after the first department of anthropology was opened in Calcutta University. Since then, anthropology has made great strides as an integrated science of man.

Studying anthropology and the process of becoming an anthropologist are, therefore, now generally well understood. But, why an individual prefers to study anthropology, make a career in it, contribute to its disciplinary knowledge, and help promotes the growth and development of the discipline institutionally are also topics of great anthropological interest. The personal backgrounds of individual anthropologists make it clear what made them become anthropologists. To understand and analyse the contributions of anthropology's most renowned practitioners, anthropologists are keen to know about their personal backgrounds and scholarly orientations and to discuss all this in academic forums, often quite critically. Knowledge didactics becomes metamorphosed into knowledge dynamics. The biographical accounts and evaluations of individual anthropologists strongly reflect the dynamics of the discipline over space and time. Bearing in mind these considerations, this biographical study offers personal accounts of a large number of home-country anthropologists of India as narrated by their own students and colleagues in the discipline.

As humans we study humans, and that is the speciality of the discipline of anthropology, notwithstanding its disciplinary approaches from the classical to the modern to the postmodern period. Anthropology, defined as the science of humans, emphasizes its holistic perspective. Man is seen in the round, not in the flat. In anthropology we study man over space and time. Anthropology started by studying human beings living in the interior of far-off countries around the world and producing ethnographies about them. The growing interest was in mapping out 'other societies' and 'other cultures' from micro- as well as macro— perspectives. Toeing the line of colonial-era anthropologists, Indian anthropologists in India even began their teaching by encouraging their students to conduct first-hand fieldwork among the so-called 'primitive tribes' inhabiting different parts of the interior of the Indian subcontinent. Methodologically fieldwork was taken for granted as the *sine qua non* for an anthropologist to establish herself or himself as an anthropologist, meaning that at the disciplinary level it was considered a field science, with the field as its laboratory.

During the course of their careers, anthropologists have made contributions to various fields and subfields of anthropology, as well as to interdisciplinary collaborative studies. It may be pointed out here, however, that there are some areas of interest which Indian social and cultural anthropologists share with Indian sociologists. In the fields of specialization, social anthropological, biological and archaeological studies are the most prominent. Some have contributed simultaneously to bio-cultural studies, psychology, linguistic anthropology, cultural ecology, gender studies, medical anthropology, applied and action anthropology, impact and change studies, development anthropology and quite a number of emerging areas of sub-disciplinary and sub-sub-disciplinary knowledge, where they have established their reputations. At the interdisciplinary level they have collaborated with sociology, history, political science, economics, genetics and the clinical sciences, as well as a host of other sciences and humanities. Some of them have shifted their interest from a focus on tribal societies *via* caste societies and peasant studies to examining urban societies, disaster risk assessment and reduction studies, environmental studies and studies of topics of nascent global interest. The discipline thus centres round the study of humans, their past, present and future. In sum, it is indeed a 'what it is not' discipline! Scholars in social-science and humanities disciplines often evince an interest in anthropological approaches to understanding and analysing man and society from various angles and have appreciated how this has enriched their disciplinary knowledge beyond their own boundaries. Field-based knowledge is an additional interest and source of data for them. The growing interest in anthropology and the emerging trends in anthropology speak of its value as a body of disciplinary knowledge that can be appropriated by all under the rubric of "Anthropology for All".

In India itself in the past hundred years, anthropology as a body of disciplinary knowledge started growing through an appreciation of how anthropological endeavours could bring to the fore the rich and fascinating Indian Adivasi cultures and their significance for understanding Indian society and politics. The prime ministers of newly independent India, as well as intellectuals with influence at the government policy-making level, in their conviction of the diversity of Indian Adivasi cultures, became so much concerned with them that they wholeheartedly patronized the establishment of academic and research institutions to carry out anthropological studies. Anthropological research was given a priority, and avenues started evolving for the teaching of anthropology as a recognized university discipline. Concern for tribes, tribal cultures, their populations and their rights as dignified citizens became one of the main issues, and special provisions were made for them in the Constitution of India. The irony was that, in order to integrate the Adivasis into the mainstream of Indian society, bring about change and development, and spur the implementation of economic development in rural areas, government policy and planning bodies sought out experts in the fields of economics and sociology, the macro-social science disciplines. Since, as usual, the government formally approved of the macro-disciplines, anthropology was relegated to a secondary position, as it was seen as less adaptable to macro-scale policy and planning. In the process, the dominance of macro-social scientists led to anthropological viewpoints being undervalued. Of course, compared to anthropology, economics and sociology as academic disciplines were better known, and scholars in these fields were numerically dominant over anthropologists. Nonetheless anthropologists as members of policy-making and planning bodies also had this interactive experience.

To meet these challenges, anthropologists need to pursue their studies at the micro-level from a comparative perspective, focus on their mission of excellence in interdisciplinary collaborative research studies, win the confidence of scholars of all hues, sciences and humanities, and record the open admiration of all those with an influence in promoting disciplinary knowledge in anthropology. Individual anthropologists need open minds to understand and analyse the facts, problems and issues concerned with and concerning humans and to fulfil the requirements to gain exposure to wider fields of knowledge. Especially, when it is broadly a matter of 'Man in India', Indian anthropologists must examine what has been done and what has not been done so far. Anthropologists pursuing studies in their respective specializations in different university departments of anthropology and research institutes in India must for practical reasons bear in mind the crucial and fundamental value of integrating the sorts of disciplinary knowledge we espouse in anthropology. At the same time, they must also forsake their own idiosyncrasies and personal squabbles over sub-disciplinary differences in order to raise the image of anthropology in India.

The present book, in providing biographical accounts of leading Indian anthropologists, examines the personal, academic, research and administrative aspects of their professional lives. It is evident that anthropology as a discipline was not a matter of choice for most Indian anthropologists as they generally came to its study accidently. However, once they had adopted this discipline, they enriched the subject with their research and erudite scholarship, thus contributing meaningfully to the knowledge base of the discipline.

1
A. Aiyappan

Vineetha Menon

Dr. A. Aiyappan was born on 5th October, 1905 at Pavaratty, Thrissur district in the Kerala State of South India. He hailed from the Izhava community, now recognised administratively as other backward community, about which he later came to do doctoral research and write a Ph.D. thesis. Although his family members did not follow the traditional caste occupation of the Izhavas and his childhood was far from affluent, having lost his father in an early age, he could pursue his education with the help of an elder brother. His family was interested in education and Aiyappan had the fortune of being exposed to classic texts in Sanskrit and literary works in Malayalam.His initial college education was in Palakkad Victoria College from where he got B.A. (Hons). Then he moved to Madras Presidency College and pursued post graduate education in Economics under the University of Madras. He got his Ph.D. in the year 1937 from the London School of Economics under Prof. Raymond Firth who was a student of Bronislaw Malinowski.

Aiyappan's career break in anthropology was as Superintendent in the Government Museum, Madras in the year 1929.He was the first Indian to be appointed to this post. He had been a research assistant with the Zoological Survey of India when the Madras Government Museum was being established. In the absence of qualified anthropologists, Aiyappan was appointed as anthropological assistant in the museum and got trained in anthropology. His training in anthropology under Diwan Bahadur K. Rangachari gave him good grounding in the anthropological techniques of fieldwork and got him exposed to anthropological monographs. In 1940 he rose in his career and became the Head of the Madras Museum and continued in that capacity till 1960. At around this time, he was also Visiting Professor in Cornell University (1954 to

1956).Thus, his career in anthropology began with a show casing of culture in museums during a historical time period when anthropology was closely linked to museums. However, he soon had opportunity to take up another major mission of his life, i.e. establishing teaching departments in anthropology. In 1958, as Professor and Head of the Department of Anthropology, Utkal University and from 1966-67, as Professor and Head of the Department of Anthropology, Andhra University, he turned his attention into teaching anthropology and advancing anthropological research for the knowledge it created and applying that for the benefit of the marginalised and society at large.

Dr. Aiyappan's Ph.D. thesis was published as "Iravas and Culture Change" in the Bulletin of the Madras Museum in 1945.As noted already, his Ph.D. was from the London School of Economics. He was attracted to this prestigious place by a chance reading of Malinowski's classic "The Argonauts of the Western Pacific". Being stationed in London gave him the opportunity to interact with many doyens of anthropology not only in the London School of Economics, but also those associated with the Royal Anthropological Institute, London. In his doctoral work, Aiyappan projected the idea that 'studies of contemporary culture contact will help the "historian of culture" understand better how customs were propagated in the past'. The influence of the Malinowskian idea that the process of diffusion is poorly understood in its contemporary manifestations and that an empirical study of contemporary diffusion is essential for understanding its past history is evident in this approach. The suggestion to study the Irava culture was given by Prof. Raymond Firth, himself a student of Malinowski. The topics dealt with in Aiyappan's thesis—propagation of culture and culture change—had been discussed in Prof. Firth's seminars where students from different parts of the world expressed their views. These crosscultural classroom discussions impressed upon Aiyappan the need for a microscopic study of caste practices from the focus of a single caste.The evaluation of cultural traits by functional analysis was insisted upon by Malinowski and by Firth. In the Preface to his book "*Iravas and Culture Change*" Aiyappan has acknowledged his debt to these two professors who gave him the necessary grounding in anthropological theory and method. It is interesting to note that although Aiyappan studied the Izhavas or Iravas, the community of his birth and upbringing, there was no reference to "auto ethnography", a term which became popular much later, under "post-modern" influence. Even if the term had been in use in those days, it is doubtful if Aiyappan would have used it to refer to his work. He did not highlight subjectivity as a significant factor in the study of culture or culture change. On the contrary, he emphasized "a scientific study of society" following the footsteps of Malinowski. He also subscribed to an ethnological approach to ancient Indian culture. In this he was appreciative of the works of Das, Elwin, von Furer-Haimendorf, Chattopadhyay, Ghurye, Grigson, Karve, Majumdar, Nirmal Bose, and Rai Bahadur Roy.

His early career was as research assistant in Zoological Survey of India and later with the Madras museum in various capacities. Thus show casing material culture and zoological specimens was an early career interest which soon gave way to study of culture change and setting up institutions for teaching and research in anthropology.

Aiyappan's Ph.D. thesis submitted to London School of Economics in 1937 under the title "Culture Change in South-western India" was published in book form as "*Iravas and Culture Change*" in the Bulletin of Madras Museum in 1945. A study of the same village where he conducted Ph.D. fieldwork after almost three decades in 1965 was published as "Social Revolution in a Kerala village – A study in Culture Change". This study was an enquiry into the impact of social reform movement on the Irava caste. An earlier book titled "*Social and Physical Anthropology of Nayadis of Malabar*" published in 1937, the very same year he submitted his Ph.D. thesis, was a study of the lowly untouchable community that adopted begging for a livelihood.

In 1948 he published the "Report on the Socio-economic Conditions of the Aboriginal Tribes of the Province of Madras". This report is used in the training of administrative officers in South India. In 1963 he wrote on some social aspects of the recent race mixture in Kerala and on Prehistoric India. In a radio talk delivered by him in 1952, Aiyappan tried to present the human history of Deccan over a vast stretch of time and space to highlight that "mankind even in this small area of the Deccan is an amalgam and that the communal and religious cleavages which now loom so large are just superficial cracks in its very thin crust" (Aiyappan 1952 in Mohanty, U. (ed.), 1988:17). His writings on voluntary death and confession among some Hindu communities as possible survivals of Jainism, sociology of avoidance comparing Orissa and South India, fraternal polyandry in Malabar, meaning of tali rite, sociology of friendship, etc. try to offer explanations for these customs and practices. Another set of his writings are on various dimensions of marginal existences like racial minorities, ex-slave caste, beggary and so on. Yet another group of publications of Dr. Aiyappan deal with applied dimensions of anthropology. In this group of literature, problems of "primitive" tribes, anthropology and tribal welfare, experiment in the rehabilitation of a beggar caste, applied anthropology, anthropology and practical affairs, etc. find a place. In the article on "Anthropology and practical affairs", Aiyappan urges that "the difference between the tribesmen and the rest of the Indians is mostly cultural, but even in this respect, we share with them hundreds of common traits. This is point on which the Indian public and the educationists, teachers and authors of school books should be educated. It is a basic background knowledge which should be part of the mental equipment of the social workers and others who have anything to do with the tribesmen"(in Mohanty (ed.)1988 : 186).Teaching aids form yet another category of Aiyappan's writings. Handbook of Museum Techniques is an example.Thus the articles and other publications of Dr. Aiyappan are testimonies to the multifaceted responsibilities that he took upon seriously in the course of his professional journey. In a section on "Academic anthropology and welfare work". Aiyappan addresses the question whether scientific objectivity would be fogged and one's value as social scientist would suffer if anthropologist gets involved in tribal affairs. His answer is very clear on this, he says, "…it is possible to be scientific and at the same time, love your neighbour……; the anthropologist has his human right and also his scientific right to stand up for the rights of the tribesmen" (in Mohanty (ed.), 1988: 187).

The book "*The Personality of Kerala*" published in 1982 is a collection of lectures delivered in the University of Kerala as Tagore Lectures. Examining the commonalities and differences between Tamil Nadu and Kerala, he concludes that "for the best part of their long history, Kerala and Tamil Nadu shared a common language and culture, but relatively the recent development of divergencies has crowded out memories of the common heritage" (Aiyappan, 1982:4). The discussion on early history of matriliny in Kerala and how matriliny affects the personality structure of Kerala presents interesting thoughts that stem from a comparison of the two regions' ethnic and cultural compositions and histories.

The posthumously published book titled "*Ecology, Economy, Matriliny and Fertility of Kurichiyas*" is perhaps one of the most noted contributions. The painstaking fieldwork for this book was started by Aiyappan in the 1940s and continued for four decades. The work was completed and published by K. Mahadevan in 1990 after the demise of Aiyappan in 1988.

"*Bharathapazhama*", a book in Malayalam also deserves special mention among his contributions.

Dr. Aiyappan was recipient of the Sarat Chandra Roy Gold Medal of the Asiatic Society of Bengal.

He was also Honorary Fellow of the Royal Anthropological Institute, London.

Dr. Aiyappan is to be recorded in history undoubtedly, as an institution builder with great administrative acumen and vision. The Departments of Anthropology in Utkal University and Andhra University were established and developed under his visionary leadership as Head of the Department. In 1970, he became a sponsoring founder of the Centre for Development Studies, Thiruvananthapuram.He was also a sponsoring founder and Director of the Department of Rural Welfare of Odisha. He undertook the reorganisation of Odisha museum as a multipurpose museum with natural history, mining and geology and anthropology galleries. As special officer to organise tribal research and training centre in Kerala, Dr. Aiyappan had a major role in the setting up of KIRTADS, the Kerala Institute for Research, Training and Development Studies. Dr. Aiyappan also made known his administrative experience in his capacity as the Vice Chancellor of Kerala University from 1969 to 1972. He was associated with the Kerala State Planning Board as Chairman of the Task Force on the welfare of the backward classes and with the Union Planning Commission as member of the steering committee on social welfare. With profound knowledge and interest spanning from prehistoric archaeology on the one hand and social and cultural changes on the other and an interesting mix of career opportunities that came his way, Dr. Aiyappan had a rich cross-cultural experience, both at the theoretical and empirical levels, the benefit of which he brought into his administration and institution building.

In the two decades of work as Director of a premier museum in India, Dr. Aiyappan had opportunity to express his integrative approach to culture. Prehistoric and historic archaeology and history, environmental factors, demography, linguistics, folklore, all aided Aiyappan in his work. His reflections and hypotheses in these areas have enriched those disciplines also. Economics and political science benefited from his discussions on consumer culture, impacts of outmigration in a community and village, political leadership and other issues that shape cultural dynamics. Aiyappan believed in the urgent need for applied anthropology. His contributions to trigger public discourses through publications in newspapers, delivering lectures, radio talks, writing review articles and serving in different committees for State and Central Governments are contributions that went beyond anthropology. His contributions for improving administration, social work, industry, public health and medicine are noted.

International Collaborations

Dr. Aiyappan's international collaborations were through the London School of Economics and the Royal Anthropological Institute, London and in the course of his career with Zoological Survey of India and the Madras Museum. Notable among them were undoubtedly, Bronislaw Malinowski and Raymond Firth. Although no formal collaborations were forged, he could associate with Max Gluckman, Meyer Fortes, S.F. Nadel, Paddington , Morris Ginsberg, Karl Mannheim, A.C. Haddon, Seligman, etc.

Dr. Aiyappan passed away on 28th June, 1988.

REFERENCES

Aiyappan, A.1945. "Iravas and Culture Change" in the *Bulletin of the Madras Museum*.

Aiyappan, A. 1965. *Social and Physical Anthropology of Nayadis of Malabar.*

Aiyappan, A. 1948. Report of the socio-economic conditions of the aboriginal tribes of the Province of Madras. Chennai: Government Press.

Aiyappan, A. and Satyamurthy, S.T. (eds.), 1960. *Handbook of Museum Techniques*. Chennai: Government Press.

Aiyappan, A. 1967. Voluntary Death and Confession among certain Hindu Communities: Possible Survivals of Jainism. Paper presented at the Conference on Medieval History, Andhra University.

Aiyappan, A. 1968.Sociology of Avoidance: Orissa and South India Compared. L.K. Ananthakrishna Iyer Birth Centenary Endowmnent Lectures, Madras University.

Aiyappan, A. 1971. "Sociology of Friendship", In Dr. V. Raghavan Shashtyapurthi Felicitation Volume, Andhra Pradesh: Kuppuswami Sastri Research Institute, pp. 242-261.

Aiyappan, A. 1981. "Beggary in India: An experiment in the Rehabilitation of a Beggar Caste", *International Journal of Asian Studies*, Vol. I, pp. 21-51.

Aiyappan, A. 1982. *The Personality of Kerala*. Trivandrum: Valsa Printers.

Aiyappan, A. 1985. *Bharathapazhama*. Calicut: Mathrubhumi Printing and Publishing Co. Ltd.

Aiyappan, A. 1988. "Tribal Situation—Southern India", in Dr. U.C. Mohanty (edited), *Tribal Culture and Tribal Welfare*, Selected papers by Dr. A. Aiyappan, Chennai: University of Madras. pp. 1-11.

Aiyappan, A. 1988. "The Deccan Plateau: Ethnology", in Dr. U.C. Mohanty (edited), *Tribal Culture and Tribal Welfare*, Selected papers by Dr. A. Aiyappan, Chennai: University of Madras. pp. 12-17.

Aiyappan, A. 1988. "Applied Anthropology", in Dr. U.C. Mohanty (edited), *Tribal Culture and Tribal Welfare*, selected papers by Dr. A. Aiyappan, Chennai: University of Madras. pp.167-174.

Aiyappan, A. 1988. "Anthropology and Practical Affairs", in in Dr. U.C. Mohanty (edited), *Tribal Culture and Tribal Welfare*, selected papers by Dr. A. Aiyappan, Chennai: University of Madras. pp. 185-191.

Aiyappan, A. and K. Mahadevan. 1990. *Ecology, Economy, Matriliny and Fertility of Kurichiyas*. New Delhi: B.R. Publishing Corporation.

Aiyappan, A. 1992. "The Paniyas, an ex-slave tribe of South India". *Centenary Souvenir (1851-1951)*, Chennai: Government Museum.

2
Biraja Shankar Guha

Nabakumar Duary

In early fifteenth century Ramanath Guha Majumdar, one of the ancestors of Dr. Biraja Sankar Guha moved out of Daulatpur in Khulna district of undivided Bengal, i.e. now in Bangladesh. Joysankar Guha, grandfather of Dr. Guha was an eminent lawyer, who also served the Ahom Raja as law adviser and permanently settled in Guwahati in 1824. Biraja Sankar was born on 15th August, 1894, in a respectable and renowned Kayastha family at the then Shillong, capital of Assam. His nick name was Makhan. He was the second child among the ten children of Srimati Khirodabala and Rai Bahadur Abhayshankar, a renowned civilian. Khirodabala was a disciple of Swami Vivekananda and once Swamiji met her in the residence, Guha Lodge, at Pan Bazar in Guwahati.

Biraja Sankar inherited the spirit of learning and dedication from his father and grandfather. He showed signs of his intellectual calibre and keenness from his early childhood and acquired distinction in his academic career in school and college. In February 1908 Biraja Sankar passed Prabesika Examination securing first position from the Cotton Collegiate School, Guwahati. In January, he passed the Intermediate Arts from City College and was placed in first division. In January 1912, he passed Bachelors of Arts with Honours in Philosophy along with Sociology from Presidency College and passed Master of Arts in Mental and Moral Philosophy along with Sociology from the University of Calcutta in January 1915. Guha joined as lecturer in Sociology and Philosophy in Bangabasi College Kolkata and later joined in Cotton College, Guwahati for two and half months during 1915-16. The names of the principal teachers were Dr. A.N. Mukerjee, Dr. Brajendranath Seal in post graduate level. Dr. Guha frequently wrote letters (in Bengali) to his mother in Guwahati and shared about his education and some events or incidents in India and abroad. He wrote last letter to her on

9.8.1961 from Europe. His mother passed away at the age of 102 years.

Biraja Sankar showed interest to know about Archaeology as well as to know about the indigenous people. Later he took interest in Anthropology. He became in close contact with some luminaries like his mentor Sir Brajendranath Seal, Sir Asutosh Mukhopadhyay, Sir Jagadish Chandra Bose and a few other stalwarts. Brajendranath Seal recommended Guha for a research scholarship of the Government of Bengal in 1917. His first anthropological fieldwork was among the Khasis of Assam.

Dr. Guha had married twice, first in 1920 to Labanya Prabha Das. They had one son Aloke Sankar. After the sudden demise of Labanya Prabha, he married Srimati Uma Bose on 28th May, 1931. She was the daughter of Sudhansumohan Bose, MA (Cantab), Bar-at-Law, Member Public Service Commission, Bengal and granddaughter of Ananda Mohan Bose, who was the founding member of Indian National Congress. They had two sons Bhaskar Sankar and Rupal Sankar and one daughter Alta. Dr. Guha resided in several places in India along with family members at 10, Hungerford Street, Kolkata-16, Kaizer Cassel at 64 Cantonment, Varanasi during his service life where some times Verrier Elwin was also staying. One day Sarvapally Radhakrishna visited his place and gifted his book Indian Philosophy on 7th January, 1942. After his retirement Dr. Guha stayed at Banasree, Purulia Road, Ranchi from 1955 to October 1961.

Biraja Sankar was interested by the work of Professor R.B. Dixon of Harvard University. He became Hamenway Fellow in 1920 and obtained A.M. in Anthropology with distinction in 1922 from Harvard University. His teachers were Professor E.A. Hooton, Professor R.B. Dixon and Professor A.M. Tozzer and studied different branches of Anthropology. B.S. Guha was awarded Ph.D. by the Harvard University for his thesis "The Racial Basis of Caste System in India" in 1924. His thesis was supervised by Professor R.B. Dixon. Dr. Guha was the fourteenth recipient of Ph.D. in the discipline of Anthropology from the Harvard University. He was the first career Anthropologist having his Doctorate from the Harvard University in the United States. Between 1934 and 1935, he was on study leave to Europe where he studied the latest trends in anthropological research with Professor Arthur Keith of Royal College of Surgeons, Professor Elliot Smith, Professor Rivet and few others.

His scholastic aptitude earned him a number of fellowships from India and abroad. Like two years research fellow in Anthropology in India; carried on ethnological investigation on behalf of the American Bureau of Ethnology during the summer of 1921. He studied foreign languages like German and French. Dr. Guha was a Research Associate in the Natural

History Museum, Boston and New York; Museum of Anthropology, Colorado and Bureau of Ethnology of the Smithsonian Institute, Washington in 1922-24 and carried out field investigations in Red Indian Reservations of Colorado and New Mexico. The Harvard University provided him with a Teaching Assistant in Anthropology from 1923-24. In 1924 Dr. Guha read a paper in Anthropology Section of the American Association for the Advancement of Science by special invitation. The Harvard University awarded him the Winthrop Scholarship in 1925.

Dr. Guha was aware of the strength of fieldwork in anthropological studies. His experience in field investigation was phenomenal. He continued the anthropological fieldwork from student life (since 1920) up to his service life in the Zoological Survey of India (June 1927), Office of the Census Commission (on deputation, 1930-33), Anthropological Survey of India (December 1945 to July 1954), as well as during retirement assigned job in Social Education Organiser's Training Centre (SEOTC), at Ranchi and Bihar Tribal Welfare Institute (March, 1956 to March, 1959).

Dr. Guha's first fieldwork was among the Khasis of the erstwhile Assam in 1920. During 1926-27 he was deputed to go to Burma border for the abolition of human sacrifice in Naga Hills. He did fieldwork among indigenous tribes of Colorado and New Mexico. He studied from time to time on excavated remains of human and animal skeletons in Mohenjodaro, Harappa, Maski and other prehistoric sites of India with Lt. Col. B.R. Seymour Sewell between 1927 and 1932. He also conducted field investigation on racial structure of the population in Central, Western and Southern India and few selected areas in the North and the East India during 1930-1933. He studied the tribal populations of remote areas like Lepcha of Darjeeling 1936-38, Jaunsar Bower in the then Eastern Simla Hills (1947), Andaman and Nicobar Islands (1948 and 1949), the erstwhile Travancore, Cochin State (1949-50), the then Naga Hill (1950-51). Dr. Guha also investigated the life and culture of other tribal groups like the Nagas, Khasis, Garos, Riangs, Kaipengs, Uchai and the Rankhols of North-East region. In 1950 he also conducted field survey in two Bengali refugee settlements, namely Azadgarh in Tollygunge, 24 Parganas (now in Kolkata) and Jirat in Hooghly district in West Bengal.

However, one of the important fieldworks of Dr. Guha was among Abor in Assam. He received a proposal under consideration in collaboration with the Government of Assam for carrying out a systematic anthropological survey on Abor tribe in the Dadiya Frontier Tract in Assam. He organised multidisciplinary research team number of times to work among the Abors in 34 villages during 1948, 1949 and 1952. The team had to encounter several fieldwork hazards. He himself stayed in camps along with team members. Dr. Guha collected data and helped others for collection of data through demonstrations. In the evenings, he would play music for the villagers over record player. He also joined in local cultural activities and festivities. The Department of Anthropology (Anthropological Survey of India) also participated in the exhibitions in the field sites. Photographers had taken thousands of important photographs, which illustriously documented the daily life, culture and surrounding nature of the Aboras as well as activities of the researchers from camp to study area. Perceiving the importance of music in the lives of the tribals, Dr. Guha also documented it on double-sided gramophone disc and also made two silent documentary films, namely "Abor of NEFA" and "Abor Dance".

On coming back to India he became lecturer in Physical Anthropology at the University of Calcutta in 1926. Lt. Col. B.R. Seymour Sewell, Director of Zoological Survey of India (ZSI), Kolkata, took permission from the Government of India for appointing a trained Physical Anthropologist in ZSI. Then Dr. Guha left Calcutta University and joined as Anthropologist and sectional Officer-in-charge in the newly opened Anthropology Section of the Zoological Survey of India, Kolkata in June 1927 for taking adequate and proper care of valuable ancient human skeletal remains and other anthropological collections. During 1927-28, he studied primitive tribes of Travancore and Cochin, namely the Kadars, the Irulas and the Paniyans. Their spirally curved hair, dark skin colour, broad flat nose and averted lips led him to his important discovery of the Negrito racial strain in the sub-stratum of Indian population. Dr. Guha took part in scientific expedition, and sent by the Government of India to Central and Eastern Kaffirstan in 1929 along with Professor Morgentierne. Dr. Guha served with the Census Commission of India on deputation in 1931. Anthropological measurements were taken on 34 population groups on each individual and on 18 different characters besides a large number of observations including the tints of skin, eye and hair colour. His epoch-making work in the Census of 1931 and his concept of Indian races brought him instant world fame. Dr. Guha was suggested the following main six-fold classifications of the Indian population like the Negrito, Proto-Australoid, Mongoloid, Mediterranean, Western Brachycephalic and the Nordic.

Guha's contributions cover a great depth and included various aspects of anthropology. He had published number of research articles on primary field data on different subject matters, like. race, racial origins, racial affinities, racial ethnology, human skeletal remains, stone age, basketry, progress and development of anthropology, culture contact, nation building, tribal welfare, social welfare, aborigines and administration, refugee problems, biography of Thakkar Bappa, etc. In fact, he had touched almost all major facets of Indian anthropology. He published these individually and with co-authors or joint authorship in edited books, memoirs, academic journals and bulletins in India and abroad between 1926 to 1962.

Guha published a book entitled Racial Elements in the Population in 1944. In 1950 published a book entitled *Bharatiya Jati Parichaya* in three languages, namely, Bengali, Hindi and Tamil by Government of India. Besides, Dr. Guha jointly edited one book entitled Essays in Anthropology, presented to Rai Bhadur Sarat Chandra Roy (with co-editors J.P. Mills, K.P. Chattopadhyay, D.N. Majumdar and A. Aiyappan, 1942). The names of the co-authors of his papers are, Lt. Col. R.B. Seymour Sewell in a number of papers, primarily on skeletal biology of different ancient populations. and his joint authorship with J.P. Mills, P.C. Basu, S.S. Sarkar, A.K. Mitra and H.K. Bose. Dr. Guha's papers published in following journals like *Man in India, Vanyajati, Science and Culture, Anthropos, Nature, Journal of Asiatic Society, Bulletin of the Department of Anthropology, Sociological Bulletin, Social Welfare in India, Bulletin of the Bihar Tribal Research Institute and Mankind Quarterly*. As an Anthropologist he studied almost all branches of anthropology and sub-disciplines of Anthropology. Regarding tribal administration his brilliant report to the Governor General of India in 1949 is an eye-opener and it is very relevant even today.

Some of the important research papers of Dr. Guha are, A comparative study of the human crania excavated at Adittanallur (1927), Negrito racial strain in India (1927), Some anthropological problems in India (1928 a,b), Report on bones excavated at Nal (1929), The racial types and social institutions of the Kaffi and Khalash tribes in Central and Eastern Kaffistan (1929), Racial affinities of the peoples of India, (Census of India, 1931). Human remains, in Mohenjo-Daro and the Indus Civilization (1931a,b), Report on the human relics recovered by the Naga Hills-Burma expedition for the abolition of human sacrifice during 1926-27 (1931), A note on somatic characters of the Brahmans and other groups of the Kannada people (1932), New light on the Indus Valley Civilization (1936), An outline of the racial ethnology of India (1937), The racial composition of the Hindukush tribes (1938), Human cultures in India during the stone age (1941), Racial elements in the population (1944), Progress of anthropological research in India (1946), Aboriginal population and their place in the national life of India (1949), Indian aborigines and their administration (1951), Tribal welfare in India (1955),

The role of social sciences in nation building (1958), Race and nationality (1959), Studies in social tensions among the refugees from Eastern Pakistan (1959) and so on. On 13 April, 1944, he delivered a radio talk on Culture Contact which was broadcast by All India Radio, Lucknow.

Dr. B.S. Guha's contributions in the field of anthropology is great. He is famous for his contribution in race study and racial classification of the people of India. In Guha's own words those are racial origin, racial affinities or racial elements. He is widely recognized for his skill and mastery in anthropometric techniques at his time as he was an author of Techniques Somatometry for the International Committee of Standardization of Anthropometric Measurements. However, he was criticized for his racial classification by his teacher Professor Arthur Keith and his junior colleague and physical anthropologist Professor Sasanka Sekhar Sarkar. The concept of race has become controversial all around the world, yet if applied appropriately, keeping in mind the extent of intermixing of population; it can still serve as a marker of human types (Bhattacharya and Sarkar, 1996: i). People are recognising Dr. Guha for his works and appreciate him of his zeal, pertaining to anthropology, have been made by the scholars, both from India and abroad. In this context Dr. B.R. Ambedkar wrote-Guha's explanation of racial classification in India is more authentic than Risley's work. Professor D.P. Mukherjee wrote Guha's objective reports will remain as treasure in the annals of Indian anthropology for ever.... (1996:74) and Asok K. Ghosh wrote that it is perhaps only Guha who had made efforts to work simultaneously on both modern and ancient populations. Further works may be helpful for greater confirmation, with application of modern sophisticated techniques (1996:15-33).

Dr. Guha was given a special honorarium of Rs. 750 by the Governor General Council in recognition of the Anthropological work done by him in connection with the Census of 1931. The Asiatic Society awarded him the Anandale Memorial Gold Medal in Anthropology for his distinguished work in Asiatic Anthropology in 1942 for conspicuously important contributions to the study of Anthropology in Asia. He had received this medal from the Dr. Shyamaprasad Mookherjee, President of the Royal Asiatic Society of Bengal. He addressed "...kindly accept it with the Societies' and my heartily congratulations. I thank you very much for coming over Benaras to receive the medal personally this evening" (1943:7-8). Dr. Guha gave a course of Lecturers in Anthropology to the ICS probationers at Dehra Dun at the invitation of Sir Theodore Tasker in 1944. A short biographical sketch was included in the third edition of the International Biographical Encyclopaedia in 1945 as a leading scientist of India.

Dr. B.S. Guha had the vision to establish a separate institution which should devote itself exclusively for the co-ordinate research in various aspects of anthropology in the nation. Therefore, he had submitted a proposal to the Government on the 30th December, 1944 for the establishment of an independent Anthropology Department. This proposal was supported by Dr. R.B. Seymour, Director of ZSI. The scheme of research in the Survey right after it was founded reads:

- To study tribes and other communities that forms the population of India both from the biological and cultural points of view;
- To study and preserve human skeletal remains, both modern and archaeological; and
- To collect samples of arts and crafts of the tribes in India.

On 11th May, 1942 the Zoological Survey of India was shifted from Calcutta to Varanasi, Kaizer Cassel at 64 Cantonment on the bank of river Varuna for its safety during Second World War. The nucleus of the Anthropological Survey of India was formed on 1st December, 1942 and Dr. Guha was appointed Officer on Special Duty. The Survey was located at Varanasi with six staff members at the initial stage of its origin. A separate library was set up with 1039 books. The Survey's journey started as a specialized centre for advanced scientific anthropological research involved in the study of human being holistically and was to collect complete scientific information about the people of India for the use of researchers, planners and administrators. Here Dr. Guha developed friendship with Sarvapalii Radhakrishnan, the then Vice-Chancellor of Banaras Hindu University. On 1st August, 1946, he was appointed as the Director of Anthropological Survey of India with additional assignment of Anthropological Adviser to the Government. Dr. Verrier Elwin was appointed Deputy Director on 1st October, 1946. Dr. Guha established various sections for multidisciplinary field based research like physical and cultural anthropology, human biology, osteology, radiology, biochemistry, linguistic, geography, psychology, photography, sound and cine sections on priority basis. The name of the Survey was changed into Department of Anthropology in January 1948. At the end of May 1948 the Department moved from Varanasi to Indian Museum, Calcutta where it had opened its Ethnographic gallery. The cinematography unit was started in the Survey in 1949 and the Cine unit in 1953. Additionally, an independent printing press was established in 1950 for publication of research results in institutional bulletin and books. His endeavour resulted in appointing

Professor Lidio Cipriani from Italy as the first Travelling Fellow in 1950. Dr. Chi Nakane a Japanese Scholar and Dr. E.C. Buchi, from Zurich University joined Department of Anthropology as Foreign Fellows on invitation from Dr. Guha. They contributed substantially in imparting training of fieldwork and laboratory work to young physical and cultural anthropology scholars for three years. He established two substations of Department of Anthropology at Port Blair (December 1951) and Shillong (May 1953). Dr. Guha established the Ethnographic Museum at Calcutta in 1952. The Port Blair museum started with the rare exclusive artefacts of the Onges. In all, he collected 744 artefacts of 31 types. One such artefact was 'Wooden effigy of the Khalash of Hindukush' which is worth mentioning.

Dr. B.S. Guha was nominated as an Editor and Executive member of several journals and bulletins in India and abroad like Bulletin of the Department of Anthropology, Bulletin of the Bihar Tribal Research Institute, Mankind Quarterly, Homo, Journal of the Indian Anthropological Institute and The Anthropologists.

Dr. B.S. Guha retired from the post of Director of Department of Anthropology on 31st July, 1954. There were 189 office staffs at that time. Fund allocation was 1.34-7.88 lakh rupees. Number of publications were 145. Library had more than 20,000 books and 543 periodicals. He took special interest in creating separate departments for Anthropology in Delhi University (estd. 1947) and Gauhati University (estd. 1948).

Dr. B.S. Guha was attached to many academic and research institutes in India and abroad in various capacities till his death. He also participated in many academic forums all over the globe. Dr. B.S. Guha was the member of the Board of Trustees of the Bose Research Institute of Science, Calcutta since 1931, elected a member of the Council of The Asiatic Society, Calcutta in 1930 and served as its Anthropological Secretary from 1931 to 1934. He was the President of the Anthropology section of the Indian Science Congress twice – in 1928 and 1938, elected a fellow of the Royal Anthropological Institute of Great Britain and Ireland, a member of the Permanent Council of the International Congress of Anthropology in 1934, elected a Foundation Fellow of the National Institute of Sciences of India (now Indian National Science Academy, Delhi) in 1935 and selected Honorary Treasurer during 1938-1942, elected member of Committee of international preparation scientifique de L'Institute International d'Anthropologiede de Paris, founder member and Hon. Secretary of the Indian Anthropological Institute, Calcutta since 1936. Elected a member of the Comitato Internal per L'unificazionedei Metodi E per la Sintesi in Anthropologiaed Engenica of Bologua in 1937, elected

President of the Anthropology Section of the Joint meeting of the British Association for the Advancement of Science and the Indian Science Congress held in Calcutta in January 1938, elected Vice-President of the Section of Physical Anthropology and Human Biology of the Second Session of the International Congress of Anthropology held in Copenhagen in August 1938, he was also made a member of the Selection Board for the appointment of a Lecturer in Anthropology of the Cambridge University in 1938 and also that of Professor of Anthropology of the Calcutta University in 1938, elected a Fellow of the Royal Asiatic Society of Bengal in 1939. Dr. Guha was selected as a member of the International Committee of the teaching of Anthropology and Ethnology of Utreckt in 1939. Dr. Guha was closely associated with the Asiatic Society. He became the council member and Anthropological Secretary and first Indian Honorary General Secretary from 1931 to 1942. Government of India representative at the Third Meeting of the International Congress of Anthropological and Ethnological Sciences in India held at Brussels. He was the Vice President of Adimjati Sevak Sangh in Delhi and was attached with many other professional bodies in India and abroad.

In between work of Dr. Guha would visit the house of Bengali famous writer Rajsekhar Basu at 14, Parshibagan Lane for adda i.e. rendezvous. The people who gathered there were eminent historian Acharya Jadunath Sarkar, writer Prabhat Kumar Mukhopadhyay, Sarat Chandra Chattopadhyay, prominent archaeologist Rakhaldas Bandyopadhyay, Professor of linguistics Sunitikumar Chattopadhyay, artist Purnachandra Ghosh, Pulinchandra Kundu, Acharya Jogeshchandra Ray and others. This association indicate the intellectuality and interaction level of Dr. Guha and sometimes he earned ideas through the typical constructive adda.

In August 1934, Dr. Guha went to London to the first meeting of the International Congress of Anthropology as a Government sponsored delegate in 1934. He was on study leave in Europe from Zoological Survey of India for a year and a half in 1934-35 during which he studied the latest developments of the Anthropological science and its technique under Sir Arthur Keith in the Royal College of Surgeons and Professor Elliot Smith from July to October 1934. He read a paper before the Anthropological Institute of the University of Zurich by special invitation in May 1935. Dr. Guha worked in the Anthropological Institute of the University of Zurich under Professor Otto Schlaginhanfen during May and June 1935 and worked with Professor Th. Mollison from July to December 1935. He delivered two lecturers on Racial Biology before the Anthropological

Institute of the University of Munich in September and November 1935. Dr. Guha took part in the scientific deliberations and read a paper by special invitation at the XVI Session of Institute International d' Anthropologie held at Brussels in September 1935. He worked with Professor Rivet and Professor Marcelle Boule in the Institute of Human Palaeontogy in University of Paris from November 1934 to April 1935. Dr. Guha was one of the members of the Research Committee of the Standardization of Anthropological Methods and he participated in the International Congress of Anthropology in 1935. Dr. B.S. Guha presided over the Anthropology Section of the joint session of the Indian Science Congress and the British Association of the Advancement of Science, held in Calcutta in 1938 and in the same year served as the Vice-President of the section of Physical and Racial Biology, International Congress of Anthropology, in its second session held in Copenhagen, Denmark in August 1938. He was Fellow of Royal Anthropological Institute, Great Britain and Ireland during 1934-1939. Dr. Guha was invited to attend the Sixth Pacific Science Congress of the Pacific Science Association held at Berkley, USA during July and August in 1939. In 1939 he went to Zurich for attending an academic meeting of the International Congress of Anthropology for revision of the technique of measurements on the head with Professor G. Dahlberg of Upsala and Otto Schlaginhanfen and also invited to attend the XVIII Session of the International Congress of Anthropology and Prehistoric Archaeology held at Istanbul in 1939. Dr. Guha attended the third meeting of the International Congress of Anthropological and Ethnological Sciences at Brussels as a Government of India representative in 1942. In 1956, he attended the International Anthropological meeting at Philadelphia in 1959 and visited Pennsylvania.

After his retirement he was actively engaged in the anthropological research under the Government of India's Retired Scientist Scheme. However, he continued his research activities in various fields of Anthropology. He joined the Social Education Organiser's Training Centre at Ranchi as Director from 1955 to 1956. He organized the training centre under the Community Development Scheme for training the people to work in tribal areas. Then Dr. Guha tookover as the first Director (1st March, 1956-1st March, 1959) of Bihar Tribal Research Institute located in Katwin House, 40 Morabadi Road, Ranchi. He established tribal museum, library and published the first bulletin of the Institute.

Dr. Guha was the *ex officio* adviser to the Indian Government in Tribal Welfare. On 20th October, 1961, when Dr. Guha was returning from Calcutta to Ranchi after a meeting of the Anthropology Advisory

Committee he met with a tragic train accident near Ghatsila and died on the spot. The news of his untimely death spread widely across the nation. He left behind his old mother, wife, children, relatives and innumerable bereaved friends and anthropologists. The Anthropological fraternity deeply mourned the great loss of a towering anthropological personality. The condolence meeting was held at Rammohan Hall in Calcutta, on 5th November, 1961. Obituaries were published in several reputed national and international anthropological journals. Dr. D.K. Sen wrote – His death removes one of the chief architects of Indian anthropology. N.K. Bose wrote–By his death the society has thus lost a distinguished fellow, and an outstanding scientist.

Commemorating Dr. B.S. Guha's Centenary year and the Golden Jubilee of Anthropological Survey of India (1994), seminars, lectures, exhibitions were organised in collaboration with the Indian Museum. A book was published by Anthropological Survey of India and also by the Asiatic Society. A Lecture Hall was named after him in the Dehradun office of the Anthropological Survey of India. A national seminar was organised by the Indian Anthropological Society at Visva-Bharati, a Silver Medal is awarded in the memory of Dr. B.S. Guha by the Department of Anthropology, University of Gauhati.

Antanas Paskevicius Poska, (24 March, 1903 to 16 October, 1992) was a prominent Lithuanian motorbike traveller and physical anthropologist. He is best known for his journey to India in early 1929 to 1936. In 1936, he submitted his Ph.D. thesis to the University of Calcutta under Dr. B.S. Guha. The title of the thesis was "Physical Affinities of Shin Speaking People of the Western Himalayas". On 28th November, 2014 Poska's D.Litt. Certificate was posthumously received by his daughter Laimute Kisieliene in the university convocation.

Dr. Biraja Sankar Guha is an architect of 20th century in Indian Anthropology and a great institution builder. By remembering Dr. Guha, we can critically appreciate the process of implantation of the roots of present day anthropology in India in history. His contributions to the progress of anthropology in India are multidimensional. They include leadership and vision in organising multidisciplinary research work at national level in government set up. Dr. Guha will be remembered in the world of anthropology for his pioneering research, his academic brilliance, research contribution and administrative capabilities. Now it is indispensable to do more studies on his life and works in different dimensions through research, deliver lecturers, organize seminars, exhibitions and publications. However, we may introduce a memorial award in the memory of Dr. B. S. Guha from government organizational level for cheering young scholars in anthropology for their outstanding work. In this way we can shows a proper tribute to the commemoration of 125th birth anniversary of Dr. Guha as well as it will be significant to celebration of 100 years teaching in anthropology in India (1920-2019).

NOTE

On 15th August, 2019 a few anthropological organizations celebrated the 125th Birth Anniversary of Dr. B.S. Guha. Present author of this article made a documentary titled Untiring Mind: Dr. Biraja Sankar Guha – life and anthropological journey on the occasion of his 125th birth anniversary tribute and celebration of centenary year of teaching in anthropology in India (1920-2019) and this documentary was inaugurated at Vivekananda Auditorium, Vinoba Bhave University, Hazaribagh, Jharkhand on 14th October, 2019 on the occasion of 49th Annual Conference of the Indian Anthropological Society.

REFERENCES

Ambedkar, B.R. 1970. *Who Were Sudra*?, Thackers, First Published in 1946, pp. 100-101.

Anthropological Survey of India. 1996. *Souvenir*, Anthropological Survey of India Golden Celebration-1945-1995, Calcutta.

Banerjee, Sudeshna. 2014. Bengal Honour for Baltic Biker Boy, *Telegraph*, Calcutta, Sunday 23 November 2014, p.14.

Basu, Rajsekhar. 1992. Parasuramer Galppasamagra, M.C. Sarkar & Sons Private Limited, Calcutta, p.15, First publication 1969.

Bose, N.K. 1962. *Year Book of The Asiatic Society*, For 1961, Calcutta, Vol. IV, p.150.

Bose, N.K. 1963. *Fifty Years of Science in India – Progress of Anthropology and Archaeology*, Indian Science Congress Association, Calcutta.

Das Gupta, Bimankumar. 2007. *Biraja Sankar Guha, Anthropological Perspectives*, Creative Data Centre, Kolkata.

Duary, Nabakumar. 2019. "Untiring Mind: A Documentary Film on Biraja Sankar Guha". *South Asian Anthropologist*, Vol.19(2), pp 177-179.

Duary, Nabakumar. 2019. "Poska and Biraja Sankar Guha: An Unexplored Tale in Indian Anthropology, Brief communication", *Anthropos India*, Vol. 5, No. 2, July-December.

Elwin, Verrier. 1948. The Anthropological Survey of India, Part-I, History and Recent Development, *Man*, No. 78 & 79, June, pp. 68-69.

Elwin, Verrier. 1948. Department of Anthropology, Government of India, *American Anthropologist,* N.S. 50, pp. 576-581.

Elwin, Verrier. 1951. *Dr. B.S. Guha, Illustrated Weekly of India*, 25 November, 1951.

Ghosh, R.R. 1993. *Biraja Sankar Guha, Biographical Memories of Fellows of the Indian National Science Academy*, Vol. 17, Indian National Science Academy, New Delhi, pp.1-8.

Ghosh, Asok K. and Priyadarsini Sengupta. 1996. Human Types in Indian Population: Present and Past Anthropology of B.S. Guha, Eds. R.K. Bhattacharya and Jayanta Sarkar, Anthropological Survey of India, Kolkata, pp. 14-35.

Guha, Abhijit. 2018. "Social Anthropology of B.S. Guha: An exploration", *Indian Anthropologist*, Vol. 48, No.1, pp. 1-12.

Guha, B.S. 1946-49. "Progress of Anthropological Research in India", *Anthropos*, Vol. XLI-XLIV, pp. 607-613.

Institute for Research, 1948. *World Biography – Biographical Encyclopedia of the World Biography International Biographical Encyclopaedia*-1945, 3rd Edition.

Kundu, Kamal Kumar. 1994. Ananya Biraja Sankar, *Desh* (Bengali magazine), Year 61, No. 24, Calcutta, 24th September,1994, pp.41-50.

Majumdar, D.N. 1953. *India, Pakistan and Ceylon, International Directory of Anthropological Institutions*, Edited by William L. Thomas, Jr. and Anna M. Pikelis, Wenner-Gren Foundation for Anthropological Research, Incorporated, New York.

Mukherjee, D.P. 1996. *Some Anthropological Contributions of Biraja Sankar Guha: A study in retrospect,* Eds. R.K. Bhattacharya and Jayanta Sarkar, Anthropological Survey of India, Kolkata, pp. 3-83.

Royal Asiatic Society of Bengal.1943. *Year Book of the Royal Asiatic Society of Bengal*, For 1942, Vol. IX, 1943, pp.8-9.

Sen, Dharani. 1974. "Proceeding of the Seminar on Indian Anthropology Today",

Sen, D.K. 1962. Biraja Sankar Guha 1894-1961, *Eastern Anthropologist*, Vol.15, No. 2, May-August,1961, pp. 170-171.

Sinha, D.P. 1963. "Biraja Sankar Guha 1894-1961", *American Anthropologist*, Vol. 65, No.1, February 1963, pp. 382-385. Department of Anthropology, Calcutta University, Calcutta.

Syamchaudhuri, N.K. and Shyamal Kumar Ray. 1973. "The Growth of Faculty of Anthropology in the University of Calcutta", *Bulletin of the Anthropological Survey of India*,Vol. XXII, Nos. 1 & 2, pp.1-85.

The Asiatic Society. 1994. *The Asiatic Society and Anthropological Studies in India,* this publication is dedicated to the memory of Biraja Sankar Guha on the occasion of his Birth Centenary, The Asiatic Society, Kolkata.

Zoological Survey of India. 2016. *Souvenir*, Zoological Survey of India Hundred Years Celebration-1916-2016, Kolkata.

3
Kshitish Prasad Chattopadhyay

Abhijit Guha

Kshitish Prasad Chattopadhyay was one of the most distinguished anthropologists of India. He was born on 15th December, 1897 and had a brilliant academic career. Chattopadhyay was a descendent of two great social reformers of 19th century Bengal, namely Raja Ram Mohan Roy and Pandit Ishwar Chandra Vidyasagar and he was an affine of the famous family of Rabindranath Tagore. He was educated in Metropolitan School in Kolkata and then in Vidyasagar and Presidency Colleges of the University of Calcutta in Physics. Kshitish Prasad ranked seventh in Matriculation in 1913 and stood First in his I.Sc. Examination in 1917. He earned a First Class Honours degree in Physics from the University of Calcutta. Chattopadhyay was a student of the famous Indian scientists like Meghnad Saha, Satyen Bose and Acharya Prafulla Chandra Roy. Thereafter, he worked as a research student of C.V. Raman (Basu, 2011).

In 1919, he went to United Kingdom and took his admission at Cambridge University in Physics and began his studies under famous physicists like Thompson and Rutherford. But soon he changed his subject and obtained his Masters degree in Anthropology in 1922. He came in contact with the famous British anthropologist W.H.R. Rivers, who was his teacher and Chattopadhyay was awarded the Anthony Wilkins Fellowship to carry out his research on the Newar community of Nepal. The fellowship was later withdrawn because of his activities with the Indian Seamen's Union (London), which were regarded as objectionable and he was not allowed to visit Nepal for his fieldwork by the then colonial government. He came back to India in 1922 with M.A. degree in Anthropology from Cambridge University.

After his return to India, Chattopadhyay joined as a Lecturer in Anthropology at the University of Calcutta in 1923 but within a short period of time he left the university and joined as an Education Officer of the Corporation of Calcutta being inspired by C.R. Das and Subhas Chandra Bose when the Congress party was running the Civic Body. He worked at the civic body during 1924-1937 and trained 1500 primary school teachers to impart free education to children. In 1924, there were very few primary schools under the Calcutta Corporation. K.P. Chattopadhyay took special initiatives to establish more primary schools and before he left the job 232 primary schools came up in which more than 50,000 children belonging to the poor families were being educated. Chattopadhyay also wrote two primers in Bengali named *Lekhapara* using the most advanced teaching methods. While working at Calcutta Corporation he actively participated in the Civil Disobedience Movement of Mahatma Gandhi. In 1937, he rejoined the University of Calcutta as Head of the Department of Anthropology until his retirement in 1962. He was not only the Head of the Department of Anthropology at the University of Calcutta but was also a life-long fighter for civil liberties movement in West Bengal before and after the independence of India. His researches on the jute mill workers and the workers of the then Calcutta Corporation were pioneering in anthropology which broke away from the colonial anthropological tradition.

Chattopadhyay's range of interest in anthropology was extremely varied and he was a prolific writer with sound command in statistical sciences as well as in Sanskrit. He wrote more than hundred scientific articles in English and also popularised anthropological themes in the vernacular. His posthumous book *Ancient Indian culture contacts and migrations* was published by Sanskrit College of Calcutta in 1965 and it was reviewed with admiration by C.von Furer-Haimendorf in the *Bulletin of the School of Oriental and African Studies*, London in 1968 (vol. 31, issue 2, pp.450-451). The articles he wrote were published in many international and national level professional journals, like *Man, American Journal of Physical Anthropology, Ethnos, Journal of the Royal Asiatic Society of Bengal, International Journal of Comparative Sociology, Sankhya, Man in India* and *Modern Review* on the theoretical and core areas of anthropology like anthropometry, material culture, kinship, marriage, social organisation, inheritance of property as well as on the applied areas, namely culture contact, culture change, personality and culture, social conflict, tribal development, rehabilitation, education and national planning. He most intensively studied the Santals of Bengal and his Report on the Santals was published by the University of Calcutta in 1947. Apart from Santals he also conducted studies on the social organisation of the Khasi and Korku. The influence of W.H.R. Rivers on Chattopadhyay's works on kinship study was evident but he was also critical of the applicability of several western anthropological categories, which he found inadequate for the interpretation of Indian reality. Rajatsubhra Mukhopadhyay succinctly observed that K.P. Chattopadhyay could not find any advantage to use the term 'nuclear family' since it did not play any role comparable to the nucleus of a cell in the Indian context. He also strongly suggested treating 'joint' and 'extended' family types as structurally and organizationally two different types of social institutions in the Indian situation.

Although, his major area of interest was in kinship, family and marriage in the tribal societies but he was not confined to either in these areas or among the tribal populations only. As early as 1923, he wrote an article on the history of Newar culture in Nepal in which Chattopadhyay combined historical data with contemporary social practices to show the past continuity of the Newar caste system and social divisions down to the present time. In the same vein, his three important papers on the history of Indian social organisation (1935), Social organisation of Satkarnis and Sungas (1927) and Dharma worship (1942) were attempts to explain some ancient institutions and customs with the help of social anthropological methods of inquiry. Chattopadhyay's another area of interest was the study of material culture of the tribal and non-tribal populations and he published quite a good number of articles and abstracts on this important topic in Anthropology. He wrote on Korku house types, plough and clod crusher, Bondo and Korku tree-press, Santal fish-traps and bird net, Bengal coiled basketry, Indian rafts, toe-peg sandals of India and Korku dress and ornaments.

N.C. Choudhury, a former Director of the Anthropological Survey of India, and one of the illustrious students of K.P. Chattopadhyay perceptively noted that during the 1950s Chattopadhyay shifted his interest to social and cultural changes in traditional culture, which started with his 1949 Man in India article on changes in Santal economy. In this period he wrote on the culture contact and changes in Vedic age (1955), study of changes in traditional cultures (1957), Sari border changes (1957), changes in Santal songs (1957), some changes in Khasi culture (1960), structural changes in family in Bengal (1959).The paper on Sari border changes is quite unique. In this paper Chattopadhyay had shown how the introduction of mill made saris (a piece of long cloth worn by Indian women) gave an upper hand to the *mahajans* (money lenders who loans money at much higher rates than banks) who forced the traditional weavers of Bengal to adopt new designs and ultimately made the latter dependent upon the former and turned the weavers into wage labourers.

An unorthodox kind of study undertaken by K.P. Chattopadhyay and his co-workers dealt with the problems and living conditions of undergraduate students at the University of Calcutta. During the early 1950s, Chattopadhyay in collaboration with the Statistics Department of the University of Calcutta conducted a survey on the living conditions of the undergraduate students and the report of this pioneering survey was published by the University in 1954. Another study jointly conducted by K.P. Chattopadhyay and P. Bose of the Department of Statistics dealt with how the guardians planned education for their children and this study was also published by the University of Calcutta in 1962. Both these application oriented empirical surveys were not only unusual but this kind of surveys is still very rare in Anthropology and other social sciences. With these studies K.P. Chattopadhyay laid the foundation stone of educational anthropology in India, which has not yet come into existence in Indian anthropology.

One of his most remarkable contribution beyond anthropology was on the rehabilitation of the people affected by the Great Bengal Famine of 1943 in which he collaborated with the famous statistician P.C. Mahalanobis to work out a plan for successful rehabilitation of the famine affected families of the then undivided Bengal. The jointly authored book *Famine and rehabilitation in Bengal* (1946) by P.C. Mahalanobis and K. P. Chattopadhyay is still regarded as one of the best known early applied researches on Bengal Famine. Chattopadhyay's two other remarkable applied social researches were on the Municipal labour in Calcutta (jointly with G.S. Roy in 1947) and a socio-economic survey of the jute mill workers of Bengal in 1952, which were published by the University of Calcutta. Chattopadhyay developed an early interest in the study of caste and class in Bengal villages. His two unpublished papers read at Gokhale Institute, Poona on changing values and social patterns in caste society in West Bengal villages (1961) and class relations in Bengal villages (1962), a conference paper in Calcutta bear testimony to this fact.

His knowledge and interest in the application of Statistics in Anthropology was also pioneering in Indian anthropology. As early as 1941, Chattopadhyay published an article entitled "Application of Statistical Methods to Anthropological Research" in the famous journal *Sankhya: The Indian Journal of Statistics* edited by P.C. Mahalanobis. In this pioneering article Chattopadhyay discussed the problems of sampling in Physical and Social Anthropology with the help of simple examples. In this paper he also cautioned the anthropologists about the importance of considering the environmental and historical factors while they collect and/or define their populations and societies. In 1951, he wrote another interesting methodological paper entitled "The racial composition of Bengalees" which was published in a supplementary volume of Census of India 1951 edited by A.Mitra on The Tribes and Castes of West Bengal. In this article he dealt with the differences of same anthropometric measurements recorded by the physical anthropologists on similar population groups. Here he criticised H.H. Risley's measurements, which according to Chattopadhyay "suffered from a serious defect in that his assistant was not properly trained" and Risley did not carry out any cross-check "regarding the comparability of measurements taken". Chattopadhyay's another area of interest was social psychology and he wrote articles in the *Indian Journal of Psychology* on temporary loss of memory (1939) and personality and culture (1957) as well as on juvenile delinquency in Calcutta in *International Journal of Comparative Sociology* (1962).

K.P. Chattopadhyay represented India at the International conferences of the anthropologists at London, Vienna and Paris in 1934, 1952 and 1960, respectively and delivered the keynote address in the international seminar on the problems of juvenile delinquency in London organised by UNESCO in 1960 which was published in 1962 in the prestigious *International Journal of Comparative Sociology* (vol.3, no. 2, pp. 221-228). He was a Fellow of the National Institute of Sciences of India and Honorary Fellow of the famous Sanskrit College of Calcutta. Chattopadhyay was actively engaged with the Asiatic Society of Bengal and served as the Anthropological Secretary of this renowned Institute of the country.

During 1937-1962 K.P. Chattopadhyay served as the Head of the Department of Anthropology at the University of Calcutta in its formative phase. During this period, the department flourished in all the three major subdisciplines of Anthropology, namely Physical Anthropology, Prehistoric Archaeology and Social-Cultural Anthropology. In 1955, the Department of Anthropology at the University of Calcutta was chosen by the University and the UNESCO to hold a conference on the Study of Changes in Traditional Culture and with the able academic and administrative leadership of K.P. Chattopadhyay the conference was not only held most successfully but the whole proceedings of the conference along with the discussions were also meticulously recorded and published in the form of a book by the University of Calcutta in 1957.

Under the encouraging guidance of Chattopadhyay many of his students and teachers acclaimed national and international recognitions. Some of his students who later became famous at the national and international arenas were Ramkrishna Mukherjee, Surajit Sinha, B.K. Roy Burman, André Béteille and many others.

K.P. Chattopadhyay was an anthropologist with nationalist and humanist spirit who dedicated himself to the welfare of humanity. In an obituary of Chattopadhyay, which was published in *Man* (vol. 53, nos.193, 194; 1963, pp. 155-156) the eminent anthropologist J.H. Hutton noted:

> Apart from his academic work he was always active in promoting the welfare of his fellow men. As a student in England he had worked among seamen in the East End of London; in India the free primary education system in Calcutta was largely his work; as Treasurer of the People's Relief Committee, famine relief and rehabilitation work in the rural areas of Bengal owed much to him, and during the communal riots of 1946 he organized a 'Peace Corps' to restore order.

K.P. Chattopadhyay remained active after his retirement from the University of Calcutta. Just before his fatal cerebral thrombosis in May 1963 he had been working on his book on the Santals and a volume on the culture contact and migration in ancient India which was published in 1965. Chattopadhyay passed away on 31st May, 1963 in Calcutta.

REFERENCES

Chattopadhyay, G. 2000. A critical appreciation of professor K.P. Chattopadhyay's work on education, in Life and times of an Indian anthropologist: K.P. Chattopadhyay, ed. G. Chattopadhyay, pp.1-7. Calcutta: The Asiatic Society.

Chattopadhyay, K.P. (Ed.) 1957. Study of changes in traditional culture [Proceedings of the Conferences held by the University of Calcutta in Co-operation with the UNESCO]. Calcutta: The University of Calcutta.

Chattopadhyay, K.P. 1941. Application of Statistical Methods to Anthropological Research. *Sankhya*: *The Indian Journal of Statistics* (1933-1960), Vol. 6, No. 1, Proceedings of the Indian Statistical Conference 1941 (1942), pp. 99-104.

Chattopadhyay, K.P. 1951. The racial composition of Bengalees. The Tribes and Castes of West Bengal, ed. A. Mitra. Census of India, 1951. Calcutta: Government of West Bengal.

Choudhury, N.C. 2000. Professor K.P.Chattopadhyay: The teacher and an anthropologist, in Life and times of an Indian anthropologist: K.P. Chattopadhyay, ed. G. Chattopadhyay, pp. 52-59. Calcutta: The Asiatic Society.

Haimendorf, von, C. 1968. Review of Ancient Indian culture contacts and migrations. (1965), published by Calcutta Sanskrit College: Calcutta. *Bulletin of the School of Oriental and African Studies*, vol. 31, Issue 2, pp.450-451.

Hutton, J.H. 1963. Obituary. *Man*, vol. 53, nos.193, 194; 1963, pp.155-156.

Kshitish Prasad Chattopadhyay (1897-1963). 1964. *Notes and News. International Journal of Comparative Sociology*. Vol. 5, Issue 1, January, 1964, pp. 111-112.

Kshitish Prasad Chattopadhyay.1976. *Samsad Bangali Charitabhidhan* (Vol. 1), p. 168. Kolkata: Sishu Sahitya Samsad Pvt. Ltd.

Mukhopadhyay, R. 2000. K.P. Chattopadhyay and the study of kinship, in Life and times of an Indian anthropologist: K.P. Chattopadhyay, ed. G. Chattopadhyay, pp. 39-49. Calcutta: The Asiatic Society.

Ray, S.K. 1974. Kshitish Prasad Chattopadhyay (1897-1963), in Bibliographies of eminent Indian anthropologists (with life-sketches), pp. 45-55. Calcutta: Anthropological Survey of India & Indian Museum.

Roy Burman, B.K. 2000. Professor K.P. Chattopadhyay — A scientist with social concern, in Life and times of an Indian anthropologist: K.P. Chattopadhyay, ed. G. Chattopadhyay, pp.50-51. Calcutta: The Asiatic Society.

4
Anthropology's Folkloristic Root
Sarat Chandra Mitra and Anthropology in India

Sumahan Bandyopadhyay

Development of Anthropology in India has a history which has roots in several academic traditions, activities of different societies, academic-administrative and missionary approaches, and initiatives of independent scholars before the formal beginning of the discipline as an academic programme in the university system. In the attempts to document the history of anthropology in India, we have seen commendable exercises in narrating the institutional development, trends of research and individual contributions (Guha, 1938; Bose,1963 c.f. Danda, 2019; Roy, 1974; Vidyarthi,1978; Joardar, 2001; Uberoi, Sundar and Deshpande, 2007; Danda, 2019; Sarkar and Dasgupta, 2019). In spite of the best of the efforts, it is a fact that contributions of many of the pioneering scholars of anthropology in India remained unsung or under-evaluated (Guha, 2011). Guha (2011) has referred to this kind of 'academic amnesia' with regard to T.C. Das and Sarat Chandra Mitra, both senior in age and as colleague to Das in the Department of Anthropology of University of Calcutta probably suffered rather more academic neglect in spite of making enormous contributions to the development of anthropological studies in India. His contribution is seldom evaluated or acknowledged. However, we find that among the departmental members of anthropology who manned the department when it was established, only Sarat Chandra Mitra had the formal academic linkage with the first institutional set-up dedicated to the anthropological researches in the country[1]. The name of this organization was Anthropological Society of Bombay which was set-up in 1886. However, we may be surprised to find that there is hardly any comprehensive discussion on his life and works so far in the major encyclopaedic collection or compendium of anthropology published

(Roy,1974; Vidyarthi,1978; Uberoi, Sundar and Deshpande, 2007; Sarkar and Dasgupta, 2019). However, we see that Guha (1938) referred to his works just as mentions. Only Joardar's (2001) book has discussed about his life and works in brief and included him as one of the pioneers in Indian Anthropology. However, his scholarship has been acknowledged by the folklorists (Sengupta, 1965; Siddique,1974). The present chapter, within its limited scope will try to find answers to these questions along with providing a biographical sketch and works of S.C. Mitra. Moreover, the paper argues that the contributions of Sarat Chandra Mitra built up one of the major foundations of anthropology in India, which was based on the study of folklore. Therefore, the discussion on S.C. Mitra would unravel the nature of anthropology at its beginning of the formalization in our country.

Mitra should better be seen as an 'armchair anthropologist'. He was at best a 'Tylorian folklorist' (Stocking,1996) as Andrew Lang was in the West. In fact he was an avid reader of Andrew Lang and referred to Lang's works frequently in his articles. This tradition of anthropological folkloristic was a main current of academic exercise when Mitra was actively engaged in research and studies. Many of his colleagues in anthropology contributed largely to the enrichment of folkloric study that was well included in the syllabus. In fact, the anthropologically oriented foreign scholars during colonial period used to write on folklore at length and published these in the anthropology journals. The popular anthropology or public anthropology of the period was mostly represented in English and vernacular languages through the writings that now we refer to as more folkloristic than anthropological. The presence of folklore in the anthropological discourses may also be indicated through this simple statistics: For eight years, from 1922 to 1930, if we consider the total 179 articles published in *Man in India*, we would see that 43 per cent of the total papers dealt with folklore which included discussion on folktale, myth, legends, folk literature, folk deity, magic, taboos, beliefs, customs, superstitions, craft, folk dance, folk games, folk medicines etc. Of the total 77 articles during the above-mentioned period, Mitra singularly contributed 35 per cent of the total articles published. In 1925, the Syndicate resolved to purchase only one book for anthropology,that was R.E. Enthoran's *The Folklore of Bombay*.[2] Therefore, it can be well surmised that Mitra represented one of major contemporary trends of studies in anthropology in the department. Many of the topics studied by him were either subsumed under anthropological studies that gave emphasis on fieldwork or abandoned altogether by the anthropologists for the folklorists in later years. The new trend of fieldwork-based studies was gradually gaining ground in the discipline. Some of his departmental colleagues who later became towering figures in anthropology developed the intensive fieldwork tradition in the Malinowskian fashion. Nirmal Kumar Bose (1963) who was a direct student of Sarat Chandra Mitra in the department of anthropology in the university and worked on the spring festival which was also studied beforehand by Mitra (1915), did not mention about him in his historical treatise on the fifty years of development of anthropology. This clearly indicates that the types of studies done by Mitra were getting out of fashion in anthropology along with the ebbing of the theoretical position of a kind of evolutionism forwarded by Tylor, and popularized by scholars like James Frazer and Andrew Lang. With the emergence of functionalism, structural-functionalism, civilization studies/study of complex society, neo-functionalism immediately after the demise of Mitra, the social cultural anthropological studies drifted towards fieldwork-based ethnographic study from ethnological one. In this background, Sarat Chandra's works were being appropriated by the emerging field of folklore that was moving towards formalization in academic curriculum. The folklorists of the period, however, paid greater attention to his works and penned a more or less rounded notes on him (Sengupta, 1965; Siddique,1973). Despite all these rise and eclipses, we cannot undermine the contributions of one tall, fair-complexioned nearly sexagenarian faculty of the newly established department of anthropology in Kolkata, who had around five hundred articles to his credit. The versatility of interest and skill of prolific writing have been garbed in an upbringing that is outlined in the following biographical sketch.

Sarat Chandra Mitra was born in a reputed (*kulin*) Kayastha family on 15th November, 1863. It is said that one Kalidas Mitra who was the son of Aditya Mitra of Kanauj of North India migrated to Gour which was the then capital of Bengal during twelfth century A.D. The ninth descendent to Kalidas Mitra, Dhananjoy Mitra came to Barisha (which is now a part of Kolkata), a settlement in the south-western part of present day Kolkata. At the fear of Burgi (Marhatta) invasion, the family shifted to a more centrally located portion of Kolkata, known as Hogolkuria. The family was later came to be known as Hogolkuriar Mitra Paribar (Mitra family of Hogolkuria). Sarat Chandra's grandfather Tarak Chandra Mitra was very enthusiastic about educating his children. It is to be kept in mind that University of Calcutta was set up just a few years ago in 1857 and Western education system was gradually setting in. His family was one of the few families of the city that imbibed this newly established education system. Tarak Chandra learnt English with his own effort since there was no scope for learning this in formal system in his time. But he did not hesitate to employ private tutors for his sons Bireswar and Narsingh once the opportunity opened up. Moreover, he had a great love for books, which we see permeated to the later generations up to the present. Sarat Chandra was born as the second son of Narsingh Chandra and Nistarini Devi with another son Amulya Charan elder to him and Shailabala, a daughter younger to Sarat Chandra.

Narsing was graduated in Law from the University of Calcutta and worked as a pleader and legal adviser in Huthwa Raj (a principality more or less corresponding to the Saran district of present day Bihar). Sarat Chandra, after a brief education in Calcutta Training School also studied at Zilla School of Chapra in Bihar. However, later he was admitted to schools in Kolkata. It appears that Sarat Chandra was a good student throughout his academic career. He passed Entrance examination in First Division. In F.A. examination, he stood 18th among all the candidates from Metropolitan Institution founded by Pandit Iswar Chandra Vidyasagar, the great social reformer and educationists in 19th Century Bengal. He showed brilliance in B.A. with honours in English which he studied in the same institution (now Vidyasagar College located in Kolkata). He passed B.A. securing second position in first class in 1885 and was awarded Pandit Iswar Chandra Vidyasagar Scholarship for one year with an amount of Rs.30 per month. It can be mentioned here that he also studied with scholarship at the secondary and higher secondary levels. He got M.A. degree in English in 1886 and passed Bachelors of Law in 1888. His M.A. in English had some stylistic effect in his articles which at times sparkled with marvelous quotes from Tennyson or any other English writer.

Sarat Chandra's marriage with Sarasibala took place, when he was twenty two. They had ten children – five sons and five daughters, though their two daughters and one son died at their early childhood.

After passing law, he started his career as a lawyer in the Chapra Bar where his father was already established as a government pleader. He joined as Superintendent of Survey and Settlement under Huthwa Raj estate in 1894. He also became the Law Superintendent in the same principality. Here, he continued up to 1904 when he returned to Chapra Bar as legal practitioner. He was again appointed as the Assistant Manager of Huthwa Raj in 1911. He continued till 1920 when he came to join the newly established Anthropology Department in the University of Calcutta.

As per the Report of the Syndicate (1920), the post-graduate Department of Anthropology had seven teachers in the academic session 1920-21: Ramaprasad Chanda, Dr. Anathnath Chatterjee, Rai Bahadur B.A. Gupte, Rai Bahadur L.K. Anathakrishna Iyer, B.C. Mazumdar, Panchanan Mitra and Sarat Chandra Mitra. It is clear from the salary statement that Sarat Chandra joined the University in 1920 and continued till 1925. He used to draw the highest salary among his colleagues in the department till L.K. Ananthakrishna Iyer joined in 1921. Sengupta (1965:54) writes that "He was the first professor of the first department of anthropology in the country". In absence of any explicit reference to the headship or professorship, it may well be inferred that he led the newly born department of anthropology in the beginning as the worthiness of his appointment is concerned. He mentioned his affiliation as Lecturer in Social Anthropology in the articles published in the journal *Man in India* during his tenure in the University of Calcutta. During this time, Sir Asutosh Mookerjee, the then Vice-Chancellor of the University of Calcutta was the Chairman of the first Board of Studies in Anthropology which was one among several Boards of Higher Studies in Arts at that time.

Well before his joining the University of Calcutta, he earned a great deal of reputation in scholarship. He became a Corresponding Member of the Anthropological Society of Bombay in 1895. On his association with this pioneering institution of anthropological studies in the country, Sir Basil Scott, the then Chief Justice of the Bombay High Court said in his presidential address in 1912 that :

> "I refer to Sarat Chandra Mitra who is, according to Mr. Modi's resume of the society's work, the most prolific of our members, having actually supplied a larger number of papers to the Society's journal than Mr. Modi himself".

It is really a matter of fact that he published as many as 183 articles in the above mentioned journal between 1892 and 1906.

During his years of teaching in the department, he also actively participated in various seminars and conferences across the country, most notable of these, however, was his participation in the Science Congresses held in Lucknow, Varanasi among other places.

His style of fieldwork or field studies did not match the contemporary standard of anthropology. It was more like a survey kind of field exposure. However, he had a great penchant for travelling and visiting new areas. He used to go about places in different parts of northern Bihar when he was in the service under Huthwa Raj. In these visits, he had observed many things of the life and culture of the rural people beyond the areas of his immediate concern that his service demanded (Mitra,1302 BS,1304BS). He used to visit regularly these areas even after he left that service and joined University of Calcutta. In his retired life, he lived with his sons in different places of the greater Bengal and adjoining areas where his sons had to stay for their service. His eldest son Satkari Mitra was a lecturer of Economics in Carmichael College in Rongpur (now in Bangladesh). His second son Panchkari was a Deputy Magistrate and third son Tinkari was an engineer who retired as Chief Engineer of the West Bengal and had been posted in different parts of the state in the early years of his career. Sarat Chandra often visited his sons. He used to collect oral narratives and folkloric items through informal talks with simpleton masses met around. This kind of approach to primary data is more folkloristic than anthropological. The folklorists used to become typically a narrator of his or her own culture. Thus, folklore has been a kind of 'auto-ethnography' of a culture presented by the insiders of the particular culture. Sarat Chandra had a pioneering role in this enterprise.

Though primarily accepted as a folklorist among the anthropologists, Sarat Chandra Mitra's interest was wide and limited to the cultural anthropology alone. Although, very few in number, he wrote on prehistoric archaeology and physical anthropology apart from folkloristic writings. He has, unlike many of his contemporaries who wrote in similar topics in English, very few writings in vernacular language. Most of his articles were published in academic or scholarly journals like *Journal of the Anthropological Society of Bombay* (183), *Quarterly Journal of the Mythic Society* (126), *Man in India* (34)[MII], *Journal of the Asiatic Society of Bengal* (30), *Journal of the Bihar and Orissa Research Society* (45), *Journal of Department of Letters*, University of Calcutta (12), *The Journal of the Royal Asiatic Society of Great Britain* and *Ireland* (1, Mitra, 1897) [JRASGBI], *Folklore* (1, Mitra,1898) and in magazines like *National Magazine* (37), *Hindustan Review* (21) and Bengali magazine *Bharati* (5)[3].

Joardar (2001:173) has classified the works of S.C. Mitra into nine categories following Siddique's classification without acknowledgement (Siddique,1974:126), however, Joardar changed the order of arrangement of the genres originally done by Siddique. The classification ran as: 1. Belief and Superstitions, 2. Games and Rhymes, 3. Magic and witchcraft, 4. Myths, 5. Obscure Religions, 6. Proverbs, 7. Riddles, 8. Songs, and 9. Tales. I do not find this classification as much encompassing or comprehensive since it glossed the varieties of his writings. Thus, it failed to accommodate some of the varieties of Mitra's writing. For this reason, I have taken a more type based classification rather than the genre-based as done previously. It is a fact that all classifications may have a tendency to overlap, still a more refined classification of his works would be given for the present purpose as the following:

1. Formalized folklore – folktale, proverbs, legends, riddles, rhymes, myth.
2. Material folklore – folk craft.
3. Folk religion – folk deity, magic, superstition, folk beliefs, taboos, totems, customs, festivals and ceremonies.
4. Performative folklore – folk games, dance, folk song.
5. Folk medicine.
6. Prehistoric Archaeology.

His area of study, so far as the spatial distribution was concerned was mainly extended over northern Bihar, Odisha, West Bengal and eastern Bengal (now Bangladesh). In this regard, it can be said that he paved the way for comparative folklore in Bengal, which later became one of the major domains in the syllabus of folklore (Ghosh,1997). His folkloric studies covered the oral traditions of the tribal, peasants and the Muslim people.

He wrote a good number of papers on folk-medicine (Mitra, 1898, 1915a, 1915b,1916). These articles dealt with curing charms practiced by the people in Bihar in dealing with diseases, like diarrhoea, dysentery, hydrophobia, scorpion-stings, fever, rheumatism, etc. Another topic on which he wrote profusely was human sacrifice. He made a number of studies on ceremonies and festivals like Chawk Chandi and Panchami Brata, Harparouri of Bihar, Gaidara ceremony of the Ahirs of Bihar, Dharma festivals in north Bihar etc. He had interest in place-names and made some investigations into it.

Mitra published quite an exhaustive number of birds and plants myths mainly in the Quarterly Journal of the Mythic Society (QJMS). Of his total 126 articles published in this journal, 62 articles were on bird-myth and 44 articles dealt with plant myths. He presented these stories either from their published texts in Bengali (Mitra,1923) or his own collections from the field (Mitra,1924). In this regard, he used to find those stories which could be an addition to the existing knowledge and not published before. If the collected tales did not fit to the classification so far being followed, he suggested new categories or 'story radicals' for the new texts. Owing to his contribution, many of the elements of Indian and Bengali folk literature were cited in the English references for the global readers and thus making them familiar about the richness of folk culture of India. Most of the folk tales or myths he wrote about were aetiological that means these were mainly the origin myths or causation myths. Besides myths, he used to collect a good number of drolls which were basically comic stories of ludicrous adventures. In her book, Cox (1895: 284) mentioned mainly the German examples of drolls, had Mitra's publication been there, we could have reflect upon the treasures of drolls available in India. Mitra (1923) also published cumulative folktale which is another category of folktales 'pilled up by repetition of all the preceding steps upon the addition of each new one' (Cox 1895: 284). In fact, he spotted the crucial knowledge gap in our collection of folktales and attempted fill them by his own works. Apologue is a type of moral fables or animal stories with moral teachings. Mitra (1925) wrote on a Meithei apologue and its Bengali variant. In this article, he compared the stories and came to the conclusion that the original form was in Meithei, which was later adopted by the Bengali people when they came in contact with the Meithei in Assam. Therefore, it is not the case that the Hindus always influenced tribals who absorbed the culture of the former, but the reverse did happen as reflected from the analysis of Mitra. In this way, we must say that Mitra made a tremendous contribution to the storiology, i.e. the systematic study of folk tales. Besides folktales, his contribution can be counted upon other forms of folk literature, namely riddles, proverbs, rhymes, ghost-lore, legends, dream-lore etc. He wrote about the riddles of Bihar, Chittagong and Pabna (now in Bangladesh), riddles found among the Hos, proverbs of Tangail (now in Bangladesh).

Mitra's another major area of works was folk religion, cult, beliefs, magic, witchcraft, customs, and superstitions. In the study of folk religions, he discussed about some unique folk deities and associated beliefs and worships. For examples, we may mention his articles on gods and goddesses of diseases like Ekachura, Bara Kumara, Lalasa Bisesvara, Khala Kumari (Mitra, 1923) etc. Besides them, he also published on the deities which are little known today such as Uttama Thakura, Andheswari, Garsi, Mangalchandi, Kalarayi phul of Balasore, Sonaraya of Rajshahi (now in Bangladesh), Khsetrapala of Chittagong (now in Bangladesh), Gorakhnath, Mahakala of the Rajbanshis, Dakshinaraya of Sundarbans, Turhar of north Bihar, Kasi Baba of the Binds of Bihar, and Bir Kuar of Palamau and Katha Deota of Patna, Bihar, Maharani of Bhuiyas of

Hazaribag along with Satyapir, Saraswati, Durga, Hanuman, Siva etc. The peculiar customs of dog-worship, worship of jujube tree and its presiding deity of Itokumar, the worship of Makdum Pir brought out the myriad cultural life of the people of Bengal and eastern parts of the country. Mitra has described a number of rituals and ceremonies observed in eastern India. Of these most elaborate study has been done on rain-making rituals. Two of his studies on this topic were published in very prestigious journals, namely *Folklore and Journal of the Royal Anthropological Society of Great Britain and Ireland* (Mitra,1897, 1898). In both the papers, he has shown how the rain producing ceremonies were linked to Vedic rituals at one hand and a kind of sympathetic magic on the other. Mitra also published on various cult practices like ones in Champaran of North Bihar, Orissa or Sambhu Chandi Sect, Musalman Sect of North Dinajpur, Nath sect and Jugi caste.

Apart from his enormous number of writings in English, he wrote a few articles in vernacular Bengali. These articles, though infinitesimal, are important for two reasons. First, these show the way he used to gather information on the life and culture of the people. Second, the very lucid and facile Bengali may well serve exemplary in referring to the ideal of vernacular communication of anthropological writing. The five articles written in Bengali deals with the rural life of Bihar, worship of tiger, the legend of Raja Rasalu, travel on the elephant back, and the Hindu burial custom. It can be mentioned here that some of these articles were published in English. The two of them, one on the rural life of Bihar and other on the travel on elephant-back appear original Bengali articles. The articles were written graphically in first person. Though basically descriptive, like one writes a diary, and his personal reflections are quite interesting in these articles.

Now, if we try to analyze the academic orientation of Sarat Chandra Mitra, we identify at least the following features of his theoretical position—evolutionism, diffusionism, psychic unity of mankind, parallelism and comparative method. Some of these features are interlinked undoubtedly. He held that many of the customs, myths, deities and rituals were of aboriginal origins. In connection with the discussion of Bana Durga and Sakambhari in his article on the cult of tree-goddess, he came to the conclusion that many non-Aryan elements had been appropriated by the expanding Brahminic culture or Hinduism. He wrote (Mitra, 1922: 239-240):

> "The non-Aryan aborigines, who lived in these forests, believed them or rather the trees contained in them to be

> inhabited by an invincible shadowy spirit or goddess whom they adored and prayed to. When this cult was absorbed into orthodox Hinduism, the exponents of the orthodox faith dubbed the spirit or tree-goddess with the names of Bana Durga, Bana Devi or Burha Thakurani."

In order to prove the borrowing, he used to follow the comparative method. In this method, the apparently irrational or anomalous custom of a country was compared with the similar custom elsewhere where it was meaningfully performed. This idea of comparative method as advanced by Andrew Lang was followed by him to a great extent (Lang, 1884). The parallelism is a common technique in folklore, that helps to see the similarity in customs or practices. Mitra (1923b) identified a number of parallels of practices across cultures in different parts of the world. In explaining the similarities in these cultures, he took to two kinds of explanation: one, that similar culture might have originated independently. In his study of the folk tales found among the Santals and the Bengalis by using comparative method, he came to the conclusion that the tales were of independent origin (Mitra,1930b). Following Lang (1893), he attributed this similarity to the 'mental similarities of man across cultures'. Two, there might be cultural contacts that led to the borrowings of elements between cultures. In the first explanation, he adhered to the view of psychic unity of mankind. He also used Tylor's concept of 'survivals' in explaining some the queer rituals and customs. His studies in this regard were of pioneering value in the sub-branch of comparative folklore which became a full-course later when formal study of folklore began in India (Ghosh, 1997).

He made ample references to anthropological literatures particularly when he studied the ceremonies, totemism, witchcraft, sorcery, magic, superstition and popular religion. It is interesting that he used the term 'popular religion' much before the beginning of 'Popular culture'. Unlike the social anthropological orientations of some of his fellow colleagues in the department in Calcutta University, he was much attracted to the cultural aspects. Besides this, he also wrote on the prehistoric archaeology which fell so far by its approach ethno-archaeological (Mitra, 1905, 1907).

He dealt with the issues which he found to be of anthropological in nature as the prevalent fashion at that time. In one such article on the cannibalism, he referred to A.C. Haddon and quoted the following statement of A.C. Haddon to focus its anthropological significance :

> "Cannibalism for magical purpose of this sort has probably been extremely common and is possibly at the base of good deal of anthropology." (c.f. Mitra, 1930: 481)

His folkloristic inquiries were basically informed by the anthropological issues relevant at that time. In the sense of the period, his investigations were anthropological. In the book *The Mind of Primitive Man* (Boas,1938; first published in 1911), Boas wrote (p.169):

> "Perhaps the best proof of transmission is contained in the folklore of the tribes of the world."

Mitra took this path to know human society and culture like many of his contemporaries in India and abroad. Of course, this was ethnological which formed a part of anthropological studies. Many of the classic anthropological works of the period gave much emphasis on these studies. Two major examples of the importance of this approach can be discerned in *Tylor's Anthropology* (1896) which contained a chapter on history and mythology and Boas' General Anthropology (1938) in which chapter thirteen was written on mythology and folklore by Franz Boas himself. Laurence Gomme's book *Ethnology in Folklore* (1892) acknowledged the anthropological concerns of the folklore studies. One can easily notice how Mitra followed the issues discussed in the books of Tylor, Lang, Burne among others. He very often opened the discussion in his articles by referring to the anthropological implications his articles were going to hold. In his article on the human sacrifice to water-spirits, he started discussion by quoting Tylor in the following words:

> "It is Sir E.B.Tylor who, in his great work, *Primitive Culture*, promulgated his theory of religion which is known as "The Theory of Animism"."(Mitra, 1922: 397)

Following this, he passed on to discuss the animistic elements in the belief of water spirits personified in the names of Shata and Jatha found in the Kandi of Murshidabad district in West Bengal.In another article on the Lurik ballad sung in the district of Malda in West Bengal, he linked the underlying thought to Tylor's concept of soul.To quote Mitra (1934-35: 129):

> "Competent anthropologists like Sir E.B.Tylor are of opinion that the custom of *sati*...which was known to the ancient Indo-Aryans and is mentioned in the Rig-Veda, also

originated in the aforementioned belief of the primitive peoples."

It needs no further elaboration to show how anthropologically inclined he was. In fact his broader reputation in the academic journals, even in journal that would publish mostly folklore staffs, was established as an anthropologist. *The Quarterly Journal of the Mythic Society* mourned at his demise by saying the following words (1939: 510):

> "By his death on the 15th of December, 1938, at the age of 76, the Indian Anthropologists have lost in him a most devoted and erudite scholar".

His contribution to anthropological studies was eloquently acknowledged by noted folklorists like Ashraf Siddique (1973: 216):

> "It was largely due to Mitra's stimulation that a subsequent generation of native folklorists not only in Bengal but throughout India, attached importance to anthropological methods, to scientific collecting of all the available variants, and above all, to the methodological analysis of their materials."

It is said that the development of anthropology in India has been fashioned along three traditions – Colonial, Hindu and Nationalist (Guha, 2019). It should be added that folklore studies represented one major foundation of anthropological investigations in the country cross-cutting all the above-mentioned traditions. The anthropologically oriented folkloristic works done by scholars like S.C. Mitra, S.C. Roy, V. Elwin, T.C. Das, D.N. Majumdar, K.P. Chattopadhyay can mostly be taken as examples of Hindu and Nationalist enterprises. However, the Indian scholar who laboured most to the laying of this folkloristic foundation of Anthropology in India was none other than Sarat Chandra Mitra.

NOTES

1. In this connection, it should be mentioned that noted sociologist A.M. Shah of Delhi University made a very serious mistake in his article published in the journal *Sociological Bulletin* by referring to S.C. Mitra as R.C.Mitra (Shah, 2014). However, he was unstinted in acknowledging his contribution in paper when he wrote: "…I may observe that JASB became the principal forum

anthropological work of two outstanding scholars, Jamshedji Modi and Ramesh Chandra Mitra (2014:361)". I wonder how Shah failed to mention S.C. Mitra properly when latter's complete name was written below the title of each of his 183 papers, probably highest among all the contributors to the journal. In this paper, Shah gave the total number as about 170 as he mentioned that he could not check the entire archive. Shah also mentioned the year of Mitra's demise as 1936 instead of 1938.

2. 'Syndicate resolved that the book '*The Folklore of Bombay*' by R.E. Enthoran be purchased.' Pp.933, Minutes of the Syndicate for the Year 1925, No. 24. Dated.18.05.1925.
3. The total number of his publications mentioned by Sengupta (1965) and Sidiqque (1973) has been changed with my checking of the archives. The information presented here can be said to be most updated before we find any of his other writings. My investigations revealed at least three major changes over the past counting, QRMS and JRASB returned 126 and 30 articles respectively instead of 97 and 21 mentioned by them. They also did not mention the JRASGBI and Folklore articles published from England and United States of America respectively. I find his five Bengali publications in *Bharati* of which Sengupta (1965) mentioned only of three. I think, there are more vernacular writings by him.

REFERENCES

Basu, P. 2011. *Bangla Bhasay Samajvidyacharcha*. Kolkata: Charchapad.

Boas, F. 1938. *The Mind of Primitive Man*. New York: Macmillan Company.

Boas, F. (Ed.).1938. *General Anthropology*. Boston: D.C. Heath and Company.

Bose, N.K. 2019 (Orig. 1963). "Fifty years of Science in India: Progress of Anthropology and Archaeology". In Danda, A.K. (Ed.). *One Hundred Years of Anthropology in India*. Pp.41-90. Jhargram: Indian National Confederation and Academy of Anthropologists.

Burne, C.S. 1914. *Handbook of Folklore*. London: Sidgwick & Jackson.

Danda, A.K. 1995. *Foundations of Anthropology: India*. New Delhi: Inter-India Publications.

Danda, A.K. (Ed.). 2019 . *One Hundred Years of Anthropology in India*. Jhargram: Indian National Confederation and Academy of Anthropologists.

Cox, M.R. 1895. *An Introduction to Folk-lore*. London: David Nutt.

Ghosh, S. 1997. *Lok Samaskritir Anginay*. Kolkata: K. Ghosh.

Gomme, G.L. 1892. *Ethnology in Folklore*. London: Kegan Paul,Trench, Trubner & Co.

Guha, B.S. 2019. (Orig. 1938). "Progress of Anthropology in India During the Past Twenty-Five Years". In Danda, A.K. (Ed.). *One Hundred Years of Anthropology in India*, pp. 3-38. Jhargram: Indian National Confederation and Academy of Anthropologists.

Guha, A. 2011. "Tarak Chandra Das: A Marginalised Anthropologist". *Sociological Bulletin*, 60(2): 245-265.

Guha, A. 2019. "Colonial, Hindu and Nationalist Anthropology in India". *Sociological Bulletin*, 68(2):154-168.

Joardar, B. 2001. *Anthropology in the Making: The Indian Experience*, New Delhi: Inter-India Publications.

Lang, A.1893. *Custom and Myth*. London: Longman, Green and Co.

Mitra, S.C. 1897. "On the Har Paraurī, or the Behāri Women's Ceremony for Producing Rain". *The Journal of the Royal Asiatic Society of Great Britain and Ireland*, 29: 471-484.

Mitra, S.C. 1898. "A Rain Ceremony from the Murshidābād District of Bengal". *Folklore* 9(3): 277-280

Mitra, S.C. 1302. B.S. Behārer Grāmyachitra. *Bharati* 19 (Āswin): 319-329.

Mitra, S.C. 1304. B.S. Hasti Prismṭhe. *Bharati* 21(Baisakh): 11-21.

Mitra, S.C.1898. "On the lizard in Indian superstition and folk-medicine". *Journal of the Asiatic Society of Bengal*, 67(3): 44-52.

Mitra, S.C. 1915a. "North Indian folk-medicine for hydrophobia and scorpion sting". *Journal of the Asiatic Society of Bengal*, 11(N.S.): 217-230.

Mitra, S.C. 1915b. "On north Indian charms for securing immunity from the virus of scorpion stings". *Journal of the Asiatic Society of Bengal*, 11(N.S.): 305-310.

Mitra,S.C.1916. "Some North Indian Charms for the Cure of Ailments". *Journal of the Bihar and Orissa Research Society*, 2(2): 215-229.

Mitra, S.C. 1922. "On Some vestiges of the custom of offering human sacrifices to water-spirits". *Quarterly Journal of the Mythic Society*, 12(4) : 397-405.

Mitra, S.C .1923. "Bengali Cumulative Folk-Tale of "The Old Dame Lousy Type". *Quarterly Journal of the Mythic Society*, 13(4): 767-775.

Mitra, S.C. 1923b. "Parallelism between Malay and a Chiru aetiological folk-tale". *Man in India*, 3(3 & 4): 243-245.

Mitra, S.C.1924."On a Santali Aetiological Folktale of the "Mann und Fuchs" Type". *Quarterly Journal of the Mythic Society*, 14(3): 211-216.

Mitra, S.C. 1930a. "A note on the prevalence of cannibalism among the Birhors of Chotanagpur". *Journal of the Anthropological Society of Bombay*, XIV(4):489-483.

Mitra, S.C. 1930b. "The Cockroach's relatives – A study of Comparative Storiology". *Man in India*, 10(1): 58-64.

Mitra, S.C. 1934-35. "Ballad of Lurik". *Quarterly Journal of the Mythic Society* 25(1-3) :122-135.

Roy, S.K. 1974. *Bibliographies of Eminent Indian Anthropologists* (With Life-sketches). Calcutta: Anthropological Survey of India.

Sarkar, A. and S. Dasgupta, (Ed.). 2019. Doyens of Indian Anthropology. Delhi: Agam Kala Prakashan.

Sen Gupta, S. 1965. *Folklorists of Bengal – Life-sketches and Bibliographic Notes*. Calcutta: Indian Publications.

Shah, A.M. 2014. "Anthropology in Bombay, 1886-1936". *Sociological Bulletin* 63(3) : 355-367.

Siddique, A. 1973. "Sarat Chandra Mitra and his Contribution in Bengali Folklore". *Folklore,* 14(4): 125-135; 14(5): 165-177; 14(6): 204-216.

Stocking, Jr. W.G. 1996. *After Tylor–British Social Anthropology 1888-1951*. London: Athlone.

Tylor, E.B. 1871. *Primitive Culture.* London: John Murray.

Tylor, E.B. 1896. *Anthropology*. New York: D. Appleton & Co.

Uberoi, P., N. Sundar and S. Deshpande (Eds.). 2007. *Anthropology in the East: Founders of Indian Sociology and Anthropology*. Ranikhet: Permanent Black.

Vidyarthi, L.P. 1978. *Rise of Anthropology in India—A Social Science Orientation*. Vol.I. New Delhi: Concept Publishing Co.

5
Rai Bahadur Sarat Chandra Roy

Abhik Ghosh

Sarat Chandra Roy was one of the first batch of Indian Anthropologists who began to study the social and biological diversity of Indian communities from scratch. There is still some dispute after A.C. Haddon wrote in a letter that S.C. Roy was the Father of Indian Ethnology. Aiyar was also known as the Father of Anthropology. He was also colloquially known as '*bada baap*'. Biswanath Joardar claims that perhaps one might see Sarat Chandra Roy as being '*chhota baap*'. Whatever be the case, it is no longer in dispute that these Anthropologists became the new wave of Indian Anthropologists who took over the job from the British, giving it a more nationalist and Indian direction.

Sarat Chandra Roy was born on 4 November, 1871 at Nonnagar, Manikpur (some articles say this is Gholgholé or Kadapada) in Khulna district to Purna Chandra Roy and Rajlakshmi Devi. His father, a Bengal Government Judicial Service member, died in 1885 when he was just 14 years of age, the eldest of 5 sons and 3 daughters. This made him responsible for educating and marrying off all his brothers and sisters. Though his family was well-off, through zamindari property, all of it was taken away from the hapless family by other family members, leaving Sarat Chandra Roy to cope with it.

Under these circumstances, while taking tuitions to eke out a living, he continued to study and completed his matriculation in 1888 at the age of 17 years from City Collegiate School in Kolkata. He then completed his B.A. (Honours) in English from General Assembly Institute (now Scottish Church College) in Kolkata. In 1893, he completed his M.A. in English from the same College in Kolkata. He then shifted his attention to following his father's occupation, obtaining a B.L. degree from Rippon College (now Surendranath College), Kolkata in 1895.

It was as a lawyer that he learnt about the problems faced by the tribals of India, who were stuck in a legal system whose language they did not understand. To figure out their problems, he began to learn about them. To figure out how to do it, he started teaching himself Anthropology, getting books from England ordered so that he could study them.

In 1896, he became the Headmaster at Mymensingh High School at Dholla (now in Bangladesh). From there, he became the Principal of the G.E.L. Mission High School at Ranchi for a brief period of eight months. In 1897, he began his legal career in the District Court of Alipur Bar, 24 Parganas. He shifted to Ranchi in 1898 due to his illness and began as a lawyer at the new courts of the Chotanagpur Judicial Commissioner. In 1903, he built a large house in Ranchi, even as he built a very large library in Anthropology. In 1908, he wrote his first article on the Mundas which appeared in Indian World.

For him, the struggle was to develop a uniquely Indian understanding of tribes and other communities. This understanding would fit into a larger metaphysical goal of the general meaning of human life and existence. It would show the 'trend, direction and aim of human culture and civilization'. In his opinion this was the 'eternal spiritual reality behind life and society' and the ultimate goal of Anthropology. He thought of it as the Truth that hid behind the Untruth and of the underlying causes of human behaviour in society.

Roy's obsession about Indians doing Anthropological work in India was seen from his analysis in a paper. He found that in the Journal of the Asiatic Society of Bengal published between 1784 to 1883, only three out of 100 articles were written by Indians. Between 1843 and 1883 in the Calcutta Review, again only three out of 53 articles were by Indians. No monographs had been published solely by Indian authors.

So, Sarat Chandra Roy began by attempting to record the history, mythology, family, kinship and other practices in Munda society. This was the tribe seen mostly around the area of Ranchi town. He took the time and effort needed to learn the dialects of the tribes of the region. He even took some informal coaching through his known circle of friends and acquaintances.

He managed to acquire the habit of getting good rapport among those he worked with in spite of the fact that he had no formal training in Anthropology. There were few roads to many of the interior villages that he travelled to. There are photos of him travelling on elephant back with all his camping equipment. Later, as he became older (and, perhaps, wealthier) he bought large touring cars and they had all kinds of field equipment tied in bundles to the vehicle, resting on the broad footboards at the sides.

While in the field, initially, he requested the tribe to build him a small mud house in the village, where he stayed, eating their own food. However, he had a sensitive stomach, often causing him much discomfort. Later, he would take his own tent and hire some helpers. He would also take his own raw materials and cooking equipment along with a cook. The cook made him simple boiled vegetables, pulses and plain boiled rice. His penchant for buying such vehicles at a time when they were a rare sight made him the cynosure of all eyes. His family remembers that all his life was a series of an unending line of field trips, both long and short.

In 1911, he was awarded the Certificate of Honour by the Lieutenant Governor of Bengal. This was in the name of George V, the Emperor of India, on the occasion of His Majesty's Coronation Durbar, in recognition of his ethnographic work. Surprisingly, this was before he had published a single book on the tribes of Chotanagpur, as yet. It was only in 1912, that the first monograph ever written by any Indian on a major tribe was published as *The Mundas and their Country*. This was published for many years by him and his family, now by others. In this work, he discussed their history as well as their land systems in detail, from an insider's perspective. In this work we get a view from the tribal perspective, unlike the work of Baden-Powell on The Land Systems of British India. For this work funding was given by the Bihar Government under Sir Edward Gait, who was the then Governor of Bihar.

In 1913, he was awarded the 'Kaiser-i-Hind' medal by the Government for his services. In 1915, he completed *The Oraons of Chotanagpur*. He also became the Secretary of the Bihar and Orissa Research Society. From 1916, he wrote a series of articles in the Journal of the same society on his excavations and discoveries of the Asur sites in Chotanagpur. In 1918, he was the curator of Patna Museum at Bankipore. In fact, he began to take classes in Physical Anthropology and Archaeology there. Sadly, apart from his collection of lectures called *Principles and Methods of Physical Anthropology* published in 1920, we have no records of what elapsed at the time as yet. The lectures were titled Readership lectures which were delivered in Patna University between January and March 1920.

In 1919, he was bestowed the title of 'Rai Bahadur' with two certificates of Honour and two medals. In 1920, he also became an Honorary Member of the Folklore Society of London. In 1921, he began a new journal which he called *Man in India*. He spent his own money bringing it out and later his daughter spent her own money on publishing it till 2006-07. This was part of his agenda to begin a peculiarly Indian School of Anthropology. Such a School would give its own evidence, data, analysis and interpretation for evolution, racial affinities, mentality and culture. To this end, he began to make it available to all by making it cheap. He also made the information accessible by giving a simply written summary of each year's anthropological work in the journal. He became the President of the Anthropology and Ethnography Section of the Indian Science Congress Association as well as a Member of the Bihar Legislative Assembly till 1937.

In 1925, he published *The Birhors*. In 1928, his second book on the Oraons, called *Oraon Religion and Customs* was published. This work showed how the Oraon culture was rapidly transforming and acculturating. One example was the Bhagat movement. At this time, he became a member of the Provincial Committee, sitting with the Simon Commission that year. He was also a member of the Indian Franchise Committee headed by Lord Lothian. In 1932-33, he was elected President of the Anthropology and Folklore section of the All India Oriental Conference. In February 1933, he was elected Fellow of the Bose Research Institute after which he gave up his legal practice.

In 1934-35, he published the book *Caste, Race and Religion in India*. In 1935, he became the foundation Fellow of the National Institute of Sciences in India. He also published *The Hill Bhuiyas of Orissa*. In 1936, he was elected Member of the Permanent Council of Congress International des Anthropologiques et Ethnologiques. In 1937, he published *The Kharias* in two volumes with the help of his son Ramesh Chandra Roy. The data on anthropometry was analysed by P.C. Mahalanobis, the internationally renowned statistician also called the 'Father of Indian Statistics'. This book was detailed in having a monographic study with both social and physical anthropological data of one community. In 1941, a homage was paid to him by the Indian Science Congress.

He did much more than just this. In his life, he never took up a case that was against any tribal, even when it was a case of murder. This made him trusted by the tribes and hated by many who were landlords. He had built a set of ante-rooms with a toilet where his tribal clients could stay while he fought their cases and also collected ethnographic data from them. He learnt the language to understand the culture and thought of the tribals. He further ensured that many of the problems of the tribes that he was familiar with were resolved through his offices. It is often said that the tribes of the region call outsiders or exploiters as diku in a pejorative manner. This never happened with Sarat Chandra Roy. In fact, especially in cultural matters, he was often called upon to resolve conflicts.

He wrote many papers on a variety of issues that he found interesting to the Black Bhils of Jaisamand Lake to caste to many other things. However, whenever he wrote, he corrected and checked the data again and again, as well as his expression, language and spelling. This ensured that each paper written was word-perfect. However, this habit of his annoyed many of his students, like Nirmal Kumar Bose, who felt that he could have written many more papers had he been less fastidious. This would have perhaps ensured far more issues covered by him through his writings.

He was also a lawyer who prepared detailed briefs of his cases. In later years, he trained his sons by preparing briefs for issues relating to tribes. These were detailed, annotated with information of relevance and with much data and references relating them to other cases. It made for a document well-worth reading. It was no wonder that he rarely lost cases pertaining to tribal culture and was often rèferred to, even by the British government.

Sarat Chandra Roy built up the discipline of Anthropology from scratch. He taught Anthropology at Calcutta University in its very inception, along with L.K.A. Iyer. He also took classes on Physical Anthropology at Patna University. However, this does not mean that he gave up on fieldwork. He continued to conduct his field researches. As seen from his house, he had marked a large map with his red ink pen the areas which he had visited. The map contained all the villages in the present state of Jharkhand. It was a mass of red though it was almost impossible for people to travel on foot and on elephant back for such long distances over days where roads were not available. He not only worked himself but tracked anthropological and archaeological work being conducted all over the country. He introduced two basic articles in each issue of *Man in India*. One was about the extent of work conducted by Anthropologists in India in the past year. Another was to give his students a basic outline of anthropological issues and concepts. These issues were discussed at length with Nirmal Kumar Bose as well as his youngest daughter Mira Roy, who died in February 2006.

For him, in his later years, his works on the overall aspects of culture, were a beginning, something that needed a major change. His experience taught him that what was now needed was a work on the Oraon that had the diversity and variation from each region and each village to show how varied the tribe was in its behaviour – something we know today as an essential component of post-modernism. To fulfil this monumental task, he had prepared a note of each village, classified into separate tehsils and thanas, into several notebooks. These notebooks had at least one page dedicated to each village beginning with its census, numbers, different communities and castes, arranged often in hierarchical order. Each page was numbered and the village thana number was also noted. They showed individual differences and variation as well as village-level differences in the observance of cultural norms.

So deeply did he get into Oraon society that he became united with its ambitions and goals, and so was able to relate them to others as if he belonged to them. This was also not an intrusion into an 'other' society, because instead of seeing him as an outsider the Oraon took to him. They would often call upon him to solve their problems. For instance, a problem came up while a bridge was being constructed over a river at Lohardaga:

> "The river side had Hindu and Oraon settlements. Since the bridge was washed out twice earlier, the contractor wanted to placate the Gods of both the villages. He repaired an old dilapidated temple of Hindus and presented a flag with a railway engine painted on it to the Oraon which was a symbol of power to that parha of Oraons in the Jatra festival. But envious of this, one of the neighbouring parha made a same kind of flag having the emblem and led [to] trouble at the annual Jatra festival at Bhasko. Two persons were killed. Fearing similar trouble next year, Roy was consulted by the Sub-divisional Magistrate and he then presented a flag emblemed [*sic.*] with an aeroplane and explained the superiority of it to the senior members of the parha of the latter village next year. A happy solution came out and no trouble occurred at the jatra that year." (Roy; 1980: 215-216)

Thus, when he was called upon to teach Anthropology at the Universities at Calcutta and Patna, he was able to talk of Anthropology as a subject that he had not only learnt, but something he had learnt while practicing. He thus became a well-loved teacher who was known very much for his intensity as well as his knowledge of various communities. He went on to thus establish the Anthropology Department at Patna University first and then Calcutta University next in order for teaching Anthropology. It seems Patna University perhaps could not sustain this interest in Anthropology, but Calcutta became a major centre for learning in the subject. Ironically, S.C. Roy himself had never attended a single class in Anthropology!

Roy eventually became a Member of the Legislative Council in the Jharkhand region (then South Bihar) and was dealing with issues relating to the tribes. He was very sincere and was often consulted for issues relating to tribes. At one time, he was asked whether the Tana Bhagats were fighting against the British. Roy had worked among the Tana Bhagats. The District Commissioner then went on to put together a document showing how the Tana Bhagats (an Oraon sect) had sung songs in praise of the Germans and the Kaiser. S.C. Roy then took this document and showed how line-for-line it showed the advance of a social movement within the Oraons rather than a movement against the British. This was then accepted by the British.

In this and in many other ways, S.C. Roy saved the lives of the tribes and other Indians who were often being accused of sedition against the British. He showed how legitimate protest against their conditions, ethnic groups, or even language was being misinterpreted and so quietened the fears of the British.

Eventually, a copy of the ethnographic raw data of the census operations in large trunks was sent over to his house so that he could use it for his researches. As a result, he had at hand a huge store of data on different communities from India at his disposal. However, he also collected data on tribes in different regions by sending questionnaires and requests for maps of different feudatory states which were sent back to him filled by the heads of the different states.

His fieldwork was something that showed how Anthropological rapport establishment was useful over generations. His student, D.N. Majumdar, in 1921 visited the area around Khunti with his students and he commented that:

> "How far this was true was seen by us in 1921, when some of us, then students of anthropology at Calcutta visited the Munda country with Dewan Bahadur L.K. Anantakrishna Iyer, Reader in Anthropology, Calcutta University. We visited hamlet after hamlet, we went into the interior villages of the Munda country, we enquired about the intimate social life of the people and everywhere we visited we felt the invisible presence of Roy. Every village we passed through, we were greeted with shouts of Sarat Babu Ki Jay. It is no wonder that Roy represented the tribal people of his district in Bihar Legislature for successive terms." (in Roy; 1980: 210)

It is a fact that Sarat Chandra Roy never formally did a course in Anthropology. Yet, he became such a good practitioner of it that when he began to write his books beginning with Mundas and their country, he was feted both in India as well as abroad, in Britain. As noted already, J.H. Hutton stated in a lecture that he was the 'Father of Indian Ethnology'. He was awarded the Kaiser-i-Hind medal, among others. Many other great Anthropologists wrote letters to him, praising his works, asking for details or sharing their own books and ideas. This included A.C. Haddon, among others. This made him truly an International figure rather than just a local Anthropologist.

The times were different and his own innate sense of nationalism drew him to take pride in the works of Indian Anthropologists, to which he mostly dedicated his new journal *Man in India* which is still in print. He would always locate his research within the larger body of the theories and structures seen in an International anthropology. Thus, he saw a range of studies from simple societies (or primitive societies, as they were called then) to the idea that, "primitive society exhibits the ground-plan on which the more complex structure that we call civilization has been built up" (Roy, 1937: 249). For him, different levels of society should be understood and then the entire structure of civilization could be organized from such beginnings (Roy, 1937: 249).

Since, Roy began by using Anthropology for tribal welfare he always saw Anthropology as being for use, for nation-building, helping the oppressed and thus emancipatory, and for creating fellow-feeling for a better future in the eternal history of humankind (1937). Thus, he intended that Anthropology should be included within all Universities and in the Administrative and bureaucratic offices as an integral part of their work.

For S.C. Roy, the first editions of Anthropology books that he had collected and read painstakingly by buying through orders from London, arranged in his room full of shelves, became his anchor. When he fell ill, he turned the shelves toward himself so that he could see all his books from the bed where he lay. From this vantage point, he could look at references and order them to be brought to him. Using these references he kept on writing, including a file of poetry that he created to introduce Anthropology to the uninitiated. This was to be published much later in *Man in India*.

From here, perhaps he recalled the passing faces of his informants who came in for court cases and he spoke to them as a lawyer and also the different villages which he had visited. He may have remembered Budhu Birhor who had saved his life while crossing the swollen Damodar River near Rajrappa to visit a village for a cultural function. He might have seen the faces of the students he had taught as his health failed. His students wished that he would do more, write much more about the issues that impassioned him.

In his zeal and enthusiasm, he infected students to take up Anthropology. Perhaps, far more became his adherents than if he had been a Ph.D. and taken on research scholars. Today, his work stands up to our current scrutiny. He was the quintessential all-rounder as an Anthropologist. He worked in all the sub-fields and his work was applicable to administrators, bureaucrats, politicos, scholars, tribes and development activists, all at the same time. We do not have his like even today. This was why when he died on 30th April, 1942 on the holy day of Buddha Purnima, he left a yawning emptiness.

REFERENCES

Roy, Sarat Chandra (with Ramesh Chandra Roy). 1937a. *The Kharia*. Ranchi: Man in India Office.

Roy, Sarat Chandra. 1908. *The Mundas, Their Country, Their Character and Their Poetry in Indian World*, VII, April.

Roy, Sarat Chandra. 1912, 1995. *The Mundas and their Country*. Calcutta: City Book Society.

Roy, Sarat Chandra. 1914. "Magic and Witchcraft on the Chota Nagpur Plateau" in *The Journal of the Asiatic Society of Bengal*, September, New Series, Vol. 10, No. 9, pp. 349-353.

Roy, Sarat Chandra. 1915. *The Oraons of Chotanagpur*. Ranchi: Bar Library.

Roy, Sarat Chandra. 1920. *The Principles and Methods of Physical Anthropology*. Patna: Patna University.

Roy, Sarat Chandra. 1921. "Anthropological Researches in India" in *Man in India*, Vol. 1, pp. 532-533.

Roy, Sarat Chandra. 1922 (b). "The Gods of the Oraons" in *Man in India*, Vol. 2, No. 3, pp. 123-140.

Roy, Sarat Chandra. 1922(a). "Anthropological Research in India" in *Man in India*, Vol. 2, pp. 11-55.

Roy, Sarat Chandra. 1925. *The Birhor: A Little Known Jungle Tribe of Chotanagpur*. Ranchi: Man in India Office.

Roy, Sarat Chandra. 1926. "The Oraon Feast of Sal Flowers" in *The Journal of the Bihar and Orissa Research Society*, June, pp. 1-27.

Roy, Sarat Chandra. 1927. "Death and its Attendant Ceremonies Among the Oraons" in *the Journal of the Bihar and Orissa Research Society*, September-December, pp. 278-291.

Roy, Sarat Chandra. 1928. *Oraon Religion and Customs*. Ranchi: Man in India Office.

Roy, Sarat Chandra. 1932. "A Message of Hope and Goodwill to the "Adi-Bashi" in *Adibasi*, Vol. I, February, pp. i-ii.

Roy, Sarat Chandra. 1932. "The Study of Folk-Lore, and Tradition in India" in *the Journal of the Bihar and Orissa Research Society*, Vol. 18, Parts III-IV, pp. 353-381.

Roy, Sarat Chandra. 1935. *The Hill Bhuiyas of Orissa*. Ranchi: Man in India Office.

Roy, Sarat Chandra. 1937. "The Study of Anthropology from the Indian View-Point" in *The Journal of the Benaras Hindu University*, pp. 243-256.

Roy, Sarat Chandra. 1938. "An Indian Outlook on Anthropology" in *Man*, September, Nos. 171-172, pp. 146-150.

Roy, Sarat Chandra. 1938. "Anthropological Studies in India" in *The New Review*, February, pp. 136-150.

Roy, Sarat Chandra. 1939. "The Cultural-National Outlook" in *The Behar Herald*, p. 23 (Presented at the Lahore Indian Science Congress in 1939).

Roy, Sarat Chandra. 1946. "The Aborigines of Chota Nagpur: Their Proper Status in the Reformed Constitution" in *Man in India*, Vol. 26, No. 2, pp. 120-136.

Roy, Sarat Chandra. 1961. "The Administrative History and Land Tenures of the Ranchi District Under British Rule" in *Man in India*, Vol. 41, No. 4, pp. 276-323.

Roy, Sarat Chandra. 1966. *Studies in Indian Anthropology. Calcutta: Indian Studies: Past and Present*. Edited and introduced by Nirmal Kumar Bose.

Roy, Sarat Chandra. 1971. "A Historical Documents" in *Man in India*, Vol. 51, No. 3, pp. 191-207.

Roy, Sarat Chandra. 1972. *Oraon Religion and Customs*. Calcutta: Editions Indian.

Roy, Sarat Chandra. 1982. "The Effects on the Aborigines of Chotanagpur of Their Contact with Western Civilization" in *Man in India*, Vol. 62, No. 1, Mar., pp. 65-100.

Roy, Sarat Chandra. 1984(a). Magic and Witchcraft on the Chota-Nagpur Plateau – A Study in the Philosophy of Primitive Life in *Man in Life*, Vol. 64, No. 1, March, pp. 91-129.

Roy, Sarat Chandra. 1984. *The Oraons of Chota Nagpur: Their History, Economic Life and Social Organization*. Ranchi: Man in India Office

6
An Ideal Teacher
Dr. Abhimanyu Sharma

Vinay Kumar Srivastava

Dr. Abhimanyu Sharma, Reader in Anthropology, University of Delhi, was barely forty-eight when the cruel hands of death snatched him from us. His only child, a son, had just started reading for a degree in Economics in St. Stephen's College (University of Delhi) at that time. Half-a-year before Dr. Sharma's sad demise, he was diagnosed with a cardiac ailment, the hardening and calcification of his aortic valve. The eminent surgeon of those days, Dr. Nagarur Gopinath, who had founded the cardio-thoracic centre at the All-India Institute of Medical Sciences (AIIMS), New Delhi, conducted a valve-replacement surgery on Dr. Sharma, the valve being imported from New Zealand. The family of Dr. Sharma was also planning to fly him to New Zealand for surgery, but then thought that the AIIMS would be the best option in India for this.

Dr. Sharma, however, could recover from the surgery, as is said in the medical parlance, 'the operation was successful', but had jaundice while convalescing in the hospital, and passed away on 25 September, 1978. Vivid to my memory is a meeting with him – Professor P.C. Joshi was with me – a couple of days before the scheduled date of his operation. In a feeble voice – this man whose robust voice could be heard several metres away from the room when he was lecturing – he advised us to dedicate ourselves to the growth of anthropology. His commitment to anthropology was exemplary and infectious.

I knew some of his doctoral students. Closest to the graduate students of the department those days was his disciple, Dr. Surinder Nath, who later served as a teacher in the Delhi Anthropology Department. Dr. Nath worked for his doctoral thesis under Dr. Sharma's astute supervision, on the pattern of human growth and development among the Jat of

Haryana villages. Dr. Nath often described his supervisor as stern, mathematically sophisticated, and impeccably correct in his usage of the English language. He expected his students to gradually imbibe these characteristics, and those who made sincere efforts in this direction were dear to him, and the rest who failed to live up to his expectations, fell from his eyes. That was the prime reason why he did not have an entourage of students around him as was the case with some other teachers of the department who were less exacting. Those who worked under Dr. Sharma's supervision for a doctorate had bittersweet relations with him, because of his challenging schedule and a battery of unending constructive criticisms on their research writings, which often seemed to these students enervating and demoralising. Those of his students whom I knew often whinged about the rough supervisory treatment they invariably received, but the same persons after having finished their doctoral theses often spoke admiringly of the unparalleled learning experience they had under Dr. Sharma's tutelage, and those who stayed in teaching – as did Dr. Nath – were at the forefront of transmitting what they had learnt from Dr. Sharma to their respective research students. Thus, Dr. Sharma continued to remain alive for generations. In fact, Dr. Sharma often used to quote a statement from the Talmud: "If you teach your son, you are in fact teaching your son's son."

The other student of Dr. Sharma I knew was Dr. G.D. Gupta, who wrote a thesis of palmar dermatoglyphics, and later joined the Central Forensic Science Laboratory as a scientific staff, from where he finally retired. He has always registered his indebtedness to Dr. Sharma for teaching him the methodology of scientific investigation. Another of his student, Dr. Kusum Taneja, was relatively quiet, absorbed in her work, and contributed several papers to international journals, in joint authorship with Dr. Sharma, on palmar prints.The last one I knew was Ms. Parakh Sachdeva who had started her research work under Dr. Sharma on growth and development. Many of his students, like me, who did not read for a Ph.D. under him, were profoundly impressed by his academic acumens and the vast trove of his knowledge, which he generously distributed in his long classes on anthropometry, material culture, Indian ethnology, human palaeontology, and pair-bond relations. He was keen to supervise me for a doctoral work on the growth of pelvis, and in this work, he wanted along with him, an anatomist or a radiologist to be my co-supervisor, for the data would include in addition to anthropometric measurements, radiological material on pelvis. However, my destiny lay elsewhere.

Dr. Sharma was the only researcher from the department who carried out fieldwork for his doctoral thesis in Myanmar, encompassing both the biological and socio-cultural aspects of the people. However, his doctoral thesis, titled 'A Study of Palmar Dermatoglyphics of Burmans: Certain Fresh Methodological Approaches as based on Burma Data', was on an anthropological specialisation which was destined to be his life-long commitment. He studied the palmar prints quantitatively, describing his specialization as 'metric dermatoglyphics'. He used to tell us an episode in our classes. In a conference of 1961 in Rome, on the mathematical study of dermatoglyphic patterns, Dr. Sharma was one of the invitees. He presented a couple of papers in it, which impressed the audience greatly with the sophistication of his analysis and interpretation. One of the participants in that seminar asked him a question, addressing him as 'Dr.'. Being outspoken, he intervened before the asker could complete his question. "Please don't call me Dr., as I have not yet earned my Ph.D. You may call me Mr., or just call me by my first name," was Dr. Sharma's intervention. The audience was so overwhelmed with his reply that each one of them dropped the titles (Dr. or Prof.) before his or her respective name. Later, one of the participants in the seminar said the following: "If you can produce such an erudite work without completing a Ph.D., then I am sure you'll excel in all departments of knowledge after you have earned your doctorate." Dr. Sharma was awarded his doctoral degree in 1962; and indeed, he excelled in all academic activities – teaching, supervising, writing.

Dr. Sharma was born, as I learnt from his brother and son, in jail. His grandmother was jailed for participating in the national freedom struggle. Along with her went to the jail Dr. Sharma's mother, who was pregnant at that time. Dr. Sharma had four brothers and two sisters. His father worked for the *Hindustan Times*. The family lived in a New Delhi neighbourhood called Hanuman Lane (Connaught Place). For schooling, Dr. Sharma went to D.A.V. High School, and later he studied science subjects at Hindu College, University of Delhi. Of the subjects he studied at college, his most favourite was Physics. This would partially explain his deep interest in quantification, and the application of rigorous methods of study to palmar prints and human growth. He then studied for his master's and doctorate in anthropology, under the supervision of Professor P.C. Biswas. I came to know from his family that he enjoyed cycling a lot and untiringly would cycle from his residence to the towns neighbouring Delhi.

Dr. Sharma's travel to Rome was perhaps the only academic visit he carried out after a long stint of fieldwork in Myanmar, the pictures of which he had systematically arranged in an album and would bring it to his class on the ethnology of India to speak to the students on the ethnic types. His family members told me about his private visits to some other foreign countries, including Germany.

To the best of my knowledge, Dr. Sharma did not have any collaboration with a foreign or Indian scholar, though he did write some articles jointly. Neither did he apply for a project to any funding agency. Besides perhaps holding the superintendentship of practical and theory examinations, which in any case one has to do on a rotational basis in a teaching department, Dr. Sharma did not occupy any administrative position. He could also not become a professor of anthropology; for the first time the post (which fell vacant because of the retirement of Professor Biswas) went to Professor Indera P. Singh. The second professorship the department got from the university was in social anthropology, for which Professor J.D. Mehra was selected; Dr. Sharma, being a physical anthropologist, was not eligible for this position. He remained a reader (now, equivalent to associate professor) in anthropology till his death. Sometimes he described him as a 'Reader in Applied Physical Anthropology', because he thought that physical anthropology had no meaning except when it was put to use, to help in the management of human affairs, to give a fresh understanding to the designing of human-friendly appliances, and to explode several myths that had been plaguing human existence.

Dr. Sharma certainly would have been a good administrator, for he was well aware of the norms and procedures of running departmental affairs. He was cordial towards the non-teaching staff. He was perhaps the only teacher in the department those days who extracted the best out of the photographic laboratory (called Dark Room). Now the same room has been converted into a laboratory of Visual Anthropology and is sometimes used as a class room for conducting tutorials and lectures for a smaller number of students. Those days the Dark Room was almost a forbidden place. Black paper was glued to the glasses of the rooms, including the ventilators. Only a couple of people used to go there. And one of them was Dr. Sharma. The photographer, Mr. O.P. Sahni, was a dedicated man, truly beholden to Dr. Sharma. After his classes were over, Dr. Sharma would sit in the Dark Room. The other person who would join him there was the statistician of the Department, Mr. S.M. Thukral. Although Dr. Sharma was very friendly with them, and through them to some other non-teaching employees (especially, the head of the instrument room, Mr, N.C. Jain), much to the annoyance of the teaching faculty in a hierarchy-ridden department, it was much more than a simple relationship of friendliness with them.

By contrast to the other teachers of the department, Dr. Sharma gave great importance to the display of visuals in his class lectures. The other teachers preferred to dictate their notes to the students, or give a lecture continuously looking at their notes, or had memorised their lectures which they delivered in the class, or had ingeniously composed the lecture in the class, involving the students and covering a broad area of knowledge resourcefully. To this, some of the academic entrepreneurs today send their notes to their students by email, advising them to read them and approach the teacher in case of doubts. Till early 1972, Dr. Sharma followed the method of lecturing the students, often referring to his notes, but from late 1972, visual material constituted an integral part of his lectures.

Let me give at this juncture a glimpse of Dr. Sharma's pre-1972 classes. Before he came to conduct his lecture, one of the laboratory attendants brought to the classroom the teaching material he would require. Besides his notes, it included bones or their fragments, plaster casts of fossils, albums, measuring instruments, material objects (including archaeological tools), charts, sketches, and diagrams. However, the things brought to the classes differed with respect to the topic he was going to teach. Suppose, it was a class on fire-making technology, as was the case in 1970 when he taught my B.Sc. (Hons.) Second Year class some portions from a paper on material culture and technology, he would bring from his personal collection some fire-producing instruments, such as pieces of flint, materials used in bow drill method; and if it was a lecture on human evolution, then primate skulls, plaster casts of early man, pictures, and hand-drawn charts of the evolutionary tree, would be his accompaniment. In a class of somatometry, sliding and spreading callipers would come, and painstakingly, Dr. Sharma would talk about the merits of these instruments.

His notes were a wad of papers (of different sizes and colours), some handwritten, some typed, some printed, some were clippings from newspapers, all tagged. To the notes, he initially prepared for his classes, he would keep on adding newer material, so the papers would swell; in fact, these notes were also a testimony of how knowledge in that area had expanded over years. He would bring all his notes to the classroom. It seemed to me that perhaps he was going to write an article in the class for which he had brought with him the reference material. Each of his classes was focused; he gave the most recent information, and also the questions that could come in the mind of an inquisitor.

Mr. Sahni earlier prepared charts for Dr. Sharma's classes, and Mr. Thukral extended him help in statistical packages. When the technology of preparing slides came, Mr. Sahni was busy in doing that. Dr. Sharma was the first teacher in the department to make use of this novel teaching devisė, which was an ineluctable part of his post-1972 teaching style. Later, the other teachers in the department took lead from him.

Dr. Sharma was unconventional, iconoclastic, and took great delight in teaching (and researching) new areas in anthropology. Among the topics he took great interest while teaching was the foundation of human behaviour. Like the other scholars of those days whose interest lay in this field, Dr. Sharma was also closely examining the nuances of primate behaviour and evolution. Among its aspects, he paid a lot of importance to understanding sexual relations, the pair-bonding between males and females. Although the other papers did deal with sexuality (particularly the ones concerned with kinship and marriage, old world and new world monkeys), the teachers teaching them were shy of talking about it in their class lectures – thus, mating behaviour and sexual violence among higher apes was conveniently skipped and so was a discussion of pre-marital sexuality. I cannot forget the blushes on the face of a young, unmarried, social anthropology teacher, while he lectured on Verrier Elwin's study of the Muriya ghotul. And, at this point, I remember that in many libraries of the world Bronislaw Malinowski's Sexual Life of the Savages was kept under lock and key, to be issued to the readers under the strict instruction of the higher authorities.

Dr. Sharma was, however, different. He had closely read Desmond Morris' *The Naked Ape*, and used to quote from it profusely, sometimes annoyingly, in his classes. In 1973, I accidentally found Desmond Morris' *Intimate Behaviour* (1971) in Delhi Public Library, Old Delhi Railway Station, which I used to visit frequently, and I got it issued for Dr. Sharma. I recall the joy on his face when he saw that book, for he had not read it. A couple of days later, I saw one of the office assistants typing out some pages from the book, as photocopying was non-existent at that time. Next I saw those pages being appended to his notes.

As I said earlier, a bulk of Dr. Sharma's research papers was on palmar dermatoglyphics, quite a few written jointly with his doctoral student, Dr. Taneja. Those days the division of labour with respect to dermatoglyphic studies was that Dr. Sharma worked on palmar prints, Dr. P.K. Datta, on sole prints, and Dr. H.K. Kumbnani, on finger prints, although the possibility of shifting from one specialization to the other was always there. Of these three dermatoglyphic patterns, sole was not a part of the course.

Most of the papers of Dr. Sharma were published in the journal that the Delhi Department of Anthropology started in 1954. Titled *The Anthropologist*, it was the third anthropology journal to have started in India after *Man in India* (1921) and *The Eastern Anthropologist* (1947). These articles of Dr. Sharma were on different, but interrelated, aspects of palmar prints, such as geometric basis of main line index determination, symmetry of four main lines, effects of variable digital spreading on radio-ulnar trends of deviation quotient, and the palmar dermatoglyphics of different communities. With Dr. A.K. Kalla, he wrote a paper on palmar prints of Kashmiri Pandits. Many of his publications were on the data from Burma, including a short article on kin terms of the people he had studied.

In 1964, he published a short paper in *Man* (Item 19, 64: 18-19) on a new instrument he had devised for measuring angles directly. Two years later, in 1966, he contributed a paper to Current Anthropology (7[2]: 235-39) titled 'The Linear-Coordinate-cum-Angle Measure: A Multi-Purpose Tool.' One of his most perceptive comments titled '*On Theoretical Models of Natural Selection*' appeared in Current Anthropology (19[11]: 188), where in the context of model-building, he spoke of "intuition [striking] one's mind like lightening". In the same comment, quoting Galton's idea of a 'cold-blooded examination of facts', he also considered the maintenance of objectivity in a research pursuit as a principal requirement. One of his most popular articles was on the Negrito problem in India, published in Bala Ratnam's Anthropology on the March (1963). In this highly referenced article, Dr. Sharma rendered a summary of the different views on the autochthonous status of the Negrito in India, including his correspondence with Dr. B.S. Guha. For ethnologists, working on the formation of races, it is still a relevant contribution.

Dr. Sharma reposed full faith in the time-tested instruments of physical anthropological investigation, such as the anthropometric rod, different types of callipers, and appliances used for printing dermal ridges. He believed in an integration of different branches of anthropology. Many of the anthropological puzzles required drawing insights from the other branches. Although he described himself as a 'physical anthropologist', it did not mean, as he always said, that he was 'pigeonholed'. He looked beyond his specialization to borrow methods and approaches from other cognate branches. This is clear from the concluding sentence of his article on Negrito problem: "The answer lies not only with physical anthropology and human genetical investigations...., but with the spade and brush as well." Here, the reference is to the archaeological enquiry. He was arguing, as is clear, for an interdisciplinary exploration of anthropological questions.

Dr. Sharma's faith in traditional anthropology, which has withstood the test of time, was most clear when in 1971, a German geneticist, Dr. Friedrich Otto Vogel, came to the Delhi Department of Anthropology to train the faculty members and research students in cytogenetic techniques. The teachers specializing in physical anthropology, including the then head of the department, joined his workshop; and so did a number of young researchers. The laboratory-based anthropology was flying high then, so much so that the head of the department got a microscope installed in his room, to carry on with research during his leisure, when he was relatively free from his administrative duties. Dr. Sharma kept himself out of the 'new fad', as for him the 'entire human world was his laboratory'. He perhaps knew that the cytogenetic research was bound to deflect us from the investigation of fundamental questions of human evolution and survival in a holistic manner.

7
An Excellent Theorist
Professor Gopala Sarana

Vinay Kumar Srivastava

Professor Gopala Sarana made a difference to my life. When I met him in early 1984, I was a lecturer in sociology in a college affiliated to the University of Delhi. Before that I had seen him in December 1978 in a well-attended session on post-colonial anthropology of the International Congress of Ethnological and Anthropological Sciences (held in Delhi), which was chaired by Professor Surajit Sinha. Professor A.L. Basham was also there; so were Professors Agehananda Bharati and T.N. Madan. Professor Sarana attended the two hours' session, rather restlessly, sometimes feverishly turning the pages of a book he had carried with him. As soon as the discussion on the presentations made in the session began, Professor Sarana was the first to give a long comment on the fate of anthropological theory after the Second World War, and before the session could be concluded with the final remarks of the Chairperson, he left, and was not to be seen in Vigyan Bhawan, the venue of the Congress.

In early 1984, Professor Surinder Nath introduced him to me. In a short interaction of less than quarter of an hour, I found him extremely amiable. He advised me to 'return' to the Department of Anthropology, University of Delhi, where I had studied for five years. He said anthropology needed 'good people' to save it from being 'hijacked' and 'engulfed' by sociology. What he said on that day has been said by some other people in different contexts. When Indian sociologists visit universities in Europe and America, they identify them as 'anthropologists'. Among the sociologists, they become anthropologists, and among anthropologists, they become sociologists. 'The double-faced sociologists have caused a lot of damage to anthropology,' were Professor

Sarana's words spoken loudly and clearly. When saying this, one could easily guess that Professor Sarana had some particular people in mind.

That fortuitous meeting with Professor Sarana was the commencement of a long relationship with him, lasting till 2010 when he breathed his last. During this period of twenty-six years, he stayed in my house on umpteen occasions, and I had a golden chance to learn from him about the issues in philosophical anthropology in which he was greatly interested those days, and also about the fraternity of anthropologists. I could see he always preferred me over others. In December 1984, he organized a seminar on the birth centenary year of Bronislaw Malinowski (1884-1942), inviting a select group of people to speak on this occasion. I was fortunate to have been included in the list of the invitees, such as Professors N. Subba Reddy, R.K. Srivastava, N.K. Behura, and Dr. V.C. Channa. I read out in this seminar a paper that ran into sixty handwritten pages. Not even once was I reminded of time. Later, Professor Sarana said that never has there been a seminar in which the paper-readers truly had the luxury of time. It was singularly because of fewer participants, where each one of them could give a total view of his paper, without pruning anything, and also could have an insightful discussion on his presentation, which would subsequently help in its revision. My present-presentation began at ten in the morning and with discussion finished at two in the afternoon, when we broke for lunch.

These papers were supposed to be published in Professor Subba Reddy's newly founded journal titled South Asian Social Scientist. After returning from Lucknow, where the Malinowski Seminar took place, I thoroughly revised my paper, and was in a hurry to publish it. Since one did not know when Professor Subba Reddy's journal be published, I sent my paper (which was on Malinowski's ideas of freedom and civilization) to Sociological Bulletin, which readily accepted it, and one portion of this paper was sent to Dialectical Anthropology, which also published it later. Professor Sarana was not happy about this decision of mine, for he thought that all these papers on Malinowski should have been published together in an issue of a journal, and later this issue could have been converted into a book.

Professor Sarana was extremely happy when he learnt that in January 1985, I was selected for the post of lecturer in Social Anthropology at the University of Delhi. I immediately wrote to him that I was always indebted to him for inspiring me to return to my parent subject, my parent department. From then on, since both of us were now in the same subject, our relationship strengthened further. He wrote a recommendation for me when I was seeking admission in the University of Cambridge for a doctorate; the other recommenders were Professors André Béteille and D.K. Bhattacharya. Whenever I went to Lucknow for a lecture, he always came to attend it, even if it was on a topic not related directly to anthropology. I remember once I delivered a lecture on the subaltern approach, illustrating it with the work of David Hardiman, in a workshop that Professor B.R.K. Shukla had organized on research methods. Professor Sarana came to attend it and gave one of the finest comments on the relationship between anthropology and history.

In late 2005, I mustered courage to tell Professor Sarana that he might think of assembling his papers on anthropological theory for a compendium, which should also have an introduction demonstrating how these papers were interconnected. Professor Sarana was convinced about this idea when I gave him several examples of anthropologists and sociologists who had attempted the same and came out with well-known books. I submitted before him that different research papers could be considered as different chapters of a book – the articles have to be transformed into chapters, and a book would then eventually result. The introduction to the book would organically knit it together. I also told him what I had learnt from those who had the experience of producing books from a collection of their articles that when one is reading one's papers, one should not do anything to them except correcting the spelling mistakes and grammatical errors. The original flavour of the article should remain intact.

Professor Sarana, who otherwise fancied disagreements, and was not shy of being acerbic during arguments, agreed on all that I had told him. Within five months or so, he got me delivered his manuscript, well bound, with twenty-four chapters ('articles') and an introduction. He wanted me to have a look at it, and if I thought that it was worth publishing, then I should negotiate with Delhi publishers. For a foreword to his book, he wished to contact Professor David Maybury-Lewis, and in case he remained un-contacted or could not do so because of other engagements, then he thought he would write to Professor Clifford Geertz. He wrote aerogrammes to them, sent reminders as well, but his communications remained unanswered. [Later, he came to know that Professor Maybury-Lewis was severely ill with Parkinson's disease, and breathed his last in December 2007, and Professor Geertz had passed away in October 2006.] Then, Professor Subba Reddy contributed a foreword to his book.

I submitted the manuscript first to an international publisher, a big name in social sciences, and their comment was that Professor Sarana's papers were on 'old theories', some of which would not capture the attention of the readers. Another international publisher was not interested in publishing on anthropological theory because the market for such books was sluggish. The third one was a well-known Indian publisher, whose response was that the manuscript comprised papers which were 'pretty old' and had 'outlived their utility'. Finally, it was Rawat Publishers who went ahead with the project and two years before Professor Sarana's death, the book titled *Method and Theory in Anthropology* was released. I received a signed copy of this book from Mr. Kailash Rawat, the founder of Rawat Publishers. For my readers, I have given a succinct account of how Professor Sarana's book was produced, and how books of similar type can be contemplated for publication.

After his master's in anthropology, Professor Sarana taught at Lucknow. His indebtedness to Professor D.N. Majumdar was expressed in the following words: "I learnt anthropology sitting at the feet of Professor Majumdar." Then, Professor Sarana proceeded to Harvard University to read for a doctorate under Professor Cora DuBois. His doctoral thesis was unconventional but on a familiar subject. It was unconventional because it was not a fieldwork-based research, and it was a meticulously-undertaken comparative study of different varieties of comparative methods that had emerged in anthropology at different points in time beginning with classical evolutionism.

Anthropology was (and is) unthinkable without empirical research; statements like the following are respectfully held among the fraternity of anthropologists: 'an anthropologist is worth his salt if he has an ethnographic monograph to his credit', 'an anthropologist is an anthropologist if he has conducted a lengthy fieldwork among the members of a community (own or different) and written about it', and 'ideally an anthropologist should carry out intensive field studies in at least two communities, for this will give him an opportunity to compare the social situations he has studied.' Professor Sarana wrote several papers on how anthropologists should carry out their studies and the ethical standards with which they should conform. But he was often criticised in the academic circles for not having a lengthy field study to his name, although he re-analysed the ethnographic writings of others – for instance, for a definition of marriage, he closely looked at the Nayar case, for an understanding of rebellion, at the Swazi case, and in both cases, he ventured on to give novel interpretations. Although Professor Sarana never spoke about it, his printed curriculum vitae, of which I have a copy, states that he carried out a fieldwork among the Oraon of Ranchi. However, to the best of my memory, he never published an ethnographic piece on it.

Professor Sarana's love for anthropological theory and method was unparalleled – I have not come across any anthropologist in my life whose commitment to theory and method could match his; but he confined his interests to classical philosophical writings and those of some new philosophers, and within anthropology, he restricted him to functionalism, structuralism, and comparative methodology, and within the first two, to the British tradition, and Claude Lévi-Strauss. Once, in 1986, he also organized a seminar on Marxism and Anthropology in Poona, where his friend, Professor Srivastava, was teaching, but its proceedings were not published, and I am not aware of what Professor Sarana spoke there. One of his regrets was that wherever he taught [Karnataka University (Dharwar) or Lucknow University], he did not come across any student who was truly devoted to learning social science philosophy and pure theoretical traditions. Some of his students in Dharwar and Lucknow were exceptional, but none took delight in pure theory. His concomitant interest was in linguistic anthropology, mainly because he had closely studied the French structuralism. He was one of the few who had delivered at several places worth-reading lectures on structuralism.

Professor Sarana always desired to be in a place where he could teach courses of anthropological theory and methods to a batch of students who were really interested in learning it. He thought that in India, Delhi University's Anthropology Department would be the best place, and also, he would be able to work here till the age of sixty-five, for that was the age of retirement. He was keen to join but his condition was that he would neither send his application for the post of professor nor he would appear for interview before the members of the selection committee. In other words, he wanted to be selected in absentia.

Professor Upendra Baxi was Delhi University's Vice Chancellor from 1990 to 1994. As he was keen on bringing the best minds as teachers to the University, I thought he might respond positively to the suggestion of appointing Professor Sarana to the Department of Anthropology. I had developed a little familiarity with Professor Baxi because I had been teaching a course on research methods at the Faculty of Law, University of Delhi, which was introduced by him, and on many occasions, I had sought his wise counsel on the topics I was teaching. Since I also wanted Professor Sarana in my Department, for I knew it would bring about a qualitative change in the standard of teaching and research in social anthropology, I sought an appointment with Professor Baxi and handed over Professor Sarana's curriculum vitae. In this brief meeting, I told Professor Baxi about Professor Sarana's academic contribution and how the department would be academically strengthened with his joining.

Later, I learnt that in the interview held for the posts of two professors in social anthropology in August 1990, one of the experts placed before the selection committee Professor Sarana's curriculum vitae for consideration, but it did not want to consider anyone in absentia. The University of Delhi remained deprived of his services, but in my own humble way, I introduced my students to his work, particularly his lectures on structuralism, human nature, and a booklet on introducing anthropology to the beginners. Professor Sarana retired from Lucknow University in June 1995, and continued working on the subjects of his interest.

Professor Sarana was very fond of intelligent students and colleagues. He could even tolerate their idiosyncrasies and unhesitatingly engaged with them in unending debates, which would often become acrimonious, but this did no damage to their interpersonal ties. I was a part of one such debate between Professor Sarana and Professor Ajit Pandey (a sociology teacher) on Naxalism. It just did not seem to end, because new arguments and polemics were surfacing, but at no juncture, Professor Sarana seemed to lose his cool, although he was making his points aggressively and pointedly. Eventually, we decided to split. In spite of such heated discussions, when Professors Sarana and Pandey were walking out of Professor Sukant Chaudhury's house, where all this took place, they were as friendly as they ever were.

In his own humble way, he promoted his students and younger colleagues whom he thought were promising. He motivated Professor Pandey to publish his work in *The Eastern Anthropologist*. For a brief period of time, he was appointed the editor of *The Eastern Anthropologist*, and one could notice a remarkable change in the quality of the journal. In 1991, in *The Times of India*, I read an article on the Andamanese tribes, which carried pictures of anthropologists in their swim suits playing banter with the Onge. The pictures and the write-up accompanying them annoyed me to such an extent that I immediately wrote a long protest letter to the editor of the newspaper, and also sent its copy to Professor Sarana. To my pleasant surprise, some months later, I saw that letter printed as a 'brief communication' in *The Eastern Anthropologist*, under the title 'Anthropology is not a romantic pedagogy'. *The Times of India*, however, did not publish it. When later I told Professor Sarana that had I known that it would be published in an anthropology journal, I would have written it more 'academically' and more 'carefully'. His answer was that one must always value the spontaneity in writing!

Professor Sarana's major work was on an anthropological understanding of the comparative method. Not only that his doctoral dissertation on comparative methods was published by the Wenner-Gren Foundation for Anthropological Research (New York), and several papers of his on this topic appeared in well-known journals, he was also invited by Alan Barnard and Jonathan Spencer for an article on the comparative method for their Encyclopaedia of Social and Cultural Anthropology. His salient argument in these works was that there are several comparative methods, each designed to serve a particular purpose. Here, he disagreed with A.R. Radcliffe-Brown's contention that there was only one comparative method – 'the comparative method' – the aim of which was to move from the particular to the general. Professor Sarana distinguished between comparative method as used in anthropology from that in linguistics, a theme to which he contributed some of his papers.

One of the major issues in social anthropology is of conceptual clarification, and to this, Professor Sarana paid central attention. He meticulously addressed the concepts of his days in his writings. That he was prodigious may be guessed from the fact that at the age of 21, he wrote a paper on "Radcliffe-Brown's contribution to Kinship Studies" (1956) and at 22, on "British social anthropology and its American appraisal" (1957). Those days Radcliffe-Brown was a celebrated anthropologist; Edmund Leach wrote that in England, in the late 1920s and 1930s, the budding anthropologists would come to Malinowski's seminars in London to learn the art and science of fieldwork, and once they were confident of conducting their independent fieldwork, they would shift to Oxford to learn the theoretical approaches from Radcliffe-Brown. Professor Sarana's essays 'de-mystifying' Radcliffe-Brown, and also showing that the latter did not use the words like 'gems', as said M.N. Srinivas, a doctoral student of Radcliffe-Brown, were highly appreciated by Sir Raymond Firth, and the 'founder of the science of culturology', Leslie A. White.

That Professor Sarana was indeed ahead of his time can be gauged from his essay on the methodology of Austro-German diffusionism, written in the 1960s, when he was a student at Harvard. Those days not much was written in English on Kulturkreiselehre; Professor Sarana took the lead, not only in familiarising the English-speaking world with these ideas, but also examining the impact of this school on American anthropology.

One of Professor Sarana's unforgettable contributions was that he promoted an 'integrated anthropology'. He knew full well the scrimmages and quibbles that endured in anthropology departments between physical and social anthropologists. Sometimes, this 'cold war' used to turn rancorous when issues of appointment and distribution of funding came up, adversely affecting the interpersonal relations that eventually thwarted the progress of the department and the subject. He believed that the best way was not to counsel the members of the department and pontificate on the virtues of living with amity, but to create a context where the social anthropologists wrote on issues of physical anthropology, which they could handle competently, or on archaeology; and in a similar vein, the physical anthropologists might write on cultural factors affecting growth and development or the profile of health and illness. I remember the animated discussion he had with Professor Nath on the political economy of physical growth. Keeping the spirit of integrated anthropology alive, he wrote a booklet introducing anthropology, in which all the branches of anthropology were adequately covered. Professor Sarana also wrote a book on prehistoric archaeology in Hindi which was published by the Directorate of Hindi Medium Implementation, University of Delhi. Incidentally, he was one of those few Indian anthropologists (like Professors S.C. Dube, Yogesh Atal) who excelled in writing in Hindi. Almost all the letters he wrote to me were in Hindi and his handwriting was exceptionally beautiful, which many of his students tried to emulate. Further, while writing in English, he unfailingly took care to use the diacritics.

Although his interest in physical anthropology did not wane even when it had become 'highly medicalized', he remained a hard-core cultural anthropologist. Once he wrote: "Men are incomplete or unfinished. Culture makes them complete." The process of 'humanization' transforms 'man – the animal' into 'man – the cultural being'. Professor Sarana often quoted Malinowski's statement: 'Culture is uniquely human'; so culture makes a 'particular man', not a 'general man'. There is no culture in general; culture is always particular. Here, Professor Sarana lent support to Geertz's idea of culture as a symbolic system, and this became the bulwark of his study of human nature.

Besides several perceptive essays on functionalism and causality, Professor Sarana spent a long time learning the nuances of anthropological and linguistic structuralism. As I said earlier, his lectures on structuralism – which have been published – still constitute a good reading material for students. Although he did not concentrate much on Lévi-Strauss's study of myths and totemism, he examined the structural methodology in historical and comparative perspective. Of particular interest to Professor Sarana was the similarity that Lévi-Strauss found between the thoughts of the 'primitive man' and the 'modern man' – for both think in immoderation and their thoughts are equally condemnable. The view of the West that it has created a complete society is grossly erroneous, because a number of small societies have been able to solve the problems with which the West is grappling till today.

Professor Sarana's theoretical bent of mind has been inherited by his son, who is a distinguished political scientist at Lucknow.

8

Professor Indera Paul Singh

P. C. Joshi

Prof. Indera Paul Singh was born in Amritsar, Punjab on 20th February, 1928. His father Shri Jawahar Singh served in Indian railways. His first name was Indera closely resembling the first name of Jawaharlal Nehru's daughter. His early education was in Delhi. He did his Higher Secondary from Ramjas Higher Secondary School, Delhi in the year 1943 in five subjects, namely, English, Urdu, Science, Mathematics and Commerce. For his I.Sc. (Medical), he joined Hindu College of Delhi University and passed it in 1944 with four subjects – English, Biology, Physics and Chemistry. He then went to Khalsa College in Amritsar to do his B.Sc. with four subjects – Botany, Chemistry, English and Punjabi. He then joined the newly opened Department of Anthropology in the second batch and completed his masters in Anthropology in the year 1950. While doing masters his affiliation was with most famous hostel of Delhi University, the Gwyer Hall. Prof. Singh was well versed in Punjabi, Urdu, Hindi, English, German and Russian. Prof. I.P. Singh was married to Mrs. Balbir Kaur and had three sons from her, namely, Jatindra Paul Singh, Varindra Paul Singh and Manindra Paul Singh. His sons are well placed, being pediatrician, Neuro-Surgeon and Merchant Navi officer. Prof. Singh said that he took anthropology by chance. After doing his graduation, he had come to Delhi University to learn Russian language as it was very popular course at that time. While doing Russian, he came across the subject of anthropology which he eventually made into a career.

Prof. Singh did his doctorate in the year 1959. He was the first one from the department to successfully defend his thesis. A few theses submitted to the department prior to his were rejected. Research scholars were very much worried for their doctorate. Prof. Singh had the good fortune to visit Frankfurt to receive advanced training in Anthropology from Franz Weidenreich Anthropologische Institut in 1952 and Dr. B.S. Guha, who invariably was the external examiner for the Ph.D. theses of the department, was impressed with Prof. Singh's training in Frankfurt. The title of his thesis was 'Inheritance of Finger-ball Patterns' which was a study in dermatoglyphics among the Khatri caste of Punjab in north India. He studied a total of 75 families of two generations with 268 children (147 males and 121 females).

While Prof. Singh had written his thesis on dermatoglyphics, the specialization of his supervisor Prof. P. C. Biswas, he was very critical and innovative in his thesis. I would like to quote from his thesis (p. 12), "Whorls have been divided by Wilder into Inner, Meeting and Outer sub-types on the basis of the radiant of left delta meeting the radiant of the right or passing above or below it. The author does not agree with this accepted basis of dividing whorls into Inner, Meeting and Outer. The same whorl becomes "Inner" on the right hand and "Outer" on the left hand; because the delta from which the radiant is to be traced is always the left one." His thesis is full of calculations trying to trace inheritance of finger ball prints between generations. The presentation of results in the form of figures and charts is also quite impressive indicative of the hard work and labour involved in writing a thesis in the 1950s.

Prof. Singh was one of the onouring students of Prof. Biswas. He was also liked by Dr. B.S. Guha who was a frequent visitor to the Delhi's Anthropology Department. He proudly showed to us a testimonial that he had received from Dr. B.S. Guha, the then Director of the Department of Anthropology, Government of India. For his visit to Frankfurt, Germany he was greatly helped by the German teacher of the Department, Ms. Freda Mukharjee. His assistantship to Dr. Oscar Lewis, who had come to India on a Ford Foundation grant to study rural India had greatly helped him, especially in having a good grasp on cultural anthropology. Dr. Oscar Lewis, an accomplished fieldworker himself, trained Prof. Singh in the finer nuances of ethnographic fieldwork. The study of Rani Khera, a village in the outskirts of Delhi gave him a good insight of doing ethnography. According to him, most of the photographs given in the book on Rani Khera were taken by him. It was Rani Khera study which inspired him to do the ethnographic study of Daleke, a village in Punjab which was also restudied by him after sixty years under ICSSR grant. The supervision of Oscar Lewis inspired him to write path-breaking papers in cultural anthropology.

Prof. I.P. Singh has contributed to all branches of anthropology. He was a natural collaborator and connoisseur of pursuing advanced research in diverse fields of anthropology. While he was doing his research on dermatoglyphics, he got an opportunity to work with the legendary Oscar Lewis, who was invited by the Planning Commission of India to investigate the social and political dynamics of Indian villages. On a grant from the Ford Foundation, Oscar Lewis came in contact with the Department of Anthropology and decided to work in a Jat village located in the western periphery of Delhi. He hired students from the department to help him in his village study. Prof. I.P. Singh was one such student hired by him. Lewis was extremely impressed by the ethnographic acumen of Prof. Singh and therefore, wrote a joint paper with him titled "Ceremonial and Festival Cycle in a Jat Village" which was part of the Proceedings of the American Philosophical Society. Inspired by Oscar Lewis, Prof. Singh embarked upon ethnographically exploring a Sikh village called Daleke. He wrote two outstanding papers titled "A Sikh Village" published in Journal of American Folklore and "Religion in Daleke– A Sikh Village" published in Majumdar Memorial volume. He had a knack for writing in topics related to cultural anthropology. His paper on the topics such as "Dynamics of Change in a Sikh village", "Life in a Pepsu Hill Village", "Effect of Urbanization in Delhi Suburban Village", "Caste and Occupation in Simla Hills", "Leadership in India", "Social Work in Ladakh" and "Concept of Health and Disease among Some Communities of Eastern Uttar Pradesh". As a hardcore physical anthropologist, he had extensively published in various branches of physical anthropology. Starting with publishing in the field of dermatoglyphics initially (he had published on the finger and palm prints or inheritance till 1906s.

He was a regular contributor to the Department of Anthropology, Delhi University's journal – The Anthropologist. He published a total of 12 papers in this journal. His other notable papers were in *American Journal of Physical Anthropology* (3 papers), *Human Genetik* (2 papers), *Acta Genet. Med. Gemellol., Human Biology* (2 papers), *Journal of Heredity* (2 papers), *Z. Morph. Anthrop.* (9 papers), *Anthropologischer Anzeiger* (5 papers), *Acta Anthropolgenetics*, *Human Heredity* and many more journals. He believed in collaboration and encouraging younger colleagues and students from the very beginning of his career as professional anthropologist, he wrote joints papers with P.K. Dutta, A.S. Seth, H.K. Kumbnani. H.L. Harit, Darshan Singh, M.K. Bhasin, P.K. Ghosh, S.L. Malik and many more students. Besides dermatoglyphics and human genetics, he substantially contributed in the field of serology, physiological anthropology, cytogenetics, human growth and development and anthropology of high altitude.

From the very beginning of his career, he was keen in doing research projects for national and international agencies. Between 1953 and 1955, he did a research study on the 'Ex-criminal Tribes of Delhi State' – the study done with Prof. P. C. Biswas supported by a grant from the Planning Commission, Government of India. His second study commissioned by the Planning Commission was in the year 1966-1972 on studying the Socio-economic, and Cultural Study of the People of Ladakh – A Polyandrous Society. For the Anthropological Survey of India, he initiated a study on Genetic and some Physical and Bio-Chemical Traits in certain Population Groups of Western and Central Himalayas in the year 1973. He was the investigator-incharge of the DST supported study titled "Impact of Technological and Economic Development programme on Bio-Cultural Heritage of Gaddis and Pangawalas Population Groups of Himachal Pradesh". He did another important study for the Department of Science and Technology, Government of India on Cytogenetic Studies on Newborns. With financial support from the Ministry of Environment, Government of India, he did a study titled, "Impact of Human Activities on Eco-systems and *vice-versa* with reference to Sikkim Himalayas. One of his seminal research projects was the Man and Biosphere project supported by the UNESCO.

His association with M.K. Bhasin was quite special. Bhasin came from a family of publishers in old Delhi. The book '*Anthropometry*' by I.P. Singh and M.K. Bhasin became a landmark book for anthropologist, nutritionists, clinicians and sport scientists. He also co-authored two books with Prof. P.C. Biswas – one was on the '*Ex-Criminal Tribes*' of Delhi and other titled '*Aspects of Indian Anthropology*', the proceedings of the Summer School in Dalhousie. Prof. I.P. Singh was an academic leader having capacity to organize people around an idea. He served as Head of the Department of Anthropology in Delhi University for 14 years. During this period, he established cytogenetics, physiological anthropology, ergonomics and kineanthropometry laboratories in the department. By virtue of his contacts with the foreign scholars he was able to get his students scholarships for advanced studies in state-of-the-art laboratories of the world. He had done extensive fieldwork in the Northwest Himalayas – Bharmour Valley, Simla Hills, Kulu, Manali, Chamba, Dharmashala, Dalhousie, Jammu and Kashmir and Jaunsar-Bawar. He was Editor-in-Chief of the journal *Research Proceedings* and *Manav Vigyan* – a Hindi journal of Anthropology; Associate Editor and later Editor of the journal *–the Anthropologist*. He had visited many foreign universities such as Keel, Munster, Heidelberg, Hamburg, Bonn and Newcastle Upon Tyne, Institute of Child Health, London, Aberdeen University and Institute of Physiology, Glasgow.

He was intensely associated with many important academic bodies. He was a sectional member, Recorder and President of the Anthropology and Archaeology section of the Indian Science Congress Association in 1956 and 1965; 1966-68 and 1968-69, respectively. He was co-sponsor with Prof. David Mandelbaum of the conference of Indian and American Anthropologists held in Delhi in 1963. His international academic leadership is amply reflected in his being the Secretary of the International Union of Anthropological and Ethological Sciences in 1973 and Organizing Secretary of the International Congress of the Tenth International Congress of Anthropological and Ethnological Sciences in 1978.

Prof. Singh played a very crucial role in building of the Department of Anthropology at University of Delhi. He was always part of the University bureaucracy holding the post of University proctor for longest period in the history of Delhi University. He was twice the Dean of the Faculty of Science; Dean, Students Welfare, Chairman, Board of Studies in Science Faculty, Member of the Delhi University's Executive Council, Academic Council and University Court, Chairman, Board of Residence, Health and Hygiene and member of governing bodies of seven university colleges and five hostels. He was a trouble shooter for DU Vice-Chancellors. He looked after the issues of security and order during 1975-77 emergency period.

For the Department of Anthropology, he made sure that the classes are held in time and the department is able to excel in frontline areas of research. He was always keen in inviting foreign anthropologists to the department. Scholars like Mandelbaum, Owen Lynch, Margaret Mead, Fredrick Barth, von Furer-Haimendorf, John A. Endler Sunderland, Napolean Wolanski, George Foster, F. Vogel, H. Walter not only visited and gave lectures in the department but also inspired young researchers to embark upon exploring new areas for research.

He was a person of good network in the academia, research institutes, government departments and bureaucracy. He was also very good at making use of the networks. He collaborated with Government of India's Defense Science Laboratory to train young scholars in human physiological experiments to start with. He then sent students to United Kingdom to receive advanced post-doctoral training in physiological anthropology to set up state-of-the-art laboratory in the Department. He sent another research student to Germany to receive advanced training in ergonomics while one student was sent to receive advanced training in visual anthropology and yet another to receive training in cytogenetics. For students returning after receiving advanced training, he would make arrangements to set up laboratories with necessary equipments. Quite often he would organize workshop for training faculty and research scholars from Indian universities. The present laboratories in the area of physiological anthropology, ergonomics, kinanthropometry, cytogentics are single handedly created by him. A large number of students have benefited by these facilities for gaining their M.Phil. and Ph.D. and research publications. He had friends across all research organizations and government departments.

He also played a very important role in promotion of anthropology across India. He was a member of the University Grants Commission's panel on Anthropology as well as Union Public Service Commission's panel on making syllabus of Anthropology subject for the Indian Administrative Services. He was chairman of the seminar on teaching of physical anthropology in Panjab University. He was invited as expert by various Indian universities to advice on syllabus and curriculum formulation. He was member, Faculty of Moral Science and member, Committee of Courses and Research Studies in Anthropology of Poona University; Member, Committee of Courses in Human Biology and Faculty of Social Sciences, Punjabi University, Patiala. He was also member, Nutrition Society, United Kingdom and Member, Human Biology Council, United States of America.

Prof. I.P. Singh had a multi-dimensional personality. From the very beginning of his career, he had a commitment to volunteering work. While in West Germany in 1951, he attended UNESCO's Youth Leaders Training Camp at Oberhansen; he also participated in A.F.S.C Youth and Work Camp in 1951-52. He was the chairman of 11th UNESCO Conference of International Voluntary Work Camp Organization, 1958. In collaboration with War on Want and Freedom from Hunger Campaign, he was the Chairman and Treasurer of Rural Welfare Works Committee, Jhatikra, Delhi, from 1960 onwards. He was particularly keen in popularizing anthropology beyond academics. He delivered talks in places like Maulana Azad Medical College, New Delhi; Gandhi Bhawan, Delhi; National Institute of Family Planning , New Delhi; Institute of Criminology and Forensic Science, New Delhi; Central Forensic Science Laboratory, New Delhi; Vigyan Bhawan; Deshbandhu College, New Delhi; Constitution Club, New Delhi; Rotary Club, New Delhi; Atma Ram Sanatan Dharam College, New Delhi; Indian National Science Academy,

New Delhi; India Environmental Society, Agra and many more institutions. His talk would cover popular themes like inheritance of genetic traits, human evolution, application of anthropology, high altitude populations, chromosomal abnormalities, human heredity, genetic engineering, personal identification and many more topics of general interest.

Prof. Singh was truly an international scholar. Right from the early research days when he was able to get a scholarship to receive advanced training in physical anthropology; his career is full of relentless efforts in international collaborations. He got the first chance to work with Oscar Lewis who was a highly acclaimed cultural anthropologist of United States of America. Prof. Singh used his association with Lewis not only in honing his fieldwork and qualitative methodology but also in writing papers based on ethnographic information. With Prof. P.C. Biswas, who was a recipient of Humboldt Fellowship, Prof. Singh helped many students of the department to visit West Germany to receive training in advanced methods in physical anthropology. While he was Head of the Department in Delhi University, he was always keen that foreign anthropologists who were in India pay a visit to the department and interact with the faculty and research students. While Margaret Mead was visiting India at the invitation of the Government of India, Prof. Singh made it a point that she is received very well while she is in India. Prof. Singh met her in her US office and assured her that she will have no problem while in India. He made sure that someone is available to receive her at the Delhi airport and she is comfortably taken to her hotel. Margaret Mead had a very successful and memorable visit to India with Government of India honouring her with national award for her courageous work in the area of women liberation. He made a large number of presentations on the transhumance Gaddi and Pangawalas tribes of Himachal Pradesh in a number of European universities like Bremen, Hamburg, Mainz, Durham and Newcastle Upon Tyne. With all these universities, he established collaborative ties for exchange of faculty and students.

Prof. I. P. Singh retired from active service on 19th of February, 1993. After retirement, he was quite active initially but went into depression a little later. He stated that his grandchildren infused new energy in him and he became active again. He was very regular to the Department of Anthropology of Delhi University whenever he would be in Delhi. He would also attend conferences and seminars in the department and outside. While he was not well versed with power point presentations and computer typing, he would not hesitate to come to the department and ask young research students to help him in his papers and articles. His enthusiasm led him to apply for a grant from ICSSR to do the restudy of the Sikh village Daleke which he had studied more than forty years ago. He had left behind an array of worthy students many of whom have made notable contribution to the subject. His first student was R.S. Bali who taught at HS Gaur Sagour University. His second student I.J.S Bansal was a pioneer of the Department of Human Biology, Punjabi University, Patiala. Some of his students such as R.S. Mann, P.K. Ghosh, S.L. Malik, etc. joined the Department of Anthropology in Delhi and retired as professors. Four of his students, namely, Ratan Jeet Singh, Ravinder Kumar Kenue, Veena Bhardwaj and K. Sudhakar went abroad as professionals. Indeed his students were in government, non-government, academia and research institutions carrying forward his name. Prof. Singh will be known to the upcoming generations for his untiring zeal towards promoting the cause of anthropology and his dedication to the subject which was so dear to him.

9
Professor Irawati Karve

R.K. Mutatkar

> "We may be betrayed or shown ingratitude by our colleagues, peers and kin on certain occasions. But, we will never be betrayed by our work. The work shall ever remain loyal to us and will always stand by us." —Irawati Karve

I

Irawati Karve in her book, '*Hindu Society—An Interpretation*'(1961) discussing her lifetime work about the structure and organization of Indian Society, has mentioned only one anthropologist in 'Preface', Prof Clyde Kluckhohn, author of the classic, '*Mirror for Man*,' acknowledging him posthumously, that he had read her book on '*Kinship*' and offered helpful comments. She regretted, Prof. Kluckhohn was no more to read the book on '*Hindu Society*' and offer comments. She belonged to that generation of classical anthropologists on the global scene.

Famous American Cultural Anthropologist, Prof. Margaret Mead visited Bombay (Mumbai) in the 70s. while she died in 1978. The Indian Council of Social Science Research (ICSSR) through its Western Regional Centre, Bombay (Mumbai) organized a seminar in her honour whereby the social scientists from western region were invited to meet her. I had travelled to Mumbai directly from the Madia tribal field from the Aheri-Allapalli area in Chandrapur district (now Gadchiroli) and had private audience with her as the only anthropologist among the invitees. She inquired about the tribal ethnic group. In her presentation, she expressed concern about industrialization-urbanisation in the West which accentuated environmental degradation. S.N.D.T. Women's University organized a special Convocation in her honour and conferred the honorary D.Litt to her. Margaret Mead was introduced and addressed repeatedly by the lady dignitaries connected with the University as a great woman. She walked to the stage, with the support of the wooden trident-shaped tribal stick in her hand and boomed without addressing any courtesies, "I am not a woman, I am an anthropologist." Irawati Karve belonged to the same breed as an Indian Anthropologist.

Irawati Karve, named after the river Irawaddy was third sibling of the six, born in Burma (now Mynmar) on 15 December, 1905. Her father, Hari Ganesh Karmarkar was serving in a British Oil Company at Rangoon. She was admitted to a Huzurpaga Girls' School at Pune at the age of seven and was nurtured in the family of Wrangler, Sir R.P. Paranjpe, a great rationalist and liberal, who was Principal of Fergusson College and later became the Vice-Chancellor of Pune University, before becoming India's High Commissioner to Australia.

Irawati Karve graduated in philosophy from Fergusson College in 1926, and completed post-graduation in Sociology, under Prof. G.S. Ghurye at Bombay University, submitting a dissertation on "Chitpavan Brahmins—An Ethnic Study". She went to Germany for Ph.D. during 1928-30 and worked on "The Normal Assymetry of the Human Skull" under the guidance of Prof. Eugen Fisher.

From 1931 to 1936, she functioned as Registrar of S.N.D.T. Women's University which was actually the creation of her father-in-law, Maharshi Dhondo Keshav Karve. She told us that she was a failure as an administrator.

She joined as Reader in Sociology at the Deccan College Post-graduate and Research Institute in 1939, which was revived from the earlier Deccan College, closed down in 1934,by the Government, due to poor enrollment of students, as a result of emergence of several other colleges in Pune. Irawati Karve expired on 11th August 1970 due to cardiac arrest in sleep. Her academic career as a classical anthropologist blossomed at the Deccan College due to networking with the peer scholars in Archaeology, Linguistics, Sanskrit and History, such as respectively Prof. H.D. Sankalia, Prof. S.M. Katre. Prof. A.D. Sankaran and Prof. T.S. Shejwalkar. I joined as a University Lecturer in Cultural/Social Anthropology at the Deccan College on 22nd July, 1960 and had the privilege of witnessing the interaction of these scholars. She participated in several archeological excavations with Dr. Sankalia and had joint publications with him. This also led to one literary piece whereby Irawati Karve was imagining herself with the identity of a female skeleton as her own, as per the Hindu concept of rebirth, with an exclamation. "Am I you. Are you me ?"

She was married in 1926 in the family of social reformer, Maharshi Dhondo Keshav Karve, to his son Dinkar, a faculty in Fergusson College who later became the Principal of the College. With the reformist background, both from the families of orientation and procreation, it was not surprising that she publicly addressed her husband by first person singular name. She had the advantage of not being subjected to second class citizen treatment as daughter-in-law in a patriarchal society. She was probably the first lady scooter rider in India taking males on the pillion.

As a feminist, she expressed regrets over the sufferings of her mother-in-law and the wives of public figures such as Lokmanya Tilak, mentioning about Gautam Buddha also, who were busy with their public work. Probably, as a protest of seeing the child widows and the plight of widows in general, she would not normally adorn the symbols of Maharashtrian married women, *mangalsutra*, *kumkum* and bangles. However, for *darshan* and paying obeisance to Dnyaneshwar *paduka* carried in a palanquin, passing by the Deccan College, or in case, she was asked to unfurl national flag on 15th August or 26th January at the college, she would put on the *kumkum* on her forehead, following the cultural tradition. There was no contradiction between protesting against inhuman traditions against widows and following benign cultural traditions on ritualistic or ceremonial occasions.

She was greatly fond of Vithoba (Vitthal, i.e. Vishnu), the presiding deity symbolizing the cultural identity of Maharashtra, situated at Pandharpur, having ritual connection with Balaji (Vishnu) of Tirupati. She participated in a pilgrimage walk referred to as Dindi for a fortnight (anthropological participant observation) to Pandhapur, with thousands of people, what is referred to as Vari and has written about it in '*The Journal of Asian Studies*'(1962), as also in her literary essays in Marathi.

To My Husband

I Place My Head On Your Feet and Ask for Your Blessing.

She publicly acknowledged her gratitude to her husband. She said, she could work and contribute since, she always had the protective and supportive umbrella cover of her husband over her head. Her dedication of the book '*Kinship Organisation in India*' to her husband is worth documenting.

> While dedicating to you this book which would never have been either thought out or written but for you, let me express my feelings in the traditional Hindu manner:

I had seen her husband Principal D. D. Karve who was known for his 'stern' face, having uncontrolled weeping at her funeral at the Omkareswar crematorium on 11 August, 1970.

I had the privilege to work as a University appointed lecturer in Cultural Anthropology, under the supervision of Prof. Irawati Karve, Head of the Department of Sociology and Anthropology at the Deccan College Post-graduate and Research Institute, during July 1960 until she passed away on 11 August, 1970. I first saw her at the Sociological Conference in 1959 at the Indian Statistical Institute, Kolkata, where, as a final year Master's student from Sagar University, I presented a paper on 'Caste Dynamics in a Gwalior Village'. Dr. Leela Dube introduced me to her at the Conference. She wrote to the then Vice-Chancellor, Prof. D.G. Karve, from Berkley, recommending me for the faculty position, since she could not be present at the Selection Committee meeting in the summer of 1960.

Irawati Karve was like our mother. So, we had no boss-subordinate relationship. We had the realization that we could not follow her model of scholarship of classical anthropology combining biological, cultural, archaeological and linguistic aspects of the Study of Man, Culture and Society, in the historical perspective. She publicly acknowledged her orgnisational deficiency about building a Department or a School on lines of what Dr. Sankalia or Dr. Katre could do, respectively for Archaeology and Linguistics. In a lighter vein, she remarked that as the Registrar of S.N.D.T. University, her administrative lapses had not yet been fully rectified. U.G.C. gave building fund for a separate Anthropology building which she surrendered to Dr. Sankalia seeking two halls, one for laboratory and another for tribal museum in the Archaeology building at the Deccan College. However, she gave total freedom jointly to me and my biological anthropology colleague, Dr. R.K. Gulati in organizing the distinct postgraduate teaching programme in Anthropology in 1963 at the Pune University and she formally communicated this to the Registrar of the University. Earlier, it was a mixed programme for Sociology and Anthropology with a Masters degree in Sociology. Deccan College as a Research Institute was then affiliated to Poona University, which is now a Deemed University under the U.G.C. Act. since 1990.

Unlike all classical and peer anthropologists, Irawati Karve did not produce a tribal or a village monograph. She travelled widely for anthropometric measurements in Maharashtra and Karnatak. Her travels were more directed to collecting data for biological anthropological analysis. The experiences and observations during travels have also been expressed in literary writings by her. Towards the end of her career, she had taken up a project in Tamil Nadu and among the Dhangars (shepherds) in Maharashtra. The statistical analysis of her anthropometric data was done by the famous statistician-economist, Prof V.M. Dandekar and published jointly (1951). Relevant anthropometric data has been presented for describing the ethnic groups in Maharashtra in the Maharashtra State Gazatteer (1968) which she authored as 'Maharashtra, Land and its People', in which she has analysed the culture and society of Maharashtra. Karve has analyzed the evolution of Maharashtra as a culture region, the uneven progress within different regions, about the caste composition, about villages and their localities and hamlets, and about the language and literature.

She acknowledged Vithoba of Pandharpur as the presiding deity of Maharashtra. The places from where people go to meet Vithoba is the boundary of Maharashtra as per her hypothesis. Another identity is the boundary up to where the Mahars (dominant Scheduled Caste to which Ambedkar belonged) reside. She went with the people for a fortnight, walking all the way to Pandharpur, with the Vari, about which she has written separately as a literary piece. That is her anthropological fieldwork with participant observation and informal, open-ended interviews, which we normally do in our early years of fieldwork training, living with the people in a tribal village.

Prof. Irawati Karve chose to analyse the civilisational and cultural aspects of the macrocosm. It was not considered necessary to develop scientific objectivity by undertaking fieldwork in a remote area as is commonly done in anthropology. India with its rich plurality and ancient history, as also textual knowledge, was sufficient to subject it to anthropological objective analysis. Even the tribal communities in India had linkage with the mythological scriptures of *Ramayana* and *Mahabharata*, unlike the isolated island communities in Pacific Ocean, studied by Western pioneer anthropologists. Irawati Karve's studies could not be classified under colonial anthropology, which have been strongly rooted in Indian mythology and Indian culture, analysed through qualitative research methods, expressed also in her literary works, acknowledged under Humanities.

Irawati Karve chose to analyse the Indian Social Organization at the macro level, at the national level, through historical times. She has discussed Indian civilization in the context of region, caste, kinship and family linking Mahabharata times to the contemporary scenario. Irawati Karve's documentation and analysis of Kinship Organization in India, acclaimed internationally, covers the plurality and geographical coverage of India, never tried on such a wide scale. We are aware that in the ethnographic writings of pioneer anthropologists, kinship and religion have been discussed as the hard core of traditional cultures. Her analysis gave rise to her definition of 'Caste as a kin-group of actual or potential kin' and the difference between 'caste and caste-cluster', replacing the prevalent classification of sub-caste and caste. She has analysed her classification of 'caste as an endogamous group' having its distinct ethnic identity, by citing examples of Brahmin endogamous caste groups as also of the Marathas, Kunbis and Potters in "Hindu Society—An Interpretation" (1961). This analysis conforms to ground level functioning reality. The generic terms, such as Brahmins, Maratha, Dhangar (shepherd), Kunbi, Kumbhar (potter), Sonar (goldsmith), etc. as in Maharashtra and in other linguistic regions in India are caste-clusters which are further agglomerated in the Varna system, as a pan-Indian phenomena. This classification would be much helpful in adjudicating the claims of pseudo social groups to constitutional reservation categories.

Although Irawati Karve was known as a classical anthropologist and did not directly get involved in the applied aspects, she has written a full chapter on the national issues and problems in her book 'Hindu Society'. She has expressed her opinion about the linguistic states, issue of link language, about caste reservation and its after effects. I have personally experienced her promotion of applied aspects. While she was called upon to speak at the Armed Forces Medical College about socio-cultural aspects of health to the postgraduates in Preventive and Social Medicine in 1963, after one visit, she drafted me to the institution. My association for thirty years with AFMC and later with B.J. Medical College developed medical anthropology in India, different from ethno-medicine.

Irawati Karve had a literary flair. She wrote several short literary essays presented in three Marathi books. While writing research papers, a strict discipline about objective presentation is necessary. However, during field travels for research work, one's subjectivity and emotional responses are also responding to your inner self. These could not be expressed in scientific terminology, although based on objective observations. Irawati Karve expressed these responses and insights which could be called literary in nature. Her literary short essays could be termed as common man's anthropology or anthropological expressions and insights for common man.

Her book '*Yugant*', an anthropological interpretation of *Mahabharata* unfolded through analysis of personalities, is her life-time contribution acclaimed widely as an excellent piece of literature recognized as 'Sahitya Akademi Award' in 1968. The anthropological interpretation of Culture and Personality has contributed to the analysis of Mahabharata personalities in the context of prevalent values in the pastoral economy and society of Mahabharata times. Her feminism is projected in her analysis of Bhisma's personality, who was charged with forcibly bringing the princesses to marry the princes in his family. The discussion about woman as the field and man as a seed in '*Niyoga*', probably indicates the transitional stage from pastoralism to agriculture, symbolised with a plough as weapon with Krishna's brother, Balram. Plough continues to be a weapon if an isolated farmer is attacked on his field.

Irawati Karve as a classical anthropologist could analyze the biological and cultural distance among various endogamous caste groups in a caste-cluster, as also among the endogamous castes across the caste-clusters. There could be several similarities among the Deshastha Maharashtrian Brahmins with the Maratha or Kunbi than with the Chitpavan Brahmins. Regional similarities and variations would similarly be prominent in a linguistic region which have been carved out as political states. It is to her credit that she did not follow the Western ethnographic model of studying an isolated community which had no written text about their history.

Not addressing the microcosm of one tribal community or a village as an ethnographic monograph, there is no reference to structuralism and functionalism in Irawati Karve's analysis. Irawati Karve analyzed India and Maharashtra as a cultural region developed through historical process, having organic links with the values from mythology. In doing so, the classical holistic model of anthropology connecting biological, cultural, linguistic, ancient history and archaeology has been portrayed.

Although Deccan College was redesignated as a Research and Training Institute in 1939, no research funds were available. Data besides Census was needed for planning development schemes with the establishment of Planning Commission. Research meant quantitative survey. Anthropology was and continues to be miles away from quantification, except in biological anthropology where data is subjected to statistical analysis. Irawati Karve as Professor of Sociology and Anthropology got involved in survey research in collaboration with Sociology colleagues like, Y.B. Damle and Hemlata Acharya, as also some Ph.D. students. Her first such survey was among the Bhils of West Khandesh for which she travelled herself with an assistant to fill in the questionnaires and simultaneously take anthropometric measurements (1958). "Group Relations in Village Community" (1963) with Y.B. Damle and

"Social Dynamics of a growing Town" with her Ph.D. student, J.S. Randive (1965), "The Role of Weekly Markets in Tribal, Rural and Urban Setting" with Hemlata Acharya (1970) and "A Survey of the People displaced through the Koyna Dam" with her daughter Jai Nimbkar (1969) have been some examples of survey research in which she participated marginally. Some of these projects were funded by the Programme Evaluation Organisation of the Planning Commission.

Irawati Karve presided over the Anthropology section at the Science Congress in 1947 at Delhi. She was visiting faculty at the University of London (1955) and in California University, Berkley during 1959-60. However, she earned the respect of the common people and elites due to her book, '*Yugant*' which was awarded the highest literary award in India. *Yugant* has been translated in several languages. She has penned her travel experiences and her subjective responses to the realities of life in Marathi in a literary style. She got experience as honorary magistrate of the family court, about which she has written in Marathi. Irawati Karve was a good conversationist, enjoying the company of P.C. Biswas, Mahalnobis, M.N. Srinivas, S.C. and Leela Dube, as also the Marathi Sahitya Akademi award winners and other literary luminaries.

Irawati Karve supervised several Ph.D.students in Sociology and Anthropology.The notable who remained in the profession in Sociology were Sunanda Patwardhan and Vidyadhar Pundlik, in Anthropology, K.C. Malhotra, R.K. Gulati and Vijay Bhanu, all three in Biological Anthropology.

Irawati Karve who was brought up in liberal and reformist families had deep understanding of Indian civilization and values as followed by common people. She said, she owed a 'debt' to the society which she was paying by way of research. She did not owe anything else to anybody.

We have been advocating through documents such as UGC model curriculum in Anthropology (2001), that we are not satisfied with Anthropology in India, but we look forward to developing Indian Anthropology. Irawati Karve with her initiative to analyze Indian Civilization and unravelling the culture region as big as Maharashtra has been a pioneer Indian Anthropologist. Irawati Karve's scientific and literary writings justify the quote by Eric Wolf that "Anthropology is a most humanist of all sciences and most scientific of all humanities." We need to follow her tradition to analyse the macrocosm as a whole.

10

Krishna Chandra Tripathy

A Pioneer in Odishan Prehistory

Kishor K. Basa

Professor Krishna Chandra Tripathy was born on 7th September, 1938 in the village Bira Krishna Saran Pur Sasan, otherwise known as Batagaon, near Khalikote block in the district of Ganjam in south Odisha. His father was Late Godabaris Tripathy and mother Late Rama Tripathy. He was the fourth child in the family. The village was a gift of the King of Khalikote. His father was the village chief or Karji.

Tripathy passed Matriculation from Mardaraj High School, Khalikote, Ganjam in 1954, I.Sc. from S.K.C.G. College, Parlakhemundi in 1956—now in Gajapati district, and B.Sc. (with Chemistry, Botany, Zoology combination) from Ravenshaw College, Cuttack in 1959. The subject of anthropology had been opened in Utkal University in 1958 with Professor A. Aiyappan, formerly Superintendent of Madras Museum, as the founder Professor, with eight students in each batch. Besides Aiyappan, there were two other teachers – Nityananda Pattanaik teaching Social Anthropology and Kamala Kanta Das teaching Physical Anthropology. P.D. Prasad Rao was the demonstrator. Taking admission in 1959 Tripathy belonged to the second batch in the Department of Anthropology, Utkal University and completed M.Sc. in 1961 with Physical Anthropology as his specialization. After K.K. Das left for London for higher studies, the post of lecturer in Physical Anthropology fell vacant and Tripathy joined the Department on 20.11.1961 as a lecturer, initially on an *ad hoc* basis. As suggested by Aiyappan, Tripathy started teaching prehistoric archaeology and museum studies, besides Physical Anthropology. He completed Ph.D. in 1972 from Utkal University on prehistory of south western Odisha. It is primarily to the credit of Tripathy that prehistoric archaeology was opened as a special paper in 1975 and the first batch came out in 1976. He became Reader in prehistoric archaeology in 1976 and Professor in 1990. He was the Head of the Department from 1.6.1993 to 31.5.1995 and was superannuated in 1998. From 1975 to his superannuation in 1998 he devoted his professional life in studying Odishan prehistory out of his total service period of 37 years in Utkal University. Six students were awarded Ph.D. under his academic supervision.

Tripathy published his Ph.D. work with the title *Lithic Industries in India: A study of South Western Orissa* (1980). He was one of the editors of two other books – *Science, Culture and Development: Prof. L.K. Mahapatra Felicitation Volume* (1992) and *Bio-Cultural Frontiers of Man: Usha Deka Felicitation Volume* (2001). He was the Editor for *Man in Society*, the Journal of Anthropology Department, Vol. 8, 1993-94. Besides, *Manav*, the Journal of Anthropological Society of Orissa, was published up to 1997-99 (six volumes) under the supervision of Professor Tripathy as the Secretary of the Association.

Basically, his publications belonged to two main areas of anthropology – physical anthropology and prehistoric archaeology. Until mid-seventies of the last century, he was publishing in both physical anthropology and prehistoric archaeology. However, after that he published primarily on prehistory. With regard to physical anthropology, Tripathy published on the hair of the tribal community of Saora (1963), dermatoglyphic and finger print studies on the Saora (1965), ABO blood group of the Lanjia Saora (1965-66) and some caste people (Tripathy and Mishra, 1965), a genetic survey among the Bhois (1968a), finger print designations of Lanjia Saora and Khond (1967c) etc.

Tripathy is mostly known more for his works on prehistory of Odisha. An important issue he discussed was terminology in Indian prehistory (1973-74). For example, Burkitt and Cammiade in 1930 had proposed a four-fold series (i.e. from Series I to Series IV) for Kurnool industries. Possibly influenced by African nomenclature, the terminology of Early, Middle and Late Stone Age was put forward by Subbarao in 1960. During the First International Congress on Asian Archaeology in 1961, the sub-committee on terminology accepted terms such as Early, Middle and Late Stone Ages as most suitable for India among the existing terms. But these terminologies were not uniformly used in India. For example, Ashok Ghosh in 1971 suggested terminologies like chopper-bifaces (Pebble-Core element), Flake and Flake-Blade elements, which Tripathy thought were 'rather more appropriate to study the sequential developments of lithic industries in India'. Tripathy (1980) had applied the terminology of Ghosh with slight modification while studying the lithic traits of south western Odisha. The divisions had been made on the availability of lithic tools from different stratigraphic horizons. The stone industries were arranged in their succession as Pebble Industry, Flake Industry and Flake-Blade industry.

Before we discuss any further, it is important to provide an outline on prehistoric research in Odisha until the arrival of Tripathy. While geologist Robert Bruce Foote – the father of Indian prehistory – reported palaeolithic artefacts from Pallavaram near Chennai for the first time in India in 1863, it was left to another geologist V. Ball in 1875 to lay the foundation of prehistoric research in Odisha through his discovery of lithic artefacts from four places distributed in the river valleys of the Brahmani and Mahanadi. This recovery was published in the Proceedings of the Asiatic Society of Bengal in 1876 and later in Ball's book *Jungle Life in India* in 1880. Half a century later, it was Paramananda Acharya – the first recognized Odia archaeologist – reported the occurrence of polished stone tools (neolithic artefacts) from his own village Baidipur in the district of Mayurbhanj in 1923-24. In the year 1939 P. Acharya and E.C. Worman (Jr) of Harvard University, reported a number of palaeolithic sites around Kuliana in Mayurbhanj. This led to the excavation of Kuliana – the first palaeolthic site to have been excavated in India – by Nirmal Kumar Bose and Dharani Sen of University of Calcutta before independence – which was published in 1948. This was followed by further survey by Calcutta University in 1951 and 1958 in Mayurbhanj and work on a number of sites around Kuliana. The assemblage of Kuliana was represented by pebble tools and flakes with unprepared or unifacetted striking platforms.

However, the first major work on prehistoric Odisha after the Kuliana excavation was undertaken by G.C. Mohapatra, a research scholar of Deccan College, Pune under the supervision of Professor H.D. Sankalia during 1956-1959. Mohapatra (1962) surveyed the river valleys of the Mahanadi, Brahmani, Baitarani, Khadakei and Burhabalanga in the undivided districts of Dhenkanal, Sambalpur, Keonjhar and Mayurbhanj covering an area of 38,560 km (all to the north of river Mahanadi). He showed the nature of lithic cultural succession in Odisha and tried to link them with geological contexts. He reported 22 early stone age (now known as lower palaeolithic) sites, 25 middle stone age (middle palaeolthic) and 8 late stone age sites (mesolithic).

Tripathy rightly perceived that the areas south of the river Mahanadi was yet to be explored. Hence, he began a preliminary survey of river valleys to discover prehistoric sites in the vast area of south Odisha (Triapthy, 1967a) comprising the undivided districts of Ganjam, Balangir, Kalahandi, Koraput and Phulbani. An occurrence of prehistoric tools in south Odisha was first located in 1966 (Tripathy, 2016). He reported 7 implement bearing sites in the undivided districts of Koraput and Balangir. These sites included Kalma, Chalkamba on the bank of the river Vamshadhara and Sananai in the district of Koraput, Bhuanpada, Madabhati, Ratakhandi, Khalark alam and Sandisara on the river bank of the Tel and Raul mainly with middle palaeolithic tools. Some polished stone tools were also found from the Raul river at Kharligarh. Because of such findings, Tripathy was seriously motivated to plan for a mega area survey in south western Odisha during 1969-1972.

Tripathy referred to the geological features of south western Odisha; recently included alluvium, windblown sand etc. while Pleistocene included raised beaches, older alluvium, laterite (in part). On the south of Mahanadi, the distribution of strata was as follows: alluvium, Gondwana, Cuddapah, Precamberian. For Ph.D., Tripathy studied the river Tel and its tributaries covering a wider area of about 16,750 square km in south western Odisha with detailed description of sites and relevant geological stratigraphy of cliff sections. The sites were generally located on the banks of the river Tel and its tributaries like the Suktel, Sengodi, Lant (Lunth), Kusunei Jhor, Niburti and Sandyl (Utai). The areas included were in the undivided districts of Balangir, Kalahandi, Sambalpur and Phulbani. Besides, some other river valleys such as the Jira and the Ong also were studied. Initially Tripathy used the terms such as, pebble industry, flake industry and flake-blade industry. He reported 3 sites of pebble industry with 34 tools comprising chopper, scraper, borer, points, handaxes, 16 sites of flake industry with 622 tools comprising cores, scrapers on flake and cores, points, worked flakes and miniature handaxes made on chert, jasper and quartzite, and 27 sites of flake blade industry with 1779 tools are of blades, flakes, fluted cores, scrapers, retouched blades and lunates. With regard to the flake-blade industry, chert was the most popular raw material and the industry was purely a non-geometric one. Subsequently, Tripathy (2016) equated his pebble tool industry with lower palaeolithic, flake industry with middle palaeolithic and flake-blade with mesolithic cultures.

An important aspect was his excavation (Tripathy & Rath, 1993-94) of a trial trench of 2m × 2m at Rugnia in Jira valley near Bargarh town, yielding upper palaeolithic artefacts from a stratified context. The broad stratigraphy of the Jira river valley was studied from the exposed bank section at Rugnia with the following horizons from the top: Recent humus (5cm); Sandy silt (60 cm); Upper silty clay (150 cm) (upper palaeolithic horizon); Upper loose gravel (80cm); Lower Silty clay (30cm); Bed rock. Digging was made up to a depth of 25 cm. The excavated artefacts included 12 cores (3%), 130 chips (32.6%), 57 broken tools (14.25%), 2 pebbles (0.5%) and 82 finished tools (20.5%), besides 15 baked (sun) clay pieces (3.75%). The finished tools included various subtypes such as parallel blades (22), backed blades (4), simple blades (9), convex blades (5), notched blade (1), borers (14), burins (13), side scrapers (4), end scraper (1), keel scraper (1), points (5), lunates (2), and triangle (1). With regard to raw material, chert (296) was preferred for tool making followed by quartz with jasper (1) and chalcedony (4) being occasionally used. Besides, a possible post-hole was said to have been traced at the middle of the trench. Tripathy and Rath argued that it was a manufacturing site because of the occurrence of a large number of by-products. Thus, in case of Odisha, while S.C. Nanda was the first scholar to have reported 17 sites with the upper palaeolithic evidence on the basis of his survey in the Indravati basin, Tripathy and Rath (1993-94) had attempted to study upper palaeolithic in a stratified context.

Apart from his work on south western Odisha, Tripathy also reported the occurrence of mesolithic cultural remains from the Ib valley near Sundargarh (1982-83) as well as the microlithic industry in Bhubaneswar (Tripathy & Mohanty, 1970). With regard to neolithic cultures, he undertook a typo-technological and metric study of neolithic celts from Mayurbhanj (1967b, 1968b). Besides, he reported the mesolithic and neolithic remains of Darpan Khas area, Jajpur district in coastal Odisha (Sahoo & Tripathy, 1988-89) and published on archaeology and agriculture around Tangi, near Khordha (Tripathy & Mohapatra, 1992). From an ethnoarchaeological viewpoint, Tripathy pointed out the megalithic traditions of some tribal groups of Odisha (1987-88).

Tripathy also reviewed the state of prehistoric research in Odisha in general (1986-87, 1990-91) in his presidential address of the anthropology and archaeology section of Indian Science Congress (1995) and Professor B.M. Das Memorial Oration (2016), and sometimes that of south western Odisha in particular (1973, 1980, 1992). He also wrote a chapter on Prehistory (Chapter II) in the Orissa State Gazetteers Vol. 1. For Tripathy (2016), there were two kinds of survey of prehistoric research in Odisha. While G.C. Mohapatra's work (1962) in areas north of Mahanadi during 1956-1959 and Tripathy's work in south western Odisha (1980) during 1969-1972 comprised the mega-survey, subsequent scholars conducted micro-area survey (see also various papers in Basa and Mohanty, 2000). Such scholars included S.C. Nanda in Indravati valley (upper palaeolithic and mesolithic), P.K. Behera at Dari-Dungri (lower palaeolithic) and in upper Brahmani valley in Sundragarh district (neolithic), P.K. Singh in Brahmani valley in undivided Dhenkanal district (lower palaeolithic, mesolithic and neolithic), S.B. Ota in undivided Phulbani district (mesolithic), P. Mohanty in Keonjhar district (mesolithic), B. Tripathy along the river Mahanadi and Salunki in the district of Boudh (mesolithic), D. Sahoo in the lower Mahanadi basin (mesolithic and neolithic), R.P. Prusty around Dharmagarh area of undivided Kalahandi district (lower palaeolithic), S. Chakrabarti in Mayurbhanj (palaeolithic and mesolithic), Ranjana Ray and K.K. Basa (working separately) in Palallahara, central Odisha (lower palaeolithic, mesolithic and neolithic), K.K. Basa and D. Sahoo in Duburi area (mesolithic) and a survey conducted by K.K. Basa, P. Mohanty and B. Tripathy in Mayurbhanj.

Analysing the Odishan prehistoric sites from forest eco-system perspective, Tripathy (1992-93) divided Odisha into four zones – eastern zone (coastal belt and less forested areas), northern zone (moderately forested), western zone (comparatively highly forested), and southern zone (comparatively highly forested) and tried to correlate them with the distribution of prehistoric sites in Odisha from palaeolithic to the neolithic. For example, no lower palaeolithic site had been reported from the eastern zone of coastal Odisha. Moderately forested zone was the preferred habitat for the lower palaeolithic man as inferred from the distribution of such sites. During the middle palaeolithic period, early man gradually extended his habitational localities even to the comparatively highly forested zone for better exploitation of natural resources. The shift in the habitational pattern may be, Tripathy thought, due to population pressure and compulsion for exploitation of new facets and regions for their subsistence. The above situation of early human habitation gradually took a new and distinct orientation during the mesolithic period. Moderately forested ecological surroundings were not preferred by the people and they gradually moved towards the heavily forested regions. There was further extension of habitat in the neolithic period since all the four zones were associated with the neolithic relics. However, the northern zone with moderately forested areas was the preferred landmass for the habitation of the neolithic man. This trend of occupation was not much altered during the metal age. Tripathy suggested two things for a better understanding of prehistoric cultures in Odisha from such a forest eco-system perspective; firstly, mapping the distributional concentration of the tribal population in zonal basis and secondly, undertaking eco-system mapping at two levels – macro ecological and micro-ecological situations:

Tripathy also published text books in Odia language. *His Adimanav* (1973) is thought to be the first text book in Anthropology in Odia. He also authored *Byabaharik Nrutatwa* (1974) (with two others), *Nrutatwa Prabesh* (1974) (with two others), *Nrutatwa O Pragitihas Sanskruti* (1979), *Nrutatwa* (2002) (with two others), *Byabaharik Nrutatwa* (with three others) (2004). Along with six others, he also prepared a *Glossary for Anthropology in Odia* in 2003. He also translated S.C. Dube's *Indian Society* into Odia titled *Bharatiya Samaj* (1990) published by the National Book Trust. He was also writing a column on Anthropology in the Odia daily *Matrubhumi*.

Tripathy had obtained a Certificate in Rock Art in 1981 from Cantro Comuno Di Study Prehistoric, Capondi-Ponte, Brasaia, Italy. As a part of Indo-USSR Cultural Exchange Programme, he had visited Institute of Archaeology, Leningrad, Department of Archaeology, Dushumbe, Tajikstan from 17.8.1985 to 31.10.1985. He had also participated in the XIV Congress of the Indo-Pacific Prehistory Association at Jogyakarta, Indonesia during August-September, 1990 and presented a paper titled 'Fresh Light on Lithic evidences from the Eastern Ghats, Orissa'.

Tripathy invited scholars from the Scandinavian Institute of Asian Studies for working on neolithic cultures of Odisha. Along with Dr. Knut Odner, Institute of Anthropology, University of Oslo, Norway, Tripathy made a joint survey from 13.1.1983 to 7.2.1983. Similarly, a second fieldwork was undertaken with Dr. E.M. Mikkalsen, Department of Social Anthropology, Arhus University, Denmark from 20.10.1988 to 15.11.1988.

Tripathy was a Recorder and subsequently the President of the Anthropology and Archaeology Section of Indian Science Congress Association in the 82nd Session of ISCA in 1995, held at Jadavpur University, Calcutta. He was invited by the Indian National Confederation and Academy of Anthropologists (INCAA) to deliver the Professor B.M. Das Memorial Oration in 2016. He was Secretary, Anthropological Society of Orissa and was responsible for bringing out its journal *Manav*. Besides, he was a Member, Advisory Committee, Anthropological Survey of India, Member, Advisory Council for Orissa State Museum, Archives and Archaeology and Consultant, Prehistory Section of Jayadev State Museum, Government of Orissa. He was also associated with UPSC.

In Utkal University, he was given a number of assignments, such as N.C.C. Officer (1963-65), Hostel Assistant Superintendent (1964 -66), Vice-President, Post Graduate Athletic Club (1978-79), Chief, Employment

Information-*cum*-Advisory Bureau (1985-1987) and Chief Editor, *Vani Vikas* (1995). Besides, he was Joint Secretary, Utkal University Teachers' Association (1966-67). While he was the Head of the Department of Anthropology, the Birth Centenary Celebration of Padmashree Paramananda Acharya was organized in Utkal University in 1993. He was also Secretary of Children Centre of Integral Education (CCIE) which has a Public School at Acharya Vihar, Bhubaneswae (where he lives) based on the educational philosophy of Sri Ma and Sri Aurobinda. At present, he is the President of Utkal Anthropology Alumni Association.

He married Late Swarnalata Devi who was a teacher in Odia in D.M. School in the Regional Institute of Education, Bhubaneswar. She passed away on 27.5.2016. He has one son Tarun, an engineer based in California, USA, and two daughters – Tanushree an economics student based in Bengaluru and Tanuja, a psychology student now based in USA.

A student of Professor A. Aiyappan, Tripathy published in both physical anthropology and prehistoric archaeology of Odisha during 1960s and early 1970s. Like D.K. Bhattacharya in Delhi University, he specialized in physical anthropology as a student, but moved to prehistory later. From mid-1970s onward, he published primarily on prehistory. In physical anthropology, his publications were related to hair, dermatoglyphic and finger print studies, ABO blood group and genetic survey etc. For prehistory, like G.C. Mohapatra's work earlier for areas north of the Mahanadi, Tripathy also conducted a mega-survey in south western Odisha for his Ph.D. covering an area of about 16,750 sq. km. An encouraging colleague and an excellent class room teacher with a good sense of humour, he had opened and led the specialization in prehistoric archaeology in the Anthropology Department in Utkal University since 1975 and continued until his superannuation in 1998. As to terminology, although he initially used terms, such as pebble-tool, flake and flake-blade industries, subsequently like other scholars, he used terms such as lower, middle, upper palaeolithic, mesolithic and neolithic cultures. He began his survey of prehistoric sites in Vamsadhara valley in south Odisha and continued surveying in different parts of Odisha reporting sites from lower palaeolithic to neolithic cultures. He provided a stratigraphic context to the upper palaeolithic phase in Odisha. Besides, he published on ethnoarchaeology by taking note of megalithic traditions of various tribes. Theoretically, his approach was culture historical. A major limitation – which is also true even now for much of Odissan prehistory – is the lack of absolute chronology for any site he had studied. He was also responsible for establishing a small museum on

Odishan prehistory in the Department primarily as a teaching aid. In short, like Paramananda Acharya and G.C. Mohapatra before him, K.C. Tripathy was a pioneer of prehistoric research in Odisha. The tradition of having a specialization in prehistoric archaeology – now known as archaeological anthropology – and conducting annual fieldwork initiated by him is being continued and expanded by the Department of Anthropology, Utkal University. For example, the Department along with Centre for Heritage Studies, Bhubaneswar, Deccan College, Pune and Odishan Institute of Maritime and South East Asian Studies had excavated a neolithic-chalcolithic site at Bang-Harirajpur about 30kms from Utkal University, involving multidisciplinary specialists. Since the site had yielded three skeletons – no other excavated site in Odisha has this number so far, study is under process even to determine their DNA. I wish Professor Tripathy a healthy life.

REFERENCES

Basa, K.K. & P. Mohanty (ed). 2000. *Archaeology of Orissa.* (2 vols.) Delhi: Pratibha Prakashan.

Mohapatra, G.C. 1962. *Stone Age Cultures of Odisha.* Pune: Deccan College Post Graduate & Research Institute.

Sahoo, D. & K.C. Tripathy 1988-89. "Archaeology of Coastal Orissa: A glimpse". *Manav*, vol. 3: 269-73.

Tripathy, K.C. 1963. "Middle Phalangeal, Hair among the Saoras of Puri, Orissa". *Eastern Anthropologist,* XVI (No. 3): 133-137.

Tripathy, K. C. & N.P. Mishra. 1965. "ABO Blood Group Distribution Among Some Orissan Castes". *Adivasi*, 17-21.

Tripathy, K.C. 1965. "Dermatoglyphic Studies of the Sa-ara, Orissa". *Eastern Anthropologist*, XVIII (No. 3): 154-158.

Tripathy, K.C. 1965-66. "ABO blood group of Lanjia Saora", *Adivasi,* No.2: 13-16.

Tripathy, K.C. 1967a. "Report on exploration of Prehistoric Sites along the Vamshadhara, Koraput, Orissa", *Prakruti*, Utkal University Journal- Science, 4(1):55-59.

Tripathy, K.C. 1967b. "Type- technology of Mayurbhanj neoliths, Orissa". *Prakruti*, Utkal University Journal - Science, 4: 61-70.

Tripathy, K.C. 1967c. "Fingerprint Designations of the Saora (Linjia) and Khonds", Orissa. *Archaeology & Physical Anthropology in Oceania*, Vol.2 (No.3):236-240.

Tripathy, K.C. 1968a. "A Genetic Survey among the Bhois (Bauris) of Bhubaneswar, Orissa". *Adivasi*, Vol. X, No. 1: 1-8.

Tripathy, K.C. 1968b. "A metric study of the Neolithic Celts of Mayurbhanj, Orissa". *The Orissa Historical Research Journal,* Vol. XIV (No. 2): 13-30.

Tripathy, K.C. & U.C. Mohanty, 1970. "Microlithic Industry of Bhubaneswar", *Prakruti*, Utkal University Journal-Science, Vol. 7(1): 72-92.

Tripathy, K.C. 1973. "South Orissa Prehistory: The First Record of Stone Age tools". *Asian Perspectives*, Vol.XV, (4): 47-59.

Tripathy, K.C. 1980. *Lithic Industries in India: A Study of South Western Orissa*. Delhi: Leela Devi Publications.

Tripathy, K.C. 1982-83. "Preliminary Archaeological Survey of the Ib". *Manav*, Vol.I (No.1): 60-66.

Tripathy, K.C. 1986-87. "Archaeology of Orissa". *Manav*. Vol.II (No.1): 190-199.

Tripathy, K.C. 1987-88. "Mortuary sites and Lithic Associations Among the Tribes in Orissa". *Man in Society*, Vol.3: 31-41.

Tripathy, K.C. 1990. *Fresh light on Lithic evidences from the eastern Ghats*, Orissa. XVI IPPA Congress.

Tripathy, K.C. 1990-91. "Early Man in Orissa: Material Culture and Artistic Creativity". *Man in Society*, Vol. 5: 87-93.

Tripathy, K.C. *Orissa State Gazzetters,* Vol.1, Chapter II, Prehistory of Orissa, pp. 147-182.

Tripathy, K.C. 1992. *Prehistory and Proto-History of Western Orissa – A Study. in Ethos*, Sambalpur University 226-240.

Tripathy, K. C. & S.K. Mohapatra 1992. "Archaeology and Agriculture around Tangi". *Man in Society,* Vol. 6, 107-118.

Tripathy, K.C. 1992-93. "Man and Forest Eco-System in Orissa: A chronological Interpretation from past to present". *Man in Society,* Vol.7:110-116.

Tripathy, K. C. & Alok Rath. 1993-94. "The Upper Palaeolithic Industry of Rugnia, Jira River Valley, Orissa". *Man in Society,* Vol. 8, 85-88.

Tripathy, K.C. 1995. "Some Aspects of Regional Prehistory". Presidential Address, Anthropology and Archaeology Section, ISCA, Jadavpur University, Calcutta.

Tripathy, K.C. 2016. "Spectra of Odisha Lithic Cultures. Professor B.M. Das Memorial Oration", Indian National Confederation and Academy of Anthropologists (INCAA).

11
K.S. Mathur

Nadeem Hasnain

Kripa Shankar Mathur may rightly be described as one of the doyens of Indian anthropology. I cherish his memory as an outstanding teacher and mentor of several anthropologists including me.

Born on 9th April, 1929 in Shahjahanpur, Uttar Pradesh, he had his schooling in this district where his father was serving in the Department of Agriculture, Government of Uttar Pradesh. Later, he had his education in Bareilly, Uttar Pradesh. Born and brought up in a traditional Kayastha family he imbibed traditional values but marched with modernity. During this time Allahabad and Lucknow were the best centres of higher education and their universities were also known as Oxford and Cambridge of the east. He joined Lucknow University for his under graduate and post graduate studies. Popularly known as KSM, he married Vimla (Mathur) in 1953 and had a pleasant and popular family of two sons and a daughter.

Dr. Mathur came to anthropology *via* commerce and economics at Lucknow University. Several people may not be knowing that up to 1951, there was no independent department of anthropology in this university. Sociology and anthropology courses were being taught under the umbrella of economics. D.N. Majumdar was the only teacher of Anthropology in this department appointed in 1928 to teach the paper on primitive economic system. While taking his classes, he was able to attract a number of his students who later on became his illustrious disciples and made name in the discipline of sociology and anthropology. KSM was one of his students drawn to him and stayed with him till his sudden death in 1960.

After obtaining his masters degree in 1950 with specialization in Anthropology. Dr. Mathur decided to do his Ph.D. in social/cultural anthropology. He was keenly interested in the Dudhi region of Uttar Pradesh for his anthropological research in future. This was an eventful decade for anthropology in Lucknow as well as for Dr. Mathur. Lucknow University administration took years despite the persistent efforts of Dr. Majumdar for getting a separate department of anthropology. It was only in the year 1951 that the department of anthropology emerged with Dr. Majumdar as its founder head of the department. In the very year K.S. Mathur was appointed as lecturer in the department. He worked closely and tirelessly with Dr. Majumdar to develop it as a prominent centre for anthropological research and teaching centre in Asia.

In the year 1953, Mathur was awarded a research fellowship by the Australian National University, Canberra. The Department was still in a nascent stage and he was reluctant to leave but his teacher and mentor D.N. Majumdar encouraged him to join this research assignment for his personal as well as departmental well-being. He left for Canberra along with his wife. He was fortunate to get the guidance of one of the most prominent anthropologists of his time, S.F. Nadel who took him under his wings for his Ph.D. work. This was the time when Nadel was keenly interested in extending his department's research programme to South Asia. Adrian C. Meyer was already in central India working on the secular aspects of caste, Mathur was persuaded to do his research work on the religious aspects of caste in Malwa region of central India. Mathur had to reluctantly drop his proposal on Dudhi. While he was still engaged in field for data collection Nadel passed away. He later completed his dissertation and was awarded the degree of Ph.D. in Anthropology under another prominent anthropologist J.D. Freeman in 1960. His Ph.D. dissertation was published in 1964 under the title Caste and Ritual in a Malwa village.

This work was acclaimed internationally as a seminal contribution to this field of knowledge. Published by Asia Publishing House from New York in 1964, this work attracted international attention. It was a systematic attempt to interpret the local beliefs and practices in terms of universal Hindu values. It was long needed. As several of his international reviewers opined, his attempt to relate ideology and structure was indeed admirable besides it containing a wealth of ethnographic information. His thesis that 'Hindu philosophy' was the principal determinant of caste behaviour was established ethnographically.

Besides his academic pursuit the couple, Mr. & Mrs. Mathur, was extremely popular on the campus of Australian National University as well as the city of Canberra because of their involvement and promotion of cultural activities. They were like the 'cultural ambassadors' of India.

After the completion of his Ph.D. work in ANU, Canberra, Mathur returned to Lucknow in 1957 and resumed his duties in the department.

The discipline of anthropology in India, Department of Anthropology of Lucknow University, Mathur and other close associates of Majumdar received a major setback when D.N. Majumdar passed away suddenly in 1960. He was like a banyan tree for the nascent department. Recovering from this shock Mathur involved himself in conducting a comprehensive survey of primitive tribes of Madhya Pradesh on their socio-economic condition. This was sponsored by the National Council of Applied Economic Research, New Delhi. The survey was spread over the period of 1960-62. Later, he became the Head of the Department of Anthropology in 1962 and continued to occupy this chair till his sudden death in 1977. His devotion to the Department of Anthropology, Ethnographic and Folk Culture Society and its various activities was seen to be believed. As head of the Department he was managing the department, as general secretary of the EFCS he was actively involved in its various affairs and activities and as the editor of *The Eastern Anthropologist* he almost single handedly published the journal regularly without fail. He sacrificed his own academic pursuits for the sake of the legacy of the master. Several opportunities came in his way when he could become fullfledged professor with better emoluments (because the only post of professorship was entangled in litigation and he remained a Reader/Associate Professor) but he was in no mood to leave Lucknow and the Department of Anthropology. As S.C. Dube wrote in his obituary, "towards the end Mathur was tired and unhappy although he did not accept defeat. He had learned to face the perversities of human nature and institutional disincentives with a degree of stoicism. The realization of the cherished ambition of a university chair seemed within sight, but each time, by a cruel joke of destiny, it receded into an uncertain future. That he did not loose heart speaks volumes of his optimism and courage." Mathurs' close knit family played an important role in helping him not losing hope and courage despite the fact that life did not treat him kindly.

D.N. Majumdar founded Ethnographic & Folk Culture Society in 1945 and the research journal *The Eastern Anthropologist* in 1947. Mathur was one of the closest associates of Majumdar in both these ventures and inherited both these responsibilities and worked tirelessly since the death of his mentor in 1960 till his death in 1977. In a short span of 17 years the society became a recognised organization especially of ethnographic research. Most of the eminent anthropologists and sociologists became the life members of EFCS. Some distinguished life members from abroad have been Louis Dumont, Cora Dubois, Mckim Mariott, Harold Gould etc. Among the Honorary Fellows of the EFCS the names of C. Von Furer. Haimendorf, David Mandelbaume, Sol Tax, Fred Eggan, Levi-Strauss and others may be mentioned. The organ of EFCS, *The Eastern Anthropologist* made rapid strides during his tenure and counted as one of the best known journals of Anthropology in the world. During his tenure two more research journals – *Indian Journal of Physical Anthropology, Human Genetics* and *Manav*, the first and the only research journal of Anthropology and allied sciences in Hindi were started adding another feather to his cap.

In 1972 Mathur got the EFCS to initiate a biennial lecture series in memory of Majumdar. It had already became a prestigious academic event in his own life time.Stalwarts such as H.D. Sankalia, S.C. Dube, Haimendorf, T.N. Madan and others had delivered the lectures. The show goes on. Just before he passed away the institution builder had one more institution to build. It was D.N. Majumdar Museum of Folk Life and Culture, another wing of EFCS, established in 1975. It has galleries exhibiting ethnography and material culture mainly of the folk and tribal communities of Uttar Pradesh. It was the first and the only museum of its kind in Uttar Pradesh.

Since the Department of Anthropology was located in the heart of Hindi land and students were coming to the University through Hindi medium background there should have been some text books and translations of standard English books to cater to the requirements of such students. Because of his persistent persuasion the Uttar Pradesh Hindi Academy published some books of Anthropology as well as the translations of some books. He himself wrote books in Hindi to motivate and inspire others.

Mathur's contribution was not confirred to only anthropology or academia. Even his world beyond anthropology was widespread so was his areas of interests. When Lucknow Festival was started in 1975 by the Government of Uttar Pradesh, he was actively involved in its organization. He took keen interest to propagate the culture of Lucknow and its arts and crafts. Because of his passion for Lucknow's *Tehzeeb* (culture) Amrit Lal Nagar, the legendry Hindi novelist and himself an epitome of Lucknow's culture and especially its *Ganga-Jamuni Tehzeeb* (composite culture), often called Mathur as Majnu-e Lucknow (meaning by implication a passionate lover of Lucknow). Mathurs' refinement and sophistication justified this title. He was also deeply interested in the lives of the artisans and their crafts and skills and always supported their cause. He felt sad about the plight of these artisans who create beauty but lived a life of deprivation. Mathur was also involved with mass media and wrote articles in newspapers and magazines. His talks on All India Radio, Lucknow were very well received. When Doordarshan made its debut in Lucknow in 1975, Mathur was invited to host a couple of programmes which were quite popular. He also delivered popular talks in various fora including for the probationers of state services and Rotary Club members.

Mathur also enjoyed international repute. He was a member of the permanent council of the International Union of Anthropological and Ethnological Sciences and Vice President of Indian Anthropologist Association and was associated with as member of academic bodies.

A super organizer, an outstanding anthropologist, a visionary mentor and inspiring teacher, he has left behind hundreds of his students, some of whom are now his illustrious successors based in different parts of the world.

12
L.P. Vidyarthi

V. S. Sahay

This extraordinary internationally acclaimed anthropologist of the Third World spent his childhood very ordinarily (Sahay, 1988, 2001). Born in a remote village of Bariyarpur, under the police station Barh, District Patna in the state of Bihar, Vidyarthi learned the initial alphabets under the shade of a tree in a gurupinda (a village school of traditional type). From this rural background, within a short span of fifty-six years of his active life, he became one of the most distinguished anthropologists of the world, whose contributions in the discipline of anthropology was internationally acclaimed. A leader of world anthropology, an advocate for the just cause of anthropology, an anthropologist who propelled the Indian anthropology since mid-fifties, and gave maximum momentum to anthropology in India during the post-Independent period; the man, who perhaps produced the largest number of professional anthropologists in the country after Independence; the man, who was elected as the President of the Xth IUAES[1] and ICAES[2]; the man, who lifelong remained as the President of the Indian Anthropological Association; the man, who received the 'Distinguished Service Award' in anthropology from the University of Chicago, died suddenly on December 1, 1985. In the death of Professor Vidyarthi an era of Indian anthropology came to an end.

I had been associated with him under different capacities for over a decade and a half. My initial interaction was as a postgraduate student of Anthropology from 1970-72; then gradually as a doctoral student from 1973-1978; as a Research Associate in the Department of Anthropology, Ranchi University from 1979- 8 I; and finally, as a lecturer and colleague from 1981 onwards; till he breathed his last. It was during the Xth ICAES in New Delhi in December 1978, that I apprised Professor Vidyarhi of my intention to write his biography. Thereafter, in a series of discussions with him at his residence in this regard, he narrated accounts of his childhood and early education; his schooling in Mahabir Middle School and matriculation in 1946 from City High School (Rajendra Vidyalaya) Gaya; graduation from Patna College in 1950; M.A. (Part I) in Geography in 1952 from Patna University; his somewhat accidental shift from geography to anthropology in Lucknow University; his flair for writing; his inclination towards anthropology, sociology and social psychology; his political awareness at Lucknow; his association with D.N. Majumdar and Acharya Narendra Dev—the then Vice Chancellor of Lucknow University, and so on. Vidyarthi was the 100th Ph.D. in Anthropology from the University of Chicago in 1958. During my long association with him I had the opportunity to observe Professor Vidyarthi from quite close quarters.

Out of those discussions I had prepared a biographical account of him in 1981. However, at the behest of Vidyarthi, this biographical account was sent to Shelley Porteous, who was then working on the same line in Canada. In her article on Vidyarthi, Porteous (1986) extensively quoted from my write up, which appeared in an edited volume entitled *L.P. Vidyarthi: Contributions to the Development of Anthropology* by M.K. Gautam and A.K. Singh. The book contains valuable articles with regard to Vidyarthi's contributions to anthropology, contributed by Mario D. Zamora, Charles Frantz, Baidyanath Saraswati, L.M. Prasad, Shelley Porteous and Ajit K. Singh.

Even earlier, a brief article by me, particularly discussing about the contributions of Vidyarthi in Anthropology, appeared in a book *Development of Anthropological Researches in India* edited by L.P. Vidyarthi and V.S. Upadhyay, under the title '*In Search of Ranchi School of Anthropology*' (Sahay, 1981). Before its publication, the paper was first presented in a national seminar organized by the Ranchi University. After its presentation, it was so hotly debated that I still remember, while stepping down the stairs of the seminar hall, the Chairman (who prefers to remain anonymous) putting his hands on my shoulder said to me, "Well, Dr. Sahay, I too don't agree with any such concept as 'Ranchi School of Anthropology', but you have, at least sown the seeds of that school."

To begin with my personal experiences with him, I would start with some anecdotes. I was standing on board M.V. Andamans that had anchored at the harbour of Port Blair. It was a bright sunny morning in the winter months of 1971. It had been a tiresome and arduous journey of four days and four nights from the Port of Calcutta. Everyone on board the ship was in a hurry, jostling for quick disembarkation. I was quite fatigue; more so, because I got seasick during the tiresome four-day journey. Therefore, resting my elbows on the railing of the ship-deck, I was just looking at the greenery around the Port Blair harbour. Meanwhile, I heard Vidyarthi asking me from behind, "What are you thinking Vijoy?" "I am thinking about the future, Sir" I said. "Instead, you should think about the present," sharp came the reply from him. I was left speechless. On another occasion during the same trip, our ship had anchored near the Katchall Island in the Nicobar Archipelago. The sea was turbulent, and the weather very rough. Everyone looked tired and exhausted, except Vidyarthi. He looked as fresh as ever. I asked him, "Sir, don't you feel seasick?" Putting his hands on the railing of the ship-deck, he looked around the turbulent sea, and with great delight answered, "Well, I am a sea man." He was a great fieldworker. I am reminded of yet another incidence. On our trip to Andamans for fieldwork, we found a number of tribal labourers from Ranchi on board the ship. I reported it to Vidyarthi. Immediately he became interested, and within a short time prepared an inventory and asked us to collect as much of information as possible. Frankly speaking, at that time we were in no mood to interview the labourers on board. But now I feel nostalgic today to recollect how Vidyarthi was then moving up and down the stairs of the vessel with a small group of students in search of information of anthropological interest. He mixed freely with the poorly clad labourers. It only reflects Vidyarthi's love and dedication for fieldwork and anthropology. He would extend hero's welcome to any of his students/scholars who returned from the field.

There are many people from every walk of life, at least in Ranchi, who would claim that they were most close to Vidyarthi. It was perhaps an outstanding feature of his personality that people in distress or unable to take decision in their personal problems always confided with Vidyarthi, who gave them a very patient hearing. What he did for anybody in distress is a different matter, but his patient hearing and a few words of sympathy proved to be more encouraging than any material help. More especially, if any student was in trouble during his anthropological fieldwork, Vidyarthi would rush to the field camp and extend all possible help as a friend and a guardian. The hard-taskmaster Vidyarthi of the department, was very friendly, sociable and naive outside. One who has seen Vidyarthi playing *Kabaddi* (a rural Indian game) along the sprawling beach of Digha can hardly miss to see the social and friendly aspect of him. It was during an excursion trip in February 1970, that the staff and students had gone to Digha, a beautiful sea beach of Bay of Bengal in the coastal Midnapore district of West Bengal. While strolling along the beach in the evening, Vidyarthi suggested all of us to play *kabaddi*. He immediately took off his *kurta* (long shirt), and wearing only *pajamas* and undershirts was soon lost in play with us.

Some people think that Vidyarthi neglected his family owing to his pressure of work. In my opinion his family front was as successful as his professional front. He imparted thorough education to his two sons and two daughters. He got his daughters married very timely, which is considered very necessary and appreciable in a Hindu society. He very much enjoyed the company of his grandsons and daughters and often spent some time with them. He was quite an affectionate grandfather. Some people alleged that Vidyarthi seldom attended any social function with his wife. True, he was not uxorious. But the author has witnessed moments of Vidyarthi talking to his wife quite tenderly and warmheartedly. Once Vidyarthi said about his wife to this author, "With her undergraduate degree (she) proved to be a very successful housewife with two daughters and two sons" (Porteous, 1986:32). According to his family members, no family affair of some importance could escape his attention. He took care to see that confrontation does not arise between his family life and professional life. For this he maintained a certain amount of 'passiveness', though not 'negligence' in any case, in his family affairs. His family members had also become accustomed to his 'busy routine', and in due course it had become the accepted and adjusted natural pace of the family life.

Vidyarthi believed in the maxim 'Work is God'. He virtually venerated his work. He remained so absorbed in his works that he could seldom leave his house in the first half of the day. He remained in his study room till midday dictating articles, letters, or speeches, which he had to deliver on different occasions. He used to derive great pleasure and self-satisfaction in his work. His labour bestowed upon him one success after another, and thereby, his academic aspirations and organizational capabilities also moved step by step ahead as the years passed by. He not only worked hard, but also knew how to organize and get the work done, and that was the basis of his success. The successful holding of the Xth International Congress of Anthropological and Ethnological Sciences in New Delhi in 1978 under his Presidentship is a great testimony of it. He had developed a fabled reputation for hard work. It seems incredible though, but it is true, that even just two days before his death (when doctors advised him for complete rest), and only a few hours before falling into coma, he worked for four hours.

His public relations were very extensive. It included anthropologists as well as scholars of other disciplines, philanthropists, social workers, missionaries, industrialists, businessmen, administrators, bureaucrats and leaders of political parties; and thus, in general people from all walks of life. Obviously, such an extensive public relation was not developed in a few days; he had nurtured it for decades. Once this author had the experience of Vidyarthi's extensive and prolific correspondences. In connection with the Xth ICAES in 1978, one day he dictated me more than fifty letters, which ranged from the Prime Minister of the country to the State Chief Minister, and to almost all the important political personalities of that time; as well as to all the senior anthropologists of India and abroad. And to the other extreme, he also responded to a fresh matriculated rural teenager from Bero (a village 21 miles west of Ranchi) who had enquired of him about the prospects of studying anthropology, as an optional subject in an Intermediate college. He would respond to all letters, be it that of academicians, or VIPs, or mere social onefrom an ordinary person. He had built up an excellent relationship with the press, the local as well as national. He was very friendly with the pressmen; and the pressmen too made it a point to invariably attend the functions organized by him.

Some of my professional colleagues and senior students of Vidyarthi often say that Vidyarthi did not take much initiative to see that the subject developed in other institutes/universities in Bihar during his life time. But I think it is not true. In 1981, the Selection Committee in Ranchi University under Vidyarthi's headship, appointed lecturers in anthropology in almost all the colleges of the University. However, the man who trained so large number of professional anthropologists in the country during his life time, failed to produce equally competent and dynamic anthropologists form among his students in his home state to carry on his banner. Soon after his demise, the legacy of Vidyarthi began waning from the Department of Anthropology, Ranchi University. Sometimes one wonders whether Vidyarthi was like a banyan tree. He would give shelter to all, but would not allow anyone to grow or to become at par with him. Perhaps, for this reason there are many, who though sadly felt the absence of Vidyarthi after his demise, but were much disappointed and despaired in the Department due to such frame of his mind. In a way his method was dictatorial. We have seen that when a heated discussion arose during a seminar or general meeting and the members did not arrive at any conclusion, Vidyarthi made sweeping remarks and propositions and brought the discussion to an end.

Ranchi has twice led the anthropological researches in India. It has been the home of two 'veteran anthropologists of international repute', namely, S.C. Roy and L.P. Vidyarthi. With a band of disciples, they brought to light many of the unexplored fields of Indian life and culture. Their conceptual frameworks and methodologies have given light to many young researchers of their respective times. They, however, represent two different 'eras' of anthropological development in the country. While Roy focused his attention primarily on the tribes of South Bihar (now Jharkhand), Vidyarthi's interest went throughout the length and breadth of the country; from Badrinath in the Himalaya's in the North to Rameshwaram in the south; and from the State of Meghalaya in the east to the sacred city of Dwarka in the west. Vidyarthi's manifold anthropological interest went as far as the island culture of Andaman and Nicobar Islands, where till now the Sentinelese live in complete geographical and social isolation. If Roy brought international repute to India by his selection as a member of the Council de Honour of the International Congress of Anthropological and Ethnological Sciences, Vidyarthi's election as the President of the Xth IUAES & ICAES (1973-78) marked the advent of a 'new era' in Indian anthropology. The basic differences between these two geniuses of Indian anthropology lie in their intellectual background and general anthropological outlook. While Roy's researches in anthropology reflect complete British influence; Vidyarthi, initially reflected explicit American influence, but soon made a departure, and became a champion of "Indianness in social science in general and anthropology in particular."

Having been trained initially under the leadership of D.N. Majumdar at Lucknow, in India, and later in the University of Chicago in America, Vidyarthi entered as a professional anthropologist understandably with American influence. However, soon he realized that the methodologies developed in the study of the Occidental cultures were not accurately suited to the study of complex Oriental cultures. Hence, he began to advocate to bring 'Indianness' in anthropology. In his presidential address at the Xth ICAES (1978) in New Delhi he said "India's ancient scriptures like the Vedas, the Upanishads, the Smritis, the Puranas and the other great epics provide a sensitive insight into the social realities. Therefore, the Indianness in social science has to emerge with a proper appraisal of these ancient texts, whose influences on the behavioural pattern of our countrymen cannot be neglected." About the ancient scriptures of India, he further said, "these ancient scriptures reflect the wisdom and provide guidelines for shaping the sociocultural life in India. The patterns of nature-man relationship, man-to-man relationship and man-to-spirit relationships are explained in great depth. The basic elements of Indian's life-style lie in their traditional practice of the four Ashramas, four Purusharthas, 16 Sanskaras, etc. which still continue to influence the ethos, worldview and the life of an average Indian. Dharma (wrongly translated as religion) is the first of the four fundamental principles of social ethics of man in the form of Purushartha – the word literally means 'the meaning of man' or the 'aim of being human'. The other three principles are: *Artha* (wealth), *Kama* (desire) and *Moksha* (salvation). It is man's duty to fulfill the first three in order of priority and live with purity to achieve the last" (*ibid*). In the same Presidential Address, he also categorically lashed out against the comments of some of the Western scholars like Gunnar Myrdal, who said that there was dominance of religion only on the thinking and practice of Indian folks. He also attacked the Western scholars who held that the Third-World countries were not capable of pursuing research works. Thus, we find that Vidyarthi, quite often, hit the traditional trends of anthropological inquiries to discover some stimulating and new trends of researches for the coming generations.

Vidyarthi's contributions to anthropology are exhaustive to behold. He authored 35 books and edited 37 volumes; wrote 159 articles for different national and international journals;and supervised three D. Litts., and 35 Ph.D.s. Thematically, his contributions could be summed up under the following heads: Village Studies, Applied and Action Anthropology, Study on Scheduled Caste, Folklore Researches, Urban-Industrial Anthropology, Study on Leadership, Anthropological Theories; besides, of course, formulating two very significant concepts in Indian Anthropology, viz., the Sacred Complex and the Nature-Man-Spirit Complex.

Vidyarthi first proposed Sacred Complex (1961), and thereafter, Nature-Man-Spirit Complex (1963). He obtained his doctoral degree from the University of Chicago on Sacred Complex. We find very apparent influence of Chicago School of Anthropology of the 1950s and 1960s in his both the concepts. Robert Redfield, Milton Singer, and McKim Marriott were then teaching anthropology in Chicago University, while Vidyarthi was engaged in doing Ph.D. there. Julian Steward was though not associated with University of Chicago under any capacity, but Vidyarthi seems to have been very much influenced by him and his theory of 'cultural ecology' also; to the extent that Julian Steward wrote the Foreword of Vidyarthi's second book, *The Maler: A Study in Nature-Man-Spirit Complex of a Hill Tribe in Bihar* (1963).

After Vidyarthi's study of Hindu Gaya, a number of scholars, such as, B.N. Saraswati, who studied the Holy Circuit of Nimsar (1962) and Temple Organization in Goa (1965); Makhan Jha of Janakpur and Ratanpur (1971, 1978); K.N. Sahay of Tanginath (1975);Sachindra Narayan of Deoghar (1972); V.S. Upadhyay of Dwarka (1974); M. Mohapatra (1971) of Lingraj Temple; Vidyarthi and Saraswati of Kashi (1978); A.B. Saran and Gaya Pandey (1992) on Sun Worship at Deo, and many others worked on the concept of sacred complex. It was observed that the concept of sacred complex was not only a useful anthropological tool in the study of complexities of ancient pilgrimage centres of India, but it was useful in examining the spirit-world of the tribes of India as well. The concept of sacred complex incorporating 'sacred geography', 'sacred specialist' and 'sacred performance' reflected a level of continuity, compromise and combination between great and little traditions. He also provided such terms as 'sacred centre', 'sacred cluster', 'sacred segment' and 'sacred zone' to describe the 'sacred geography' of a 'local', 'regional' or 'universal' aspect of the great Indian civilization.

Likewise, the concept of Nature-Man-Spirit Complex was also tested and verified as a very suitable tool for the study of the tribes by various scholars in their researches. Mention can be made of Man (1978) on Bhils of Rajasthan, Morab (1978) on the Soliga of Karnataka, Ramesh Chandra (1978) on Kinners of Himachal Pradesh, Sandhwar (1978) on the Korwa of Palamau, Prasad (1978) on the Parahiyas of Santhal Paragana, Sahay (1981) on the Nicobarese, Pradip Singh (1981) restudied the Maler, Prabhat Singh (1986) on Kurmis of Chotanagpur, and Ashok Pandey (2016) on the Baigas of Madhya Pradesh, Banita Basu (2012, unpublished) on Sunderban Delta, and Mayank Prakash (2018, unpublished) on the Rabha. P.K. Singh in his restudy of Maler (1981), introduced a mathematical computation in the concept, and thereby, giving a new dimension to it. He claims that nature-man-spirit complex is constant.

To sum up, Vidyarthi is known for his volumes of works, but very few people know that he died much before completing two of the most ambitious projects of his life. The first, was on 'Anthropological Thought', incorporating the views of the eminent Indian social thinkers and those written in the ancient Indian scriptures. This work he intended to do with my assistance. The second was on the 'Civilization'. He believed that India alone was a country where the people of all the stages of civilization could be found. Once he told this author that he wanted to complete these two projects by 1992. It is to be noted that he was to retire in 1991. This also suggests his well-calculated and time-bound work programme. It is quite an irony that he left for heavenly abode much before even actually starting these two ambitious projects. Professor Vidyarthi is no more today. Regardless of all polemic, he has left his imprints in the annals of anthropology for the posterity.

NOTES

1. International Union of Anthropological and Ethnological Sciences.
2. International Congress of Anthropological and Ethnological Sciences.

REFERENCES

Gautam, M.K. & A.K. Singh (eds.), 1986. *L.P. Vidyarthi: Contribution to the Development of Anthropology*. Concept Publishing Co. Pvt. Ltd., New Delhi.

Porteous, Shelley. 1986. "Experiencing Vidyarthi". Gautam and Singh (eds.), *L.P. Vidyarthi: Contribution to the Development of Anthropology*. Concept Publishing Co. Pvt. Ltd., New Delhi.

Sahay, Vijoy S. 1981. "In search of Ranchi school of anthropology". In L.P. Vidyarthi and V.S. Upadhyay (eds.), *Development of Anthropological Research in India*. Concept Publishing Co. Pvt. Ltd., New Delhi.

Sahay, Vijoy S.1988. My Guru as I Saw Him. *South Asian Anthropologist*; Volume 9, No. 1.

Sahay, Vijoy S. 2001. "My Guru as I Saw Him (Revised version)". *The Oriental Anthropologist*, Volume 1, No. 1.

Vidyarthi, L.P. 1978. "Presidential Address". Xth International Congress of Anthropological and Ethnological Sciences.

13

Leela Dube

Pioneering Gender Studies in India

Subhadra Mitra Channa

Anthropology is one discipline in India, where even in the present times, when women are seen as dominating many disciplines, there is a dearth of known women scholars. For many decades after the subject was introduced in India during the colonial period, there were only men, who could be counted as representing the discipline. The few women, who did dare to enter the discipline had to leave without leaving much mark, with the sole exception of Iravati Karve. However, Karve was concerned with the conventional fields of anthropology and although could be interpreted as a feminist (Channa, 2007), was never overtly or expressly, specializing in gender.

It was the eighties, when Leela Dube was established as a scholar, that the first step towards gender studies in sociology and anthropology was taken. A generation of feminist and gender studies specialists followed Western feminist like Pat Caplan, Maria Mies, Helen Safa and Eleanor Leacock (to name a few of the leading influences) to highlight gender as an essential component of both epistemology and analysis. Dube can be considered as a pioneer of gender studies in India. At the Xth ICAES held in 1978 in Delhi, she was actively engaged in understanding anthropology from a non-conventional non-patriarchal premise, especially the gendered character of kinship. In the volume that emerged out of that meeting, Visibility and Power, she had contextualized gender relations in India to the textual analogy of seed and earth; emerging out of the agricultural base of Hindu cosmology.

Till the publication of this book, one can hardly identify any work where there was a conscious effort to mainstream gender into the analysis. Indian anthropology was the product of a line up of male scholars, who kept to positivist and male focused analysis exactly as was done by their colonial predecessors. Dube too was following the Western trend of gendered scholarship but she did not follow her Western counterparts absolutely, and turned the gaze onto Indian world view and cosmology, highlighting the social and philosophical contexts of gender construction. She draws eclectically from field data, existing social conditions, literature, art, folk sayings and folklore and a variety of sources to indicate the rich cultural sources of how a society constructs gender.

However, the journey to the Xth ICAES, was a long one and one needs to understand the biographical roots of her scholarship as well as her try to assess the genesis of her academic inclination.

Leela was born in the year 1923, the fourth daughter of a well to do Brahmin family of Maharashtra. However, her family had moved to Middle India, in the heyday of the Peshwas in the latter part of the nineteenth century, in what is known today as Madhya Pradesh. As can be expected the upper caste Maharashtrians were landlords and well established. When the colonial rule brought in formal education, it was this stratum, that first took advantage of Western education and the opportunities it provided. At the same time women's education was seen as essential for the Indian family had always valued the role of the mother and wife. From the last part of the 19th century, there were girl's schools opened in some parts of India, beginning with Bengal. Women in families like that of Leela Dube, went to school in the natural course of things. However, education was not directed towards career or money earning but towards self-improvement and for value addition as wives and mothers. Most women obtained education so that they could be fit wives for men of high status.

Her three elder sisters were educated up to a point and then married. The renowned classical vocalist Sumati Mutatkar, was her elder sister. The process of arranging a match in those days was somewhat derogatory to the self-esteem of the bride to be. She was often made to feel embarrassed and there was also the custom of dowry. Leela rebelled against this process and refused to get married by arrangement. She continued her education and after doing her graduation she enrolled for her Masters degree in Political Science in Nagpur University.

She had been an avid reader of books, novels and fictions and was full of ideals of womanhood that she read in Marathi and Bengali novels of that time as well as from mythology and Hindu epics. Yet as she herself acknowledges; her mind was not ready to accept everything in totality. There was always an element of of criticism, of debate, in her, "a tacit acceptance of traditions and an implied agreement with customary ways made me quite uneasy" (2000: 4038). Her aim was to marry a person who would be her intellectual superior so that she would not have to strain herself to be deferential to him. She had realized that a woman had to accept her position as inferior to that of her husband, and if it was supported by the actual situation then acceptance would be easier. When she met the brilliant Shyama Charan Dube in Nagpur, she was immediately attracted to him. She persuaded her family to arrange her marriage to him. He joined Ph.D. in Anthropology after standing first in Political Science, and she also did the same after marrying him. Their families seemed to have readily agreed to the marriage facilitated no doubt by the fact that both were upper caste Brahmins. In her description of her father, we see a reflection of Prof. Dube as she describes him as impeccably dressed in Western clothes, with a pipe dangling from his mouth and speaking flawless English. Her father was a judge in the service of the British, a fact that somewhat jarred her nationalist sentiments. But she admired him, his talents as a musician and his importance in society.

Her anthropological research work began after her marriage. Her Ph.D. was a study of Gond women in Madhya Pradesh. Her exposure to the lives of Gond women, opened her eyes to the existence of a world that was completely different from her own. Here women could speak and sing about sexuality, about love, about having affairs. Widows remarried and many men and women had contracted second marriages after divorce. However, what really impressed her and later guided her interest into gender studies was the lack of fit between norms and practice. There was always a scope for manipulation, of subtle remoulding of relationships, of the exertion of power and influence that made different kinds of space available than what was legitimate and sanctioned. In other words gender relations could never be understood by simply referring in a positivist manner to the rules and norms of society. One had to go into subjective depths, into case studies and details of interaction that were not always available on the surface.

In her family life too, like in all Indian families, there were the stories, sometimes hushed, about deviations, breaking of norms, exertions of power and influence to get what one wants, or the opposite, the breaking of hearts, the cruelties and deprivations. She realized that in all kinds of societies, including the Gonds, she had studied, there were depths that were not accessible on the surface. She completed her Ph.D. in 1953 but it remains unpublished till date. It presented an account of three tribal societies in Madhya Pradesh, with its focus on the lives of women. Deeply impressed by the comparison of these women with the upper caste and class women she knew, this thesis laid the foundation of the comparative study of gender, which became her specialization in later life.

The initial period of her married life was spent like that of most Indian women, that is playing second fiddle to her illustrious husband. She became an unpaid assistant to him, helping in his fieldwork and research work, keeping a low profile, working as an honorary teacher, in Sagar University, where he taught for many years. As described by their son Saurabh Dube (2007), she had helped S.C. Dube collect material for his work on the Kamars. She was especially useful to him by getting access to data on women. Later Leela Dube had also received a regular teaching post in the same university, but she went on to do other things. She had two sons, and would perhaps not have distinguished herself much if she had not been overpoweringly impressed by Iravati Karve.

Iravati Karve was a domineering personality, both physically and in terms of her fearless attitude towards expressing her own opinions. Leela Dube had many chances of interaction with her as they also belonged to the same city, Pune and spoke the same language. Under her influence, Leela Dube slowly came into her own and carved out her own path in academics. "Iravati Karve emerged as a towering figure, particularly in contrast to my shyness and halting self-confidence" (2000:4041).

Since Karve's major contribution to anthropology was her work on comparative kinship in India, and her recognition of the regional nature of kinship, Dube too became interested in the comparative study of kinship. Malinowski and Kathleen Gough also influenced her interest in the study of kinship. Earlier she had prepared grounds for a possible study of law (in her father's footsteps) by attaining a degree of proficiency in Sanskrit, Philosophy and English Literature. This training later helped her in her analytic and writing abilities in the field of social anthropology and sociology. Although grounded in anthropology, several outstanding anthropologists of the sixties and seventies became known as sociologists as they were studying the institutions of their own society, such as caste and kinship. This list includes names like S.C. Dube, M.N. Srinivas and Andre Beteille. Leela Dube, too, although doing work like an anthropologist, is often known as a sociologist and was active in the sociological forums.

In the early sixties, when she was teaching at Sagar University, a student from Kerala came to do Ph.D. under her. This student, Abdul Rehman Kutty, wished to study an island Kalpeni, which was relatively isolated from the coastal main region, but was home to a unique community. Although Muslims by faith, these people followed the Nayar system of kinship with the custom of matriliny and visiting husbands. As a young man, he was fired by the spirit of adventure and collected substantial demographic and social data from these island people. Dube was fascinated by this unique system of kinship and religion. Among them, the ancestral properties were inherited according to matrilineal rules while self-acquired properties were passed on according to the Sharia laws. At the time of the fieldwork, over 76 per cent of the men were visiting husbands. Although Dube published a book, *Matriliny and Islam*, along with A.R. Kutty, she was not satisfied. Quite rightly she felt that justice has not been done to the extraordinary field data. She also felt that a lot more work could be done. So, in 1969, accompanied by her young son, she went to Kalpeni to do another bout of fieldwork and collected a large amount of data, on legal disputes and marital problems, that were bound to occur under two such divergent normative systems operating together. Even at this time, her interests were mainly on the data on kinship and legal matters, and gender was not a central concern. She never wrote another book on Kalpeni, but a large amount of data and analysis pertaining to her Kalpeni material went into her later writings on Kinship and Gender.

In 1970-72, she did a project on kinship and family in India, from the Indian Council of Social Science Research, that was later published as a book, *Sociology of Kinship: An Analytic Survey of Literature* (1974). While scrutinizing the enormous data on kinship and marriage in India, she became interested in gender relations, in the myriads of ways in which women were affected by inheritance rules, marriage practices and other customs that gave them certain roles within the family and kin group. In 1976, she founded the Commission on the Anthropology of Women, within the global body of anthropologists, then known as ICAES (International Council of Anthropological and Ethnological Sciences) which is today known as IUAES (International Union of Anthropological and Ethnological Sciences). In 1978, the ICAES held its major congress in New Delhi, one of its largest and most well attended. Here Dube brought the Commission on women into prominence, attending with her were prominent gender specialists and feminist scholars like Maria Mies, Pat Caplan, Eleanor Leacock, Helen Safa and others, and they held several panels and had wide ranging discussions. As a result of this Congress a number of books were published that established Leela Dube as an authority on gender studies.

The book *Visibility and Power: Essays on Women in Society and Development*, published by Oxford University Press, Dube wrote the Introduction along with her co-editors, Eleanor Leacock and Shirley

Ardner. She also wrote her well known essay where she locates the genesis of gender construction in South Asia, in the Hindu cosmology of Seed and Earth, where the men are symbolized as seeds and women as earth. The entire philosophy of the interdependence of seed and earth in producing a good crop or a good offspring is reflected in the Indian system of caste. Thus, while women as mothers are very important in providing nurturance to the children, the role of the man or the father remains supreme. It is the seed that determines the nature or identity of the crop or the offspring. A child derives its main identity from the father and its healthy growth and development is dependent on the nurturing done by the mother, just like a seed needs nourishment from good soil. For this reason, in South Asian society, the role of the mother is the most important than a woman can play and since society is mostly patrilineal, the mother's role is enhanced, when she is the mother of sons (Channa, 2013).

As her career graph in gender studies and women's studies developed, Leela Dube visited ASEAN countries and carried out a comparative analysis of South Asian and South-East Asian countries. This work resulted in the book *Women and Kinship : Comparative Perspectives on Gender in South and South East Asia*. She also played a key role in the 1984 World Sociological Congress in which women scholars and activists played a crucial role. By this time Leela Dube had emerged as one of the foremost social scientists of India who was an authority on gender and women's studies. She was a feminist at heart although her writings did not reflect feminist approach as much as they reflect a shift away from positivist approach. Most of her writings are on conventional anthropological themes such as kinship and marriage but she quite rightly was able to show that one cannot describe social institutions in a gender-neutral way.

Moving away from the purely positivist analysis that is reflected in the work of male anthropologists of that time, Dube, advocated a dialogic approach in anthropology, following her colleague Eleanor Leacock. She made a pioneering effort to show that gender constructs in South Asia have completely different premises than those in the Western cultures. Moreover, most feminists in India, although intellectually opposed to patriarchy rarely followed the radical feminist path. In India even feminists have been concerned with issues of suffering, cruel customs, injustice and structural inequalities, more than that of liberty and sexuality. The influence of Gandhian, Marxist and socialist thoughts have predominated over hard core feminist thinking.

Social activism, issues of female infanticide, neglect of female children, dire poverty and deprivation of a large section of society, age old modes of inequality, such as caste, have occupied most of the attention of Indian feminists. Moreover, Indian women rarely have to content with relations of power only with their sexual partners. Radical feminism is meaningless when women are embedded within the larger social network of joint families and extended kin networks, where the most important men in one's lives are more likely to be one's father and brother and brother-in-law. Even in the 1980s Leela Dube had predicted that with rampant female infanticide and female foeticide, the disproportionate sex-ratio will lead to escalation in crimes against women. Her prediction is chillingly coming true in contemporary Indian society.

She played a key role in introducing women's studies into Indian academic curriculum by the contribution made by her to the 'Towards Equality' report of the Parliamentary Committee on the Status of Women in India (1974). She joined in the year 1980, as a senior faculty in the Institute of Rural Management, Anand (Gujrat, India). Here she conceptualized how anthropological fieldwork methods could be introduced into management studies especially with regard to rural management. The last part of her career was spent in this institute.

Leela Dube made a lasting impact on sociology and social anthropology in India by making a generation of feminist anthropologists aware of the gender equation in methodology. Many of us, women scholars were under her direct influence, and I took up as the Chair of the Commission on Anthropology of Women, at the Kunming Congress in 2009. I visited her at her home in Delhi, to seek her blessings and also to inform her that after her, I was the second Indian woman scholar to assume this responsibility. As I have already mentioned Indian feminism went in the direction of social activism rather than the sexual liberation that was the prime agenda of Western feminists.

Indian women had to fight at the frontiers of poverty, neglect, violence and sexual exploitation. Gender in India is deeply intersected by caste, class, ethnicity and religion. Yet women had never been the kind of secondary citizens as they were in the West. When formal education was introduced in India, many fathers were motivated to get their daughters educated and that is how we had scholars like Iravati Karve and Leela Dube. Although both were married to enlightened and very scholarly husbands, each had carved out their own path. Although never overt, her ambivalent attitude towards her married life is expressed in her own words, "At the level of personal and social experience (and incessant soul searching), I had always found marriage intriguing and baffling" (Dube, 2000:4042). Leela Dube, was overshadowed by her husband for quite some time, but later came into her own, both under the influence of Iravati Karve's dynamic personality as well as by her close association with Western feminist scholars. It is noteworthy, that in the presence of many outstanding and dynamic scholars, she was chosen to be the first Chair of the Commission on Women, of the most global anthropological association, in 1976 and continued in this position till 1993.

She, along with several other feminist scholars, under the guidance of Vina Mazumdar, drafted the Towards Equality, report on the status of women in India for the government. This report, submitted in 1974, changed the lives of women by making women's questions and issues an integral part of the state's planning. These women pointed out that society is not the same for men and women, they lead different lives and have separate domains that need to be addressed separately. At the same time, by taking a comparative approach and a field- based methodology, Dube and others were able to also show the internal cleavages of women. As she had realized during her first fieldwork among the Gond women, women's lives were not the same across the entire social fabric of India. Another dimension that deeply influenced gender studies in India was colonization as expressed in the classic volume by Sangari and Vaid (1989) and other important ones like Ghosh (2007). The nationalist fervour also created the critical attitude towards established institutions and also inherited values of society. As women scholars came into their own, the silencing of women in all spheres of society became more and more a matter of discourse.

Leela Dube (like Iravati Karve) made good use of the literature, mythology and folklore of the Indian subcontinent to create gender constructs that were local and socially contextualized. They were also deeply influenced by a nationalist consciousness, a sentiment of being part of a non-Western indigenous culture, which was significantly different from the West and needed to be understood as such. Indian women had their own scripts and narratives that needed to be understood in their own context. Dube has the distinction of doing a wide range of comparative analysis even extending beyond South Asia into South East Asia. Her wide-ranging scholarship has rarely been matched in the field of women's studies. Her work as well as her personality remains an inspiration for women scholars both in India, and also globally. She remained active and alert till the end of her life, passing away in 2013, leaving a rich legacy for the future generations.

REFERENCES

Channa, Subhadra Mitra. 2013. *Gender in South Asia: Social Imagination and Constructed Realities*, Cambridge: Cambridge University Press.

Dube, Leela, 1956. The Gond Women (unpublished Ph.D. dissertation of Nagpur University.

Dube, Leela, 1969. *Matriliny and Islam: Religion and Society in Laccadives*, Delhi: National Publishing House (In association with A.R. Kutty).

Dube, Leela, 1974. *Sociology of Kinship: An Analytical Survey of Literature*, Bombay: Popular Prakashan.

Dube, Leela, 1980. *Studies on Women in Southeast Asia*, Bangkok: UNESCO

Dube, Leela, 1997. Women and Kinship: Comparative Perspectives on Gender in South and South-East Asia2000 "Doing Kinship and Gender: An Autobiographical Account" In *Economic and Political Weekly*, Vol. 35, No.46: 4037-4047.

Dube, Leela, Eleanor Leacock and Shirley Ardner (eds.). 1986. *Visibility and Power: Essays on Women in Society and Development*, Delhi: Oxford University Press.

Dube, Saurabh, 2007. "Ties that bind: Tribe, Village, Nation and S.C. Dube" in Patricia Uberoi, Nandini Sunder and Satish Deshpande (eds.), *Anthropology in the East: Founders of Indian Sociology and Anthropology*, New Delhi: Permanent Black, pp. 444-495.

Ghosh, Anindita (ed). 2007. *Behind the Veil: Resistance, Women, and the Everyday in Colonial South Asia*, New Delhi: Permanent Black.

Sangair, Kumkum Sangari and Sudesh Vaid (eds.). 1989. *Recasting Women: Essays in Colonial History*, New Delhi: Kali for Women.

14
Der Wissenchaftler Professor Dr. L.K. Mahapatra

Prasanna K. Nayak

What could be more ecstatic for an alumnus than recounting reminiscences of his alma mater, glory of his pedagoguery and singing in praise of his teacher! The teacher-taught conviviality in ancient Indian society bears testimony to the remarkable importance of the teacher in everyday life of the student. In the Indian ideological system veneration to the teacher-preceptor is conceptually regarded as ethereal and carrying forward his supreme command is espoused as blissful. The prideful place of the teacher in the society can never be rendered embittered. The universal value bestowed on the teacher is not for the sake of being and becoming a teacher but for help producing the right kind of student. A teacher takes pride in his pupil and becomes enamoured of the glory that accrues to him (the student). A teacher is credited the most only when his own student excels him. A teacher could be the fountainhead of all intellect. He could be an institution by himself. The sustainability and ubiquity of this institution depends upon how best and with what rigour the teacher has been able to cut the analytical teeth of the taught. A teacher not only stimulates the mental faculty of the student but also inculcates in him the required dynamism to ensure the growth of knowledge through a process of self-falsification. The singular aim of this prefatory thought to the essay is to appraise and felicitate my teacher, my research guide, my intellectual stimulator, my Professor, Professor Dr. Lakshman Kumar Mahapatra, and to recapitulate some of the fundamental anthropological questions which, quite often modestly he addresses to and as I have perceived them well within the ambience of my doing 'anthropology' commensurate with the precincts of the discipline.

It was some time in 1973 I happened to come across a black suited, spectacled, clean-scalped, and fairly graceful man rushing to our departmental premises. The whisper accentuated, "Professor Mahapatra, the Head of the Department". That time he was resuming the Headship after a period of research leave. I was amazed to see that within a few months' time, he organized guest lectures and conducted seminars and the entire department was surcharged with hum of academic activities. At a personal level I felt as if the department had a breakthrough and we all students were exposed to a broad sphere of academy. Up until then, I did not discern myself that I was being taught in a University department. The underlying assumption is that pursuit of knowledge in a University is affected more through seminars, symposia and commissioned lectures than through mere class-room teaching. "Knowledge-didactics" gets metamorphosed into "Knowledge-dynamics" in a University institution. The Germans quite often define knowledge (Wissen) in their own tongue by quoting Socrates, "ich weiss dass ich nichts weiss", the English translation of which is that "I know that I know nothing". The search for pure knowledge becomes the main pursuit of a student in a University, and for this, creation of viable and congenial conditions and opportunities becomes the sole responsibility of a University Faculty. Professor Mahapatra has successfully discharged his responsibilities: the growth of five specializations in anthropology and the present faculty strength of Anthropology Department at Utkal bear testimony to that. His wider outlook, broad vision, and farsightedness among the first-second generation of anthropologists in India have earned him and his Department undisputed national reputation. Because of stewardship of Professor Mahapatra, during his heydays, Utkal-Anthropology continues till date the source of inspiration for others, the magic wand being "craze for quality".

Professor Mahapatra's class-room teaching is an exemplar. If he enters the class nobody knows when will he leave the class. He starts with questioning a few on a precise topic, goes on simplifying them till he realizes his limit and discusses the full-range of the topic in tandem, knotted with illustrations, partly his own and partly textual, quoting authorities and thus gets himself engrossed and immersed, slowly but gradually getting momentum, and performs his class-room job. In social anthropological theory, methodology and anthropological analytical enterprise he is second to none in the department. His style of teaching is simple, method of teaching "associative" and mode of deliberation and presentation absorbing. Besides his full grasp of the whole gamut of social .anthropological questions and issues, he used to demonstrate sanguine interest and concern for the allied sub-disciplines in anthropology. He is an integrationist as far as specialization is concerned.

In higher academic fora and research platforms he is an admirer and votary of the unity of sciences. He is not only strong believer of the interdisciplinary approach and collaborative research but also a practitioner in the arena, and in the whole of University he is singularly known for his efforts in this direction. The Centre for Regional Studies (CRS), Population Research Centre (PRC), and the Specialization, South-East Asia Culture Area Study in Anthropology at Utkal University are his own creations, in which he involved quite a good number of sister departments to work in collaboration with anthropology. Knowing fully well the academic bureaucracy and politicking in the University he ceaselessly works for reaching his goal and attaining his cherished mission. In spite of all odds, internally and externally at work, he forges ahead and never breaks down. His patience, perseverance and diligence hardly fetters away. During his tenure as Head of the Department, Professor Mahapatra has spared no efforts in seeing that the students undergo rigorous training in the field and prepare standard field reports. He never has allowed dilution of the discipline. In the Field-Methods class he acquaints the students the problem of study with clarity and surfeit. The hard-task master insists time and again on revision of writings till the point of perfection. His corrections in his own hand-writing can be emulated as models for the learner. He possesses a kite's eye in pointing out mistakes and picking up the point of argument. From his logical dissection of field-data and their pin-pointed analyses the research student learns the skill and acquires knowledge in a much more perfect way than otherwise he would have acquired. Professor Mahapatra is a live wire. Quite sharply he reacts to situations unhealthy, circumstances inert, conditions stultified, happenings unwarranted, practices unlawful, working habits sluggish and prepares the ground to overtake and step forward. He loves having powers, acquiring positions and exercising authority but intends not to infringe the norm and devalue the standard. By birth, Mahapatra is a stubborn Oriya, by dealings a polite and gentleman Bengali, and by temperament an advanced-looking German. To reify the above qualification it may be pointed out that having acquired his Intermediate degree in Orissa he spent the most crucial and formative period of his academic career in Calcutta University earning B.A. Hons., and MA. in Anthropology and completed his D.Phil degree within a couple of years having been exposed to higher level of research-learning in Germany. Among his contemporary Indian colleagues he is one of the anthropologists by choice and among them he is the only one who has to his credit first class academic career throughout. The man has ingrained in him the outlook of a scientist in his personal life unparalleled among his peers, scientists and non-scientists alike. Even when in higher academic positions hardly has he undeservedly groomed anyone to grow; rather he has all the while championed the cause of those who help themselves. As an examiner he affords not to be prejudiced on any count and in evaluating answer scripts, he is very tuff to the better-off than to the worst-off. He is regarded not only as a teacher of teachers but also as a master-teacher. He is communicable at any wave-length and makes explicit his point of view to intellectuals, administrators, technocrats, professional of all hues. He is inquisitive about almost everything, earthly and heavenly, and has been gifted with an intrinsic knack for knowing and learning things by self. Relation between "anthropology and its social environment" is of great consideration for we professionals. Moreover, what is taught does not depend only on the syllabus, but also on the tendencies dominant among those by whom the instructions given. Professor Mahapatra's training in ethnology and sociology in Germany dominated anthropological teaching and thinking at Utkal for about a quarter-century (1967-1989) and his legacy, in some measure continues to fervour around even today. Way back in 1988, at Oxford, I met Professor Rodney Needham, the world famous anthropologist of England and interacted with him at a personal level soon after his seminar lecture on 'Indian Religion' was over. When he came to know that I was from Utkal, immediately he asked me about Prof. Mahapatra and enquired about him. Then, I asked him whether he had met Professor Mahapatra at any time in the past! He replied, no. But confided to me that he had been impressed by one of L.K. Mahaptra's articles on "Gods, Kings and Caste System in India" and that way he remembers his name. That time onwards, our friendship grew and we were meeting frequently during my three months research stay there, and on one occasion, he invited me to have dinner with him at Wolfson College Guest House. From this, one could guess the name and fame earned by L.K. Mahapatra at the world academic forum.

Professor L.K. Mahaptra was born on 29th October, 1929 in Rajanilgiri, Baleswar district, Odisha. All through, he has struggled very hard to pursue his education and finally achieved what he wanted to have. He finished his school education in 1946, got first class and stood second in the list of the best-10 students. He passed the intermediate course in 1948 from Utkal University in first class, securing second position. He chose to study Anthropology and moved to Calcutta University and passed Honours in Anthropology in 1950 and secured First Class First position in 1950. He obtained Masters Degree in Anthropology from Calcutta University in 1952 and stood first class second. Being a brilliant student throughout, he acquired a pride of place among all the anthropologists of India. In 1960, he was awarded D.Phil degree in Social Anthropology in the grade of Magna-cum-laude from Hamburg University, Germany.

After retirement, he lived in his home 16 Satyanagar, Bhubaneswar with his wife, son and daughter-in-law. His daughter, Sila Mahapatra did study Anthropology and completed her M.A. from Utkal Univesity in 1997 and after her marriage she has been blessed with a twin.

Professor Mahapatra has had a very chequered career since 1953. He was Joint Secretary, Tribal Research Bureau, Odisha, served as lecturer in Anthropology, Lucknow University, Government of India (Community Develoment Training Centre for Tribal Areas), Gauhati University and Utkal University. He joined Utkal University as Reader in 1964 and subsequently took the headship from Professor Aiyyapan in 1967 and continued as Professor and Head of the Department of Anthropology unti1989.

Professor Mahapatra is a multifaceted and multidimensional personality, who due to his scholarship, wider outlook and broad vision has excelled as a distinguished teacher, researcher and administrator in the field of Anthropology in India. He earned a number of laurels in his long academic career. He was Visiting Professor, Hamburg University, UGC National Lecturer, National Fellow, Indian Council of Social Science Research and Visiting Fellow, Anthropological Survey of India. He was Vice-Chancellor of Utkal University and Sambalpur University after which he assumed Directorship of Nabakrushna Choudhury Centre for Develoment Studies, Odisha and became UGC Emeritus Fellow attached to Utkal University.

During his academic career, he has done extensive research on all branches of social anthropology and produced sixty research papers. He was the editor of two research journals and has published seven books. He remained actively engaged in research and guidance of research studies in various disciplines till 2015.

As a reputed scholar known in India and abroad he has contributed a lot in extending the horizons of social anthropology and sociology through his numerous studies. He has made significant contributions in the studies of castes, tribes, social types in tribe/caste-continuum, ritual kinship, role of Hindu princes in the caste system in Odisha, Swidden cultivation, social movements etc. Professor Mahapatra's doctoral dissertation was on the Hill Bhuiyan of Odisha, an illuminating work in the field of social anthropological research. In his study he brings to the fore that given the self sufficiency and autonomy of the village community it is imperative to study it as a whole, as a unit, as Redfield has tried to depict in his little community, and in addition, it has to be supplemented with and integrated into an analysis of its relations with the outside towns and villages and this approach is unavoidable. The conceptual framework and the methodological perspective in Professor Mahapatra's study of the Pauri Bhuiyan shows his academic excellence, uncontroversial conviction and constructive predictions for future researchers. The sub-section on 'the settlement history and village plan' is so very informative that one feels tempted to go through the description uninterruptedly. It sets a pertinent example for the future ethnographer to be conscious in incorporating the minute and significant details. He discusses how shifting cultivation as a means of livelihood has influenced the entire fabric of socio-cultural, political and religious life of the Pauri Bhuiyan.

The seed of interest and ardent zeal in shifting cultivation which sprouted during his early days of doctoral research lead him to organize the Post-Congress ICAES symposium on Anthropology of Shifting Cultivation as Co-chairperson in the Department of Anthropology, Utkal University in 1978, with the collaboration of UNESCO, where the focus was on quality of life and environment connected with shifting Cultivation. In 1979, he participated in a meeting of social scientists in Bangkok. Professor Mahapatra highlighted on swidden cultivation in India from a comparative perspective and contributed his paper, "An Overview of Swidden Cultivation in India" to the UNESCO publication on '*Swidden Cultivation in Asia*' in 1983.

Professor Mahapatra's interest in the study of Ex-princely States of Orissa, especially of Mayurbhanj, Keonjhar and Bonai contributes to our understanding of tribal politics. His chief concerns are the ethnic components and tribal polities, rulers with alleged tribal ancestry, rulers sponsored by tribes. The characteristics of Ex-Princely States are discussed in the contexts of techno-economic and socio-political management, territorial division and general administration, socio-ritual regulation and defence system.

Professor Mahapatra evinced sanguine interest in study of tribal as well as caste societies of Odisha from a kingly perspective, and put forward his view that historical documents or other evidences should be combined with and reinforced by local myths or legends and living cultural institutions for reconstruction of a fuller and more reliable social history of the tribal polities in conjunction with ex-princely states systems prevalent in Odisha and for that matter in other parts of India.

His paper on "The Role of Hindu Princes in the Caste System in Orissa" (1984) is another significant contribution which throws light on Caste Councils and the Raja, the highest caste court and the Raja and the Caste Dynamics. His major findings show that the Raja had major roles in the preservation of the caste order and the Hindu society, in caste status mobility, in the creation of new castes etc.

Professor Mahapatra's scholarly contribution in the field of the caste system in India is reflected through his outstanding paper, "Gods, Kings and Caste System in India" published in *The New Wind – Changing Identities in South Asia,* edited by Kenneth David (1977). He opines that Orissa as a cultural region exemplifies the parallelism between king's court, estates and services, and the State deity. He goes beyond Hocart's (1970) notion of the caste system serving both king and god. He mentions about the identification of king and god wherein the king is called the god-king (Thkur-raja) and prevalence of such a conception of divine kingship continued for a long time in South-east Asia. He has also described the situation of castes in princely states of Orissa and gone one step forward to show the role of kings in the Hinduization of tribes.

On 'ritual kinship', Professor Mahapatra contends that ritual kinship is the institutionalised friendship. He has critically discussed ritual kinship from cross-cultural perspective. While hinting at the place of ritual kinship in peasant societies he has also discussed its importance among the tribal communities and interpreted 'ritual kinship' as a "fictive extension of actual kinship". He has also discussed the ritual kinship in the context of interethnic group social relationships between the Hindu castes and tribes.

Mahapatra's outstanding paper on Social movements among the tribes in eastern India with special reference to Orissa (1968) discusses a schematic history of social movement in Eastern India and analyses the nature, types, activities and trends of development of social movements among the Scheduled Tribes during the post-independence period.

Consequent upon the construction of river dams, installation of factories in different tribal areas of Orissa some of the Pengo paraja, Jharia paraja, Bhatara villages bordering Kalahandi, Koraput districts and a few other tribes of Koraput, Sundargarh and Sambalpur districts were facing the problems of displacement and rehabilitation. By then there was no government effort to study the problem of the people in order that their miseries would have been alleviated in right earnest. A group of Post-

Graduate students of the Department of Anthropology under the stewardship of Professor Mahapatra studied the foreseeable socio-cultural, economic and psychological problems of the denizens of the Indravati Dam Project area. The study showed that very casual attention was given by the government towards their problems and people on their own were leaving their home and hearth to settle in the non-project area. The study revealed that unless something in very concrete terms were done for the rehabilitation of these people with proper planning, the future of the people would be in dark. One prosperous Jharia Paraja burst into tears when he was interviewed by one of the students on the problems of their future displacement; he came all the way from his village to see this student off in the field camp with all the hopes that on his return to Bhubaneswar he would ventilate their worry and agony to the government. With Professor Mahapatra's personal appeal to government authorities concerned immediate attention was paid to depute a development scientist to alleviate their problems. That speaks of Professor Mahapatra's concern with people's problems and his conviction of application value of anthropology in rescuing people from distress.

15
A Brief Memoir of Life and Works of Prof. M. Kodanda Rao

B.V. Sharma and *N. Sudhakar Rao*

Before I introduce Prof. M. Kodanda Rao's (Prof. MKR) life and work, I believe my association with Prof. M.K.R. first as a student and subsequently as his colleague in the Department of Anthropology at University of Hyderabad (UoH) deserves a mention[1]. I divide my association with UoH (since 1982) into three phases. The first phase that I term 'the GT phase' of about four years was when I was an M.Phil. and Ph.D. scholar in the Department of Sociology and Anthropology under the research supervision of Prof. M.K.R. The second is 'the HCU phase' of about three years, when I was a student of Prof. M.K.R. as well as a faculty (temporary appointment) in the Department of Anthropology, UoH. The third phase that I call 'the UoH phase' is when I was faculty (permanent) of the Department of Anthropology, UoH. These phases have been like the phases of separation, segregation and integration, which Van Gennep noted in Les rites de passage. At each of these phases, my intimacy with Prof. M.K.R., my understanding of his academic potential and contributions, my appreciation for his empathy for his students, my grasp on his willingness to use all his resources for building a department of social anthropology of some repute and many others varied.

What I have stated below about Prof. M.K.R.'s life is based on the anecdotes and narrations provided by Mrs. Omkar Devi, the wife of our beloved teacher, his classmates in the Department of Anthropology, Andhra University, Visakhapatnam, colleagues in the Department of Sociology and Anthropology, UoH and our own experience with him. The untimely death before superannuation of Prof. M.K.R. without leaving behind any personal account of his past has left us with no other choice in this regard.

Prof. M.K.R. (1939–1995), the founder head of the department of Anthropology, UoH in 1985, had an obscure and difficult early life. He did not have the right conditions for education, being the eldest of nine children born to a young, sickly mother and a timber businessman. His caste and social background made life tough for Prof. MKR, and his wife Mrs. Omkar Devi recalls that his decision to pursue higher education was bitterly opposed by his father.

It is not clear from the interviews with his colleagues and family members whom Prof. M.K.R.'s mentors for higher education were, nor what inspired him to pursue Anthropology. He appears to be self-made in this regard. Evidently his passion to understand the social life of the downtrodden communities and particularly the fishing communities that he had been interacting with from his childhood contributed to this decision. His friends like K.V. Ramana (served as Professor in the Department of Social Work and Vice Chancellor of Andhra University) who joined Social Work in Andhra University at the same time seem to have contributed to his decision to explore the 'new' discipline of anthropology rather than the 'traditional' ones like history or political science.

Prof. M.K.R. completed Master's in Anthropology from Andhra University in the year 1963. Prof. N. Subba Reddy, Dr. Chakravorty, Dr. Golla Reddy and Dr. Prasada Rao were the faculty of the department then. After completion of Masters, Prof. M.K.R. left for Netherlands as he received a fellowship for P.G. Diploma in National Development at the Institute of Social Studies, Hague, during 1965-66. Subsequently, Prof. M.K.R. joined as Research Fellow, Department of Social Anthropology, University of Bergen, Norway for a brief period and then for his Doctorandus in Cultural anthropology, State University of Utrecht, The Netherlands during 1966-67. He also received a Research Fellowship from Norwegian Agency for International Development in 1967-68 for doing pre-doctoral work under Professor Barth, a stalwart in European anthropology whom Prof. M.K.R. considered his Guru, in the University of Bergen. At Bergen, he also met other scholars such as Gunner and Randy Holland, Ion Broegger, and Leif Mangar. He also came into contact with another great figure, Georg Pfeffer of Frei University, Berlin, West Germany.

Prof. M.K.R. returned to Andhra University and pursued his Ph.D. working among the Jalari (fishermen) community on a traditional but tough topic, 'marriage and family among the Jalari'.[2] He had registered for

Ph.D. under the guidance of Prof. N.Subba Reddy. Dr. G. Prakash Reddy, Dr. Raj Pramukh and Dr. Yatiraj Kumar, who served as faculty in Andhra University, Dr. D.V. Raghava Rao Dr. MVT Raju who served as faculty of UoH, and Dr. M. Suryanarayana who served as faculty in S.V. University, Tirupati were the other research scholars along with Prof. M.K.R. at that time. While he was pursuing his Ph.D. on Jalari family and kinship, Prof. Kazue Koda of the Department of Sociology, Osaka University, Japan visited Visakhapatnam in connection with his research work among the Jalari community in the year 1973. Prof. M.K.R. was associated with the project. In Prof. Rajpramukh's opinion, this collaboration not only helped Prof. M.K.R. to establish useful contacts but also 'to evolve into a man full of ideas' both in terms of choosing the research areas and conducting in-depth research.

Prof. M.K.R. started his career as Lecturer in 1970 in the Department of Anthropology. However, he could not complete his thesis under Prof. N. Subbareddy allegedly due to personal differences. He approached Dr. K. V. Ramana who had returned from the US and joined the department of Social work, although he did not have any anthropology training or any notable publications in his area of interest. Prof. M.K.R. finally submitted his thesis in 1975. A year after that he left Andhra University to join the Department of Anthropology and Sociology at North Easter Hill University (NEHU), Shillong that was headed by Prof. Aurora that time. His other colleagues there were Prof. A.P. Sinha, Prof. A.C. Sinha, Dr. Nikhilesh Kumar and Mr. C. Nunthara. He was promoted to Reader in the same university in 1978. While he was serving NEHU, he was invited by the Osaka University in the year 1979 to collaborate as Visiting Research Fellow.

In 1979 he moved to the combined Department of Sociology and Anthropology, UoH, Hyderabad, a new central university, in the same position as Reader and became a full Professor in 1985 . . . MKR's spell in UoH lasted about 14 years—as Reader (1979-1985) and as Professor (1986-1994). His other senior colleagues in the department at UoH at the time of his joining the department were Prof. G.S. Aurora, Prof. Ratna Naidu, and Prof. Vijay Kochar; the junior colleagues were Dr. C.H. Bhat and Dr. Mithilesh Pande. Of course, others like Dr. Umaramaswamy, Dr. Vidyasagar Reddy, Dr. M.V.T. Raju, Dr. K. Laxminarayana and Dr. P. Venkata Rao joined the same department later as his colleagues.

Prof. M.K.R. was instrumental in the establishment of the Department of Anthropology in UoH. He represented to University when Prof. B.H. Krishna Murty was the Vice Chancellor for the bifurcation of the

Department of Sociology and Anthropology, which was not, as some of his colleagues in the School of Social sciences in the UoH and others in anthropology circles in the country alleged, for his personal gain (to gain the status of Head of the Department early). As the proposals he made for the five-year plans of the department during his headship show, the bifurcation was to achieve a specialized Department of Social Anthropology. He was not in favour of an integrated, Anthropology Department with due emphasis on physical anthropology. His vision was to particularly strengthen the research and teaching in the specializations of Family and Kinship Studies, Ritual and Symbolism and Ecological Anthropology. In spite of stiff opposition from majority of the faculty of the combined Department of Anthropology and Sociology for the bifurcation, he mustered the support in the academic council of the UoH for his plea as well as the committee comprising of Prof. N.Subba Reddy, and Prof. Gopala Sarana.

Thus he became the first Head of the Department of Anthropology in UoH that comprised only him and Prof. P. Venkata Rao who oped to join Anthropology Department from the combined department. His efforts to build a good Social Anthropology Department right from the beginning contributed to building the identity of the department within the School of Social Sciences in UoH. Prof. M.K.R. had a prominent role in establishing the compulsory course of fieldwork for M.A. and obtaining full funding for it. Most importantly, he obtained approval for permanent positions to attain today's sanctioned strength of 10. His efforts to recruit faculty of good academic credentials is also noted by many.

Prof. M.K.R's contribution to the studies in family, marriage and kinship is well recognized and cited by scholars like Louis Dumont and Anthony T. Carter. Although he seldom contributed beyond anthropology, he maintained good rapport with scholars like Prof. M.L.K.. Murty and Prof. G. Nagaraju, who were interested in archaeological anthropology, and sought their support for strengthening teaching in the Department of Anthropology. His attempts to acquire the newly-created Department of Anthropology collaborative projects with non-governmental organizations as well as government agencies such as the Tribal Cultural Research and Training Institute of the Government of Andhra Pradesh also need to be lauded. His tenure as Head of the Department also witnessed the visit of foreign scholars, particularly from the Netherlands. Notable among these was the visit of 17 students from Universities from Netherland for exposure to tribal areas in India and special sessions on Indian society. Prof. MKR's earlier contacts of with scholars in Netherlands also helped him in his appointment as Visiting Professor at the Institute Furethnologie, Free Universitat, Berlin (West Germany) in 1988 when he was Professor and Head of Department at UoH. Although he nurtured the dream of collaboration with multiple foreign universities to attain distinction to the Department of Anthropology at UoH, these plans did not materialize due to his illness and untimely death. It may not be inappropriate to state here that M.R.K. made not only several friends in his course of life but also equal number of adversaries for himself due to his straight forwardness and intolerance for any injustice and bias.

Not many students worked with Prof. M.K.R. for their Ph.D. or M. Phil. degrees. From the information that I have, only two students were awarded M. Phil. degrees under his guidance while in NEHU. During his tenure at UoH, only six students obtained their M.Phil Degrees under his research supervision. I earned the distinction of being the only student who successfully completed Ph.D. under Prof. MKR's supervision and also the first student to get Ph.D. Degree in Anthropology from the University of Hyderabad. Prof. N. Sudhakar Rao joined the Ph.D. programme under Prof. M.K.R. but he obtained Ph.D. from the University of Rochester, USA., as his Ph.D. work on kinship that he started under MKR's guidance could not be submitted to UoH for some technical reasons. Part of this work was subsequently published in Contributions to Indian Sociology. Prof. M.K.R. had suffered from kidney failure for a long time after he joined the UoH. The chronic illness surely affected his academic pursuits and prevented the full realization of his skills in teaching and research. Unfortunately, he passed away much before his retirement at the age of 60 years.

Prof. M.R.K. has a book, *Cultural and Structural Dimensions of Family* (1990) in his list of publications besides 20 research papers that appeared in various reputed academic journals during his academic journey from 1963 to 2005. There are few research reports that have not seen the light. He spent almost his entire academic career in organizing intensive anthropological fieldwork among the Jalari, a fishing community of coastal Andhra Pradesh, and writing about them apart from teaching anthropology in the university. Though he did conduct some field studies among the tribes of Andhra Pradesh in 1963 and 1975, and in Meghalaya around 1985, his interest remained largely with the Jalari from where his academic contribution comes. His deep insights in the social organization of Jalari led him to provide us with better understanding of the kinship system in South Indian communities, and perhaps he is the lone Indian scholar who engaged in the debates and discussion on the subject initiated by Western anthropologists. Along with kinship, he also dealt with the relevance of ecology to the Jalari social organization. All his papers and the book that culminates his writings are well contextualized within the contemporary scholarship and endowed with rich ethnography which exhibits his hold on the chosen subject. They do reflect very clearly the impact of Professor Fredrik Barth, University of Bergen, Norway, in terms of his theoretical perspective and analytic concepts. Though most of the writings are relatively short, except one or two, they are highly analytical, and address the issue at hand very precisely. With this prelude an attempt is made to describe briefly the academic contribution of Prof. M.R.K..

Over the last two centuries the most important contribution of social or cultural anthropology to social sciences has been the significance of kinship in the human societies either of the past or present, and in this context Prof. M.R.K.'s work has immense value. His bit of contribution is towards gaining an understanding of the complex classificatory system of kinship in South India. Within this domain the most intriguing issue relates to the elder sister's daughter's marriage, which is widely practiced, along with mother's brother's and father's sister's daughter (MBD and FZD) marriage in conjunction with rank difference in the community. This problem, the co-existence of such marriage practices as pointed by Louis Dumont (1961: 90) is 'logically impossible', and Lave offers an alternative explanation of having 'wife takers' and 'wife givers' to the prevalence of such a situation. Prof. MRK shows that all the three types of marriage practices exist among the Jalari without the idea of 'wife takers' and 'wife givers' in his paper Rank Difference and Marriage Reciprocity in South India – An Aspect of the Implication of Elder Sister's Daughter's Marriage in a Fishing Village in Andhra published in Contributions to Indian Sociology (1973). His explanation is as follows:

> Of the nine local descent groups inhabiting the Jalari village near Visakhapatnam, A.P., one descent group claims the most superior status while three other claim brotherhood with this and thus of equal status but the remaining others are of lower rank. While the social ranks are permanent, the ranks engendered by marriage transactions are temporary in which the ZH is superior to WB and ZS is superior to MB. Thus, while there is no rank difference among the parallel relatives but there is difference among the cross relatives. It is to be noted that the rank difference gets neutralized when ZD marries her MB or when eZD marriage takes place. Such, rank

difference is also not insisted in cross-cousin marriage. Therefore, the overall rank difference that arises out of marriage across the intermarrying local descent groups is temporary.

The practice is that the higher ranked Jalaris prefer eZD marriages followed by MBD, and the regular practice of these marriages leaves little scope for FZD marriage. Though such marriage practices demand terminological changes, it is argued, they do not affect the terminology. As explained, the terminology draws a clear distinction between MB and FZ with mena (identity with body-own) as a prefix and FZH and MBW without mena, and similarly ZD is menakodalu which is distinct from SD (*kodalu*). Further, eZD (*menakodalu*) is different from MBD/FZD (maradalu whom the ego marries and vadina if older than ego who cannot be married) though all the three are marriageable. With the terminological differences and the choices of three types of marriages available the Jalari family selects a particular type of marriage based on the earlier marriage that is most appropriate in that instance that avoids the terminological confusion. On this ground, Prof. M.R.K. questions the equation of MBD=FZD=eZD drawn by Leach (1951) and Lave (1966) and others for the Dravidian societies that ignore the principle of generation and terminological differences that draw strength from the genealogical proximity. The kinship terminology basically is congruent with the classificatory system of marriage and hence the equation of WM=MBW=FZ holds good and can be further extended to add ZD also (WM=MBW=FZ =ZD). Though the patriarchal ideology that goes along with social hierarchy and the super status accorded to ZH and ZS the MBD and FZD marriages not only keep aside the designation of 'wife takers' and 'wife givers' but also nullify the rank differences emerging out of marriages. However, in case of the higher ranked lineage in social hierarchy tends to go for MBD while the lower ranked lineage marries the ZD in every generation.

The two papers, 'Descent and Descent Groups among Jalari' published in *The Eastern Anthropologist* (1981) and 'Kinship and marriage among the Jalari of coastal Andhra: a study of Dravidian kinship terminology' published in *Contribution to Indian Sociology* (1982) provide the complete structural properties of Jalari kinship and their social organization. Fredrik Barth's ideas of generative models, social forms, social process and so on form the theoretical basis for an understanding of the emergence Jalari descent groups that form very important forms of social organization. The ideology of descent group stems from the common ancestry through patrilines. To the members, the descent provides the rights of rights over fishing bignet, the rights to worship the lineage deity and other collective and political rights. There are maximal lineages and minimal lineages in a local descent group each of them live in a location and worship the ancestors. Upon the death of a man when his children desire to setup their own identity by worshipping their dead father independently for several reasons, they separate themselves from the father's brother who in fact has already incorporated his dead brother into the fold of ancestors that are being worshipped and venerated. Of the children yet anyone of them can also separate and establish to become senior and junior lineages over the time. Each lineage would have a head generally the position is held by the senior most member and a priest who periodically worship the deity and ancestors for their favour of good catch of fish and welfare of its members; it has bignet in which all have rights of share and members may possess different kinds of nets of their own also. In case a lineage is unable to manage the bignet on its own strength of labour of the members it may include others as share croppers. However, the brothers and agnates maintain solidarity and unity as a single body.

Prof. MRK closely follows Louis Dumont in delineating the consanguine and alliance relations and their continuity for generations with rights and obligations, prestations and counter prestations. Such classification also provides the conceptual scheme of marriageable and non-marriageable categories of relatives that 'serves as a frame of reference for the future marriage transactions'. The most preferred marriage among the Jalari is MBD followed by FZD though statically more number is found with eZD, all MBDy, FZDy and eZDy are potential spouses. However, Prof. M.K.R. rejects Good's (1980) formulation of equation FZDy=MBDy=eZDy for the terminology accommodates the rank in terms of relative age besides the distinction between genealogical and categorical identities in the ego, ego's first ascending and first descending generations. A significant terminological distinctive feature relates to male cross relatives where status implication in case ZH and WB keep the former is a superior position in the term of reference who could be cross-cousins. However, there is no status implication in case of female cross-cousins.

The paper, 'Ecological Adaptation and Maximisation among the Jalari of Coastal Andhra Pradesh, South India' (1991) found in the edited volume published in honour of Prof. Fredrik Barth, integrates the social structure, local knowledge of marine biotic and physical environment and economic pursuits of the Jalari. The highlights are about the maximization of human resource available through descent ideology and lineage solidarity and skills and the technology – different boats, fishing nets, labour organization etc., evolved over the years by experience with the vagaries of the marine ecology. This paper and also the other (1981) on various fishing castes do point out the exploitation of different ecological niches that would have certain determining effect on the social and cultural life of the human communities. In this regards the Jalari are associated themselves to marine ecology. Not many studies of this kind are available in anthropology as of now.

Finally, the book mentioned above shows the complementarily of cultural and structural aspects in family studies as most of the earlier works have dealt with the subject either of the ways. Its uniqueness can be seen in terms of explaining the fundamental processes in which the Jalari household forms are generated and reproduced along with cultural and social structural dimensions in which the changes that are taking place due to dislocation of the settlement that brought them closer to urban environment.

NOTES

1. Please note that the section I of this essay is authored by Prof. B.V. Sharma and the section 2 is authored by Prof. N. Sudhakar Rao.
2. The academic contribution of this work will be separately dealt with below.

16
Virendra Nath Misra

Archaeologist Anthropologist

Indrani Chattopadhyaya

Virendra Nath Misra (hence fourth V.N. Misra), eminent archaeologist and anthropologist of post-Independent India, was born on January 9, 1935 in village Khandauli, District Farrukhabad, Uttar Pradesh, India. He did his Under Graduation from Agra University, Post-graduation (1957) from Lucknow University in Anthropology, under the tutelage of the eminent anthropologist D.N. Majumdar. V.N. Misra had a brilliant academic career and he had topped the merit lists at various examinations and received research fellowships and research grants from India and abroad. He completed his Ph.D. (1962) in Prehistoric Archaeology under the supervision of Professor H.D. Sankalia from Poona University.

He learned Hindi (1954, Allahabad), Sanskrit (1954 & 1956, Banaras), French and German (1966, 1971, Poona) and was fluent in Hindi and Marathi. He has written more than 30 popular articles in these languages. His early training in anthropology, especially in ethnographic studies is evident in his research papers on Banjaras (1977-1985), Bhils (1977-1985), Van Vagris (1978-1985), Kanjars (1986-1991), Pardhis (1987-1990), Kuchbandhias (1987-1990) and Maria Gonds. He was interested in the funerary structures and associated rituals of the Maria Gonds (1982), a hunting-gathering and agricultural community of Bastar district of Madhya Pradesh. His ability to communicate with tribal peoples and villagers to gather relevant information, which they usually do not share with outsiders, enabled him to visualise the social dynamics of the communities in prehistoric period. V.N. Misra, archaeologist and pre-historian of international repute, took an alternative approach to archaeological understanding of the past by taking a dynamic and fluid notion of culture in which the patterned remains of the material record are used to infer social, economic and cultural processes.

After getting his Ph.D. Degree in Prehistoric Archaeology from Poona University under the supervision of Professor H.D. Sankalia, V.N. Misra conducted archaeological explorations and geological investigations in valleys of Chambal, Banas, Berach and Luni rivers and their tributaries in Rajasthan and discovered a number of Paleolithic and Mesolithic sites. He has investigated Tertiary and Quaternary geological deposits in Rajasthan and carried out exploration under the leadership of Professor H.D. Sankalia, his mentor, in coastal Bombay (now Mumbai) and in Narbada valley in central India. V.N. Misra excavated Navdatoli and Tripuri in Madhya Pradesh and Sangankallu and Tekkalkota in Karnataka under Professor Sankalia's guidance between the years 1959 to 1965. From the year 1967 to 2000 V.N. Misra conducted excavations on sites of Rajasthan-Tilwara (1967), Bagor (1968-1970), Jayal and Didwana (1981-1985) and Balathal (1994-2000); he has also excavated sites of Bhimbetka (1973-1977), Devakachar and Samnapur (1986-1990) in Madhya Pradesh.

V.N. Misra had a wide academic exposure by visiting museums and excavated sites abroad. He studied Mesolithic artefacts in the Colombo Museum, Sri Lanka, and excavated Mesolithic sites of Betadomba-lena, Balangoda, Beli-lena Kitulagala, Bellan-bandi Palassa and Historical sites of Anuradhapura, Polonnaruva and Kandy in Sri Lanka. He has also participated in the excavation of the Mousterian site of Pech de l'Aze in France (1970), studied Prehistoric artafacts in museums, research centres and visited archaeological extraction sites in Israel, Italy, France, Germany, The UK, The Netherlands, Denmark, Czechoslovakia, Australia and USA.

V.N. Misra's career started with teaching Anthropology in Lucknow University (1957-1962). In 1962 he joined Poona University as Lecturer in Prehistoric Archaeology (1962-1968) and became Reader (1968-1981). He became Professor (1981-2000) of Prehistoric Archaeology in Deccan College Post-Graduate and Research Institute, Pune. He taught Anthropology as Professor in Lucknow University from 1983-84. He was Joint Director (1986-1990) and Director (1990-2000) in Deccan College Post-Graduate & Research Institute, Pune.

V.N. Misra's interest and experiences spanned in anthropology and archaeology and his seminal work shows a breakthrough of academic barriers between these two subjects. His work, on archaeological understandings of the past have a fluid notion of culture, in which the patterned remains of the material record infer human practices and social processes in space and time. V.N. Misra's work on the Mesolithic period in central India has made significant contributions to regional issues in prehistory that step beyond the theoretical parameters of culture-history approach into cultural ecology and structural functionalism. He not only excavated and studied the distribution of sites and archaeological cultures from variety of perspectives using theory and methods for spatial analysis but also interpreted regional patterning of material culture. His methodological approaches in understanding archaeological cultures include biocultural anthropology and gender theory through ethnoarchaeological studies.

Human history in South Asia during the pre-neolithic prehistoric period is dominated by mobile hunting-gathering peoples, with the onset of sedentism around seventh millennium B.C. at Mehrgarh and later in central regions of India people settled down into permanent habitations. V.N. Misra and other archaeologists studied early sedentism and their continued practice of mobile lifestyle and subsistence strategies like foraging, pastoralism etc. Misra has shown the connections between temporary occupation of Bagor (Rajasthan) and nearby permanent settlements. His work helps us in understanding broader practices linked to mobility like subsistence/economic strategies as well as their engagement in social networks. Mobility and sedentism in continuum are difficult to study from archaeological finds alone. V.N. Misra has used his anthropological background to find answers through ethnography and studied the living tribal communities in Rajasthan, Uttar Pradesh and Madhya Pradesh of Banjaras (1977-1985), Bhils (1977-1985), Van Vagris (1978-1985), Kanjars (1986-1991), Pardhis (1987-1990), Kuchbandhias (1987-1990) and Maria Gonds. According to him:

> "As a consequence of the expansion of agriculture and loss of forests and wildlife, stone age hunter-gatherers were forced to assimilate themselves into larger agriculture-based rural and urban societies. However, some of them resisted this new economic mode. To this day they have persisted with their atavistic lifestyle but have had to supplement their resources by producing craft items or providing entertainment to the rural population." (Misra, 2001: 492)

V.N. Misra has also extensively and intensively studied Harappan culture in the areas located along the dry courses of the Ghaggar-Hakra and its many palaeochannels in Punjab, Haryana and Rajasthan states of India. Misra (1994) believes that the Harappan settlements located on the Ghaggar-Hakra and its palaeochannels could have flourished only if the

Ghaggar-Hakra was a perennially flowing river in the past, concluding that the present-day bed of the Ghaggar-Hakra is actually the bed of the ancient river Saraswati which has been eulogized in many hymns of the Rigveda as a mighty, perennial and sacred river, flowing from the mountains into the Arabian sea. In the later epics (*Mahabharata* and *Ramayana*) this river is described as having disappeared underground. This phenomenon is consistent with the post-Harappan archaeological history of the region. Misra (2001 a:504) concluded that

> "the Saraswati could have been a perennially flowing river only if the waters of the Sutlej or the Yamuna or both flowed in the past through the channel of this river rather than through their present channels. There is ample geomorphic, archaeological, historical and folkloristic evidence to conclusively establish that this indeed was the case."

V.N. Misra has six books to his name. These are:

1. 1965. V. N. Misra and M.S. Mate (eds.). *Indian Prehistory: 1964*. Poona: Deccan College.
2. 1965. V.N. Misra. *Pre and Proto-history of the Berach Basin*, South Rajasthan. Poona : Deccan College.
3. 1967. J.R. Lukacs, V.N. Misra, and K.A.R. *Kennedy. Bagor and Tilwara: Late Mesolithic Cultures of Northwest India*. Vol. I: The Human Skeletal Remains. Poona: Deccan College.
4. 1978. V. N. Misra, Y. Mathpal and M. Nagar. *Prehistoric Man and his Art at Bhimbetka*, Central India. Poona.
5. 1985. V.N. Misra and Peter Bellwood (eds.). *Recent Advances in Indo-Pacific Prehistory*. Delhi: Oxford-IBH.
6. 1992. V.N. Misra (ed.) *Indus Civilization,* a special Number of the Eastern Anthropologist. Lucknow: Ethnographic & Folk Culture Society.

V.N. Misra has written 110 research papers between 1962 and 2001. The broad theme of his papers are: Archaeological evidence of early modern Human occupation in South Asia; Palaeolithic cultures in western and central India; Stone Tool technology and industries of Prehistoric period in India; Ethnographic studies, Geomorphology, late Quaternary Stratigraphy, Paleoecology, Paleo-climatology and Chronology of Mesolithic cultures in western and central India; Chalcolithic culture in western India; Human Evolution, adaptation and settlement pattern in semi-arid region in western India; Prehistoric Rock Art in Bhimbetka, central India; Hunter-gatherers in Agrarian setting in Ganga Plains and central India, nomadic hunters of western Rajasthan; Indus civilization and identification of the river Rigvedic Saraswati with Ghaggar-Hakra paleochannel in Haryana and Rajasthan.

There are more than 29 popular articles and 10 book reviews written by V.N. Misra in English, Hindi and Marathi. He has also written 9 obituaries. He has written research papers in Ethnoarchaeology after studying the tribes of Banjaras (1977-1985), Bhils (1977-1985), Van Vagris (1978-1985), Kanjars (1986-1991), Pardhis (1987-1990), Kuchbandhias (1987-1990), Kalbeliyas (1981-2000) and Maria Gonds (1982).

V.N. Misra participated in over fifty national conferences at Dehradun, Bareilly, Srinagar (Garhwal), Delhi, Lucknow, Agra, Aligarh, Allahabad, Varanasi, Gorakhpur, Ranchi, Bhubaneswar, Shantiniketan, Kolkata, Guwahati, Shillong, Jaipur, Jodhpur, Udaipur, Ahmedabad, Vadodara, Anand, Mumbai, Pune, Sagar, Dharwad, Bangalore, Guntur, Srisailam, Tirupati, Waltair, Cochin and Kanyakumari. He has also delivered lectures and participated in conferences abroad in Sri Lanka (1969, 1990); Bangladesh (1986, 1994), The Philippines (1985); Thailand (1994); Indonesia (1990); Japan (1987); Australia (1971, 1977); Israel (1970), Greece (1979), Italy (1970, 1990, 1992, 1996, 1997); France (1970, 1976, 1982, 1990, 1992), Germany (1970); United Kingdom (1970, 1990, 1991, 1995); The Netherlands (1970, 1999); Denmark (1970, 1985), Finland (1993); Czechoslovakia (1970), USA (1973, 1984, 1985, 1992); Canada (1983); Egypt (1979); Ethiopia (1982); and South Africa (1998).

The eminent scholar V.N. Misra has received several awards since the beginning of his academic career:

1. Merit Scholarship, Government Sanskrit College, Banaras, 1954-56.
2. Bursary Scholarship, Lucknow University, 1955-57.
3. Pandit Jagpal Krishna Gold Medal, Lucknow University, 1957, for standing First in order of merit in M.A. examination in Anthropology.
4. UGC Junior Research Fellowship, 1958-61.
5. Homi Bhabha Fellowship, 1970-71.
6. Leverhulme Visiting Fellowship, Australian National University, Canberra, Australia, 1977.
7. Senior Fulbright Fellowship, University of California, Berkeley, USA, 1984.
8. Corresponding Member, Istituto Italiano per il Medio ed Estremo Oriente (IsMEO), Rome, Italy since 1994.

9. Visiting Fellow in Archaeology, Allahabad University, 1981 and 1988.
10. Visiting Professor in Anthropology, North Eastern Hill University, Shillong, 1985.
11. National Fellow, Indian Council of Historical Research, New Delhi, 2000-02.

V.N. Misra edited *Man and Environment*, the journal of the Indian Society for Prehistoric and Quaternary Studies, Pune, from its inception. He was co-editor of *The Eastern Anthropologist*, Journal of the Ethnographic and Folk Culture Society, Lucknow. He was Member of the Editorial Board of the following journals:

1. *Journal* of the Sarat Chandra Roy Institute, Ranchi.
2. *The Anthropologist*, Journal of the Indian Anthropological Association, Delhi.
3. *L' Anthropologie*, Paris.
4. *Journal of World Prehistory*, New York.
5. *The Holocene*, Cardiff, U.K.
6. *Asian Perspectives*, Hawaii, U.S.A.
7. *Geoarchaeology*, Wiley, U.S.A.

V.N. Misra's name is synonymous with the excellence of Deccan College, Pune. His administrative acumen came to light as the Secretary, National Seminar on Prehistory, Deccan College, Poona (1964); Head, Department of Archaeology, Poona University, (1968-1983); Head, Department of Archaeology, Deccan College Post-Graduate and Research Institute, Pune (1990-1995); Co-ordinator, Centre of Advanced Study in Archaeology, Deccan College Post-Graduate and Research Institute, Pune (1990-2000); Joint Director, Deccan College Post-Graduate and Research Institute, Pune (1986-1990); Director, Deccan College; General Secretary, Indian Society for Prehistoric and Quaternary Studies, Pune, (1981-1989) & (1992-2001); Member, UGC Panel on Anthropology, (1980-1983) and (1985-1988); Member, UGC Panel on History and Archaeology, (1991-2001); Member, Executive Committee, Indo-Pacific Prehistory Association, Canberra, Australia (1976-1980); Vice President, Indo-Pacific Prehistory Association, Canberra, Australia (1981-1984); President, Indo-Pacific Prehistory Association, Canberra, Australia (1985-1988); President, Anthropology and Archaeology Section, Indian Science Congress, Bangalore (1987); Member, Advisory Committee, Anthropological Survey of India, New Delhi (1985-1988); Member, Indian Council of Historical Research, New Delhi (1991-1997); Member, Standing Committee,

Association of Indian Universities (AIU) (1998-2000); Member, Central Advisory Board of Archaeology (2000 – till his demise); Member, Scientific Advisory Committee, Department of Culture, Ministry of HRD, Government of India (1999- till his demise); Member, Indira Gandhi Rashtriya Manav Sangrahalaya Samiti, Bhopal (1977-1985, 1998- till his demise); and Member, Central Sanskrit Board, Ministry of HRD, Government of India, New Delhi (1999- till his demise).

V.N. Misra has studied earliest human colonization in South Asia. In one of his archaeological research articles, 'The Role of the Ṛgvedic Sarasvati in the Rise, Growth and Decline of the Indus Civilization' published in 2001 he has pointed out that "Harappan Civilization clearly shows that this civilization was centred on the Ghaggar-Hakra river … (that) is nothing but a remnant of the Ṛgvedic Sarasvati". He along with the researchers who were thinking on the same lines are proved right by the new scientific research in 2019 when scientists from Physical Research Laboratory (PRL) Ahmedabad, in collaboration with IIT, Bombay, dated the depositional ages of the Ghaggar's flood plain and reported it as "unequivocal evidence" that modern Ghaggar is the Saraswati river as mentioned in the Ṛigveda (Chatterjee: 2019).

In ethnoarchaeology V.N. Misra's contribution is phenomenal. He has studied the emergence of food production and its consequences in archaeological and anthropological phenomenon by studying the settlement pattern and disposal of the dead in archaeological finds and living tribes like Maria Gonds (Bastar), Kuchbandhiyas and Pardhis (Damoh) in M.P.; Banjara, Bhil, and Van Vagri (Nagaur), Kalbeliya (Udaipur) in Rajasthan; and Kanjar (Farukkhabad) in U.P.

V.N. Misra studied Mesolithic material in the Colombo Museum and visited excavated Mesolithic sites of Batadomba-lena, Balangoda, Beli-lena Kitulagala and Bellan-bandi Palassa and the Historical sites of Anuradhapura, Polonnaruva and Kandy in Sri Lanka in 1969. In 1970 he participated in the excavation of the Mousterian site of Pech de l'Aze in France; he also studied Stone Age cultural materials in a number of museums and research centres and visited many prehistoric sites and excavations in Israel, Italy, France, Germany, the UK, The Netherlands, Denmark and Czechoslovakia. In 1971 he studied Stone Age collections and visited a number of archaeological sites in the States of Victoria, New South Wales, South Australia, Western Australia and Tasmania in Australia. In 1977 he studied Stone Age and ethnographic collections in a number of museums in Canberra, Sydney, Adelaide and Perth and visited the Stone Age sites on Willandra fossil lakes in New South Wales in Australia. In 1984 he collected data on prehistory and human evolution in the libraries at the University of California, Berkeley, USA. V.N. Misra visited a large number of Stone Age and Historical sites in many parts of Sri Lanka and examined Stone Age collections in the Colombo Museum in 1990.

V.N. Misra visited following countries for participation in conferences, giving lectures in universities and other institutions, conducting research, and for consultancy work: Sri Lanka (1969, 1990); Bangladesh (1986, 1994); The Philippines (1985); Thailand (1994); Indonesia (1990); Japan (1987); Australia (1971, 1977); Israel (1970); Greece (1979); Italy (1970, 1990, 1992, 1996, 1997); France (1970, 1976, 1982, 1990, 1992); Germany (1970); United Kingdom (1970, 1990, 1991, 1995); The Netherlands (1970, 1999); Denmark (1970, 1985); Finland (1993); Czechoslovakia (1970); USA (1973, 1984, 1985, 1992); Canada (1983); Egypt (1979); Ethiopia (1982); and South Africa (1998).

V.N. Misra held the posts of eminence after his retirement as Member, UGC Panel on History and Archaeology, 1991-2001; Member, Central Advisory Board of Archaeology 2000 – till his demise; Member, Scientific Advisory Committee, Department of Culture, Ministry of HRD, Government of India, 1999 – till his demise; Member, Indira Gandhi Rashtriya Manav Sangrahalaya Samiti, Bhopal, 1977-1985, 1998 – till his demise; Member, Central Sanskrit Board, Ministry of HRD, Government of India, New Delhi, 1999 – till his demise.

Notable students who have completed Ph.D. under his supervision are V. Rami Reddy (1968), Ms. Katy N. Frenchman (1972), P.K. Thomas (1977), Yasodhar Mathpal (1978), D.R. Raju (1982), Makhhan Lal (1982), Jacob S. Jayaraj (1983), S.C. Nanda (1984), Ms. Zarine Cooper (1984), Vijay Singh (1988), Md. Shafiqul Alam (1990), M.M. Hoque (1993), J.S. Kharakwal (1994), Ms. Bishnupriya Basak (1988), Sunil Gupta (1988), S.S.M. Rahman (1999), Ms. Mala Maiya Malla (1999), B.S. Harishankar (1999), A.R. Mishra (2000), Balaram Tripathy (2001), Ms. Shahida Ansari (2001), Kurush F. Dalal (2001), Abhijit Dandekar (2001).

Eminent Archaeologist and pre-historian of international repute Virendra Nath Misra, passed away on October 31, 2015 due to old-age related problems at the age of 81.

REFERENCES

Chatterjee, Anirban, Jyotiranjan S. Ray, Anil D. Shukla & Kanchan Pande. 2019. *On the existence of a perennial river in the Harappan heartland.* Scientific Reports volume 9, Article number: 17221 (20 November 2019) Open Access.

Misra, V.N. 1974. Ecological Adaptations during the terminal Stone Age in western and central India. In *Ecological Backgrounds of South Asian Prehistory*. 28-51. Eds. K.A.R. Kennedy and G. Possehl. Ithaca: South Asia Program, Cornell University.

Misra, V.N. 1996. Mesolithic India: History and current status of research. In *The Prehistory of Asia and Oceania*, Vol. 16: 321-328. Eds. G. Afanas'ev, S. Cleuzious, J.R. Lukacs and M. Tosi. Forli: ABACO Edizioni.

Misra, V.N. 2001. The Mesolithic Age in India, In *Indian Archaeology in Retrospect*, Vol.1, Prehistory – Archaeology of South Asia 2: 111-126. Eds. S. Setter and R. Korisetter. Delhi: Manohar.

Misra, V.N. 2001 a. Prehistoric human colonization of India. *Journal of Biosciences* 26 (4 Suppl): 491-531.

Misra, V. N. 2001 b. *The role of the Rgvedic Sarasvati in the rise, growth and decline of the Indus Civilization*. Annals of the Bhandarkar Oriental Research Institute, Vol. 82, No. 1/4. pp. 165-191.

Misra, V.N. 1994. Indus Civilization and the Rigvedic Sarasvati. In, Asko Parpola and Petteri Koskikallio (eds.), *South Asian Archaeology: 1993*. Proceedings of the Twelfth International Conference of the European Association of South Asian Archaeologists, pp. 511-525. Helsinki: Suomalainen Tiedeakatemia.

Virendra Nath Misra, Ph.D, Brief Bio-Data https://www.infinityfoundation.com/mandala/t_ed/t_ed_misra_cv_frameset.htm

17
N. Subba Reddy (1926-2018)

P. Venkatarao

It was the good fortune of anthropology in South India, that Prof. Subba Reddy born and brought up in Andhra region of Madras Presidency in the pre-independence period, decided to study the nascent discipline of anthropology, going all the way to North India. Prof. Nellore Subba Reddy, popularly addressed as N.S. Reddy, was born on 5th June, 1926 to Sri Kodanda Ramireddy and Srimati Bhuvanamma in a village Kalayakagollu near Butchi Reddi Palem in Nellore district of Andhra Pradesh. He obtained his M.A. degree in Anthropology from Lucknow University in 1948, and received his Ph.D. from the same university for his thesis on Depressed Castes in Andhra Pradesh, under the guidance of renowned Professor D.N. Majumdar in 1952. For the Ph.D. work, he was awarded the Bonnarjee Research Prize for best doctoral thesis (1954) by Lucknow University. After obtaining Ph.D., he worked as Research Associate in Cornell-Lucknow University Project during 1954-55. Later, he took up the position of Deputy Director for Kanpur Social Survey (A Planning Commission Project) under the directorship of Prof. D.N. Majumdar. The project report was published in 1960 under the title "*Social Contours of an Industrial City*" by Asia Publishing house in 1961 and was later reprinted in US in 1975. This book is one of the early contributions to urban anthropology in India.

N.S. Redy taught anthropology in the universities at Lucknow, Guwahati, Andhra, and Madras. Initially, he joined Lucknow University as anthropology lecturer in 1956-57 and shifted to Gauhati University where he was in charge of the Centre for Tribal Research (1957-60). He was instrumental in setting up the Department of Anthropology at Andhra University in 1960 where he took over as founder head of the Department. He continued there till 1975. At Andhra University, he was involved in a major international reserach project, 'The Medak Anthropology Project' (1970), a collaboration between Brandies University (USA) and Andhra University, to explore fertility behaviour in a backward district of rural Telangana. This was a major project where the Indian team was led by Prof. N.S. Reddy and the American team by Margurite S. Robinson. The researchers who worked in this project obtained their Ph.Ds. from Brandies University (2) and Andhra University (2) apart from producing a large number of published papers.

After establishing Anthropology Department at Andhra University, he moved on to the Madras University In 1976 and was instrumental in starting Post-graduation and Ph.D. programmes. During his tenure at Madras University, he launched as editor, a research journal by name '*The South Asian Social Scientist*' in 1985. With an international editorial board the journal gained a high degree of academic respectability in a short time. He organized a post-plenary session on religion at University of Madras in 1978 as part of World Anthropology Congress held in New Delhi in 1978. He served as chairman of Backward Classes Commission in 1983-84, appointed by the Tamil Nadu State Government. N.S. Reddy was closely associated with Madras Institute of Development Studies and was a regular contributor to its Bulletin 'Madras Development Seminar Series,' and the journal 'Review of Development and Change'. As University Grants Commission's national lecturer, he delivered lectures at various academic institutions during 1985. After his retirement from Madras University (1986), he was invited by an ICSSR institution 'Centre for Economic and Social Studies' at Hyderabad, as senior Fellow (1986-1991) and continued there as honorary professor till his death. The last major project carried out by him at this centre was the study of displacement and rehabilitation of tribals affected by the contentious Polavaram irrigation project in Andhra Pradesh.

N.S. Reddy's field experience extended over various parts of India starting from rural area of Uttar Pradesh and Andhra Pradesh to Tribal areas of Andhra Pradesh and Tamil Nadu. Prof. Reddy carried out several major research projects in his long career. His research projects covered diverse areas ranging from Culture and Fertility, Mechanization of Agriculture, Customary Laws among tribal communities, Computer literacy programmes in Tamil Nadu schools, Man-Environment relations in Eastern Ghats Ecosystem and many more. He was Visiting Senior Fellow at University of Illinois during 1970-71, where he delivered number of lectures and participated in collaborative research. He received Dr. D.N. Mujumdar Memorial Medal of the Indian Social Science Association for meritorious research in Social Anthropology in the year 1998. He was awarded R.P. Chanda Centenary Medal for his important contribution to anthropology by the Asiatic Society of Bengal on 7th May, 2018.

N.S. Reddy taught and supervised number of research students for Ph.D. degrees. His students remember him as an inspiring teacher committed to the cause of anthropology. His students occupied positions at various departments of anthropology all over South India. Notable students among them are Prof. D.L. Prasada Rao (Andhra University), Prof. D.V. Raghava Rao (Hyderabad University), Prof M. Suryanarayana and Prof. G. Prakash Reddy (S.V. University), Prof. M.A. Kalam (Madras University), and Prof. Chella Perumal (Pondicherry University). His students have been at the helm of affairs in various government organizations like Tribal Research Institutes, Registrar Generals Office, Anthropological Survey of India etc. N.S. Reddy is known as an institution builder. He played a crucial role in the establishment and shaping of Departments of Anthropology at Sri Venkateswara University (Tirupati), Calicut University (Presently at Kannur University), Hyderabad University, and Centre for Tribal Research at Tamil University.

N.S. Reddy is endowed with a wide range of scholarship as can be seen from his research work. His research covered varied topics. He published large number of papers in national and international journals and books that stand out as the examples of his scholarship. Some of the journals in which N.S. Reddy published over decades include: *Bulletin of Madras Institute of Development Studies, Contributions to Indian Sociology, Development and Social Change, Eastern Anthropologist, Economic and Political Weekly, Human Organization, Human Science, Indian Journal of Social Science, International Journal of Asian Profiles, International Journal of Asian Studies, Man in India, Review of Development and Change, Sociologist, South Asian Social Scientist.* The book titled *"Cultural Diversity and Common Humanity"* (New Delhi Academic Foundation, 2014) provides an overview of the contribution of Prof. N. Subba Reddy to the discipline of anthropology and social sciences. Apart from his writings, a number of book reviews he wrote for the Eastern Anthropologist and other journals stand testimony to his incisive analysis. He is known for unsparing criticism towards pedestrian research, absence of theoretical and methodological rigour and unsubstantiated claims.

In a short write-up like this, it will be an uphill task to render justice to the contribution of a scholar who spent his life time in the service of Anthropology in India. Instead of enumerating all his publications or providing a gist of them, an attempt is made below to capture some of his views and the essence of his contribution in selected areas.

Anthropology has been envisioned by N.S. Reddy as "The delicate task of objectively representing the ideas, meanings, and actions, as acceptable to academics, at the same time not sacrificing the distinctness of the other in terms of indigenous idiom an ethos"(2014: 102). What is universal to all humanity is the question addressed by him. In this context, N.S. Reddy raises the query that "whether in terms of rationality, all human groups are alike or there are culture-specific differences?" For him, core rationality is the same but there may be differences of degree but not of kind. According to N.S. Reddy, rational and rationally non-explainable (mystic) features exist in all societies. Logic across societies is the same, but inferences in simple societies are different due to their weak knowledge base. He expresses concern on the over-emphasis on diversities at the cost of underlining the commonalities. N.S. Reddy is strongly opposed to the arguments of socio-biologists who argue for the primacy of biology over culture. He opines that "man is unique from other animals in having an innate moral sense and ethical values". The core value of humanity is altruism. If morality and altruism form fundamental human qualities, how to explain deviance, crime, etc. is the question that remains to be addressed. For N.S. Reddy, without social bonds and norm-governed behaviour, man will not remain human.

N.S. Reddy showed zero tolerance to what he considers as "fanciful" theories. He is strongly critical of the weak conceptualizations. He systematically dissected the methodology of such works and demolished the interpretations in a logical fashion. In his writings, one can come across a powerful critique of the works of well-known anthropologists for the absence of empirical substantiation, lack of methodological rigour, and sweeping generalisations. In his pursuit, N.S. Reddy makes extensive use of the literature, facts, and logic. He undertook a critical analysis of the works of renowned scholars of anthropology like Levi-Strauss, Louis Dumont, Clifford Geertz and others. On the other hand, he offers a powerful defence of Malinowski and his functionalism and tells us to appreciate the work of Malinowski without getting distracted by his critics and admirers. In the wake of the debates on Mead-Freeman controversy, N.S. Reddy is supportive of Margaret Mead's work. He criticises Freeman for his biases, prejudices, motives, dubious methodology and lack of ethics. For N.S. Reddy, it is not the credibility of Mead's ethnography but it is of credibility of Freeman, that is in question. In the paper titled 'Conscious and unconscious models', he commented on Levi-Strauss by saying "It appears that there is no point which he cannot prove and there is no point which he cannot disprove (including the one he might have proved previously in another context). The structural method of Levi-Strauss' is maladroit. He starts with a series of contrived propositions and then chops and hews the data in a procrustean manner to fit into his theoretical frame" (2014:219). N.S. Reddy is critical of the interpretive method of Clifford Geertz. He compares Geertz to an astronaut who gazes down on earth and reads the minds of people through telepathy. The work of Geertz is labelled as literary fantasy as it lacks validation and verifiability. Empirical method, logic, and verifiability are the tenets dear to N.S. Reddy.

N.S. Reddy stresses upon giving importance to the role of the family in ensuring social and cultural stability. For him, only a stable family and an integrated society can produce a stable citizen. He does not approve new types of families and living arrangements such as single-sex families, female-headed dyads, and single person households. He indicated that they are deviant forms of family. For him, three dyads of relations: conjugal, paternal and maternal are essential for an entity to be called family. N.S. Reddy strongly emphasises the importance of saving the institution of family for safeguarding the future of mankind. His intention of safeguarding family is not to perpetuate gender inequalities but to make the family stable and less fragile.

N.S. Reddy added important insights on caste dealing with origins of caste, Jajmani system, conflicts among Dalit communities, and other backward classes (OBCs). In the paper titled 'Backward class in India the way the Mandal Commission went about its work and the anomalies followed'. N.S. Reddy criticized the survey conducted by Mandal Commission and pointed out flaws in the methodology of using six arbitrarily selected criteria for identification of backward classes. He pointed out the internal variation existing among OBCs in terms of social economic and educational disparities and advocated categorization of the OBCs. Disagreeing with conjectural accounts on origins of caste, N.S. Reddy provided an insight into the origin of the complex institution based on grassroots level data. He indicated that the caste-like system evolved in the multi-tribal villages of Paderu agency of Andhra Pradesh as necessary conditions existed there. He denied the role of contact with non-tribals in the formation of caste-like hierarchical structures. For him caste among tribals is purely an indigenous growth. Thus, he is in agreement with those who argue on the multiple origins for the pan-Indian phenomenon of caste.

N.S. Reddy took keen interest on the comtemporary processes of Globalization which he characterized as the coming together of diverse cultures and nations and the growing culture of consumption. Though globalization has been an age-old phenomenon in the form of diffusion of ideas and practices, the present form is different as one has to think of paying royalties for making use of these ideas and practices. N.S. Reddy is uncomfortable with the way in which the processes of globalisation are unfolding and critiques the free market economy advocated in the wake of globalization. Underlining the adversities faced by poorer nations in competing with others in the free market economy, N.S. Reddy highlighted the impact of globalisation on weaker sections such as threats posed to intellectual property rights of indigenous people and the growth of inequalities. He strongly pleads for an egalitarian society pointing out that "Inequality sets man against man, while equality builds cordiality and mutual confidence" (2014:137). He is seriously concerned about growing inequalities in income and wealth and the resulting social unrest in the wake of globalisation and suggests the need for appropriate public intervention. According to him, prolonged oppression, widening inequalities, exploitation of people and nations are not in the interest of the future of humanity. In this context, N.S. Reddy urges upon intellectuals to reflect upon what kind of future they want for humanity.

On the contentious issue of secularism in India, N.S. Reddy advocated that "any label we use should reflect the plurality of our society and the inclusiveness of our culture." He prefered the term Bharatiyata in the place of Hindutva. The discussion on secularism raises the question of whether secular is antagonistic to sacred/religion. Secularism for N.S. Reddy is practising one's own religion, respecting all religions while not hurting the sentiments of others through one's own actions. He observed that secular foundations have been enshrined in the Constitution of India but their actual practice by national leaders led to the erosion of secular values and suggests for disqualifying those without secular credentials from contesting elections. N.S. Reddy advocated radical secularism, i.e. secularism as a new religion.

Delineating the origin of the Post-modernist project as a response to certain conditions, N.S. Reddy elaborately discussed the features of post-modernism and the criticism of post-modernists on ethnographic practice. Describing post-modernism as a disastrous deviation. He cautions anthropologists against joining the 'fancy bandwagon'. The priority for N.S. Reddy is order and coherence against fragmentary knowledge and individualism.

In policy matters, N. S. Reddy does not stop at analyzing the problems but delves deep into the solutions. The policies and strategies for poverty eradication have ended up as a failure due to the narrow focus on income generation and provision of amenities as these are taken up without the comprehension of what N.S. Reddy labels as 'culture of poverty'. He says that sustainable reduction of poverty requires redressing the conditions that perpetuate poverty, and the use of institutions of self-help and community action among the poor. N.S. Reddy disapproved the amenities based approach that ignores the quality of community. Along with measures for poverty eradication, he stressed on the need to pay attention to healthy social life and community life, its coherence and internal harmony. A concern for social harmony, social justice, plurality and inclusiveness is evident in his writings on policy issues.

N.S. Reddy examined the debates initiated by Prof. Amartya Sen in the 1960s on the efficiency of small farms and the inverse relation between farm size and productivity per acre in India. Taking off from a discussion on reduction in the size of holdings, he delineates the marginalisation in terms of demographic pressure and partition of holdings. He traced the rise of mechanisation of agriculture through three decades and its consequences such as reduction in the number of small farms resulting from the benefits of technology flowing to rich farmers. He emphasized on the need for ensuring productivity consistent with equity. Here we can see the concern for equity, and for safeguarding small and marginal farmers in the wake of new technology.

Analyzing the problems encountered by persons affected in the Narmada project, and National testing range at Balipal, N.S. Reddy highlighted the administrative callousness and indifference to the plight of people. He emphasized on the need for a people-centred approach and cautions that unless better living conditions are ensured to the displaced people, rehabilitation is bound to be a failure. In the context of two controversial projects planned in the tribal areas of Andhra Pradesh state, N.S. Reddy raises the issues related to tribal land rights, dilution of protective legislations and resettlement of the displaced tribals without any serious consideration. In the context of these projects, he is for a comprehensive Relief and Rehabilitation Policy. N.S. Reddy recommended for bringing the tribal areas affected by the Polavaram Project in Andhra Pradesh under the VI Schedule to the Constitution of India.

In his distinguished career spanning about seven decades, Prof. N.S. Reddy made an immense contribution to the discipline. He has been an eminent scholar and able teacher who shaped the careers of generations of teachers and researchers. Soft spoken, but a powerful writer, N.S. Reddy was committed to academic rigour, intellectual honesty, and social harmony. He gave equal importance to applied aspects and policy insights along with theoretical, conceptual and methodological issues of social sciences. There is a strong message in his writings on not to get carried away by catchy concepts, fashionable and implausible theories. Most important is the focus on role and responsibilities of the social scientist in the present day scenario of divisive trends, unstable families, disintegrating social fabric, declining moral and ethical values. One cannot but admire N.S. Reddy for his scholarship, commitment to humanistic concerns and academic rigour. With the demise of Prof. N. Subba Reddy on 18-12-2018, Indian Anthropology lost one of its renowned scholar.

REFERENCE

N. Subba Reddy. 2014. *Cultural Diversity and Common Humanity*, New Delhi: Academic Foundation.

18
Nirmal Kumar Bose

Abhik Ghosh

Nirmal Kumar Bose was born to Dr. Bimanbihari Bose and Kiransashi Debi on 22 January, 1901 at Gopimohan Dutta Lane, Bagbazar in Calcutta. The house was that of his maternal uncle, Chandra Kumar Sarkar. They originally stayed at Dashghara, a village in District Hooghly of West Bengal. Nirmal Kumar Bose's father was of the lineage of the famous Kayasthas called 'Basus of Moinagar' including the illustrious physicist Satyen Bose and the revolutionary Netaji Subhas Chandra Bose. They were from a family which closely followed the teachings of the Brahmo Samaj.

He completed his schooling from the Anglo-Sanskrit School, Patna, the Sagar Dutta Free High School, Kamahati in 24 Parganas and from Ranchi Zila School at Ranchi. His father was a Civil Surgeon and was posted to different places. After his schooling, he completed his B.Sc. from Presidency College with a first class Honours. At the time Presidency College was affiliated to Calcutta University. Today, it is a Deemed University.

He interrupted his academic work in the College to participate in Gandhi's Non-Cooperation Movement in 1922. This became a long association with Gandhi. Between 1930-32, he was a part of the Civil Disobedience Movement. In 1942, he was with him during the Quit India Movement. In 1946-47, he was his Private Secretary for a walking tour of Noakhali (in Bangladesh now), Bihar and Bengal.

Around this time, he met Sri Asutosh Mukherjee, the then Vice-Chancellor of Calcutta University. He was persuaded through this illustrious person to join the University for a Masters degree in Anthropology.

Bose then completed his Masters in Anthropology from Calcutta University in 1925, being taught by H.C. Chakladhar, S.C. Roy and T.C. Das. Dewan Bahadur L.K. Ananthakrishna Iyer was the head of the Department of Ethnology. Among the theories he learnt included the Functionalist Approach of Malinowski by T.C. Das, which influenced him greatly. He also became interested in understanding the Geology of the Earth. However, his link with the freedom struggle, Gandhian and Nationalistic principles made him a follower of Anthropology.

At this point he settled down in Puri in Odisha, thus immediately being fascinated and influenced by the architecture of the temples. He then met the temple architect Ram Marasana from whom he learnt the details of Orissan temple architecture. He then became a tour guide, giving lectures to visitors to Puri. This stood him in good stead when he went on to work on the archaeological and historical background of temples. It was while he was guiding tourists in Puri that he met and was influenced by Sir Asutosh Mukherjee, the Vice-Chancellor of Calcutta University, to continue his further education in that University.

From his Masters', he was a precocious reader and was used to preparing for class well in advance. As a result he was marked out as a student who made his teachers uncomfortable, especially Iyer. It was only S.C. Roy who made him feel as if his questions had merit, patiently covering his doubts. He began to visit him at his house in Ranchi initially. S.C. Roy encouraged him and published his Masters dissertation on the Spring Festival in India in two parts in his newly-started journal Man in India. He also chose him as his mentor, though there seems to be no record of a Ph.D. He kept in touch with S.C. Roy all his life. It seems that his family lived in central Ranchi and knew Sarat Chandra Roy's family intimately.

Through the teaching in Calcutta University, Bose became aware of the theories of the Diffusionists as well as the Functionalist Bronislaw Malinowski. However, his own travels and his experiences also made him equally aware of the approaches of M.K. Gandhi, Sigmund Freud as well as Karl Marx.

Eventually, unable to reconcile himself to the theories that he saw around him at thạt point of time, he started calling himself a 'social historian', an approach which he began as a founder member.

Perhaps, his first major fieldwork was among the Juangs of Odisha in 1927. At the time, he was impressed by the simplicity of life among these poor tribals. In Bengali literature, this had become something of a trait. People often yearned to be as simple as the tribals of the region. Perhaps, this was how Bose came to know of this concept in the first hand, rather than through the words of others. The 'noble savage' of French literature was also the model on which tribe-other issues were presented in Bengali literature, from where Satyajit Ray put together his classic movie 'Aranyer Din Ratri' from Sunil Gangopadhyay's book in 1970.

In 1937, he was appointed Assistant Lecturer at the Department of Prehistoric Archaeology at Calcutta University. He then taught as a Lecturer Anthropology and Human Geography at the same University, becoming Reader from 1937 to 1959.

One of the things he strongly believed in was in conducting detailed fieldwork among the tribes of India and understanding them from the ground up. He began with Odisha but he continued to conduct field trips across many other parts of India. In this he had his grounding from his teacher in the Geology Department, Prof. Hem Chandra Dasgupta, who was a keen advocate of fieldwork.

Between 1957-58, he was a visiting scholar at California, Berkeley and Chicago. As a result, the world came to know of Indian anthropological researches in detail and this experience enriched Bose. He then eventually travelled to other Universities – Wisconsin, Michigan, Columbia, North Carolina, Howard (Washington) and Hiroshima (Japan).

Bose had his education and his work in the University often interrupted by his need to go to different parts of the country with Mahatma Gandhi. He wrote Paribrajaker Diary in Bengali in 1945 about his travels. His travels with M.K. Gandhi resulted in at least four books – Selections from Gandhi (1934), Studies in Gandhism (1946), My Days with Gandhi (1953) and Gandhiji: The Man and His Mission (1966). He was arrested and imprisoned for his protests against the British government many times. One, it was between 1931 and 1932. Again, he was arrested for three and a half years, between 1942 and 1945.

His initial encouragement and learning about Odishan temple architecture led him to continue his researches in Odisha. He began by understanding Konarak and Jagannath Puri before he could write a book on the *Canons of Orissan Architecture* (1932). Later, with this knowledge he began on his archaeological explorations in Odisha also. This resulted in *Excavations in Mayurbhanj* (1949) which he wrote with Dharani Sen.

While learning Anthropology, he wrote *Cultural Anthropology* in 1929. He also became interested in understanding the *Peasant Life in India* (1961). As he spoke to a wide variety of people, he became interested in different aspects of the social life of Calcutta (now Kolkata). Once, he was informed of how the sweepers of the city at Beliaghata were dying out due to a variety of factors. He studied them and not only identified these factors, but also suggested ways by which their life and thus their future might be assured so that they may continue to thrive. This area of Beliaghata was very important for him since Gandhiji had camped in the house of a Muslim on the Beliaghata Main Road for a while. This included both societal as well as biological factors, including fertility, mortality, and the like. So, his kind of informed social science was one method to find practical solutions for existing social problems. This enabled him to carry out one of the first city studies in India as *Calcutta: A Social Survey* (1964) on the lines of those conducted by the Chicago School. He was influenced by the American diffusionists, as well as Marx, Freud, Boas, Kroeber, Kropotkin, Malinowski and a number of literary figures both from India, the West and Russia.

When it came to the issue of Nationalism and Integration. Bose was not a hardliner. He always felt that it was more important to get an education, like Gandhi, even at the cost of nationalism. He advised Abdul Ghaffar Khan's son Ghani Khan to continue his study for painting, something his father was set against. Eventually, Ghani Khan became a painter under the famous Nandolal Bose. So, it would be difficult to put together Bose's views on Nationalism in any one statement. Further, his ideas on integration were also about diversity of cultures and practices. To this end he wrote *Culture and Society in India and Problems of National Integration* (1967), *Problems of Indian Nationalism* (1969) and *Anthropology and Some Indian Problems* (1971).

When it came to the tribes, it must be remembered that he began by studying the Juangs of Odisha and other tribes in Odisha, West Bengal, Gujarat and erstwhile Bihar (now Jharkhand) in great detail. However, he wrote a general outline of *Tribal Life in India* in 1971.

Apart from *Paribrajaker Diary*, he also wrote other works in Bengali like *Nabin O Prachin* and *Hindu Samajer Gadan* in 1949. The latter work was translated into English as *The Structure of Hindu Society* by André Beteille, still available in print. In 1941, he wrote about the Hindu mode of absorption of others into the society.

This could perhaps be said to be part of his idea about how society should be studied. Methodologically, he wanted to study in-depth the behaviour of people in society and to analyse it deeply through reassessment of notes by relating them to the rest of a larger society. This was called a civilizational analysis. Eventually, he intended to create a method for studying the history of a civilization through this process, making sense of a large area within which people co-habited together.

Further, the society was seen to be primarily a Hindu society, but Hindus were of a very large variety of cultures. Within these, there was also a sort of a high or Brahminical culture as well as the folk culture or the culture of those who were not in this category, like, for instance, the tribals. This was what created a syncretic union of many different movements and kinds of people in society. Between their joint interaction, a civilization was created. This was the basis for his historical and civilizational approach, rather than the synchronic views of the major theories developed in the West.

He loved to hold in-depth conversations and gatherings where many intellectuals of that time came and discussed issues with him. This helped his knowledge of his environment to grow in leaps and bounds, something that became apparent in his writings and lectures. The crowd that gathered around him included artists, writers, academicians, political thinkers as well as politicians.

For his efforts in 1955, he was elected a member of the National Institute of Science of India. In 1966, He was awarded the Padmashree Award by the President of India. In 1951, he became the editor of *Man in India* started by S.C. Roy in 1921, which he continued till his death in 1972.

In 1917, he participated in famine relief through the Sadharan Brahma Samaj in Bankura district. In 1919, he was an honorary member of the Goabagan Working Men's Institution. He then became the Chairman of the Palli Seva Niketan at Bangram near Santiniketan. By 1929, he had developed a seemingly functional but a more flexible approach to culture in a definition that he gave in his book *Cultural Anthropology* in Chapter 2. In 1930, he organised the Khadi Sangh in Bolpur.

He also began to be the Adviser on Tribal Affairs to the Government of India. In 1948, he was granted the S.C. Roy medal and the Annandale Medal for his researches by the Asiatic Society of Bengal in 1948. In 1949, he became the President of the Anthropology and Archaeology Section of the Indian Science Congress.

On 28 January, 1959, he was appointed the Director of the Anthropological Survey of India, a post he managed till January 1964. During his sojourn in this august institution, he could openly espouse his penchant for fieldwork. Also, he led forays into two other regions. One was a systematic study of communities that is maintained till date. This work had many ramifications. The other was an anthropological study of cities, beginning with a work on Kolkata. Here he planned out an action agenda for the organization where, in five phases, the organization would be developing an array of data on communities, their behaviour, relations, change, modernization and development for use by the government.

In other words, he grew in each area that he excelled in. He developed slowly into a very complex archaeological approach from where he had begun his work in Mayurbhanj. He became an expert on tribal studies. He became a doyen of anthropological researches and fieldwork. He also developed his own particular brand of civilizational approach to ethnographic studies. Finally, he also became a big personality within the core Gandhian group with whom he worked to actively help and create and better society.

He also propounded the idea that there needed to be an Anthropology that was not merely borne out of a Western or European background but something that was developed from within India. He wanted Indian traditions described using a uniquely Indian viewpoint and ideas that he had developed. To this end, he used traditional Hindu philosophy to spell out certain aspects of social life in India. These issues were later taken up by his student Surajit Sinha, who went on to read out papers on these issues at International Conferences.

Being a prolific writer, he wrote 40 books and 700 articles in English and Bengali. The topics on which he wrote included temple architecture, art, prehistoric archaeology, human geography, urban sociology, geology, travelogues, spring festivals in India, underlying basis of the caste system, cultural zones within India and a social survey of Calcutta. He also claimed that instead of following the West one should develop one's own indigenous models and theories based on Indian data. This would give rise to a uniquely Indian Anthropology.

Bose's interests were so wide and multi-disciplinary, that his works and ideas could not be contained just within the disciplinary boundaries of Anthropology. From the ideas on temple architecture, prehistory, biological anthropology to cultural zones in India, he managed to influence many people across disciplines. In fact, his ideas about cultural areas and zones reflected the interest in this issue by American and European social/cultural Anthropologists. Hence, it must be noted that he keenly followed the development of Anthropology in other parts of the world.

His contribution to Gandhian studies is immense in not only his closeness to the great figure but also in his writings about him where he gives tremendous insights into his behaviour, ideals and thus his philosophy.

Further, his idea that there were cultural zones even within cities and that such areas were fruitfully studied academically was another idea that was taken up more by other disciplines rather than by Anthropologists.

Finally, his studies on temple architecture and prehistoric archaeology extended beyond the discipline of Anthropology. This would be in addition to the basic ideas of a civilizational analysis that he was working towards. Such ideas would often be discussed at academic gatherings that were beyond the disciplinary boundaries of Anthropology. In this way, his writings became a lodestone for such work, since people who were not academically oriented would read his books in English or in the vernacular and often discuss them in detail at social gatherings.

For N.K. Bose, the early work of the Anthropological Survey of India under B.S. Guha was not at all important. In fact he needed to revamp their activities completely to give it new meaning. After B.S. Guha, came Dr. Majumdar, who led studies on Rupkund. After this, for thirteen months, Dr. A.K. Mitra was given charge, until finally N.K. Bose took charge. This period just before Bose joined was a period of chaos for the organization. It was Bose who took it out of its mess and gave it a new direction.

He also helped out innumerable students from abroad. One such was Eva Friedlander who had come to work on the effect of the Durgapur Steel Factory on the Bengali families of a village cluster called Gopalmath. Others influenced by him and his work included Dr. A.C. Bhagabati and the geographer Dr. Saradindu Bose.

At each of the conferences that he went to, he not only lectured well, creating a coterie of dedicated followers, but also came back from each country after learning much about their different cultures and customs, whether it was in Japan or Honolulu. In 1958, he was appreciated by Kroeber in a paper that he read out on "East and West in Bengal" at Stanford, California on 10 March. He was also in deep interaction with Haldane till his death in Bhubaneswar in 1964 as well as with Dobzhansky. With them he often discussed ideas like the concept of caste as the largest eugenic experiment. Along with them was the famous archaeologist V. Gordon Childe, who came to Kolkata between 1957 and 1958.

Though he retired in 1964, he continued to work in a number of honorary positions. In 1965, Bose represented India in USA at the Annual Conference for the Association of Asian Studies in New York. Even after his retirement, he continued to work and was a special invitee of the Study Team for the Hill Districts of Assam led by Tarlok Singh in 1965. He also looked into the educational problems in NEFA in 1966. In 1966, he was awarded the Padma Shree award by the President of India. He then became the President of the Asiatic Society and of the Bangiya Sahitya Parishad till his death.

In 1969, he was appointed the President of the Anthropology and Archaeology Section of the Indian Science Congress. Between 1967 and 1970, he served as the Commissioner for Scheduled Castes and Scheduled Tribes of the Government of India. As seen from his entire life, he was a very dedicated social worker for a number of organizations.

Among his students were Surajit Sinha, who became a very big anthropologist and took many of his theories ahead into the next two generations. Another student was the famous sculptor Meera Mukherjee, whose work he was very keen to see published, even as he lay dying.

He contracted cancer and after a long battle he died on 15 October 1972 on Mahastami.

REFERENCES

Bhattacharya, D.K. 2008. "N.K. Bose and Indian Archaeology" in *Indian Anthropologist*, Vol. 38, No. 2, pp. 19-28.

Bose, Nirmal Kumar (Reprint). 1932, 1981, 1982. *Canons of Orissan Temple Architecture*. New Delhi: Cosmo Publications.

Bose, Nirmal Kumar and Dharani Sen. 1948. *Excavations in Mayurbhanj*. Calcutta: University of Calcutta.

Bose, Nirmal Kumar, D. Sen and G.S. Ray. 1951. "Climatic Changes During the Stone Age in Mayurbhanj" in *Georgraphical Review India*, XIII, 1.

Bose, Nirmal Kumar, Dharani Sen and Gautamsankar Ray. 1979. "Geological and Cultural Evidences of the Stone Age in Mayurbhanj" in F. Raymond Allchin and Dilip K. Chakrabarti (eds.) *A Sourcebook of Indian Archaeology* vol. I. New Delhi: Munshiram Manoharlal Publishers Pvt. Ltd., pp. 178-183.

Bose, Nirmal Kumar, Pabitra Gupta and Arabinda Bose. 1960. "Palaeoliths From Monghyr District, Bihar" in *Man in India*, Vol. 40, No. 1, pp. 68-75.

Bose, Nirmal Kumar. 1929, 1953. *Cultural Anthropology and Other Essays*. Calcutta: Indian Associated Publishing Co. Bombay: Asia Publishing House (1961).

Bose, Nirmal Kumar. 1929. *Cultural Anthropology*. Calcutta: Arya Sahitya Bhaban.

Bose, Nirmal Kumar. 1930. *Nabin O Prachin*. Calcutta: Arya Sahitya Bhavan.

Bose, Nirmal Kumar. 1932. *Canons of Orissan Architecture*.

Bose, Nirmal Kumar. 1934. *Selections From Gandhi*. Calcutta: Navavidhan Publication Committee.

Bose, Nirmal Kumar. 1940, 1945, 1959. *Paribrajaker Diary (in Bengali)*. Calcutta: Vidyodaya Library Pvt. Ltd.

Bose, Nirmal Kumar. 1941. "Age of the Boulder-Conglomerate at Kuliana, Mayurbhanj" in *Anthropological Papers,* New Series, No. 6, Calcutta University.

Bose, Nirmal Kumar. 1941. "*The Hindu Method of Tribal Absorption*" in *Science and Culture*. Adapted from a lecture delivered before the Indian Science Congress, Anthropology section, at Benaras on January 3.

Bose, Nirmal Kumar. 1949. *Hindu Samajer Gadan*. Calcutta: Visvabharati Granthalaya.

Bose, Nirmal Kumar. 1952. "Current Research Projects in Indian Anthropology" in *Man in India*, Vol. 32, pp. 121-33.

Bose, Nirmal Kumar. 1959. *Modern Bengal*. Calcutta.

Bose, Nirmal Kumar. 1961. *Peasant Life in India: A Study in Indian Unity and Diversity*. Calcutta: Anthropological Survey of India.

Bose, Nirmal Kumar. 1967. *Culture and Society in India*. Bombay: Asia Publishing House.

Bose, Nirmal Kumar. 1968. *Calcutta 1964: A Social Survey*. Bombay: Lalvani.

Bose, Nirmal Kumar. 1969. *Problems of Indian Nationalism*.

Bose, Nirmal Kumar. 1971, 2002. *Tribal Life in India, Revised ed*. New Delhi: National Book Trust.

Bose, Nirmal Kumar. 1972(a). *Some Indian Tribes*. Delhi: National Book Trust.

Bose, Nirmal Kumar. 1972(b), 1988. *Anthropology and Some Indian Problems*. Calcutta: Institute of Social Research and Applied Anthropology.

Bose, Nirmal Kumar. 1972(c). "Methods in Anthropological Study of Indian Society" in *Journal of the Indian Anthropological Society*, Vol. 7, pp. 1-9.

Bose, Nirmal Kumar. 1975, 1994. *The Structure of Hindu Society*. Translated from the Bengali *Hindu Samajer Gadan* by Andre Beteille. New Delhi: Sangam Books.

Bose, Nirmal Kumar. 1994. *Nirmal Kumar Bose: Pragya Paribrajak*. New Delhi: National Book Trust.

Bose, Nirmal Kumar. 2007. *Paribrajaker Diary*. Calcutta: Punascha.

Sinha, Surajit. 1970. "Anthropology of Nirmal Kumar Bose" in *Journal of the Indian Anthropological Society*, Vol. 5, No. 1, pp. 1-22.

Sinha, Surajit. 1980. "India: A Western Apprentice" in Stanley Diamond (ed.) *Anthropology: Ancestors and Heirs*. The Hague: Mouton, pp. 275-281.

Sinha, Surajit. 1986. *Nirmal Kumar Bose: Scholar, Wanderer*. Delhi: National Book Trust.

19
P.C. Biswas

P.C. Joshi

Prof. Profulla Chandra Biswas was born in Calcutta in the year 1903. He received his early education from the suburban school in Calcutta and did his matriculation in the year 1921. The Calcutta University's Department of Anthropology had just started and he decided to undertake anthropology under the great teachers like Panchanan Mitra, Anantha Krishna Ayer and S.C. Mitra. He was a man of few words but with strong conviction and untiring dedication to his goals.

After doing post-graduation from Calcutta University he was able to get a very prestigious von Humboldt sçholarship from Germany to carry out doctoral research at the Berlin University under famous morpho-geneticist Prof. Eugen Fisher. Prof. Fisher was a very powerful intellectual of Germany of his time, although, he is not much appreciated now for his researches on racial studies and Eugenics. Biswas decided to study dermatoglyphics under Fisher's guidance. His doctoral thesis was in German language titled "Uber hand und Fingerleisten von Indern" which was probably the first Ph.D. dissertation from an Indian on the topic of dermatoglyphics. He was also a favourite of Dr. B.S. Guha who had established Anthropological Survey of India as a separate office bifurcated from Zoological Survey of India, where Guha was working initially. Trained in Harvard, Guha was a towering personality playing a very important role in the Census of 1931 and conducting a large scale anthropometric survey. When Guha was asked by Sir Mourice Gwyer to suggest suitable person to head Delhi University's Anthropology Department, P.C. Biswas was chosen as the right person.

At the time of his selection to the Delhi post, P.C. Biswas was merely an assistant lecturer in Calcutta University desperately needing a position equivalent to his qualifications and experience. He was in Calcutta

University for nearly eleven years without a dignified teaching job and so the job in Delhi was a great opportunity for him. He was not only to establish a department in Delhi University but was also required to compete with people like Thiruvengadam Rajendram Seshadri FNA, FRS of Chemistry; Daulat Singh Kothari of Physics; Panchanan Maheshwari of Botany and M.L. Bhatia of Zoology all of whom were the stalwarts in the field of science. He also faced the challenge of popularizing Anthropology, being a new and unknown subject.

He started functioning from 3rd November, 1947 from the office of the Department of Anthropology, University of Delhi under the Vice Chancellorship of Sir Maurice Gwyer. His first ten letters were addressed to students seeking admission to Anthropology. His first letter was sent to one Mr. Prithi Nath s/o Late Kali Ram at the address 119, Buru Bastian Road, Delhi. His tenth letter is interesting as it was addressed to Rup Dayal Mehra Esqr. c/o Devi Dayal, 34/3 Hanuman Road. Incidentally, Rup Dayal was brother of Prof. J.D. Mehra who did his M.Sc. and Ph.D. from the Department and later retired as professor of social anthropology in the year 1989. On 7th of November, his letter to the Station Director, All India Radio was regarding his talk on importance of anthropology indicating his zeal in popularizing anthropology as a subject in the University. In the initial years of the existence of the department, Biswas was more dependent on Anthropological Survey of India than any teaching department of anthropology. From Anthropological Survey of India, which at that time was located at 64, Banaras Cantonment, Dr. B.K. Chatterjee, M.Sc., D.Sc. (Paris) and Dr. B.S. Guha M.A., Ph.D., F.N.I. were constant external examiners for Delhi University students. His letters are an indication of the needs and requirements of an anthropology department. For example, one cannot think of anthropology department without prehistoric tools. His postage register mentions of his repeated letters to one Mr. Parmananda Acharjee, State Archaeologist, Mayurbhanj State for tools and apparatus. He was continuously writing for books to booksellers in Bombay and Calcutta and to various firms selling scientific instruments, skeletons and other teaching aids. A letter written by him on 13th January, 1951 was addressed to the Secretary, Union Public Service Commission regarding starting of Anthropology as a subject for Indian Administrative Services.

Undoubtedly, P.C. Biswas will be known as the pioneering in promoting and strengthening dermatoglyphics in India. A large number of students worked on finger, palm and sole prints under his able guidance covering issues of inheritance, disease association and other relevant topics. In 1966, he organized International Symposium on Dermatoglyphics in India. While Biswas was a versatile and prolific writer, his first article was in the field of medical anthropology. Published in the 25th issue of the *Journal of the Department of Letters*, Calcutta University, it was a full length paper on distribution of cultural traits related to beliefs and practices pertaining to disease and cure. Besides this paper, the next two papers written by him were on Chhotanagpur plateau tribal communities covering social aspects. From 1935 onwards, we see a distinctive shift in the topics of his papers. Starting with Blood Groups, he wrote series of papers on physical anthropology covering topics like dermatoglyphics, genetics, eugenics, inheritance. Later in his career, he was involved in the ICMR study on growth of school children along with D.N. Majumdar of Lucknow University.

He was obsessed with racial factors contributing to various biological traits as a legacy from his Berlin training. His papers such as "the Anthropometric Study of the Juvenile Delinquents of North India" published in the journal *The Anthropologist* was trying to look for racio-genetic factor contributing to Juvenile Delinquency. Another of his paper titled "Eugenics and Population Problems" published by the *Journal of Science Club* in 1949 was clearly suggesting controlled fertility to improve population profile.

His three monograph length studies are also significant because these books focused upon the plight of the then ex-criminal tribes, tribe and rural village. His first book titled "*Santals of Santal Parganas*" was published by the Adimjati Seva Sangh; his second book titled "*The Ex-Criminal Tribes of Delhi State*" was on the Sansi tribe of central Delhi. This study was supported by a grant from the Planning Commission, Government of India. For the Registrar, Census of India, he contributed a village study titled "Socio-economic study of Budhpur Village". Besides these books, he also published the proceedings titled "Aspects of Indian Anthropology: Proceedings of Summer School in Anthropology" and proceedings of the International Symposium on Dermatoglyphics.

He organized the first summer school in Anthropology at Grand View Hotel, Dalhousie with a financial assistance from University Grants Commission. The summer school was for 20 days starting on 5th June, 1964 and ending on 24th June, 1964. The event was one of its kind and it owes to the organizing skills of Prof. Biswas that he was able to invite participants from Universities of Delhi, Lucknow, Gauhati, Saugor, Panjab, Poona and Ranchi besides prominent research institutes, like Anthropological Survey of Indian, Registrar General, Census Operations,

Planning Commission, Defense Science Laboratory, Central Health Education Bureau, Indian Statistical Institute, Finger Print Bureau, Government of India and Tribal Research Institute, Ranchi. Besides reading of original research papers and review talks, the summer school hosted four symposia on (i) Applied Anthropology; (ii) Border Area Studies; (iii) Teaching in Anthropology; and (iv) Standardization of Anthropometric measurements for purposes of taxonomic studies as well as growth and nutrition. The summer school led to the foundation of the Indian Anthropological Association of which Prof. Biswas became the founder chairman. The meeting also deliberated on the ethical issues involved in undertaking anthropological researches. It was perhaps, one of the earliest attempts at exploring ethical issues pertaining to anthropological researches.

P.C. Biswas was the president of the section on Anthropology and Archaeology of the Indian Science Congress Association in the year 1961. He gave the presidential address titled "Studies of Physical Anthropology with special reference to India" under which he summed up the different types of physical anthropological researches undertaken in India linking them to the contemporary Indian problems and international trends.

Being the founding head of the department, P.C. Biswas had a formidable challenge in establishing anthropology as a worthy subject in the faculty of science. India had just got freedom when the department was started and there were civil conflicts all over India. At such a time, starting a discipline and attracting students for this new unheard of course was a huge challenge for Prof. P.C. Biswas. With five rupees that he got to run the dispatch register, he embarked upon his journey of building a new department amidst well established and highly reputed science departments such as physics, chemistry, botany and zoology. He was joined by Hilda Raj who was a lecturer teaching social anthropology. Starting from old Zoology building, the Department of Anthropology was shifted to the Arts Faculty building in the initial years since the Faculty of Law was housed in the present building of the department. When the Faculty of Law was shifted to a new building near Arts Faculty, the Department of Anthropology was relocated in the heritage building, the erstwhile office of Lord Mountbatten and Vice Regal ballroom. The present head of the department's office is the former while the department's ethnographic museum is the latter.

In the formative years of the department, it had very special relation with the then Prime Minister of India. Pt. Nehru was a great connoisseur of India's cultural diversity and had in-depth knowledge about the rich cultural heritage of India. He was almost like the patron of the ethnographic museum. Quite often, he would donate rare and exquisite pieces of material culture to the department. The department has a large room for housing material culture exhibits in its Arts Faculty building. Pt. Nehru paid a visit to the ethnographic museum when he had come to Delhi University to inaugurate the new Department of African Studies. The large collection from various African countries is because of this reason. P. C. Biswas was also active in promotion of the Adimjati Sevak Sangh, an organization established by legendary Thakkar Bapa. The Anthropology Department being the premier institution of Delhi indulging in front-line researches in biological and cultural aspects became a natural associate of the Adimjati Sevak Sangh. Biswas had written a monograph length book on the Santals with a funding support from Adimjati Sevak Sangh.

From the very beginning, the Delhi University's Anthropology Department was very strong in physical anthropology and ethnology because of distinctive German influence. Except for the thesis of I.P. Singh, the other theses by S.C. Tiwari and J.D. Mehra were ethnological accounts of the Raji and Shoka, respectively. Biswas tried his best to make it a complete department so as to establish all branches of anthropology. He especially sent D.K. Bhattacharya to Poona to receive training in prehistoric archaeology so that this branch may also become stronger in the department. He recruited J.D. Mehra, J.S. Bhandari, I.S. Marwah to teach social anthropology. For strengthening physical anthropology many students like S.R.K. Chopra, I.P. Singh, M.K. Bhasin and H.K. Kumbnani went to Germany and S.C. Tiwari and Raghbir Singh went to United Kingdom to receive advanced training. Department's students like J.S. Yadav and R.D. Sanwal went to USA and United Kingdom, respectively to receive doctoral training in social anthropology. Although, P.C. Biswas was not very assertive and vocal, he was patient and persuasive in guiding and helping his students achieve new heights, many of whom occupied important positions in foreign and Indian universities, research organization and government departments. North Indian departments like Anthropology Departments of Panjab University and Punjabi University, Patiala were founded by the alumni of the Delhi department.

Prof. Biswas was keenly interested in establishing links beyond anthropology and therefore, would closely collaborate with clinical scientists, social workers, basic scientists and other professionals. He had good links with the Planning Commission and he initiated some studies with the support of Planning Commission. He would be regularly going to attend Government of India's functions and speak in conferences and seminars beyond anthropology. As a provost of Gwyer Hall, he helped many students to find a home away from home.

P.C. Biswas had extremely cordial relations with foreign anthropologists starting with his own doctoral days contacts in Germany. He was always keen to use these networks for placing his students to foreign universities for advance training. He was in the editorial board of the international journal Mankind Quarterly and was Vice-President of the International Union of Anthropological and Ethnological Sciences. In the field of dermatoglyphics, he was a world renowned authority. In the year 1966, he was able to hold International Symposium on Dermatoglyphics. He hosted Oscar Lewis and provided all logistic support to him while he was in Delhi on a Ford Foundation assignment to understand the political dynamics of rural India. People like Weiner, Haldane, Mandelbaum, Haimendorf, Elwin and many more scholars of repute were hosted by him on various occasions in the department.

He was quite active in furtherance of the cause of anthropology even after his retirement. In spite of having a large house, he rented a house near Delhi University to be in touch with the subject. The department was after all run by his former students and with exception of J.S. Bhandari who belonged to Lucknow, all the faculty members were his direct students. His notable students abroad and outside Delhi were J.D. Mawalwala, Moni Nag, S. P. Sharma, P.D. P. Rao, Ramchandraiah, P. Dash Sharma, S.R.K. Chopra, J. C. Sharma, V. Bhalla, B.R. Ghosh, Narender Kumar and many more. In the department right from I.P. Singh to S.C. Tiwari, J.D. Mehra, Raghbir Singh, H.K. Kumbanani, Abhimanyu Sharma, I.S. Marwah, all were his direct students. There is a saying that a teacher is known by his students; P.C. Biswas will always be known for turning a large number of neophytes into professional anthropologists of repute, all of whom made an indelible mark in anthropology.

20

Professor Prabodh Kumar Bhowmick

An Indian Action Anthropologist

Tilak Bagchi

Prof. Prabodh Kumar Bhowmick popularly known as P.K. Bhowmick (*Mej Da* or *Jetha babu)* by the Lodhas and other downtrodden population of the Bidisha Ashram founded by Professor Bhowmick) was born on 6th September, 1926 (19th *Bhadra*, 1333 B.S.) in Amdabad, a remote village of Nandigram Police Station of the then undivided Midnapore (now in Purba Medinipur of West Bengal). He was the third child among five brothers and three sisters of Jogendra Nath Bhowmick and Sarnomoyee Bhowmick. His all the brothers were highly well placed in their respective field. His elder brother Amulya Ratan Bhowmick was the Head Master of three illustrious schools of Bengal, namely Akondobari High School of Purba Medinipur, Pathankhali High School of Dakshin 24 Parganas and Gobordanga Collegiate School of Uttar 24 Parganas. His younger brother Subhod Bhowmick was the Head Master of Amdabad Madhya Palli Vidyalaya. His fourth brother Bangabhusan Dr. Shruhid Bhowmick was a renowned linguist and noted Santali Scholar. He was the senior faculty member of Hooghly Rammohan College and Uluberia College. His youngest brother Dr. Aninda Kishore Bhowmick was a zoologist of repute and former principal of two colleges, namely Bajkul College and Tamluk College of Purba Medinipur.

His sons and daughters were also equally talented and brilliant. The eldest son of Prof. Bhowmick is Dr. Pradip K. Bhowmick, an Associate Professor of Rural Development Centre, Indian Institute of Technology, Kharagpur. His eldest daughter Professor Samita Manna was the former Professor of Sociology and Dean, Faculty of Arts, Kalyani University, and ex Vice-Chancellor, Sidhu Kanu Birsha University, Purulia, West Bengal. Both his elder son and elder daughter were awarded with D.Lit.

His youngest daughter Late Sarita Bhowmick was the most brilliant scholar among all his brothers and sisters. She was not only the Ishan Scholar for securing highest marks not only in Anthropology Honours but among all the graduate students of the University of Calcutta of that year. She also was the recipient of university Gold Medal for securing First Class First Position in Anthropology with record marks from Ranchi University. She not only got several prizes including gold medals for her academic excellence but was the author of some books and research papers. Before her death at the age of 26 she was a research scholar of the Anthropological Survey of India. His youngest son Shree Pratim Bhowmick was a very senior Geologist of the Oil and Natural Gas Commission.

Prof. Bhowmick got school education from Kalagachiya High School (now renamed as Kalagachiya Jagadish Vidyapith). The school was one of eleven schools of the then undivided Bengal were recognized as National Schools primarily due to the initiative of two great national leaders, viz. Deshbandhu Chittaranjan Das and Deshapran Birendranath Sasmal. Kalagachiya High School was one of such National Schools. Several great personalities including Deshapran Birendra Nath Sasmal and a noted chemist and founder of Bengal Chemical, Acharya Prafulla Chandra Roy visited the school and germinated the spirit of patriotism in the mind of young Prabodh. He also came in contact with several nationalist teachers viz. Jagadish Maity, Nikunja Bihari Maity, the then Head Master, Paresh Nath Maity, the then Assistant Head Master, Girish Maity, the then Assistant Teacher. Their teaching further accelerated the spirit of nationalism in the mind set of young Prabodh. As a result he used to put on *Khadi* cloths throughout his life. Prof. Bhowmick was imprisoned in jail when he was a student of Class IX by joining in the Quit India Movement and picketing at Contai. He was in jail for about two and half years. After being released he was readmitted in Class IX and passed Matriculation examination with distinction (letter marks) in several subjects including Sanskrit. After passing marticulation family members of Prof. Bhowmick insisted to admit him in Medical College to become a doctor. Prof. Bhowmick was not at all interested to join Medical College. Elder brother of Prof. Bhowmick brought him to Bangabasi College and he got admitted in I.Sc. course. In this regard it is not out of context to state that in those days Bangabasi College was the only college in Bengal which offered Anthropology at the undergraduate level. In his college days Prof. Bhowmick was highly influenced by the teaching of Prof. Satkori Mitra, the then Head of the Department, Anthropology. Swami Vivekananda, the spiritual soul of India, was the maternal uncle of Professor Mitra.

During his college days his friends and batch mates were Professor Bikram Keshari Roy Burman, former Deputy Registrar General of India (Social Studies); Sri Hirendra Kumar Rakshit, former Director of the Anthropological Survey of India; Professor M.R. Chakraborty, an eminent anthropologist; Professor D.P. Mukherjee, former Prof. of Anthropology, Calcutta University and founder of Department of Anthropology, S.V. University, Tirupati and former acting Director of the Anthropological Survey of India; Prof. Pranab Kumar Ganguly, founder Head of Anthropology, Vidyasagar University and others.

He passed B.Sc. with Anthropology Honours and M.Sc. with specialization in Social Cultural Anthropology from the University of Calcutta in 1951. He studied anthropology in University of Calcutta which celebrates 100 years of teaching in Anthropology in India in this year. Several well-known anthropologists, namely T.C. Das, K.P. Chattopadhyay, T.C. Roychaudhury, S.S. Sarkar, M.N. Basu, Dharani Sen and several others were his teachers in the University of Calcutta. Immediately after passing M.Sc. in Anthropology Prof. Bhowmick joined Bangabasi College as a lecturer in Anthropology in 1952. He then joined University of Calcutta as a lecturer in Anthropology in 1960 and superannuated from the same University on 30th September, 1994 as Professor of Anthropology. During his long teaching career he was the Head of the Department of Anthropology; Dean, Faculty of Science, and member of the Senete and Syndicate of the University of Calcutta. A sudden horrible death followed by an accident snatched him away from this earthly bondage on 5th February, 2003.

Prof. Bhowmick obtained his Ph.D. and D.Sc. degrees in Anthropology from the University of Calcutta. His anthropological insight was developed when he had the privilege of being supervised by Prof. Nirmal Kumar Bose, a doyen of Indian Anthropology and architect of Indian tradition in Anthropology. Prof. Bose was the Bengali interpreter-*cum*-private secretary to Mahatma Gandhi during his stay in Bengal during mid-1940s. Prof. Bose was also the Director of the Anthropological Survey of India (1959-1964), Commissioner for the National Commission of Scheduled Tribe (1967-1997) and President of the Asiatic Society (1972).

Gandhian approach of Prof. Bose influenced Bhowmick in his doctoral work. Prof. Bhowmick started his Ph.D. work in 1952 and was awarded Ph.D. in 1961 for his doctoral work "The *Lodhas of West Bengal : A Socio-Economic Study*" which was published in 1963 from Puthi Pustak, Kolkata. In his Ph.D. dissertation, Prof. Bhowmick observed that in earlier times *Lodhas* were no longer a purely hunting gathering group of people. As per 1901 Census Report they migrated from Madhya Pradesh as an agricultural community. However, 1931 Census Report revealed that they indulged in criminal activities. Prof. Bhowmick directly observed social, political, economic and recreational activities of the *Lodhas.* Thus the entire spectrum of life processes were pin-pointed by Prof. Bhowmick in his work. Different ritual or life cycle events from birth to death along with the participation of their kin members, shares the feeling of their belonging marked a sort of tribal identity in the cognition of the *Loddhas*. According to Prof. Bhowmick *Lodhas* feel pride in declaring them as Savara. They have a close nexus with the Mundari group of people.

Prof. Bhowmick's work revealed that the *Lodhas* must have loved freedom of the Jungle which was abandoned in Midnapore during British Colonial rule. They developed certain economic relationship with their neighbours and it is unfortunate that a wrong turn took place in this adjustment so that they were branded as a criminal tribe.

Abject poverty and social neglect were the root cause of their criminality. There can be nothing in the original cultural milieu to which they belong which would have led them into this unhappy condition. Prof. Bhowmick also observed that territorial displacement under a new setting with the impact of scheming communities all-round affected very seriously the old pattern of economic life of the *Lodhas* which was by and large pivoted around hunting, gathering, fishing and fowling mode of economy and it ultimately distorted the equilibrium of the whole society. Probably under such circumstances pilfering, petty theft, lifting of articles from the house of the neighbours and clandestine sale of jungle produces were first resorted to individual basis. This individual practice gradually crystallized a group activity. Amidst poverty, unsystematic attitude of the neighbours and stoic apathy of the rulers and Government has been responsible for their criminal activities which has cut a deep gorge in which the *Lodhas* had to role down helplessly. As a result the *Lodhas* were branded as a Criminal Tribe by the then British Government till the revocation of Criminal Tribe Act, 1952. Prof. Bhowmick on the basis of his study on 31 Lodha Villages in seven police stations of Midnapore Sadar (now in Paschim Medinipur district and Jhargram subdivision, now in Jhargram district) concluded that criminality could not be a regular profession of the human society. He also advocated that if criminality being their culture bound profession then there must be psycho-social and ritualistic attachment linked with criminality and criminal ethos which was lacking in Lodha society and culture.

Apart from academic discourse Prof. Bhowmick has worked hard in order to rehabilitate the *Lodhas* in the heart of their more advance neighbour. He has tried to clear misunderstanding, correct harmful attitude so that the neighbouring communities would be able to treat the *Lodhas* as an equal in order to rebuild a new India. His work was also an excellent and model ethnographic work on the *Lodha*. Prof. Bhowmick tried to present a picture of interlacing different aspects of culture of the Lodha community. Due to his monumental work on the Lodhas Prof. Bhowmick was often referred as Lodha Bhowmick or Messiah of the Lodha (Sahay, 2003).

Prof. Bhowmick also awarded D.Sc. in 1967 from the University of Calcutta for his monumental work "*Socio-Cultural Profile of Frontier Bengal*" which was published in 1976 from Puthi Pustak, Calcutta. On the basis of his study of the then undivided Bengal and its adjacent areas of Orissa (now spelt as Odisha) and Bihar (now Jharkhand) which formed the frontier or border Bengal, he tried to show that diversified communities with tradition bound life situation which was activated during the period of his study (in the mid 50s and early 60s of the last century) was ultimately gave vent to the exposition of different understanding which Prof. Bhowmick preferred to call the same as socio-cultural profile in the frontier region of Bengal. On the basis of his micro study of complete and cohesion as well as complete and diversified ethnic groups Prof. Bhowmick tried to establish different life-way and thought process of the people of frontier Bengal. His primary objective of study was to show the holistic socio-cultural setting of the region which encompasses the western border of the Greater Bengal. As stated earlier the specific geographical terrain which Prof. Bhowmick has selected for his study was the frontier boundary of the then undivided Midnapore district that was contiguous with the district of Balasore and Mayurbhanj of Orissa and having its spread northwards along the district of undivided Singbhum and Dhanbad of Bihar (now Jharkhand). This particular tract was also associated with Purulia, Bankura and Birbhum districts of West Bengal which both had social setting and geographical congruity as observed by Prof. Bhowmick. He also observed that this particular landmark was having a distinctive cultural background and crisscrossed political boundary. This typical geographical condition since time immemorial witnessed arrival of several kings, rulers and other groups of political dignitaries but no one could bring any devastating and significant change on the local cultural tradition because of integrity, radicalism and spirituality. Prof. Bhowmick preferred to call this territory as a frontier region also because this specific terrain like other region witnessed several socio-political and culture specific events as result of aggression, migration and conquest. He also had shown that historicity of this region witnessed colonial endeavour due to the influence of the British, the Portuguese and the French. This influence was envisaged in the rural life of the people of the contemporary region. Arrival of the Pathans and the Mughals and their political activities were deep rooted in the region.

From the remote past the area had been and continued to be influenced by the tribal groups like the Santal, the Lodha, the Munda, the Mahali, the Kora and so on along with small and isolated aboriginal derivatives like the Chirmar, Kakmara, the snake charming community Savara and so on. Besides this area was the melting pot of Odishan and Rarh Bengali culture. It formed the synthesis of cultural feature which was characterized by the tradition and the life of the people. Prof. Bhowmick strongly believed that in spite of several push and pull factors on the basis of substratum of the traditional culture and the region was by and large characterized by tribal way of life and thought. He also observed that specific tribal orientation pattern was so strong and deep rooted in the region that it could not be displaced by the influence of powerful Brahminical tradition. In his D.Sc. dissertation Prof. Bhowmick tried to show how the traditional tribal based indigenous culture reacted with different dimensions of Brahminic, Islamic and colonial thoughts and ideas and the process of inferring the concrete refinement of thinking process.

Professor Bhowmick was a prolific writer both in English and Bengali. He wrote sixteen books and more than two hundred research papers and writings both in English and Bengali. The books written by him are as follows –

1. The Lodhas of West Bengal: A socio-economic study
2. Four Midnapore villages
3. Occupational mobility and caste structure in Bengal
4. Socio-cultural profile of frontier Bengal
5. Occultism in fringe Bengal
6. Some aspects of Indian Anthropology
7. The Chenchus of the forest and plateaux : The hunting gathering tribe in transition
8. Applied, action and development anthropology
9. Primitive tribal groups in eastern India
10. Tribal literacy in West Bengal
11. Rethinking tribal culture in India

12. Caste in border Bengal
13. Customary law of Austric speaking tribe
14. Bangalar Lok Utsab (in Bengali)
15. Medinipur Kahini, later reprinted as Amader Medinipur (in Bengali)
16. Lok Samaj O Sanskriti (in Bengali)

Prof. Bhowmick in his studies throws discernible light on the question of cultural integration amidst isolation or segregation. He studied several tribes of West Bengal, Odisha, Jharkhand and Andhra Pradesh. His special interest was to study Particularly Vulnerable Tribal Groups like Lodha, Kheria, Birhor and Toto of West Bengal as well as the Chenchus of Andhra Pradesh in the context of their assimilation with the greater Hindu civilization. Besides these his interest was also on the study of population pattern and population dynamics, occultism, customary law of the tribal population, rural social system, religious centre and various festivals related to diversified folk life. He also studied several cultural traits to understand their specific significance. He envisaged social system and rural territory in terms of various thoughts and ideas. Prof. Bhowmick also made several attempts to understand thresholds of working and thinking pattern of smaller and larger communities to study special segment of the population in wider context, which was operational within the village, households and temple organizations. He studied various fairs and festivals in order to observe insider's view on village and community level and interacting patterns of diversified cultural traits which gave him an ample opportunity to examine and re-examine interaction and isolation of various infiltrated caste and community oriented cultural traits and trait complex. Bhowmick though was champion in ethnographic work but he studied many aspects of cultural anthropology in his own way.

Prof. Bhowmick founded Man and Life, a journal dedicated to study of Science of Man and he edited the journal from 1976 till 2003. He also organized several national and international seminars in Bidisha since 1974 as key organizer-*cum*-seminar Director. He also participated in several national and international Seminars in India and abroad. Notable among them was National conference of De-notified Tribal Communities in 1963. He also participated in the International Congress of Anthropology and Ethnological Scineces and chaired one session of Applied Anthropology in Amsterdam, Holland. Due to the effort of Prof. Bhowmick and his close friend Ranjit Gupta, I.P.S. (retd.), the former Inspector General and Head of West Bengal Police, the Lodhas were not only included as Primitive

Tribal Group (now renamed as Particularly Vulnerable Tribal Group) and all the police out posts made to torture the Lodhas were withdrawn. Prof. Bhowmick was the founder chairman of syllabus committee in Anthropology in Vidysagar University where he introduced non-traditional subject in anthropology in post graduate level as early as 1980s. The trend is now followed by many Indian universities. Professor Bhowmick was also the president of the Indian Anthropological Society, Kolkata and Anthropological Secretary of the Asiatic Society, Kolkata. Prof. Irwin Dustcher, Emeritus Professor of Sociology, Akron University, USA (2006) referred him as Indian finest intellectual in recognition of his contribution to the advancement of social anthropology in India. He was ever remembered as Development and Action Anthropologist. According to him Anthropology was not merely a science of man but science for the service of mankind.

Prof. Bhowmick started research work among the Lodhas since 1952. As per the advice and instruction of his mentor and Ph.D. supervisor Prof. Nirmal Kumar Bose, Bhowmick established Samaj Sevak Sangha in Bidisa in 1955. Bidisa literary meaning what diffuses light and he set up Bidisa in a presently depopulated village Bagavera meaning a path of the tiger. It suggests a state of forest dwelling path of the village and the village is located in Midnapore Sadar subdivision. The village was near to Orissa Trunk Road and a kilometre away from Narayangarh Railway station. Prof. Bhowmick started living in the village along with a group of Lodhas, Savar and other tribal groups to develop a social laboratory-*cum*-action anthropological research centre. For social work he developed Samaj Sevak Sangh while for applied and action anthropological research work he founded The Institute of Social Research and Applied and Action Anthropology. Bidisa has been identified as a role model for applied and action anthropological research in India and tried to develop Bidisa in the line of global perspective of applied and action anthropology. As per the instruction of Prof. N.K. Bose, Bhowmick established a lower primary school in Bidisa particularly for the Lodha and other downtrodden segment of people which was upgraded to upper primary school in 1968. The school was further upgraded to government aided High School after his death in 2007 and renamed as Daharpur Professor Prabodh Kr. Bhowmick Vidyalaya. Prof. Bhowmick also established an Ashram Hostel in mid 1960s for food and lodging of the Lodha children in order to transform their life style and to generate middle class mentality of the Lodha, an ex-criminal tribal group. Ashram hostel in West Bengal was one of the brain child of Prof. Bhowmick which was later taken as model

Ashram hostel by the Government of West Bengal. In this regard Prof. Bhowmick (2003) observed that Ashram hostel for boys in the form of an institutional complex was organized when the Lodha children experienced dissociation from their parents and the consequent detachment from their long pristine habit through re-socialization and enculturation into a new social milieu. In the year 1968 a riot took place between the Lodha and the Santal tribal communities. After the riot a second hostel with 20 seats was set up to provide free boarding and lodging of the riot victim Lodha boys and later on another hostel for girls with 20 seats was established. Soon Prof. Bhowmick realized that the Lodha should be provided with vocational training to make them self-sufficient. In this regard Prof. Bhowmick further observed that the expanding institutional complex at Bidisa sought to provide vocational training for the drop outs and reorganization of the life of the tribal and lower caste boys and girls through agriculture, pisciculture bee keeping, dairy farming, carpentry, tailoring and weaving. In 1977 Prof. Bhowmick set up a printing press in Bidisa. From this press he printed and published books of several luminaries of anthropology including Prof. Sachchidananda, R.S. Mann, Prof. Vinay Kumar Srivastava, Prof. N.K. Behura and so on.

Besides, Bidisa can boost off a rock garden and artificial park decorated with archaeological findings and old sculptures of Rarh Bengal, a huge tank with an island that attracts birds during winter session and a deer park, a seminar hall dedicated in the name of Prof. N.K. Bose. Prof. Bhowmick in real sense holds seminars and for the same he has constructed large rooms in brick built house as well as cottages for the guest and participants who might come to Bidisa for conference, training course and fieldwork in anthropology and allied discipline. Bidisa has also a library rich with rare anthropological and sociological books and dissertations. He also set up an open air stage in the name his beloved departed youngest daughter Sarita Bhowmick as Sarita Mancha. Prof. Bhowmick also set up Rarh Sanskriti Sangrahalaya and open air ethno-archaeological museum in 1990 with the help of two Directors of Indian Museum, namely Dr. R.C. Sharma and Dr. S.S. Biswas both of them later became the Director General of National Museum of New Delhi. The museum was inaugurated by Prof. K.L. Chopra, the then Director of Indian Institute of Technology of Kharagpur. This museum exhibited and preserved material culture and objects and objects related to art and craft of the local people including tribe and archaeological relics like a Shiva Linga of Makrana stone, old stone image of Jain Tirthankar Lord Risabh Nath, etc. and in addition he also developed Kultikri Kiarchand Sanskriti

Smarak and a guha, an artificial rock for meditation at Bidisa. In this way Prof. Bhowmick developed Bidisa, a lone model organization of applied and action anthropology. Prof. Bhowmick will be ever remembered in the domain of action and applied anthropology and for running Bidisa which had been pledged to arrange a close interaction between academic sphere and administrative domain for the welfare of the down trodden people including the Lodha. Vidyarthi (1979) observed that Prof. Bhowmick is the only anthropologist who represented fourth category of applied and action anthropology for his Bidisa experiment where he was the actual charge of the development programme of the Lodha which he and his associates had been developing and studying.

Prof. Bhowmick played a key role in establishment of Vidyasagar University along with his friend Prof. Anil Gayen. Prof.Bhowmick was also instrumental for the establishment of many colleges of rural Bengal like Pathankhali College, Bajkul College, Nandigram College and Belda College. Prof. Bhowmick was actively associated with the West Bengal Council of Child Welfare, the organization dedicated to the development of downtrodden and orphan children. He was also the editor of *Sisu Kalyan*, the Bengali journal of the Council for the several years. Prof. Bhowmick with the help of the Council established Balwadi (pre-primary) schools in Fulgeriya and Kalagachiya villages of Narayangarh police station of Paschim Medinipur, West Bengal; Dhansol village of Baripada forest range of Mayurbhanj district of Orissa. He also set up a Balwadi school in the Churachandpur district of Manipur along with his student Dr. T.S. Gangte. He was associated with several learned societies like Janasiksha Prachar Kendra, National Science Society both as President. He was also the member of the visiting team of the West Bengal Higher Secondary Council and Head Examiner of West Bengal Board of Secondary Education. As a member of the visiting team of the West Bengal Higher Secondary Council he played a decisive role for setting of plus two (standard XI & XII) schools in several places of rural Bengal. All these endeavours clearly suggest that he had genuine love for the under privileged children and spread of schools and higher education in rural Bengal in general and Medinipur in particular.

Prof. Bhowmick was also interested to study of folklore and regional history of Rarh Bengal. In this regard he not only regularly organized a seminar on the regional history and folklore and Nabanna and Pally Punorgathon Utsav (post harvest and rural reconstruction festival) regularly at Bidisa during the month of September and December respectively for the revival of folk tradition of the region in one hand and dissemination of rich cultural heritage of the region between the local intellectual and rural masses on the other hand. Prof. Bhowmick wrote several books and articles on the folklore and regional history of the marginal communities like Kakmara, Christians of Mirpur, Gajan, a regional folk festival, Tusu, Bhadu and Jhumur and other folk songs of Western part of Border Bengal. His paper on Paresh Patidar, life and creative activity of a scroll painter is also worth mentioning.

Professor Bhowmick did not made any international collaboration in his life. He however, visited Amsterdam to participate in a session of Applied Anthropology in the International Congress of Anthropological Ethnological Sciences. He also participated in several international seminar and conferences at United Kingdom, Italy, West Germany, Holland, and Bangladesh. Scholars from Bangladesh and Nepal carried out their Ph.D. under his supervision. Anthropologists and other social scientists from Russia, United States of America, Japan, Holland, West Germany, Nepal, United Kingdom and Bangladesh visited Bidisa to see his social laboratory or to participate in the seminars. In recognition of his contribution, Bill Clinton, the former President of the USA sent his best wishes and greeting card.

After retirement Prof. Bhowmick was actively involved in development of Bidisa, teaching assignment as guest faculty in several universities and IIT, Kharagpur as well as writing of books and papers in anthropology. About sixty researchers have carried out research work under his supervision for the award of Ph.D. He had supervised Ph.D. on a good number of field/topic. About fifteen scholars carried out their research work for Ph.D. degree on ethnographic account of the Mahali, Savara, Bagal, and Bauri of West Bengal, Dimasa Kachhari of Assam, Gadaba of Andhra Pradesh, Maring and Kuki of Manipur, Khond of Odisha, Bhoksa of unidivided Uttar Pradesh, Nicobarese of Car Nicobar, Rout of Chhattisgarh, Dhimal of Nepal and so on. Notable scholars who had carried out research in this line includes Prof. Rajat Kanti Das of Vidyasagar University, Dr. Shyamakanti Sengupta of University of Calcutta, Dr. Dipali Ghosh Danda of the Anthropological Survey of India, Prof. Rishikesh Rengmi of Tribhuvan University, Nepal, Niranjan Kumar Ghatak, former Director of the Ministry of Tribal Affairs, Government of India, T.S. Gangte, former Director of Education, Government of Manipur, and A.V. Subba Rao of Vijaywada Government College of Andhra Pradesh.

More than a dozen of researchers earned their Ph.D. for carrying out research on religion, religiosity, religious complex and pilgrim sites like Tarakeshwar, Holy Godavary river, concept food, disease, method of treatment and their nexus with the religion, magic, witchcraft, death rites, agricultural rituals and related topics, which may broadly be included under the canopy of magic, religion and medical anthropology. Eminent scholars who have done research on these topics include Prof. Swapan Kr. Bhattacharya of the Department of Sociology, University of Calcutta, Dr. Debasis Debnath of Indian Institute of Forest Management, Bhopal, Prof. Pabitra Kumar Gupta, former acting Vice-Chancellor and Registrar of Bidhan Chandra Krissi Viswa Vidyalaya, Nadia, Prof. Prafulla Chakraborty of Sociological Research unit of Indian Statistical Institute, Dr. Arun Kumar Chatterjee, Former Chairperson of Indian National Chapter of International Council of Museums. About four researchers including Dr. S. Chakraborty of Bangabasi College, Dr. Chittarnajan Bandyopadhyay, former President of West Bengal Board of Secondary Education, Dr. Narayan Chandra Maity, former Principal of Mahishadal Girls' College have carried out their research on joint family system, rural indebtedness, caste panchayat, rural administration which may be put under the broad category of rural social institution and administration.

About five researchers conducted research work under his supervision on the topics like methodology of development, anthropology in action tribal area, constrains of development which may be put under the category of development, action and applied anthropology. Renowned scholars who have carried out research for their Ph.D. degree in this line were Dr. Subir Kumar Biswas, IAS (Retd.), former Chairman of Uttar Pradesh Public Service Commission, D.R. Pratap, former Director of Tribal Research Institute, Andhra Pradesh, Dibakar Basak, former Joint Director of Commission for Scheduled Caste and Scheduled Tribe, Lucknow. About ten researchers carried out their research on ethnic interaction and their sequel of cultural transformation. Notable among them are Prof. Ahsan Ali of Dhaka University, Sujit Som, former Joint Director of the Indira Gandhi Rastriya Manav Sangrahalaya, Bhopal and so on. They worked on strategies of survival among the Oraon, displaced/ migrated Santals of Bangladesh, biological and cultural adaptation of the refugees of little Andaman, life in Sundarban, survival of Hindu rituals, pavement dwellers of Calcutta, social mobility, facets of historical anthropology and such other topics. About ten researchers carried out their researcher works on rural and urban problems and related issues that encompasses tribal food and nutrition, fertility and mortality, working women, urbanization and urban social situation, child labour, Naxalite movement, socio-psycho-economic problems of hospital patients, cycle-rickshaw pullers and so on. Name of some of the scholars who have carried out their research work for Ph.D. degree in those areas are Prof. Bela Bhattacharya of Vidyasagar University, Krishna Mandal of the All India Institute of Hygiene and Public Health, Kolkata Suraj Bandyopadhyay of the Indian Statistical Institute and so on. The present author has carried out research for his Ph.D. degree under his guidance on food and nutritional aspects of the five tribal communities of West Bengal which encompassed ethnographic, biological, ecological, economic, socio-cultural and developmental aspects related to food and nutrition. In short Prof. Bhowmick supervised on a wide range of aspects and areas related to anthropology and allied disciplines for the award of Ph.D. of his students.

REFERENCES

Bhowmick, A. 2004. *Sriman Prabodh Kumar: Srmitir Aloy in Adhyapak Prabodh Kumar Bhowmick, Karmajiban o Darshan*; (ed.) Pranab Roy; Bidisa; Samaj Sevak Sangha and ISRAA; pp. 44-46 (in Bengali).

Bhowmick, M. 2019. *Chirabhaswar Jnantapas Prabodh Kumar Bhowmick*; Bidisa, Narayangarh; Samaj Sevak Sangha (mimeograph in Bengali).

Bhowmick, P.K.; 1963. *The Lodhas of West Bengal : A Socio-Economic Study;* Calcutta; Punthi Pustak.

Bhowmick, P.K. 1976. *Socio-cultural Profile of Frontier Bengal*; Calcutta; Punthi Pustak.

Bhowmick, P.K. 1989. *Bidisa: An Introduction* (leaflate); Bidisa; ISRAA.

Chakraborty, B. 2019. *Amar Anubhabe Dr. Prabodh Kumar Bhowmick o Bidisa*; Sundarnagar, Purba Medinipur; Baneswar Chakraborty (Publisher).

Deb, P.K. 2006. About Prof. P.K. Bhowmick in *Exploration in Anthropology: P.K. Bhowmick and His Collaborative Research Work*; (eds.) S.K. Pramanik and S. Manna; Bidisa; ISRAA; pp. i-ii.

Debnath, D. 2012. "Bhowmick's Thoughts and Action" in *World of Development Anthropology and Society: Issues and Applications; (*ed.) Indu Talwar; New Delhi; Northern Book Centre; pp. 33-42.

Dustcher, I. 2006. Foreword in *Exploration in Anthropology: P.K. Bhowmick and His Collaborative Research Work*; (eds.) S.K. Pramanik and S. Manna; Bidisa; ISRAA, pp. iii-vi.

Koley, S.; 2019. P.K. Bhowmick in *Anthropologist;* (ed.) Koley, S.K., *et. al.*, New Delhi; Maya Publication.

Pramanik, S.K. and Samita Manna, 2006. Preface in *Exploration in Anthropology: P.K. Bhowmick and His Collaborative Research Work*; (eds.) S.K. Pramanik and S. Manna; Bidisa; ISRAA; pp. vii-xi.

Sahay, V.S. 2003. "Messiah of the Lodhas: Professor P.K. Bhowmick (1926-2003)"; *The Oriental Anthropologists*; 3 (2); pp. 164-179.

Sarkar, R.M. 2006. "Professor P.K. Bhowmick – The Field of Anthropologist

Oriented with Indigenous Vision". in *Exploration in Anthropology: P.K. Bhowmick and His Collaborative Research Work*; (eds.) S.K. Pramanik and S. Manna; Bidisa; ISRAA; pp. 41-62.

Vidyarthi, L.P. 1979. *Trends in World Anthropology*; New Delhi; Concept Publishing Company Pvt. Ltd.

21
Pranab Kumar Ganguly

Abhijit Guha

Pranab Kumar Ganguly was an outstanding anthropologist of post-independent India. Ganguly's publications, particularly in the various subfields of anthropology are not well-known in the Indian anthropological circles. He conducted remarkable fieldworks in Andaman and Nicobar Islands during 1950s and wrote thought provoking theoretical articles in a bio-cultural framework.

Ganguly received his M.Sc. Ph.D. and D.Sc. degrees from the University of Calcutta in 1951, 1966 and 1973 respectively. He joined the Anthropological Survey of India as an Anthropologist in 1969 and became its Deputy Director and subsequently, founded two new Anthropology Departments in India at Manipur (Manipur University) and West Bengal (Vidyasagar University). He retired from Vidyasagar University as professor in 1993. Ganguly was the elected president of the Anthropology and Archaeology Section, Indian Science Congress during 1976-77. He received three prestigious medals in the same year, viz., Sir Asutosh Mookerjee Gold medal (1975), Bengal Immunity Research Prize and Gold Medal (1975) and Griffith Memorial Prize (1975) for his research on various topics in Anthropology. In addition he received the esteemed Bertillon Medal of France (1973) (Directory of Anthropologists in India 1981:110-111).

The Directory of Anthropologists in India (1981) published by the Anthropological Survey of India mentioned that Pranab Ganguly was specialized in 'Physical Anthropology' although it noted that the 'Principal publications' of Ganguly included research papers on the 'Religious beliefs of the Negritos of Little Andaman' and 'Notes on the material culture of the Jarwa of Great Andaman' along with other papers on social-cultural anthropology. His D.Sc. thesis was also on the somatic variability among the Brahmins and Muslims in relation to urbanization and economic status.

Under this background, I would begin with Ganguly's contributions (some of them were written jointly with another meticulous anthropologist, Anadi Pal who was also known as a Physical anthropologist) on various topics of socio-cultural anthropology apart from his researches in the typical fields of Biological Anthropology, like anthropometry, dermatoglyphics, human genetics and dental anthropology (Ganguly 1960; Ganguly & Pal 1961, 1963b & 1974; Ganguly & Mukherjee 1964; Dutta & Ganguly 1965; Ganguly 1973a, 1976, 1978 &1979; Chaudhuri & Ganguly 1983). Because it is difficult to categorise an anthropologist like Pranab Ganguly into one of the subfields of anthropology. His solid papers in prestigious national and international peer-reviewed journals on religion, material culture, life-cycle rites and judicial system of the tribes in Andaman and Nicobar Islands during 1961-63 did not receive comprehensive treatment by the social and cultural anthropologists in India.

I would, therefore, start with one of his early papers on the religious beliefs among the Onges of Little Andaman. This paper entitled 'Religious beliefs of the Negritos of Little Andaman' was published in *The Eastern Anthropologist* in 1961. In this pioneering paper Ganguly described the cognition of the Onges about their supernatural world in vivid details. The ethnography emerged out of Ganguly's painstaking fieldwork during 1953-57 and he stayed among the hunting-gathering tribe for about eight months in total, learned their language without an interpreter and observed the everyday life of this little community. This short paper of only six pages on a difficult subject is remarkable for its clarity and density of ethnographic details through which the author finally reached a conclusion having wider significance. Let me quote:

> In the first place, though the Onge are one of the most primitive tribes of the world, the universe conceived by them is far from simple. It is indeed a remarkable creation of the unsophisticated Onge mind. The supernatural beings living in the different planes or layers of the Onge universe are, strictly speaking, neither divine nor immaterial. They eat, drink, marry, multiply and die just like human beings.....I did not find among the Onge any belief concerning a superior spirit or High God (Ganguly, 1961a: 247-248).

With Bimal Chandra Roy as the first author Ganguly wrote another ethnographic paper in Folklore in 1961 on the life-cycle customs and ceremonies of the Onges. The meticulous details of the paper in recording the Onge beliefs around birth, marriage and death were marvellous but at the same time the authors also mentioned their failure in recording the chants which were recited during the male initiation rites of the community (Roy & Ganguly 1961:370).

The next social anthropological paper of Ganguly which I would take up was an account on the material culture of the Jarawa of Great Andaman published jointly with Anadi Pal in the prestigious journal Ethnos of the Ethnographical Museum of Sweden in 1962. This study was done by Ganguly and Pal on the basis of observations and measurements made on a collection of Jarwa implements and weapons given by the Andaman and Nicobar Police Department to the researchers of the Anthropological Survey of India. This 15 page article contained detailed morphological description, measurement and diagrams of bows, arrows, bark armour, basket, bamboo vessel, bucket and resin torch. In addition we find in the article how the Jarwas used the spine of the tail of Sting-Ray (a cartilaginous fish related to sharks) to injure their enemies. The most interesting part of the article is the brief theoretical exercise attempted by the authors in the concluding section. I quote from the paper:

> Some anthropologists and linguists accept it as an axiom that language is the most stable part of culture that "linguistic changes do not proceed at the same rate as most cultural changes, which are on the whole far more rapid." But here we find that the differences between the Onge and Jarawa in respect of material culture are few and unimportant whereas linguistic differences between them are so great that the language of one is incomprehensible to the other. As we do not have adequate data on the culture history of Andaman Islanders, we are unable to offer any satisfactory explanation on the matter. It is, however, quite obvious that after the separation of the Onge from the Jarawa, which took place long ago, their languages underwent many changes in course of time, but their technologies changed very slowly, partly due to the lack of the pressure of social needs and partly due to the limitations imposed by the physical environment (Ganguly & Pal, 1962: 97).

Ganguly's other two articles on Car-Nicobarese oil press and Onge harpoon and spear (written jointly with A. Pal) also deserve attention from social anthropologists interested in the study of material culture and they were the result of his own fieldwork. These articles were published in Anthropos in 1961 and 1963 respectively. Both articles revealed Ganguly's interest in details. He never forgot to mention the measurements, in drawing the implements and describing almost graphically the method of their use. In the article on Onge harpoon and spear the authors did not hesitate to refute A.R.Radcliffe-Brown's assumption on the non-existence of harpoon and spear among the tribes of Little Andaman which included the Onge (Ganguly & Pal 1963a:557-560).The article on indigenous oil press is a beautiful example of simple description of material culture with photographs and diagrams, which are now-a-days almost absent in the writings of the social anthropologists (Ganguly,1961b: 934-935).

After material culture, I will briefly describe Ganguly's excursion in the area of political system found in one of the remote areas of Andaman Island. In 1960 Ganguly and Pal did their fieldwork in Chowra Island which was situated about 48 miles south of Car Nicobar. The fieldwork was conducted for three weeks to collect demographic and physical anthropological data but Ganguly's interest in social anthropology led him to gather useful information on the 'judicial organization' of the Chowra Islanders. The result of this social anthropological inquiry was published in an article in 1961 in Folklore under the title 'Some aspects of the judicial system in Chowra Island'. In this paper Ganguly and Pal first described the basic structure of governance in the island which was characterised by a territorial subdivision combined with ranked headmen and a supra-village chief. The chief and the 15 village headmen constituted a council (kanyu-u) which was the central authority in the island and the government administration of the Andaman and Nicobar also recognized the position of the chief and the village headmen and the government did not also intervene into the working of this tribal institution except in the cases of homicide. The most interesting aspect of this paper is the concrete case studies which were narrated in vivid details and according to the authors.

From the cases which were brought for trial to kanyu-u during the last few years several are presented....It is hoped that these concrete cases will represent the methods of administering justice in Chowra more clearly than what general statements can do (Ganguly & Pal, 1960: 155).

In the rest of the paper we find detailed cases under (a) drunkenness and assault upon wife, (b) sexual offence, (c) theft, (d) dispute about the ownership of land, and (e) homicide. If one reads the cases one will find the same remarkable clarity and logical consistency with which Ganguly described the religious life and the material culture of the Onge and the Jarwa of Andaman Islands. This paper on the judicial system, however, ended with a longer conclusion in which Ganguly and Pal noted the democratic way of dealing with allegations and disputes; although the chief of the island is the highest authority but he cannot decide a case without discussing the matter in the council. Furthermore, we learn from this important ethnographic account that in this patrilineal society of Chowra with primogeniture where women were not admitted to become head of the village or the chief of the island, women were ever punished. Even in cases of adultery it was usually the male who was held responsible (*Ibid*: 160).

Last in this series of social anthropological papers, I will mention a unique contribution of Ganguly on the ethno-history of the Nicobar islanders. In this long paper published in an off-beat journal (Journal of the Gujrat Research Society), Ganguly laboriously searched the ethnic history of the different population groups inhabiting the Nicobar Islands, which included the Shom-Pens. Unlike the typical social anthropologist Ganguly searched the ethnic origin of the Nicobarese from a bio-cultural perspective. Thus we find him collecting anthropometric and serological data as well as detailed information on demography, history, subsistence activities, social organisation and environment from all possible sources. Finally, with the help of the aforesaid data Ganguly postulated a sequence of migrations in the Nicobar Islands in a holistic framework (Ganguly, 1973: 234-270).

Ganguly's interest in the study of the Onges of Little Andaman took its final shape during the mid-seventies when he published a full-length paper entitled 'The Negritos of Little Andaman Island: a primitive people facing extinction' published in the *Indian Museum Bulletin* in 1975. This paper can be regarded as one of the finest work on policy anthropology. The paper covered almost every aspect of this small island tribe in the context of the global debate on the position of the anthropologists regarding the study of endangered and disappearing populations. Ganguly made his position clear after narrating the differences between two schools of thought on the task of the anthropologists. He quoted Sol Tax's 1971 editorial of Current Anthropology in which Tax observed a 'split' among the anthropologists on what should constitute the urgent task before them after the 8th International Congress of Anthropological and Ethnological Sciences held in 1968 in Tokyo. Should the anthropologists give priority to study the last speaker of a disappearing community to build up their theory or should they accept change as an obvious outcome and invest their time towards their development? Pranab Ganguly while studying the Onges clearly stated his position in the following manner.

> The author feels that the two approaches are not mutually exclusive, but are complimentary to each other. The study of vanishing tribes does not prevent anthropologists from being interested in urgent problems of development and change in large societies; both types of research may be carried on simultaneously (Ganguly, 1975: 8).

I will now describe how Ganguly made his attempt to combine the aforementioned approaches in his own way in the long article on Onge. Apart from the detailed and meticulous ethnography written in the classical Malinowskian style which also included the physical anthropology and demographic contours of the tribe Ganguly described the society and culture of the Onges like a professional social anthropologist. He described the material culture, subsistence activities, kinship, marriage, family, rites of passage, political organisation and the religion in a systematic and comprehensive manner. The most important part of the paper, however, is the section on the policy aspects around the major problem faced by the Onges which was their decreasing numbers. Ganguly investigated the problem of the depopulation of the Onges from a demographic perspective by carefully taking into consideration the three rival hypotheses, which were: (i) economic exploitation, (ii) assassination of the natives by the colonists, and (iii) introduction of new diseases against which the natives had no immunity. Ganguly was probably the first anthropologist who studied the Onges for a long period of time from a biosocial perspective and differed with the aforementioned hypotheses. The disagreement was based on his own observation and reading of the history of Little Andaman and he did not hesitate to state his policy recommendations towards the betterment of the tribe in a bold manner. In Ganguly's words:

> Ameliorative measures such as establishment of coconut plantations, introduction of horticulture, distribution of iron implements and other useful articles, carrying out routine health surveys and giving medical relief etc., though very useful and commendable, cannot prevent the decline of Onge population. These do not even touch the fringe of the real

> problem. Systematic investigations into the causes of Onge infertility and proper remedial measures against them are now urgently required (Ganguly, 1975: 25-26).

Finally, Ganguly proposed that as a long-term measure the Onges should be relocated in the Rutland Island 31 miles north of Little Andaman where they once lived but left the place to get away from an epidemic several decades ago. The island was capable of supporting the Onge population with their traditional mode of subsistence and Ganguly suggested that they should be allowed to live there without any outside interference because it would be increasingly difficult for them to survive in Little Andaman owing to 'the rising demands of officials and workers for pork, fish, honey, fruits, etc.' the staple food of the Onges (*Ibid*).

If we look at the works of Pranab Ganguly in a chronological order we find that during 1960-1966 he contributed in physical and social-cultural anthropology by using the methods of anthropometry, ethnography and linguistics with equal competence and his interest towards the formulation of policies was also visible in his later work on Onge, which I have just described in the previous sub-section. During the mid-seventies, Ganguly turned his attention towards macro-level data on large samples and he also organised his thoughts around the bigger problems of human adaptation and evolution in an ecosystem framework. In this context the research of Ganguly, and this was his most remarkable one, was on the gradual decline in average height (negative secular trend) in some tribal and caste populations in India. It was a remarkable finding published in an article in 1979. In this article Ganguly began this by challenging the then scholarship in biological anthropology, which presumed that the progressive increase in stature was a universal phenomenon as it happened in many technologically advanced western and non-Western countries. In this chapter he demonstrated with the help of simple anthropometric data that in India three groups out of every four have become shorter in varying degrees in course of one or two generations and it was not due to malnutrition or inbreeding but probably caused by a relaxation of natural selection against undersized individuals (Ganguly, 1979: 315-337).

In another pioneering study for which he had won the prestigious Bertillon Medal of France (in 1973) on the variation in physique in North India in relation to urbanization and economic status, Ganguly was able to show with the help of carefully controlled experimental design (rare in Indian physical anthropology) the relationship between various somatometric measurements and observations (e.g. height, weight and skin colour) and some socio-economic parameters. For example, he found that among the Brahmin and Muslim populations of western Uttar Pradesh in North India, the well-to-do men are significantly taller and heavier and have absolutely broader hips and shoulders than the poor. The increases in different measurements observed in the well-to-do clearly reflected a general enlargement in the size of the body. In the circumferential measurements of limbs and torso, the differences between the economic classes were particularly pronounced. The well-to-do men had significantly larger heads, larger in both length and breadth dimensions, than the poor (Ganguly, 1974a: 3-43).

The last remarkable work of Ganguly, which I will discuss was a theoretical paper entitled 'The problem of human adaptation: an overview' published in Man in India in 1977. In this brilliant article Ganguly viewed the major human problems of the modern world (e.g. malnutrition and inequality) from the perspective of adaptation. For him adaptation should be considered in its broadest sense which must include society and culture. Under a section in this paper entitled 'Socio-economic Milieu' Ganguly after reviewing the literature exhaustively including his own study on the Brahman and Muslim groups of western Uttar Pradesh commented.

From the foregoing discussion it should be evident that the socio-economic status effect manifests itself at every stage of life from birth to adulthood. The upper class children have significantly bigger bodies than the lower class children, and this difference persists to a remarkable degree in the final adult size. It may be argued that the genetic potential for growth of the Indian children, who suffer under the constraints of adverse socio-economic environment remains to some extent unrealized (Ganguly, 1977: 10).

But how does the poor really adapt to this adverse socio-economic deprivation? Ganguly's answer to this basic question can be found in the next section of the article titled 'Nutritional Stress'.

Adaption to malnutrition during critical stages of growth is likely to induce permanent reduction of body size which in turn will reduce the energy needs of the body. People having small body size will survive more easily on low calorie diets and they will have some adaptive advantage in areas where scarcity conditions prevail (*Ibid.*, pp. 10-11).

At this juncture one may ask a very legitimate question, which is 'Did Ganguly view poverty as a kind of adaptation only?' I would say 'yes, Ganguly looked at the unconscious strategies of survival of the poor but he also viewed the extremes of this adaptation. Let us proceed further with him through this paper.

It may be mentioned here that the survival of a population through diminution of body size and reduction of energy requirements is possible if only the nutritional deficiencies remain within tolerable limits. When the stress of malnutrition becomes very acute, the adaptive advantage of size reduction loses much of its significance and the population is threatened with the danger of extinction (*Ibid*, p.14).

Ganguly's paper on adaptation is a full-blooded bio-cultural exercise on macro-level policy issues and I regard this Indian Science Congress address of 1977 as the true successor of the lectures delivered by his teachers Tarak Chandra Das in 1941 and Sasanka Sekhar Sarkar in 1951 at the Congress. This is because like his predecessors Pranab Ganguly also dealt with the major national problems and the role of anthropology and anthropologists in providing some solutions to these problems.

Ganguly had a great interest in demography, particularly social demography. Interestingly his last article jointly written with Suvas Bose on the 'Population trends in Midnapore district, West Bengal, 1872- 1981' published in 1992 in the Vidyasagar University Journal of Social Sciences is a unique example of social demographic study of a district in India. This article is still not well known in the anthropological circles in the country. In the article Ganguly covered almost all the aspects of socio-demography of the erstwhile Midnapore district by consulting the Census reports of India. The most interesting finding of Ganguly and Bose in this paper is the decline of the population in the older townships of Midnapore district.

Pranab Ganguly visited Poland during June-July 1982 under Indo-Polish Cultural Exchange Programme for studying research methodology and recent trends and advances in physical anthropology in Poland. He was at that time employed at the Anthropological Survey of India. Many researchers from Anthropological Survey of India had gone to visit foreign countries to learn some specialised and technical matters and also for attending seminars and conferences but how many of them have written their day-to-day experience almost like an ethnographer? Pranab Ganguly wrote such an ethnography entitled 'Account of a visit to Poland' which was published in 1983 in the official journal of the Survey. This is 20 pages solid and interesting description of the author's encounter with a small European country, which at that time was governed by the communists. Ganguly's style of presentation is simple, straightforward but at the same time informative and interesting.

Pranab Ganguly as a professional anthropologist belonged to post-colonial India who practiced intensive fieldwork and published in physical and socio-cultural anthropology with equal competence . . . a rare quality among his contemporaries, which has almost vanished from the succeeding generations of anthropologists in India. Ganguly, however, was not a run-of-the-mill empirical anthropologist. His remarkable works on the progressive decline of stature among sixty endogamous population groups and the relationship of somatic variability with economic condition and urbanisation demonstrated Ganguly's ability to interpret huge mass of empirical data in a theoretical framework, which was basically bio-cultural in nature. Finally, it should be emphasised that Pranab Ganguly was not an ivory tower scholar, who only gathered knowledge but made sincere attempts to apply his findings in formulating policies for the welfare and betterment of the underprivileged sections of the Indian population whether they are the endangered Onges of Little Andaman or the vast majority of the undersized and malnourished people of independent India.

REFERENCES

Guha, A. 2016. Pranab Kumar Ganguly (In Memoriam). Anthropology News. 57 (7):e159-e160. (First Published online by The American Anthropological Association). http://www.anthropology-news.org/index.php/2016/07/25/pranab-kumar-ganguly/.

Directory of Anthropologists in India.1981. Pranab Ganguly, pp. 110-111. Edited by A. Basu, M.P. Basu, A.K. Adhikary. Calcutta: Anthropological Survey of India, Government of India.

Ganguly, P. 1960. Observations on the Teeth of Nicobar Islanders. *Bulletin of the Anthropological Survey of India*. IX (2): 43-50. Ganguly, P. & Pal, A. 1961. Morphology of Onge Foot. *Current Science*. 30(8): 300-301. Ganguly, P. & Pal, A. 1963b. Distribution of Middle Phalangeal Hair among Chowra and Terressa Islanders. *The Eastern Anthropologist*. XVI (2): 122-132. Ganguly, P. & Pal, A.1974. Secular trend in stature in India, pp.42-48. *Indian Anthropology Today*. (Ed.) D. Sen. Calcutta: Department of Anthropology, Calcutta University. Ganguly, P. & Mukherjee, D.P. 1964. Dermatoglyphics of the Shom-Pen of Great Nicobar. *Anthropos*. 59(5/6): 918-919. Dutta, P. & Ganguly, P. 1965. Further observations on ear lobe attachment. *Acta Genetica et Statistica Medica*.15 (1):77-86. Ganguly, P. 1973a. The Nicobar islanders: a search for their ethnic identity. *Journal of the Gujarat Research Society*. 35: 234-270. Ganguly, P. 1976. *Physical anthropology of the Nicobarese*. Memoir No. 34. Calcutta: Anthropological Survey of India. Ganguly, P. 1978. The physique of Nicobar islanders a study of sexual, populational, and spatial variation. *Indian Museum Bulletin*. 13:7-21. Ganguly, P. 1979. Progressive decline in stature in India: a study of sixty population groups. pp. 315-337. *Physiological and morphological adaption and evolution*. (Ed.) William A. Stini. The Hague: Mouton Publishers. Chaudhuri, Datta, S.S. & Ganguly, P.

1983. Fertility behaviour of female carriers of Haemophilia. *Journal of the Indian Anthropological Society*. 18: 51-54.

There was no recorded information on the religious life of the aborigines of Little Andaman when Ganguly conducted this study. A.R. Radcliffe-Brown's study was on the communities of Great Andaman and there were marked differences between the tribes of Great and Little Andaman as regards religious beliefs and Ganguly mentioned this fact in the first paragraph of his article (Ganguly, 1961:243). Ganguly, P. 1961a. Religious beliefs of the Negritos of Little Andaman. *The Eastern Anthropologist*. 14(3):243-248.

Three years later Ganguly published a 31-page detailed account on the vocabulary of the *Onge in the Bulletin of the Anthropological Survey of India,* which revealed his deep acquaintance with the language and its grammatical structure (Ganguly, 1966:1-30). Ganguly, P. 1966. Vocabulary of the Negritos of Little Andaman with grammatical notes and materials. *Bulletin of the Anthropological Survey of India*, 15(1-4):1-30.

Roy, B.C. & Ganguly, P. 1961. Some Ceremonial Customs in Onge Life-cycle. *Folklore*, 2(6); 368-374.

Ganguly, P. & Pal, A. 1962. Notes on the Material Culture of the Jarawa of Great Andaman: their Weapons and Implements. *Ethnos*. 27: 84-98.

Ganguly, P. 1961b. The Car-Nicobarese Oil-press. *Anthropos*. 56(5-6):934-935 & Ganguly, P. & Pal, A. 1963a.Onge harpoon and spear. *Anthropos*, 58(3-4):557-560.

Ganguly, P. & Pal, A.1960.Some aspects of the judicial system in Chowra Island. *Folklore*. 2(3): 153-160.

Ganguly's bio-cultural perspective was his life-long pursuit. At the end of his career he published an article 'The incidence of Arcus Senilis in Nicobar islands and the Nicobarese food habits' which is an example of this pursuit(Ganguly1989: 163-167). See Ganguly, P. 1989. The incidence of Arcus Senilis in Nicobar islands and the Nicobarese food habits. *Journal of the Anthropological Society of India*. 24:163-167.

Ganguly, P. 1973a.The Nicobar islanders: a search for their ethnic identity. *Journal of the Gujrat Research Society*. 35:234-270.

Under the section entitled 'Depopulation of the Little Andaman Island' Ganguly noted that there were only 121 Onge individuals in the Little Andaman Island in 1969.

Ganguly, P. 1975. The Negritos of Little Andaman Islands: a primitive people facing extinction. *Indian Museum Bulletin*. 10(1): 7-27.

Ganguly did not even exclude the sexual life of the tribe in his description. Thus we find him depicting the Onge method of sexual intercourse which was different from the typical missionary posture. At the same time Ganguly also frankly admitted his own shortcomings whenever he failed to collect any ethnographic data.

Ganguly, P. 1975. The Negritos of Little Andaman Islands: a primitive people facing extinction. *Indian Museum Bulletin*. 10(1): 7-27.

Ganguly, P. 1979. Progressive decline in stature in India: a study of sixty population groups, pp. 315-337. *Physiological and morphological adaption and evolution*. (Ed.) William A. Stini. The Hague: Mouton Publishers.

Ganguly, P. 1974a. Variation in physique in North India in relation to urbanization and economic status. In: *Bulletins et Mémoires de la Société d'anthropologie de Paris*, XIII Série, tome 1 fascicule 1, 1974, pp. 3-43.

Ganguly, P. 1977. The problem of human adaption: an overview. *Man in India*, 57(1):1-22. This paper was delivered as Presidential Address at the Anthropology and Archaeology Section of the 64th Indian Science Congress in Bhubaneswar held in 1977.

One may note that Ganguly used the term 'class' not 'caste' since his empirical findings revealed class differentiation within a caste was more important to understand the human biological variation in India—a point little recognized by the social anthropologists. It may be interesting to recall here Ganguly's comment published in Current Anthropology on Joan P. Mencher's famous article 'The caste system upside down or the not-so-mysterious East' in 1974. I quote from Ganguly, 'From my field investigations in 12 districts of western Uttar Pradesh, I have gained the impression that the North Indian Brahmans are really no better-off than the low-ranked agricultural castes of that area' (Ganguly, 1974b:482). See Ganguly, P. 1974b. Comment on J.P. Mencher. *Current Anthropology*, 15(4): 482-483.

After this statement Ganguly cited the case of the Juang population of Orissa and mentioned the findings of a biochemist, J.K.Roy of the Anthropological Survey of India who found that owing to severe malnutrition the Juang population was decreasing for the last 25 years.

Ganguly, P. & Bose, S. 1992. Population trends in Midnapore district, West Bengal, 1872-1981. *Vidyasagar University Journal of Social Sciences*, Inaugural Number, pp.1-13.

Ganguly, P. 1983. Account of a visit to Poland. *Human Science*, 32(1): 13-32.

T.C. Das's lecture entitled 'Cultural Anthropology in the Service of the Individual and the Nation' and the title of S.S.Sarkar's lecture was 'The Place of Human Biology in Anthropology and its utility in the Service of the Nation'. Das's lecture was published by the Indian Science Congress Association and the lecture of Sarkar was published in Man in India in 1951.See Sarkar, S.S. (1951).The place of human biology in anthropology and its utility in the service of the nation. Man in India. 31(1), 1-22.

Tax, S. 1971. Urgent Anthropology: Associates' views on the definition of "urgency". *Current Anthropology*. 12(2):243-254.

22
Professor J.D. Mehra

Anthropologist and Poet

Vinay Kumar Srivastava

Professor Jai Dayal Mehra, popularly known as Dr. Mehra or Mehra sahib, was a teacher of social anthropology, retiring as professor, a position he got on 11 April, 1977. In his early years, however, before Dr. D.K. Bhattacharya was appointed as an archaeology teacher, he also taught a paper on prehistoric archaeology to the master's classes.

He was born on 28 January, 1924 in Delhi, although the date of birth entered into his official records was 15 December, 1923. It was not uncommon those days that the date of birth registered in the official papers differed from the actual, and so was the case with Dr. Mehra. Each year, till he fell ill and was bed-ridden, he celebrated his birthday on 28 January, an occasion on which he invited his old friends, many of whom had done extremely well in their respective careers.

He was born to one of the distinguished families of bureaucrats and technocrats of Delhi, and was brought up in the posh, upper class, and quiet area of Connaught Place called Hanuman Lane, named so because of its proximity to the famous Hanuman Temple. He read for a master's in English literature from the University of Delhi. As was not exceptional those days, Dr. Mehra decided to do another master's, this time from a newly founded Department of Anthropology. He belonged to the first batch of students (1948, the department being founded in 1947) which was admitted to a master's programme in anthropology. His class fellows who later stayed as faculty in the department were Professors Indera P. Singh and S.C. Tiwari. Before enrolling himself as an anthropology student, neither did he visit the department nor asked anyone about the subject matter of anthropology. What he knew was the dictionary meaning of the term anthropology, which, as he once told me, paid a lot of emphasis to races and migration of people across continents. Under the garb of anthropology, it was the meaning of ethnology that was being propagated.

What actually pulled him towards anthropology was his reading of Sir James Frazer's *The Golden Bough*, which provided rich material about the non-Western societies. Frazer's lengthy, absorbing discussion of magical practices really attracted him. This was one of the reasons of his lifelong interest being kindled in the anthropology of religion, a course he taught year after year to the students of M.Sc. and M.Phil. His teachers in the anthropology department did not stimulate him enough, neither did some topics in physical anthropology which were being taught in classes, for the head of his department, Professor P.C. Biswas, was principally a physical anthropologist and gave a lot of importance to its learning. Thus, it was not just a matter of co-incidence that his class fellows (Professor Indera P. Singh and Tiwari) opted to devote themselves to physical anthropology, and so were the others from the batches of students immediately after his, who continued to pursue academics (like Professors J.D. Mavalwala, M.R. Chakravarty, and Abhimanyu Sharma). What kept Dr. Mehra glued to anthropology was the family resemblance he could see between English literature and anthropology. He carried out a field study respectively for his master's thesis, and later for his doctorate – his thesis of 1959 titled the 'Ethnological Study of the Shokas' was done under the supervision of Professor Biswas and its examiners were Dr. J.H. Hutton, Dr. B.S. Guha and Mr. Verrier Elwin. However, he enjoyed fieldwork the least, although for almost each year till the early 1970s, he accompanied the undergraduate and postgraduate students for their annual round of field study. What truly fascinated him was an array of theoretical ideas. That was the reason why he was highly dissatisfied with a plain account of facts; and that was the reason of many students not joining the specialization in social anthropology, for he was the only teacher those days who supervised doctoral theses in this branch of anthropology, and he expected a good understanding of abstract and theoretical ideas from his disciples. Students found physical anthropology far more amiable than social anthropology, and even when they did not want to study physical anthropology, they had to do it perforce, for Dr. Mehra was a demanding teacher who expected that his students would keep pace with theoretical debates and also improve upon their linguistic skills. He always insisted that one would taste success in social anthropology when one was linguistically competent and kept on improving upon one's vocabulary.

After completing his master's in anthropology, Dr. Mehra got a teaching position at Gauhati University. There, he remembered, his wit, the sharpness of his observations and comments, his comparative knowledge, and writing ability matured. Later, in 1961, he contributed an article on polyandrous Jaunsaris to the *Bulletin of the University of Gauhati*. During this stay, he also cultivated life-long friendship with the local faculty, and also with those who visited the Department of Anthropology, University of Gauhati. It was here that he met Dr. B.K. Roy Burman and remained in touch with him and his wife, Bina Deka, for years. It was in his house that I met with Professor Bhuban M. Das. Still fresh in my mind is the animated discussion these two anthropologists had on cigar, its types, the class background of its smokers, and the legendries famous for enjoying its smoke!

After spending a year at Guwahati, Dr. Mehra moved to Delhi University to teach anthropology on 26 February, 1953, becoming a reader on 25 July, 1961, and stayed with the department till his retirement on 14 December, 1988. As he had not completed his courses, since those days the University had the annual mode of examination, he wanted to continue with his teaching even after his retirement till the end of the academic year. The then head of the department, Professor Raghbir Singh, agreed to Dr. Mehra's proposal, and so the farewell party that was being organized for him on 14 December, under the convenership of Professor Aloke K. Kalla, was postponed for May 1989. I wrote a short article on Dr. Mehra for this occasion, which later I got printed with my own money for private distribution. After Dr. Mehra's demise on 29 July, 2016, it was published in *Man in India* as homage to him.

As usual after his retirement, Dr. Mehra kept coming to the department regularly, conducted all classes as per the time-table, and imparted supervisory instructions to his doctoral students. He vacated his department office quietly in the first week of June 1989, handing over a large collection of his books to his students and young colleagues, departing from the department premises with half a dozen of his books, which included Marvin Harris's *Rise of Anthropological Theory*, Harry Shapiro's edited volume titled *Man, Culture and Society*, and Claude Lévi-Strauss's *Structural Anthropology* (Volume 1). Later, these books came to me with his signatures. Needless to say, they are a part of my prized possession. Once he left the department, he never visited it. He was also not interested in knowing anything about the happenings in the department, nor its members. This sense of detachment with the department, a place he had served for more than thirty-six years, was exemplary.

During his entire career as a teacher of anthropology, Dr. Mehra was on leave for not more than a fortnight, once (in January 1971) when his wife passed away, then, when he went abroad, and lastly, when his children got married. He maintained excellent health, which he attributed to his habit of eating with frugality, and refraining from time-wasting gossips and stresses. It was amazing he would lecture a master's class for not less than three hours, standing and walking briskly from one corner of the podium to the other, without a modicum of weariness on his person and also, not drinking a drop of water, or going out to relieve himself. What an amazing control on his body! And then, after a marathon class, he would return to his room to supervise his research students, spending hours with them. He was charitable with time for his students, and did not allow any of them to go ahead with submission unless he had discussed the ideas that the dissertation endeavoured to espouse. After retirement, it was a life of leisure and cogitation that he cherished the most. However, if a former student ever visited him, he was at his best in discussing the current anthropological topics with him or her.

When Dr. Mehra began with his master's in anthropology, the department had three teachers. Besides Dr. Biswas, the other two were Mrs. Hilda Raj and Mrs. Freda Mukherjee. Dr. Mehra was respectful towards them, but did not regard anyone of them as his mentor, or one who exercised great impact on him. He cultivated a lifelong association with Professor Tiwari, with whom he also shared several personal ties. The other member of the department with whom he had academic relationship, and also used to drive him to the university campus for several years, was Dr. Sharma. Later, he developed close ties with Dr. Ram D. Sanwal, a doctorate in anthropology from London, and Professor I.S. Marwah, formerly his doctoral student. Besides this small group of his colleagues, Dr. Mehra rarely interacted with any other person, and so was often criticised for being 'elitist', 'snobbish', 'alienated', and 'aloof'.

Dr. Mehra produced a whole generation of exceptionally gifted and brilliant anthropologists, of which some are J.S. Yadav, Subhashini Subramanyam, Shalina Mehta, Subhadra Mitra Channa, P.C. Joshi, and Krishna Mahapatra. Dr. Mehra's innovativeness was reflected in the topics his students chose for doctoral work. For instance, Yadav studied factionalism in Haryana; Channa worked on urban anthropology, which was rather rare those days, carrying out an intensive study of the community of washerpersons; Mehta wrote a thesis on Hindu-Muslim realtions; Joshi was the pioneer of medical anthropological studies in the department; and Mahapatra restudied the community of Bondo

Highlanders in Odisha. There were several others whose doctoral theses Dr. Mehra did not supervise, but they were immensely benefited with his suggestions and comments. One of them was my wife, Kumkum, whose doctoral thesis on Qalandars had a distinct touch of Dr. Mehra's scholarship; and when her book was published, she dedicated it to Dr. Mehra, for teaching her the meaning of love and life. To say the least, Dr. Mehra was one of the most original, divinely-ordained thinkers, who created anthropology *de novo* in the precincts of classrooms and tutorial groups.

In a conventional sense, Dr. Mehra did not have a mentor; neither did he enjoy the patronage of anyone. He was a self-made and self-taught person. His path-showers were his books. He loved to talk on a variety of subjects in informal gatherings almost uninterruptedly. It was in these 'discourses' that he serendipitously chanced upon new thoughts, but he scarcely paid attention to writing them up. The listeners however reaped the benefits of these ideas. Many well-known anthropologists of those days (Professors V.N. Misra, S.C. Dube, S.R.K. Chopra, T.N. Madan, André Béteille, Gopala Sarana) used to visit him – some spending their evenings in his palatial house – and the conversations bubbled with ideas, discussions, polemics. I was privileged to witness some of these meetings. I used to keep a notebook with me, committing to writing any new idea that came up during their conversations.

Professor Biswas retired in 1968, and Professor Indera P. Singh became the second Head of the Anthropology Department. Those days headship was not rotated among the faculty members. Professor Indera P. Singh continued as head for eleven years, when was promulgated the principle of rotation for headship. According to the new rule, a person would serve as head for three years, and then be replaced by the next one in order of seniority.

Dr. Mehra became the Head of the Department in 1979, a position he least enjoyed. For him, administrative duty was onerous. He hardly liked sitting in the head's room, poring over the files, and exercising his authority. As the head, he was also a member of the Academic Council of the University. He once told me that during the long, unbearably boring and tedious meetings, he would solve cross-word puzzles with Professor Margaret Chatterjee (of philosophy), who was also a member of the Academic Council.

Before eleven months of his headship could finish, Dr. Mehra had to face a stiff protest from the non-teaching staff of the department concerning the payment to be made to them for conducting the practical examinations. As he could not withstand the pressure of administrative problems, he quietly went to the Vice-Chancellor's office and submitted his resignation. It was shocking to the department, but all knew that Dr. Mehra's heart was not in administration. Basically, he was a teacher, not an inspector. He was a member of cultural elite, not administrative.

Till his retirement, he did not hold any administrative position, devoting him completely to lecturing and supervising his students. He did not ever have a research project from any funding agency, nor did he have any foreign collaboration, although some foreign anthropologists were his friends, like Professors A.C. Mayer, Owen M. Lynch, McKim Marriott, David G. Mandelbaum, and F.G. Bailey. In his entire career, he travelled outside India only once (in 1974) to attend a W.H.O. meeting in Geneva. Within India, his travel was highly limited. After his wife died in January 1971, he did not accompany any group of students for fieldwork, since he had to look after his young children. When his children grew up, he consented to be a member of the selection committees for teaching positions in universities outside Delhi.

Dr. Mehra did not publish much later in his career. During this time, he did a couple of papers jointly with Professor Mehta. He wrote an article on tribal India for a popular book that Rajiv Gandhi Foundation published. However, in the beginning of his career, he was a regular contributor to the department journal titled *The Anthropologist*, founded in 1954. He also did some publications jointly with Professor Tiwari in *Vanyajati*.

In its first issue of *The Anthropologist* was published his paper on the Naiks of Ramgarh and the effect of acculturation on them. Here, in line with the other studies that had examined the deleterious effects of acculturation on small communities, he drew attention to the pathos in the lives of Naiks in following words: "The Naiks in question seem to have lost their grip in life, and their energy, confidence and gusto all appear to have been lost. They verily exist, quite unable to forge ahead in a dynamic surge as all other healthy full-blooded cultures would wont to be" (pp. 33-34). In another article in the same journal (IV [3-4]: 32-44), on the Shokas of Almora district, Dr. Mehra's frank description would stay in the mind of a reader (p. 39): "Poverty perforce leads to uncleanliness, and insanitation adds to the danger of disease and ill health. The people are very dirty and are clothed in rags and tatters. Their bodies are very often covered with festering sores." Writing on the kinship system of the Shokas (*The Anthropologist*, 1959), Dr. Mehra demonstrated that they belonged to the category of bifurcate-merging (the Iroquois system) terminology, where the father is classified with his brother and separated from the mother's brother, and similarly, the mother and her sister are lumped in the same term, and distinguished from father's sister. By this example, he demonstrated the principle of the unity of the sibling group. One of his oft-consulted papers was on the practice of snake-worship among the Nayars of South India (*Man in India*, 36: 132-39), and the other on social change, published in a book that Dr. K.S. Mathur had edited (in 1973). In addition, he also reviewed a number of books, some for academic journals, and the others for the radio programmes. His reviews are remembered for his acerbic comments; for instance, in his review of N.K. Bose's *Cultural Anthropology and Other Essays* (*The Anthropologist*, 1954, 1[1]: 53), he wrote: "[it is] a somewhat unmerited sketchy overtone." However, it was a little intriguing to note that to the Special Volume of *The Anthropologist* (1969), dedicated to Professor Biswas, Dr. Mehra did not make a contribution.

"If Dr. Mehra loved someone, he did unconditionally; the reverse was also true", said one of his students, a glimpse of which could easily be gathered from a profoundly touching obituary on him that Professor Mehta wrote for the *Indian Anthropologist* (2016, 46 [2]: 127-9). His overwhelming emotions are clear in his poems, written both in Urdu and English, but as he did with his anthropology, he did not ever contemplate their publication. But his nonchalance about publication had another facet: His actual 'texts' were his students and visitors, who like the now extinct blotting-papers, absorbed as many of his thoughts as they could and used these variously the way they liked, in their writings, speeches, and lectures. Remembering him fondly, I close this short article on him with one of his poems of 5 January, 2002.

In all of time, there is no time,
for me to tell you, how much I love you.
And all the words that ever rhyme,
can scarce define, your marvel true.

For love was an interlude fair,
A time out of time.
And the here was the there.
A believing beyond credulity.

When were you when you were not,
The very ground of my being,
The wistful light of my heart's delight,
The unseeing eye ever seeing,

The turmoil of my heart, the fever in my veins,
When came you that came you not,
To hold me by the hand,
to walk me down.
the treacherous path of a loveless barren land,
You became not,
for you ever were, the patch of blue,
in a darkening sky.

One look and I had my fill,
all the world around stood still,
Peopled but by you and me,
Our gaze, a promise unto eternity,
You the serene beauty of morning wore,
Emblazoned on your lips,
And a thousand blossoms mingling wove,
for you a garland of beauty divine.

It came to be what was not to be,
Strange marvel of illusion's reality,
Draped in the raiment of love, a resplendent dream,
Evoked visions of immortality,
It came to go and went away,
and wouldn't bide when called to stay.

Kindleless spark within my heart,
Awakened the lyre that lonely lies,
Nightly come even if with the dawn to part,
Tomorrow's bleakness I'll have the strength to bide,
In the memory of the joy that this night imparts,
Mix me a heavy opiate, with your eyes,
Enchant my being with a caressing touch,
But hasten even now, the dark night departs,
And red the dawn impatient for birth dries.
And slowly fades the vision of my dream.

All my days have gone astray,
circling in futile motion,
And step by step nears the grave,
Nemesis in annihilation.

I looked to see, if I could be
Of any relevance to the world,

But what I sought, was not my lot,
For the world went by, without me,
What then was I to do, to live this life askew.

Pointless in its irrelevancy,
Or seek to find, a kindred mind,
That likewise thrilled to its poignancy,
I looked about lost in doubt,
Went here and there, in and out,
And chanced upon a forlorn soul,
That likewise know not,
what was the goal.

Ah! Me what joy it was to be,
Comforted by each other's relevancy,
Till a gnawing doubt about us thrust,
As the world went by without us,
Two irrelevancies in infinity.

23
The Anthropological Journey of Professor D.N. Majumdar

Keya Pandey

I have a deep personal connect with Professor D.N. Majumdar. Though I was born years after he passed, I feel his keen presence in the corridors of the Lucknow University's Anthropology Department, which he established, and where I currently teach. I not only have the good fortune of working in the same chamber in the department, which was once his workplace, but also by some strange, and happy coincidence, of getting allotted the same old house, 78, Badshah Bagh, in the University, which once housed him, and where he played the gracious host of numerous happy parties.

Dhirendra Nath Majumdar was born of Bengali parents on June 3, 1903 in Patna. His father Rebati Mohan Majumdar, belonged to the landed gentry, being a Zamindar of the Kushumhaty estate in East Bengal; his mother Kusum Kumari was the sister of a magistrate at Patna. He passed his Matriculation and Intermediate Science examinations with first division in both, from the Dacca Government College, Dacca. Thereupon, he graduated with distinction from the Faculty of Arts of the University College, Calcutta. He read Anthropology for his Masters at Calcutta University, getting deeply trained in both cultural and physical aspects of the subject, and was placed in the first division and also secured the first position, in 1924. Honours started coming his way early. He started his first fieldwork, choosing the Ho of Chhota Nagpur, and recognizing the quality of his original work in 1926, the Calcutta University awarded the Premchand Roychand Scholarship to him; at the time, it was considered quite a prestigious award. In 1929, the Calcutta University further awarded him the Mout Gold Medal.

The University of Lucknow, meanwhile, had been established in 1921, and the doyen of Indian sociologists, Prof. Radha Kamal Mukherjee, the founder and Head of the Department of Economics and Sociology, was scouting for talent. By then, the promise of Professor Majumdar had been spotted not just by the venerable S.C. Roy, encouraged by whom the former was about to undertake further fieldwork in the Chhota Nagpur plateau, but also by the Government, which had nominated him to the post of Sub-Collector. The academic in him, however, rejected the Government's offer, and the bureaucracy's loss became academia's lasting gain. After Sarat Chandra Roy, it would be Professor Majumdar who would carry forward the traditions of fieldwork in India. The shift to Lucknow finally happened in 1928, when Professor Majumdar became a Lecturer in the University of Lucknow's Department of Economics and Sociology, and started lecturing on 'Primitive Economics'.

In 1933, he went to Cambridge to study for his Doctorate under Professor T.C. Hodson. For his fieldwork, he again chose the Ho in the Kolhan region of Chhota Nagpur. This study became a general basis for his study of society, in later stages. For his work on culture contact and acculturation among the Ho, Professor Majumdar was awarded his Ph.D. degree from Cambridge University in 1935. While in England, he had been invited to deliver a course of lectures on Indian culture at Cambridge, which was quickly followed, by his being elected as a fellow of the Royal Anthropological Institute of Great Britain and Ireland in 1936. During this period, he also visited Vienna for delivering a series of lectures on tribal cultures in India. In England he had attended Bronislaw Malinowski's seminars at the London School of Economics and had come under his abiding influence, and started regarding him as his teacher. Besides, the writings of Ruth Benedict had also impacted him greatly.

The doctoral work of Professor Majumdar was published in 1937, titled '*A Tribe in Transition: A study in Culture Pattern*' and is widely considered as the first scientific work in India in the field of acculturation. The dynamic nature of culture and the influence modernity can have upon simpler people, always remained a subject close to his heart and found place invariably in his monographs. The 'base' of a culture, he wrote, is a function of four variables, namely man, area, resources, and cooperation. His approach could be shortened to MARC, or Man, Area, Resource and Cooperation. The relationship between these four elements was supposed to guide the existence of any society. Man here referred to human beings having certain biological needs and physical properties. Area referred to the spaces which they occupied, the geographical referent which forms the basis of their existence. Resource signified the materials available in the spaces that they occupied. Finally, cooperation indicated the relationships between the human beings studied. The harmony among all these four elements led to a functional unity in society. He started stressing the integrated character of culture, holding that cultural stresses and strains are the outcome of a disturbance in a culture's 'base', and that this unity sometimes broke down due to external pressures. Using this model Majumdar claimed that the Hos were being influenced due to external pressures.

He could see that primitive tribes were declining and this was for him a primary concern as an anthropologist. An advanced culture impinging on a simple and passive society, according to him, was causing such a decline. He did not agree that this could be stopped by creating reserves for tribes so that they may not be influenced, or by including them very closely within the Hindu fold as a backward form of Hinduism. He advocated for their integration into Indian society, a form that he called "creative or generative adaptation."

Professor Majumdar maintained that although changes keep on taking place in a culture, it still retains its character of being an integrated whole. His view of culture was thus essentially integrationist, though not static. However, in this, he did not distinguish whether this integration was of content and function (Malinowski) or of formal integration (Benedict). He also stressed upon the importance of studying the psychological dimensions of human behaviour, particularly in the study of culture change, as he had found many such changes occurring among the Ho (Majumdar, 1937a). He believed that dominant groups should give respect to those communities that were backward or downtrodden. Social change, in his opinion, should not be disruptive, but should be in continuity with existing cultural traditions.

After his studies abroad, Professor Majumdar rejoined his post in Lucknow University in 1939. The same year he presided over the Anthropology and Archaeology Section of the 26th Session of the Indian Science Congress held at Lahore.

In 1941, Professor Majumdar became a fellow of the National Institute of Sciences. He was also elected a fellow of the American Association of Physical Anthropology. In spite of his specialization in Social Anthropology, Professor Majumdar had managed to keep up with related subjects, and while in England, had learnt Physical Anthropology from Prof. G.M. Morant and Serology from Prof. RR Gates, who taught him advanced techniques in the field (Madan, 1961). His work in the field of physical anthropology comprises mainly the extensive anthropometric and serological surveys carried out by him amongst the tribal and caste groups of Bihar, Madhya Pradesh, Uttar Pradesh, Gujarat, and Bengal, covering thousands of individuals.

Right from the beginning of his career, Professor Majumdar had started stressing upon the significance of statistical techniques for analyzing anthropometric and serological data. In 1945, he was invited by Professor P.C. Mahalanobis, F.R.S., Director of the Indian Statistical Institute, Calcutta, to undertake an anthropometric and serological survey of Bengal. In 1946-47, he was invited by P.G. Shah, on behalf of the Gujarat Research Society, to undertake a similar survey in Gujarat. Applying statistical tools to serological data, he could establish the genetic relationship of the populations of Uttar Pradesh with those of Bengal as well as Punjab. He could also demonstrate that in Uttar Pradesh there was a "biometric basis" to the caste hierarchy, and that those castes which comprised "clusters," i.e. which were close to each other in the hierarchy, were shown to be within a close range of biometric variation. Though he had used racial factors in his analysis, he was opposed to the concept of race and was not fond of single factor explanations in caste studies (Madan and Sarana, 1964).

Professor Majumdar's use of the techniques of physical anthropology did not remain confined to the distribution studies of racial characters; he was also interested in the issues of health, disease and genetic development, especially amongst school children. An important landmark in Indian physical anthropology is his study of school children of Lucknow city. (Majumdar, 1951d).

In *The Fortunes of Primitive Tribes*, Professor Majumdar provides an overview of the social and cultural life of various tribes of Uttar Pradesh. His oeuvre includes detailed ethnographies of the Ho of the Chhota Nagpur plateau, the Khasa of Jaunsar-Bawar in the Himalayas, the Gonds of Bastar, the Bhil of Gujarat and the so-called criminal tribes of U.P. Professor Majumdar's fieldwork was always conducted through local dialects and covered all the major aspects of culture – economics, kinship, marriage, religion etc. (Majumdar, 1944).

In 1946, Professor Majumdar became a Reader in Anthropology in the Department of Economics and Sociology at the Lucknow University, and as Professor in the same Department in 1950. In 1951, Professor Majumdar established a separate Department of Anthropology at Lucknow University, the third Indian university in this regard, following Calcutta (1920) and Delhi (1947); he was its Founder-Head. Due to his training in both the cultural and physical aspects of anthropology, as also pre-history, he was a firm believer in the same broad-based training in the new department. As a result, he formulated courses including physical anthropology, prehistoric archeology and cultural anthropology at both the undergraduate and postgraduate levels. He worked hard to build the Department from scratch, assembling a brilliant group of colleagues and mentoring several fine students in the years to come. His style combined research with teaching, the Department becoming a hub of various research projects, many of them respected international organisations, with Professor Majumdar himself organizing and supervising many of them.

Despite his evident stature of which he couldn't have been unaware, Professor Majumdar retained a self-effacing attitude. In his Introduction to *The Matrix of Indian Culture* (1947), which was a collection of a series of articles he delivered at the Nagpur University under the Shri Mahadeo Hari Wathodkar Memorial Foundation he wrote "I accepted the invitation of the University of Nagpur, not because I was competent to deliver the goods but because I did not want to forego [this] offer…" (Majumdar, 1947).

Professor D.N. Majumdar was acutely conscious of the need for the new political dispensation of independent India to uplift the backward and downtrodden sections of society. He wrote: "Today, when a new wave of optimism is thrilling the countryside, the fate of these voiceless millions must be simultaneously worked out from there can be no two futures for the people of the same country. These primitive tribes are living their life in inaccessible and remote hills and fastnesses and their problems which were not known or even heard of must be assessed today in the interest of social justice…" (Majumdar, 1947).

He remained a votary of problem-oriented research work based on theory rather than mere ethnography. He writes in his book *Matrix of Indian Culture*: "Mere writing an account of a tribe or some aspect of its cultural life does not make the author an anthropologist just as a protest against the infringement of the civic rights of man, does not make the man who protests, a politician." (Majumdar, 1947).

By this time, Professor D.N. Majumdar was a hugely respected figure in academia. In 1949 he was appointed as one of the honorary editors of the prestigious journal, *Man in India* from which he resigned in 1955. In 1950, the Gujarat Research Society, Bombay, decorated him with their Research Medal for his contributions to physical anthropology. The same year he was appointed as a full Professor at the Department of Economics and Sociology, at the University of Lucknow. The very next year, in 1951, he was appointed to be the first head of the new Department of Anthropology at the University of Lucknow. He was also elected a Fellow of the American Association of Physical Anthropologists in 1953. The same year he was invited by the Planning Commission, Government of India, to become a member of its Research Programmes Committee. Visiting professorships, in 1952-53, at Cornell University, in 1958-59 at the School of Oriental and African Studies, London, and at the Institute of the Social Sciences at The Hague in 1959, soon followed. In 1958 the Asiatic Society of Bengal, decided to award him the Annandale Memorial Gold Medal for his contributions to Asian Anthropology. In 1958, he was invited by the Government of India to become a member of the Central Advisory Board for Anthropology, and by the Indian Council of Medical Research to become a member of its governing body. He became a sought after presence in international conferences, attending the International Symposium in Anthropology at New York in 1952, where he represented India, Pakistan and Ceylon at the International Symposium on Anthropology organised by the Wenner-Gren Foundation, and co-chaired a session with Julian H. Steward. He attended the International Sociological Congress at Paris in 1954. Because of his interest in problems of morbidity and demography among tribal cultures, he became a member of the International Union for the Scientific Study of Population, and the United Nations appointed him as a delegate to the World Congress on Population at Rome, 1954. He also chaired a section at the International Conference on Human Relations held at The Hague in 1956. He was also elected the General President of the Second All-India Sociological Conference held at Patna.

The vast rural belt of Uttar Pradesh had attracted Prof. Morris Opler as early as 1947. This was part of the post Second World War push among academics the world over to ensure that the fruits of development reached the most needy people in the newly decolonized countries. Being the most populous state in the second most populous country made Uttar Pradesh the prime focus of this academic push. Prof. Opler's continual efforts and his repeated training programmes in Uttar Pradesh started drawing not only a number of graduate students from Cornell University, but also provided an incentive to Indian scholars like Professor D.N. Majumdar and S.C. Dube to undertake and encourage village studies in India, and specifically in Uttar Pradesh. It also made Uttar Pradesh a bastion of village studies (Vidyarthi,1976).

Having had an early interest in culture change, Professor D.N. Majumdar played a tireless role in encouraging the new field of village studies in India. From studying tribal societies, he turned to undertake the microscopic study of the villages in UP, at first in collaboration with Opler and later on, independently with his team of students. The creation of a dedicated band of student-scholars to undertake studies in this little explored area of research was also a great service by Dr. Majumdar (Vidyarthi, 1976).

His Caste and Communications in an Indian Village (1958b) presents a model of an anthropological village study: It was the first anthropological village study in India. This study was undertaken under the aegis of the Cornell-Lucknow Research Project, set up under an MoU between Cornell University and Lucknow University and financed by the Ford Foundation: It was signed by Prof. Morris Opler and Professor D.N. Majumdar, both being fellow joint directors of the project.

Mohana village of Lucknow district, with a population of 603, was chosen for a baseline study with the aim of yielding benchmark data on rural progress and social awareness. A holistic study of Mohana was started towards the end of 1953 and lasted for about two years, and was conducted with the help of field investigators. Later on, a backward village of Mirzapur district, a tribal-*cum*-rural centre, where the community development programmes were functioning, was also chosen under this project. When Cornell prematurely withdrew from its India programme at Rankhandi village in Saharanpur, the Planning Commission stepped in to fill the void, and fund this project. While Mohana saw an ethnographically oriented approach, in Dhanaura village of Dudhi Block of Mirzapur, the focus was on culture change and the impact of community development programmes on rural life (Majumdar, 1958b).

Professor Majumdar was a firm believer in applied anthropology. He emphasized that although the findings of cultural anthropologists may not be of obvious practical value as the findings of physical anthropologists are, yet the former could provide government and society with knowledge indispensable in the conscious shaping of the future. As a member of the Standing Committee of the Research Programmes Committee of the Planning Commission from 1955 to 1960, he underscored the role which the anthropologist could play in helping the Government by studying the problems of backward areas and peoples and analyzing the implementation of the various schemes meant for their welfare (Madan and Sarana, 1964). His plea, which seems a truism now, was regarding the findings of the anthropologists involved in such village studies to be deployed by the Government to the task of national development (Majumdar , 1955a, 1956b).

While the Sanskritisation model was in vogue in India, Professor Majumdar suggested a process in contrast to it in his book *Rural Profiles*. While there was a sacred status of caste, there was a distinct secular status; and the caste hierarchy worked through the mediation of both under the influence of modern conditions. While Sanskritization was a model of upward mobility, Majumdar found that Brahmins and other upper castes also try to identify and imitate other castes.He recorded that the caste mobility happens, both vertically and horizontally. His work included the description of not just the people's religious beliefs and practices, but also their leadership, factionalism and the inter-caste relationship. He also identified the reasons responsible for the formation of new social groups, for example their unity and differences. In his view the village was a concept because it was a constellation of values which changed very gradually, leading to the village retaining its identity (Majumdar, 1955, 1956).

His book *Chhor Ka Ek Gaon*, is based on the research undertaken in 1955 at village Chittora in Mirzapur district under his and Cornell's M.R. Goodall's direction as part of the Cornell-Lucknow research project. Majumdar's manuscript in English, was translated by one of his students Chandra Bhal Tripathi, who was later Deputy Director of Backward Classes Commission. This book is significant in many ways. Firstly, because it showcases Professor D.N. Majumdar's attempt to study a village type in which tribes reside with the Hindu castes, and who have got detribalised and Hinduised. Secondly, because this village is characterized by the conspicuous absence of any dominant caste unlike most villages studied by sociologists and anthropologists. Thirdly, it is the only scientific village study available in Hindi. It is also regrettable that this book is not available to the non-Hindi speaking readers and specially to the scholars of Cornell University who sponsored this project (Vidyarthi, 1976).

Professor Majumdar's concern with the ill-treatment of and injustice to the tribal and aboriginal population of India by government officials, comes through in his Races and Cultures of India, on account of their lack of knowledge and sensitivity about the former's lifestyle and problems. This book is a collection of lectures he was invited to deliver in 1942 by Sir Theodore Tusker, Supervisor of the Indian Civil Service Training Centre at Dehradun, to cover a course of lectures on Indian anthropology. It is probably his best known published work. Here is Professor Majumdar quoting S.C. Roy: "Any one having had occasion to watch at close quarters the administration of justice in certain aboriginal areas of India will be struck by the amount of injustice done, in spite of the best intentions, by judges and magistrates and police officers of all grades owing to their ignorance of the customs and mentality of the aboriginal tribes they have to deal with." Therefore, it was Professor Majumdar's strong belief that "[a] knowledge of races and cultures of the country should be regarded as an indispensable prerequisite of an efficient administrative system. Such recognition has already proved of immense benefit in countries with a large aboriginal or primitive population" (Majumdar, 1944).

He emphasized the need for administrators, the police and the judiciary to know the tribal population of India well, and try to solve their myriad problems. He wrote: "Indian administrators must know how to tackle such urgent problems of tragic mismanagement of primitive areas and decline of tribal populations, as has been evident in many tracts of India. In Africa, Oceania and other parts with primitive and backward populations, anthropology has helped the administration of these countries by throwing light on habits and prejudices which might present obstacles to economic development or the improvement of farm practices and the standards of public health and native dietary" (Majumdar, 1944).

For making officialdom responsible towards ameliorating the plight of the aboriginal population of India, training was one thing: Wouldn't it be better if students of Anthropology, already sufficiently sensitized, could themselves enter Government service? That Professor Majumdar was blessed with tremendous foresight is seen from his prescient exhortation for anthropology to be included as a subject for recruitment to a Government office: "... one expects to see our administrators, the police officers and even the teachers of schools and colleges to take an informed interest in the study of Indian culture both primitive and advanced. This can be realized if anthropology is made a subject for study also for all examinations which recruit men for the services" (Majumdar, 1944).

In 1960, Professor D.N. Majumdar, moving beyond tribes and village studies, extended the scope of his work to the largest urban agglomeration of Uttar Pradesh, viz. Kanpur by publishing Social Contours of an Industrial City. It was the result of an ambitious city survey of Kanpur, conducted from 1954 to 1956, in collaboration with Prof. N.S. Reddy, then Deputy Director of the social survey, whose earlier work amongst the Malas and Madigas of Andhra had won praise from Professor Majumdar. This survey included the history of the city, economic and social survey, and report of a family planning inquiry. The Research Programmes Committee of the Planning Commission had financed this project and the report came out a few weeks before Dr. Majumdar's untimely demise (Majumdar, 1960).

While being engaged in academic pursuits at the highest levels, Dr. Majumdar did not forget his students. For them, he wrote, with Professor T.N. Madan, a very famous textbook, An Introduction to Social Anthropology (1960), which has been reprinted repeatedly, remaining popular till date.

However, it was for his remarkable and sustained work in another sphere that his academic reputation lives gloriously on-his work on the Khasa, which has not been bettered, in all these decades. It found final documentation in his posthumously published book Himalayan Polyandry, in 1962. However, the story had begun much farther back, when as a student in England, Professor D.N. Majumdar had been asked about a polyandrous tribe called the Khasa in the Himalayas by non-other than Malinowski, a fact about which he (Majumdar) was then regretfully ignorant (Majumdar, 1962). A promise made to his *guru*, to study them, was dutifully kept: He went on to study, the Khasa of Jaunsar-Bawar in the Himalayas, during annual expeditions with his students which went on for almost twenty two long years, spending a total of about four years and eleven months in the process. There was no village in Jaunsar-Bawar which did not know him; for some Khasa, he was a "peripatetic homeopath, [for] some as a doctor, a collection of herbs, or an eccentric traveller, and [for] many as a friend" (Majumdar, 1962). Tracing their origin myth from the Pandavas, the fraternal polyandrous system of the Khasas was responsible for safeguarding their socio-economic structure. Their small precarious agricultural landholdings on terrace farms would have been divided quickly and ruinously had each brother entered a monogamous union.

Professor Majumdar used to be very fond of his students and juniors, and took personal interest in their welfare. During his stewardship of the Anthropology Department at Lucknow University, he could groom a whole host of them, many of whom became very well-known in their own right. His junior colleagues and excellent scholars, Professor D.K. Sen and Professor K.S. Mathur headed the Department immediately after him. Professor S.C. Dube, who had also taught under the headship of Dr. Majumdar….A stalwart of Indian Anthropology, Professor T.N. Madan, went on from Lucknow University and after adorning many high positions, having taught as Visiting Professor of Anthropology and History of Religion at Harvard, is currently Professor Emeritus of Sociology at the Institute of Economic Growth, Delhi University. Another junior colleague of his, the formidable Professor Gopala Sarana—a doctoral student of Cora Du Bois—under whom I was fortunate to have studied decades later, used to reverently state that he had learnt Anthropology sitting at the feet of Professor Majumdar. Prof. L.P. Vidyarthi was one of his best students, who went on to obtain a doctorate from Chicago. Among other students of Professor D.N. Majumdar, who became notable anthropologists were R.S. Gaur, who went on to Pune and later became a professor at Columbia and Berkeley; N.S. Reddy, his colleague at the ICMR Unit at Lucknow, who taught later at Madras University and Andhra University, Visakhapatnam; Ripudaman Singh, who later went on to Canada, R.P. Srivastava, who joined Pune University; and V.N. Mishra, who joined the Deccan College in Pune.

Despite being a person of the plains and quite uncomfortable in the hills, where the cold would leave his legs numb, and bring him dangerously close to totally abandoning the fieldwork (Majumdar, 1962), he persevered on, encouraging and motivating his students, and co-workers. It was his passion for knowledge which drove him, at the age of fifty three, to lead two expeditions to Roopkund Lake, located above the snow line at an altitude of about 18,000 feet, to examine a recently discovered large finds of old human remains (Madan, 1961). He was known to be interested in prehistoric archaeology, keeping up with the latest on the topic and occasionally lecturing on it. Professor Krishna Kant recounted to me the experience of Chandrasen who had gone to Roopkund for fieldwork as part of Professor Majumdar's team. He remembers that Professor Majumdar was carrying along a lot of material. One day, in the biting cold, he called everyone to his tent, and offered them all a drink. His infectious enthusiasm used to motivate his team to work alongside him on even the most routine and humdrum tasks for months on end, and produce results that were lauded for their meticulousness.

Of a slight build, Professor Majumdar was blessed with an affable temperament and great optimism. He had both unbridled curiosity and boundless energy. He could work on many projects, despite them all being very different from each other. His mind was always full of plans for future research. This, of course, is visible in the breadth of his work. A large part of his work was in new fields. His book on the Ho published in 1937 was the first Indian acculturation study. His village study published in 1958, was again a new research interest. He was also the first Indian anthropologist to bring his tools to bear on surveying a city. His work on the school children of Lucknow was also the first of its kind in India. He was, therefore, a pioneer in most of the fields he touched. Naturally, he could not stay long enough in a field in order to hone it to theoretical sophistication. (Madan, 1961). It would be more appropriate to consider Professor Majumdar as a 'seeker', whose prodigiously active mind was for ever fascinated by the desire to widen the horizons of knowledge, which he then actively shared, in order to lay down the foundation in India of a new subject with several different branches.

Professor Majumdar was an institution builder. He not only established the independent Department of Anthropology in Lucknow University, but nurtured it closely, leading to the formation of what some refer to as the 'Lucknow School'. By 1945-47, he had also laid the foundation of what was to become the thriving Ethnographic and Folk Culture Society in Lucknow. The Society's aim was to collect ethnographic data on the local cultures of rural Uttar Pradesh. Under the aegis of the Society, the quarterly Eastern Anthropologist started out as a premier journal in Anthropology, and Professor Majumdar served as its Editor right from its inception for as long as he lived. Over the years the journal has had a good readership and is still popular. The Society later started two other journals in Anthropology – *Manav* (in Hindi) and the Indian Journal of Physical Anthropology.

He had also established a research cell of the Indian Council of Medical Research within the Department of Anthropology at Lucknow University. In fact even when he passed away, he was in the midst of supervising a research project titled Process and Problems of Physical Growth among Children in U.P., a cross-sectional study of growth among children in Uttar Pradesh, under the auspices of the Indian Council of Medical Research, for which data on about 30,000 cases had already been gathered obtained by a multidisciplinary team of doctors, physical anthropologists, and statisticians (Madan, 1961). He was keen in determining both the physical as well as the cultural determinants of growth.

By 1960, the year of his death, he had managed to promote anthropology all over the country in a number of universities and also inculcated the love of the subject among many generations of students. By that time, as Professor Furer-Haimendorf (Man, Vol. LX, No. 212, 1960) writes in an excellent tribute, "His vision, wide experience of all branches of anthropology, and remarkable energy had made him a focal point of anthropological studies in India, and his department in the University of Lucknow, the foundation and development of which he always regarded as the core of his life work, has for many years been the most active department of anthropology in the whole of South Asia." (Madan and Sarana, 1964). He had then been the Head of the Department as well as Dean, Faculty of Arts. He was a young fifty seven, when after a full day's work, he went home, spoke to his daughter on the telephone, had dinner and died. His prodigious output can be assessed from the fact that several books, viz. *Himalayan Polyandry, A Village on the Fringe, Chhor Ka Ek Gaanv, and Pragithihas* (with Prof. Gopala Sarana) were in various stages of publication at the time of his death. His memory lives on in the Department he founded in numerous ways: Cornell keeps on sending me Fulbright scholars to guide; a re-study and re-interpretation of Chittora—the 'village on the fringe' has been done under my guidance, but most notably, a Majumdar Endowment Fund has been sanctioned by the Uttar Pradesh Government through the efforts of Prof. Indu Sahai. The Ethnographic and Folk Culture Society had also organized a full year of celebratory seminars, conferences and lectures to celebrate the centennial year of Professor D.N. Majumdar's birth.

From my interactions with Professors Gopala Sarana, Krishna Kant, B.R.K. Shukla (who considers himself fortunate to have gotten a chance to interact with Professor Majumdar vide the good offices of the sociologist Professor A.K. Saran), Nadeem Hasnain, A.P. Singh of University of Lucknow; Vinay Srivastava of Delhi University, and R.K. Jain of Jawaharlal Nehru University, the Anthropology Department in the days of Professor Majumdar's stewardship seems to have been a lively place. While supposedly very strict regarding his research and researchers, the cigar-loving Professor Majumdar was a very jolly person too, cracking jokes and throwing frequent parties, to which not just teachers but even the non-teaching staff were welcome. He loved being in company, was a good conversationalist and an excellent host. (Madan, 1961). In fact, Professor Majumdar had started the tradition of a monthly party in the Department, in which the high point used to be an ice cream brick procured from the fashionable Hazratganj market. There was a daily tea party thrown by him as well, which all the teachers and non-teaching staff used to attend, and which served the purpose of an effective feedback mechanism. Feedback about teaching, too, used to be obtained by Professor Majumdar from students daily, as a matter of routine. A workaholic, he took most of his lunches and dinners in the Department itself. It was no wonder, therefore, as recalled by Professor Krishna Kant that the staff of the University and the Anthropology Department were considered almost his family members by Professor Majumdar. Professor T.N. Madan and Professor Gopala Sarana writes: "Mrs. Madhuri Majumdar writes (in a letter to the editors) that her husband used to tell her that his students were his sons (his only child was a daughter). In a country in which the chasm between the proximate generations is a marked one, and the relations between teacher and student characterized by reserve and mutual aloofness, the warm relations of Majumdar with his students were something out of the usual. And the love and loyalty which his students gave him also were extraordinary" (Madan and Sarana, 1964).

In the words of Prof. D.P. Mukherjee, the doyen of Indian sociologists, "My personal relations with him were extremely cordial. The fighting qualities which noted him as marked traits did not brush against me. He looked up to me as his elder brother and I also looked at him as my younger brother. The reason of my affection, if affection had reason at all, was simple: I recognized him to be a budding scholar. In fact, he became one soon. His was the rare example of an Indian scholar who loved scholarship to the depths of his being .... He was a very hardworking man, working for ten to twelve hours a day. In the late evenings he would go to the Hazratganj shopping centre in Lucknow and meet his publishers, students and friends in the bookshops. Some of the bookshops, thanks to him, were stacked with books on anthropology. The Coffee House he would religiously attend. His students also congregated there. From nine in the morning till seven in the evening he would work and then felt himself free. In that period also he discussed all the varied problems with his students and research scholars, their projects and schemes, and helped them seriously. He collected around himself a team of workers for research. In fact, he succeeded in enlisting them for the different colleges and universities of India, and also for his journal. I think very few men in India have produced a better set of research workers than he had done. He was a friendly man, and his students were devoted to him. There was no misunderstanding with them. I have hinted above that he was a fighter, but he fought for causes, for the principles he cared for. He excused people and hoped soon to be excused. A definite mellowness was developed in later years. He had become very mature, thanks to his intimacies with his student and with European, British and American scholars. I was expecting him to be ripe, and he had got into his stride. The best was yet to be; he was only fifty seven. Dr. Majumdar was a good conversationalist and a lovable host. At first he was shy, but he soon conquered his shyness and became a good talker. He never monopolized the talk as most professors do. His wife and young daughter, their only child, collaborated with him in hostship" (Mukherjee, 1964).

To cite Prof. D.P. Mukherjee again, "One incident in the last days of his life struck me. I was with him for a week just a month before his tragic death. We talked about all manner of things, his research work and personal life in particular. He was an incorrigible optimist, but when he was elected Dean of the Faculty of Arts, at the University of Lucknow, in April 1960, he began to feel sorry. He was mindful of the honour but said he was going to lose his grip and unless he recovered it, he would be lost. At the same time he loved the life of action, notionally. But taking all into consideration he did not like the Deanship at all. The last thing he said was, 'This Deanship will kill me.' My reply was, 'You will survive. If you don't like it, give it up.' 'Yes, I will soon.' He died on the 31st of May from a cerebral hemorrhage. I have seen more than one man crumbling under the burdens of administration. And Majumdar was essentially a scholar" (Mukherjee, 1964).

I have no better way to conclude than to quote the words of Professor T.N. Madan, expressed in his obituary on Professor Majumdar's death: "His death leaves a void in the ranks of Indian anthropologists which will be difficult to fill…A British colleague wrote with feeling…that it was difficult to think of Indian anthropology without Majumdar, for he had so long been Indian anthropology" (Madan, 1961).

24

Professor Shiv Raj Kumar Chopra

The Scholar, Academician, Researcher and Administrator

Rajan Gaur

Professor Dr. Shiv Raj Kumar Chopra was a doyen of Indian Anthropology and is known as the foremost palaeoanthropologist in India. Prof. Chopra made significant contributions for the advancement of Anthropology in India and is considered among the ground-breaking anthropologists of independent India.

Prof. S.R K. Chopra was born on October 8, 1931 at Ludhiana, now an important industrial town of Punjab State of India. His father, Prof. Ronki Prasad Chopra was Professor and Head of the Department of English at Ramjas College, Delhi, and his mother, Mrs. Vidya Wati Chopra, was a home maker. His father's influence was probably responsible for his exceptional command over English. He married in 1960 to Krishna Chopra and was blessed with three children, a Son Ashish and two daughters, Shalini and Malini. All his children are well-settled and happily married.

Prof. Chopra received his initial schooling at Ludhiana. He graduated from Hindu College, Delhi with a B.Sc. Honours degree in Zoology in 1951. Subsequently, he joined the Department of Anthropology at University of Delhi for a master's course and received his M.Sc. Anthropology degree in 1953. Thereafter, he travelled to Switzerland for conducting doctoral research under the expert supervision of world famous physical anthropologist and primatologist, Prof. Adolph Hans Schultz, who was Professor of Anthropology and Director of the Institute of Anthropology, University of Zurich, Switzerland. Interactions with Prof. Schultz sharpened his understanding of primate anatomy and evolutionary biology. As a doctoral scholar Prof. Chopra carried out detailed research on the cranial suture closure in Old World and New World Monkeys, which provided new information on suture closure in relation to physiological age in monkeys. The research also provided significant baseline data for comparison with corresponding ones for anthropoid apes and humans. The findings of this research were published as Inaugural Dissertation in the Proceedings of the Zoological Society of London in 1957, which finds prominent reference in standard books on Primates. In 1955, On the basis of this research, he was awarded the degree Doctor of Philosophy by the Zurich University. From 1955 to 1958, he was awarded a University research scholarship to work at Birmingham University, Medical School. Concurrently (1955-1956), he also received the Wenner-Gren Foundation, USA award for Anthropological Research, Inc., to work with Lord Solly Zuckerman F.R.S., Professor of Anatomy, Birmingham University, United Kingdom. Under this award, Prof. Chopra designed a 'Pelvimeter' for the measurement of angles of torsion of pelvis and other bones of Primates, the details of which were published in reputed British journal '*Man*' in 1958. Mentoring, association and interactions with great anthropologists like Schultz, Zuckerman and others in United Kingdom and Europe had a significant contribution in shaping Prof. Chopra into an intellectual with a strong personality. During 1957 to 1958, he also lectured at Duckworth Laboratory, University of Cambridge, United Kingdom. After finishing his British stint, Prof. Chopra returned to India in 1959, at the invitation of the then Vice-Chancellor of Panjab University, Dr. A.C. Joshi, to set up a Department of Anthropology at Panjab University, Chandigarh, which he headed till 1981. In 1967, he became Professor of Anthropology at Panjab University, Chandigarh.

Prof. Chopra founded the Department of Anthropology at Panjab University, Chandigarh in August, 1960, with only two other faculty members, and remained its head until 1981. The sapling he planted in 1960 grew into a luxurious tree to eventually become, through several UGC Special Assistance Programme (SAP) stages, a UGC Centre of Advanced Study in Anthropology (Phase Two) in 2018. It is now recognised as one of the premier anthropology departments of India. During his time as head, he developed and fortified the infrastructure and augmented the staff and faculty strength of the department. Several laboratories, equipments, and facilities were added to the department during his tenure. Prominent among these was the creation in 1975 of a unique and nationally famous Museum of Man which at the time housed life sized models of Siwalik fossil hominoids and extant anthropoids and apes. The models of now extinct hominoids were based on the fossil remains collected under his leadership by the field teams of the department from the Siwalik deposits of northwest India. The Museum has subsequently expanded to include galleries of Siwalik mammalian fossil, models of stages of human evolution, exhibits of material culture and stone artefacts collected by department teams. In memory of its creator, the department very recently renamed the museum in 2018 as the *"S.R.K. Chopra Museum of Man*". But for his initial efforts, the department would not have reached to the prominent position it occupies today.

Prof. Chopra was a strict disciplinarian and inculcated in his students a sense of punctuality, discipline and hard work. He commanded great respect of his students, scholars, colleagues, collaborators and contemporaries. He was a wonderful orator and had a tremendous command over English language. I had the opportunity to be associated with him as a student, scholar and subsequently as a colleague. I feel he had a commanding personality, a very sharp memory and a great convincing power. As a person he also had a sense of humour and often narrated interesting anecdotes to his scholars and colleagues whenever they sat with him over a cup of tea. He was a man with aristocratic tastes and a great sense of dress. Though he liked discipline but he was also fond of outdoors in the field. During his headship, the whole department would often be taken for a few days fieldwork every few months in the hills of Himachal Pradesh, Haryana, Jammu and Kashmir and now-a-days Uttarakhand where, after a day's data collection, he would sit around a camp fire in the evening to interact with scholars, colleagues and students. His favourite field area was the Siwaliks of northwest India, where he often led teams for the collection of Primate and other mammalian fossils. His greatest contribution to Indian anthropology is the recovery of a number of hominoid primate fossils that considerably helped in understanding the early stages of hominoid, anthropoid and human evolution in south Asia. He, along with his team, made several new fossil primate discoveries from the Indian Siwaliks. He is very aptly known as the foremost palaeoanthropologist of independent India.

Prof. Chopra was endowed with great administrative skills. Apart from heading the anthropology department at Panjab University, Chandigarh, he held several important administrative positions. He remained the Dean of Foreign Students of Panjab University, Chandigarh from 1973 to 1976 and he introduced many innovative features for the benefit of foreign students in the university. His administrative prowess received due recognition when he was appointed Pro-Vice-Chancellor of Punjabi University, Patiala in March 1983, a position which he held until 1986. From 1986 to 1989 he remained the Vice-Chancellor of Kurukshetra University, Haryana. During his stint as Vice-Chancellor, Prof. Chopra brought in several key administrative and academic improvements in the University. In 1989 he returned to Panjab University, Chandigarh as its Dean of University Instructions. Professor Chopra superannuated from the Department of Anthropology, Panjab University, Chandigarh on October 31, 1991. Prof. Chopra was a strict disciplinarian and expected his colleagues, scholars, staff and students to work hard, be punctual and follow the rules and regulations. He was considered a strong administrator with a humane approach.

Prof. Chopra was a brilliant academician. He was invited as visiting Professor/Faculty/Fellow by several famous universities/institutions abroad. From 1955 to 1958 he was invited as University Research Fellow by the Department of Anatomy, Medical School, University of Birmingham, United Kingdom. He was an invited Lecturer at Duckworth Laboratory, University of Cambridge, Cambridge, United Kingdom, from 1957 to 1958. From 1965 to 1966 he was a Leverhulme Visiting Fellow at the Department of Anatomy, University of Birmingham, Birmingham, United Kingdom. During 1965-1966 he was invited as Visiting Professor by the Institute of Anthropology, Kiel University, Kiel, West Germany. In 1979, he travelled to Japan as a Visiting Professor at the Primate Research Institute, Kyoto University, Inuyama City, Japan. He also remained a Visiting Professor (1988/1989) at University of London's United Medical and Dental Schools, London, United Kingdom.

The academic and scientific achievements of Prof. Chopra were recognised by a number of prestigious international bodies and organizations which honoured him with their fellowships. The most significant of these were: Royal Anthropological Institute of Great Britain and Ireland (F.R.A.I.), Zoological Society of London (F.Z.S.), American Anthropological Association (F.F.A.A.A.), Explorer's Club, United States. He was also a Fellow of Premier scientific academies of our country, namely National Academy of Sciences (F.N.A.Sc.) and Indian National Science Academy (F.N.A.).

Prof. Chopra was recipient of many prestigious international and national awards, such as Wenner-Gren Foundation Award for Anthropological Research, Inc., New York, USA, Category 'B' (1955-1956); Research Grant from Bombay Natural History Society, Bombay (1960); Wenner-Gren Foundation Award for Anthropological Research, Inc., New York, USA (1966-67); and Silver Plaque from the Ethnographic and Folk Culture Society, Lucknow (1976).

Professor Chopra was not only an accomplished academician, administrator and researcher, but also a powerful orator. He delivered a number of distinguished academic orations, among which mention can be made of: Majumdar Memorial Lecture, Ethnographic & Folk Culture Society, Lucknow (1976); M.R. Sahni Memorial Lecture, Palaeontological Society of India, Lucknow (1985); and Dr. Panchanan Mitra Memorial Lectureship, Asiatic Society, Calcutta (1985-86). In between (1980-1981), he also remained a National Lecturer of the University Grants Commission.

The research interests of Prof. Chopra were spread over a variety of subfields of anthropology including primatology, human auxology, palaeoanthropology, palaeoecology etc. However, his distinctive and prolific contribution was in the field of palaeoprimatology. His research work on primates sought to understand the early hominoid evolution in the Indian subcontinent and explain the phylogenetic relation between lower and higher primates. He devoted a major part of his research activities to the exploration of the Siwalik deposits of northwest India and directed several national and international projects on search of primate fossils. His explorations in the Siwaliks resulted in the discovery of many new primate and mammalian taxa from several new sites located in the states of Jammu and Kashmir, Himachal Pradesh, Haryana and Punjab. He documented important stages in the evolutionary tree of fossil apes in the Indian subcontinent. His discoveries chronicling the primate evolution in the Siwaliks include fossil adapids, hylobatids, and hominoids. The major fossil primate texa reported by him include adapid *Sivaladapis (Indoadapis),* hominoid *Dryopithecus* (now *Sivapithecus*), Hylobatid *Pliopithecus* (now *Krishnapithecus*) and the world famous *Gigantopithecus*. He also published on Mio-Pliocene palaeo-environments and palaeoecology that influenced the course of primate evolution in this region.

He was a widely travelled man and had the experience of conducting research in a number of famous laboratories, musea, and institutes of Europe and Asia. Prominent among these were: Laboratory of Physical Anthropology, Zurich, Switzerland; Museum of Zoology and Palaeontology, Zurich, Switzerland; Duckworth Laboratory, Cambridge, United Kingdom; British Museum of Natural History, London, United Kingdom; Powel-Cotton Museum, Brichington, Kent, United Kingdom; Osteological Collection, St. Brides Church, London, United Kingdom; Royal Tropical Institute, Amsterdam, The Netherlands; Anthropological Institute Collection, Kiel, West Germany; Primate Research Institute, Inuyama Kyoto University, Japan; and Museum of Geology and Palaeontology, University of Florence, Italy.

He supervised twenty Doctoral theses and over fifty Master's dissertations on a variety of topics in physical anthropology. He extensively published in reputed International and national journals, such as *Nature* (4 papers), *MAN*, *Proceedings of Zoological Society of London, Primates, Zeitschrift fur Morphologie und Anthropologie, Palaeo 3, Journal of Human Evolution, Postilla* etc., and had approximately 120 scientific publications to his credit. A list of te 1 of his most prominent publications is as under:

1. 1957. The Cranial Suture Closure in Monkeys. *Proceeding. of the Zoological Society of London*.128 (1): 67–112.
2. 1958. A 'Pelvimeter' for orientation and measuremer :s of the innominate bone. *Man*, London, 58: 126-128.
3. 1961. The angle of Pelvic torsion in the primates (S.R.K. Chopra). *Zeitschrift für Morphologie und Anthropologie*, Vol. 51 (3):268-274.
4. 1969. *Gigantopithecus* (Pongidae, Hominoidea): A New Species From North India, *Postilla*, 138: (E. L. Simons & S. R. K. Chopra).
5. 1978. Geology, fauna and palaeoenvironments of Lower Sivalik deposits around Ramnagar, India. *Nature*, 275: 736-737 (R.N. Vasishat, R. Gaur & S.R.K. Chopra).
6. 1979. Miocene tree shrews from the Indian Œivaliks. *Nature*, 281: 213-214 (S.R.K. Chopra, S. Kaul & R.N. Vasishat).
7. 1979. Sivalik fossil tree shrew from Haritalyangar, India. *Nature*, 281:214-215. (R.N.Vasishat& S.R.K.Chopra).
8. 1979. A new species of Pliopithecus from Indian Sivaliks. *Journal of Human Evolution*. 8: 475 (S.R.K.Chopra and S. Kaul).
9. 1983. Palaeoecology of the Middle Miocene Sivalik sediments of a part of Jammu & Kashmir State (India). Palaeogeography, Palaeoecology, 43: 313-327. (Rajan Gaur & S.R.K.Chopra).
10. 1984. Taphonomy, fauna, environment and ecology of Upper Sivaliks (Plio-Pleistocene) near Chandigarh, India. *Nature*, 308: 353-355 (Rajan Gaur & S.R.K.Chopra).

One of the major scientific contributions of Professor Chopra is the invention of an instrument known as 'Chopra's Pelvimeter' in 1958 to measure the angle of torsion on innominate bone of pelvis and other bones of Primates, including humans. Till then, the torsion angles of pelvis were impossible to measure with conventional instruments available at the time. The pelvimeter was manufactured by M/s Blundell and Gascoigne, Birmingham (U.K.) and M/s Una and Co, Delhi. Its details were published in British journal *MAN* in 1958 (Vol. 58:126-128).

During his career, Prof. Chopra held organisational offices of a number of international and national societies and Institutions. Significant among these included Secretary Asia of International Primatological Society of USA; President, Indian Association of Physical Anthropologists; Sectional President, Indian Science Congress Association; Convener, Congress of Archaeological and Anthropological Sciences; Vice-President, Ethnographic and Folk Culture Society, Lucknow; Fellow and Foreign Secretary of the Palaeontological Society of India; Member, Rashtriya Manav Sangrahalya Samiti and its Executive Council, Ministry of Human Resource Development, Government of India, New Delhi; Member, High Powered Science and Technology Council, Punjab and Haryana; Member, State Environment Production Council of Haryana State; Member, State Advisory Board of Education, Haryana; Member, Advisory Committee on Planetarium, Science Centre and Natural History Park in Haryana. He was also member of board of Study/Control/Faculty of various subjects of a number of Universities which included Panjab University, Chandigarh; University of Baroda, Andhra University; Punjabi University, Patiala; University of Jammu; Guru Nanak Dev University, Amritsar and Pt. Ravi Shankar University, Raipur.

Dr. Chopra served as an Editor of *Everyday Science*. Prof. Chopra held membership of several international committees. Prominent among these were: Founder Member, Permanent Council, International Association of Human Biologists, Brussels; Member, International Sectional Committee for Human Adaptability (India), under the International Biological Programme; Member, International Committee for Standardization in Human Biology; Member, International Union of Anthropological and Ethnological Sciences and Member, International Committee for Ethnographic Museums of ICOM. He also remained member of a number of national advisory/expert committees, namely Member, Central Advisory Board, Anthropological Survey of India, Member, Technical Advisory Committee, All India Institute of Family Planning, New Delhi; National Committee, Museum of Man, Ministry of Education; Expert Committee Member, Museum of Natural History, Department of Science & Technology, Government of India; Member, Review Committee & Specialists Panel, University Grants Commission; Chairman, UGC panel in Anthropology; Member, Rashtriya Manav Sangrahalya Samiti and its Executive Council, Ministry of Human Resource Development, Government of India; Member, High Powered Science and Technology Councils of Punjab and Haryana; Member, State Advisory Board of Education, Haryana etc.

In addition, Prof. Chopra held organizational offices of many international/national societies/institutions. Significant among these were: Secretary, Asia International Primatological Society, USA; President, Indian Association of Physical Anthropologists; Sectional President, Indian Science Congress Association; Convener, Congress of Archaeological & Ethnological Sciences; Vice-President, Ethnographic & Folk Culture Society, Lucknow; and Fellow and Foreign Secretary, Palaeontological Society of India. From time to time Prof. Chopra also remained on the Board of Control/Studies/ Academic Council/Science Faculty of several universities, such as University of Baroda, Andhra University, Punjabi University, Panjab University, University of Jammu, Guru Nanak Dev University, Pt. Ravi Shankar University etc.

Prof. Chopra was not only a dedicated teacher, a brilliant academician, an able administrator but also an accomplished researcher and field worker. In view of his academic and research achievements he was able to secure for the department research projects from many prestigious international and national scientific organizations to conduct research on varied fields in biological anthropology ranging from high altitude anthropology, physical growth and development, skeletal changes in Primates, human origins, Neogene Hominoids, Siwalik palaeoprimatology and Siwalik palaeoecology and palaeoenvironments.

From 1967-68, under a programme of research collaboration between the Institute of Anthropology, University of Kiel, Germany and the Anthropology Department of Panjab University, Chandigarh, biological surveys on selected Himalayan populations was carried out. Government of Punjab granted a project in 1964-65 to carry out an anthropological survey of Lahaul and Spiti regions. Council of Scientific Research, New Delhi awarded a project entitled, "A study of Physical growth and development of children in the tribal populations of the Himalayan region", under which one scholar was awarded doctorate degree on the basis of data collected under this project. A collaborative project between Yale University, USA, and Anthropology Department of Panjab University, Chandigarh was co-investigated by Prof. Chopra, along with Prof. E.L. Simons of Yale University, to explore Siwaliks of north India for fossil hominoid and other primates and the world famous *Gigantopithecus bilaspurensis,* along with other hominoids, was discovered. Subsequently, from 1973 to 1976, the Indian Council of Medical Research, New Delhi, sanctioned a research project, entitled "Postnatal Skeletal age changes in Primates: eruption of teeth and order of appearance and fusion of epiphysis in primates with special reference to rhesus monkey (*Macaca mulatta*)", and one scholar was awarded Ph.D. degree on the data collected under this project. In 1968, a major collaborative research project, entitled "Search for the earliest hominoids in the Sivaliks", between the department and Anthropological Survey of India, Government of India, commenced to investigate the problem of human origins and to locate quarriable sites in the Siwalik Hills of India to recover fossil remains of early relatives of hominoids. The material collected under this project resulted in the award of Doctorate degrees to two researchers working in the project. A research project on "Anthropological variability in Himalayan populations living under varying altitude environments" was sanctioned by Indian National Science Academy (1972-74) to conduct research related to physical growth, physique and fitness in selected Himalayan populations living under different climatic conditions. Subsequently, University Grants Commission (1978-81) granted a project on "development of quarriable sites for the recovery of Neogene Hominoids in north western India" for palaeoprimatological research in the Siwalik deposits of north India. Another project related to human evolutionary studies was granted by University Grants Commission (1987-1990) on "Ecological studies and their bearing on Human Evolution in the Indian Sivaliks" to investigate the impact of environmental changes on evolution and radiation of Primates. The data generated by these projects/collaborations resulted in a number of significant research publications which were published in reputed international journals such as Nature, Postilla, Journal of Human Evolution, Palaeo3, etc.

Prof. Chopra was a captivating orator. During his academic career, he was invited by international and national academic organizations to deliver several coveted orations such as, D.N. Majumdar Memorial Lecture (1976) of Ethnographic & Folk Culture Society, Lucknow; Main Lecture at the 8th Congress of International Primatological Society at Florence, Italy (on 8.7.1980) on the invitation of Prof. A.B. Chairelli of Florence University and the President of the Society; M.R. Sahni Memorial Lecture (for the year 1984) of the Palaeontological Society of India, Lucknow; Dr. Panchanan Mitra Memorial Lecture (1985-86) of the Asiatic Society. In addition, Prof. Chopra was also appointed National Lecturer for the year 1980-81 by the University Grants Commission.

A number of students (mainly doctoral) of Prof. Chopra rose to occupy important positions in academia and elsewhere. Some of these in my knowledge are as under:

1. Prof. L.S.Sidhu, Dean Science and Head, Department of Human Biology (now Human Genetics), Punjabi University, Patiala.
2. Prof. D.P. Bhatnagar, Head, Department of Human Biology (now Human Genetics), Punjabi University, Patiala.
3. Prof. S. Kaul, Chairperson, Department of Anthropology, Panjab University, Chandigarh.
4. Prof. R.N.Vasishat, Chairperson, Department of Anthropology, Panjab University, Chandigarh.
5. Prof. Indu Talwar, Chairperson, Department of Anthropology, Panjab University, Chandigarh.
6. Prof. Rajan Gaur, Director, Centre of IAS & other Competitive Examinations, Panjab University, Chandigarh.
7. Prof. R.K. Pathak, Chairperson, Department of Anthropology and Dean Science Faculty, Panjab University, Chandigarh.

According to Mrs. Krishna Chopra, wife of Prof. S.R.K. Chopra, "*he was a man committed to his work to the core and was always dreaming of doing something for the country, his department and his students whom he loved so much. He was a hard working soul with an individual personality who wanted to see his department rise to the top in the world .... to some extent he succeeded and I wish he had a longer life to do more*" (Mrs. Krishna Chopra, Personal Communication). In the words of his son, Mr. Ashish Chopra - a well-known culinary historian—"*my father was a very open minded person who was secular to the core and liberal in his mindset and a human first and a professor later. He was a born fighter who always stood his grounds on principles and believed in fighting against the system by remaining within the system. Although he might have been apparently very tough and sometimes short tempered, but was a mellow and kind hearted person deep inside. He was also very fond of cooking and, in fact, my interest in food was influenced by my father's passion for cooking*" (Mr. Ashish Chopra, Personal Communication).

At the end, I would say that Professor Dr. Shiv Raj Kumar Chopra was a dedicated teacher, a brilliant academician, a keen researcher, an accomplished administrator, a captivating orator and above all a good human being. His demise on July 2, 1994, due to a chronic renal problem, left a huge void among the anthropological fraternity which would always be felt. He would for all time be remembered for his doughty spirit and courage of conviction and his path breaking researches in biological anthropology, in general, and palaeoprimatology in particular.

25
Sachchidananda

R.R. Prasad

Prof. Sachchidananda (1925-2012) was a towering figure in the fields of sociology and anthropology in India. Sachchidananda's contribution to the development of sociology and anthropology in India is enormous and multi-faceted. He studied the races, tribes and cultures in various regions in India. His wide ranging research interests included problem of culture changes and adaptation of tribes and their social problems, shifting cultivation, social dimension of agricultural development, Harijan educated elite, women's rights, educational problems of the disadvantaged sections of the population, voluntary action in tribal areas and socio-cultural dimensions of development.

Sachchidananda was born on 25th October, 1925 at Chhapra in Bihar State and passed away on 31st January, 2012 at the age of 86 years. In 1947, he did his M.A. in History and was appointed Lecturer in Patna College. In 1950, he was awarded a Bihar government State Scholarship in Anthropology, and went out to School of Oriental & African Studies, London University, where he took his M.A. in Anthropology. It was at this time that he came in close contact with such great masters of Anthropology as Christoph von Furer Haimendorf, Raymond Firth, Issach Schapera, Edmund Leach, Lucy Mair, Daryll Ford, John Barnes, Mary Douglas, and Gordon Childe. This experience proved immensely valuable in the making of Sachchidananda as an anthropologist.

After his return to India from London in November 1952, he established the post-graduate Department of Anthropology at Ranchi which began functioning from July 1953. In 1956, he was appointed Reader in Anthropology. At this time he embarked on a large scale evaluation of culture-change among the Munda and the Oraon, the two major tribes of Chhotanagpur. This project was financed by the Research

Programme Committee of the Planning Commission. This project gave Sachchidananda the first experience of supervising field research, and to his students, who had passed out an opportunity to receive initial training in anthropological fieldwork. The project generated a wealth of data on the basis of which the book culture *Change among the Munda and the Oraon* was published in 1964.

Sachchidananda's basic training in the history of modern India and subsequent education in anthropology stirred up his interest in social and culture change studies. After completing the evaluation of the Chhotanagpur tribes, he got associated with the sociological survey of the Bhilai region in Madhya Pradesh as an adviser during the third phase round. In this capacity he visited the field areas in this project and directed the sociological survey. This led to the publication of a book under the caption "Profiles of Rural Chhatisgarh".

Sachchidananda moved over from the Ranchi Department of anthropology in the Bihar University to the Government of India, Ministry of Community Development as the Director of Social Education Organiser's Training Centre at Ranchi. This gave him the opportunity of not only imparting supplementary specialized training in anthropology to community development efforts from all over the country, but also of observing their work in the field dealing with the problems of tribal people. In course of five hears he visited most of the tribal areas either alone or with his trainees from Rajasthan to Nagaland and Tripura. He came to realize the possibilities and the limitations of the applications of anthropological insights to the solution of tribal and rural problems. He also viewed from close quarters the functioning of welfare administration in tribal areas and the problems thereof.

This job gave Sachchidananda an opportunity to examine a tribal village in Bihar from the point of view of both as a unity and also its extensions in social, economic, ritual and political fields. This study earned for him the D.Litt. Degree from Patna University in 1961. This work was later published in book form.

In 1962 Sachchidananda moved over to the Bihar Tribal Research Institute as its Director. During his tenure, the Institute's staff produced a number of important reports in the field of tribal studies. These related to detailed ethnography of smaller and little known tribes of Bihar as well as to tribal problems such as tribal mining labour, residential schools, forest labourers cooperative societies, land alienation, tribal law and custom, tribal demography etc. A book on life and times of Birsa Bhagwan was also published.

Early in 1966, he moved over to Patna as Professor of Sociology in the newly reorganized A.N. Sinha Institute of Social Studies. There he got ample opportunities to work according to his tastes and inclinations. Two anthropological concerns which had not received adequate attention in Bihar, viz., the present position of the communal *Khutkaatti* ownership and tribe-caste continuum claimed his attention. A small report on *Khutkatti* system in Erki Block of Ranchi district was prepared. Later, a survey of Gonds in six districts of north and south Bihar was taken up with a view to tracing the process of the transition of the Gond tribe into a caste in the Hindu system. In course of time the results of this study were published in *Anthropos*.

In 1967, the Research Programmes Committee of the Planning Commission sanctioned a research proposal of Sachchidananda to study the social dimensions of the Intensive Agriculture District Programme which lead country to maximize agricultural production. Soon after this project was completed, he was involved in writing up a survey of studies on Scheduled Castes in India which was subsequently published as a chapter in the survey of research in Anthropology and Sociology of the Indian Council of Social Science Research (ICSSR).

Later in 1971, he started a study of the educated elites among the Harijans (Scheduled Castes) in Bihar in which he covered five most popular castes as the Chamar, Dusadh, Mushar, Pasi and Dhobi. The key objectives of the study included social mobility and the role of the elite in social transformation in their community. At about the same time under the auspices of the ICSSR a nation-wide study of the educational problems of the Scheduled Castes and Tribes was conducted. In Bihar, this work was entrusted to Sachchidananda. The two volumes of report of the study was submitted to the ICSSR in 1975.

In 1975, he took up the restudy of the Munda as there was no full length study of the tribe afrter the publication of Sarat Chandra Roy's book in 1912. All three groups of Munda, those living in the Munda heartland, the Christian dominated area and the Hindu influence area were covered in the study which was published in 1979 as *The Changing Munda*.

In 1980, the ICSSR decided to update its Survey of Research in Sociology and Anthropology so that the studies undertaken between 1969 and 1979 were covered. The task of updating in respect of tribal studies in India was assigned to Sachchidnanda. This work was later published as a chapter in the three volume survey by the ICSSR. Further, in 1981 he got associated with the UNESCO's project on cross-sectional study of Swidden Cultivation in Asia in which scholars from Thailand, Malaysia, Philippines also participated and prepared a country profile based on available literature. The country profile was prepared in 1981 and the case study on the Wancho tribe of Arunachal Pradesh was completed in 1983. In the same stride he also made an assessment on the impact of the government programmes on the people of Arunachal Pradesh by visiting all the districts. The study report was later published in *Man in India* in 1985.

Edwin Eames and Paramatma Saran embarked on a project in 1981 to study the role of the district officer in India before and after Independence through depth interviews. In this work Sachchidananda contributed a paper in the "District Officers in Bihar during British Rule". Under the auspices of the Ministry of Social Welfare, he conducted a very important study in which he examined the impact of industrialization on the tribals around Ranchi and Jamshedpur. In this study he also examined whether tribals suffered any social disorganization. The study focused on all aspects of this impact bringing out the emergence of such evils as beggary and prostitution, weakening of village solidarity and the influence of the family and breakdown of the traditional societal norms. The disorganization, he pleaded, could be viewed as a form of reorganization of tribal society to face the challenges of the new situations.

In 1983, Francine Frankel and M.S.A. Rao started a project for the study of caste, class and dominance in India. About fifteen scholars from India and abroad joined in this endeavour. In the book published from this effort, Sachchidananda contributed a chapter in Vol. II entitled "Patterns of the Politico-economic Change among the Tribals in Middle India". The paper revealed the changing patterns of dominance among the tribes before and after Independence.

The author of this biography had the privilege of editing the "Encycopaedic Profile of Indian Tribes" in 4 volumes which was published in the year 1996. The encyclopaedia presented a concise but comprehensive account of the socio-cultural profile of all the tribal communities who have been declared as Scheduled Tribes by the Government of India.

Sachchidananda, a close associate of Loknayak Jaya Prakash Narayan, served as the Director of the A.N. Sinha Institute of Social Studies (ANSISS) from where he retired in 1980. He, however, continued to teach sociology and anthropology at the institute until he was appointed the Vice Chancellor of Ranchi University in 1985. In 1986, Sachchidananda was appointed a member of the Bihar State Planning

Board. Between 2001 and 2004, he served as the Chairperson of the ANSISS Board of Control. Sachchidananda was also the Director of the Sulabh Institute of Development Studies. A past President of the Anthropology Section of Indian Science Congress, he was also the recipient of R.P. Chanda and S.C. Roy Medals for distinguished work in Anthropology from the Asiatic Society of Bengal.

Sachchidanand has influenced a whole generation of anthropologists. Though he did not stay long in a university system, he had guided more than thirty Ph.D. works. His pre-eminence in Indian anthropology is not the order of great theorist. But what is really remarkable in him is consistent concern with applied anthropology and his commitment to national regeneration. He combined scholarship with the feeling for the downtrodden and socially disadvantaged groups.

Professor Sachchidananda retired from National Institute of Rural Development & Panchayati Raj (NIRDPR), Hyderabad.

Acknowledgements

Author expresses thankfulness to the grandchildren of Sachchidnanda, namely Ms. Natasha Sharan and Mr. Nishant Kumar for furnishing me some unknown events of Sachchidananda's life. Due acknowledgement is also given to the Baidyanath Sarswati's paper 'Sachchidanand: An Introduction" published in the book '*Contemporary Indian Society*'.

26

Surajit Chandra Sinha

A Legend in Indian Anthropology

Sekh Rahim Mondal

Prof. Surajit Chandra Sinha is a legendary figure in Indian Anthropology. He is widely known for his significant contributions on theoretical, conceptual, methodological and empirical domains of the disciple. He was both the theorist as well as an empiricist; this unusual combination made him a towering personality.

In this chapter, the author intends to highlight in brief the life and academic works of Prof. Sinha as a tribute to remember him on the auspicious occasion of hundred years of Indian anthropology. The chapter is based on facts gathered from published materials and also on the basis of author's own experience out of close interaction with him during his student days.

Surajit Chandra Sinha was born in 1926 and died on 27 February, Wednesday, 2002. His birthplace was at Durgapur Upazila of Netrokona district in Maimansingh Division of the then East Bengal, now Bangladesh. He was the eldest son of Moharaja Bhupendra Chandra Sinha of Susang. His mother was the daughter of Jogendra Nath Maitra, a Jaminder of Sithlai in Pabna district of East Bengal (Bangladesh). His paternal uncle Maharaja Kumar Manisingha was a well-known communist leader and head of Communist Party in East Pakistan, who wrote *Jivan Singram*. At a very young age, Sinha followed the footsteps of his paternal uncle. Sinha's maternal uncle Kumar Jatindra Moitra was a distinguished singer of Rabidnra Sangit. His youngest sister Purba Dam also an eminent expert of Rabindra Sangeet. Sinha married to Purnima Sengupta (Sinha), an eminent physicist, author and music scholar. She was the daughter of eminent legal scholar and Bengal novelist Naresh

Chandra Sengupta. Sinha's family had a close interaction with Tagore and Santiniketan. Sinha carried the elite family legacy. His family members traced their landed aristocracy (landed gentry) from the region of Emperor Jahangir. Sinha's family was considered to be one of the important Zaminder families of undivided Bengal. The erstwhile Zamindari estate of Susang was considered as an important estate in protocol of the Government House of Calcutta, in British India. Moharaja of Susang was owner of the hill estate, which was one of the important states of then East Bengal (News letter, N.K. Bose Memorial Foundation, December, 1978).

Sinha completed his basic school education at Moinmansingh and then moved to Calcutta and took admission in Ballygunge Government High School, Calcutta. He started his college education in B.Sc. Physics at Presidency College of Calcutta, but later shifted to Geology and then finally completed with record marks in M.Sc., Anthropology from the University of Calcutta. At the Post Graduate, level in Calcutta University Prof. T.C. Das trained him in anthropological fieldwork and it was Prof. Das who first introduced Sinha to take up the study among Bhumij community of the then Bihar state for his intensive research.

Sinha's another mentor was Prof. Nirmal Kumar Bose, the eminent Indian Anthropologist with whom he first met for *viva-voce* examination for his master thesis, where Prof. Bose was one of the external examiner. Sinha completed his Ph.D. in Anthropology from North Western University, Illinois, in USA as a Fulbright Scholar. His thesis was on "Bhumij's of Barabhum".

Sinha specialized in the field of social cultural anthropology. After returning to India from USA, he continued to conduct field research. His main areas of interest were tribal and peasant lives in central India, when he examined and analysed in the framework of Indian civilization.

We must not forget that, while in USA Sinha did a unique field study in an American village on religion and village people and prepared a report entitled "Religion in an Affluent Society" which was published in *Current Anthropology* at his early age. In this context it is to be mentioned that Sinha was among a very few Indian scholars who had the experience of doing fieldwork in foreign land (N.K. Bose Memorial Foundation, 1978).

There are several views behind Sinha's interest in anthropology and tribes. Many hold the view that being an initial student of geology, he used to travel to hills and forests for field works and thereby came in contact with tribes and folk peoples which had grown his interest in anthropology. Some others has the view that being a member of feudal autocrat Zamindar family, Sinha had the habit of visiting forests and hills, through which he had grown interests on tribal and peasant lives. These are the probable reasons for his shifting from geology to anthropology. Still some other opined that Sinha shifted from geology to anthropology due to his mentor Prof. N.K. Bose, who himself initially was the student of geology and then shifted to anthropology. However, it is very clear that at a very young age Sinha was inclined to know the life ways of the tribes and peasants of India (N.K. Bose Memorial Foundation: 1978).

During his entire professional life, Sinha occupied several important academic and administrative positions. Such as Deputy Director and Director of Anthropological Survey of India, Calcutta. He became the Upacharya (Vice-Chancellor) of Visva-Bharati, Santiniketan. Sinha was also the Professor of Anthropology of Indian Institute of Management, Calcutta, and Director of ICSSR sponsored Centre for Studies in Social Sciences, Calcutta. In addition to the above responsible positions, he also served as an expert and advisory committee member in various Government Bodies, Research Institutions and Universities. Sinha had a very close relation with former Prime Minister Mrs. Indira Gandhi, which may be due to his family reputation and Santiniketan connections of both of them. It is also to be noted here that Mrs. Gandhi had a very keen interest on Anthropology. Sinha was also considered as the adviser to the Indian Prime Minister on tribal affairs (N.K. Bse Memorial Foundation, 1978).

Throughout the entire professional carrier Prof. Sinha had occupied many important official positions at different institutes like IIM, IIAS, ASI, ICSSR and so on. He had initiated, directed, as well as completed many significant research projects either alone or in collaboration with his research teams. The most important of them are : Levels of Economic Initiative and Ethnic Groups in Pargana Barabhum (1964), Ethnic Groups, Villages and Towns of Pargana Barabhum (1966), Research Programmes in Cultural Anthropology and Allied Disciplines (1970), Cultural Profile of Calcutta (1972), Aspects of Indian Culture and Society (1972), Tribal Thoughts and Culture (1976), Weaker Sections in India, Ascetics of Kashi (1976), Field Studies in India (1978), Tribes and Indian Civilization (1982), Tribal Politics and State Systems in Pre-colonial Eastern and North Eastern India (1971), Science, Technology and Culture and several others. Most of these project works were published as edited volume under his leadership.

Professor Sinha extended his helping hands and academic supports to many research students, who used to conduct their individual researches in different Indian Universities and other institutions under their respective supervisors. So far information is availables he himself supervised 18 scholars and they successfully completed their Ph.D. degree under his direct supervisions. The research topics those were allotted to his scholars were of varied nature, ranging from the issues of tribes, castes, occupational groups, muslims, social movements, folk culture, culture of communication, folk dance, folk music, ecological adaptation, peasant life, urban life and impact of industrialization etc. In professional life, most of his research students occupied important positions both in universities and research institutions in India and abroad.

After his formal retirement, Prof. Sinha started to minimize his involvement from anthropological affairs. During post-retirement, he used to stay mostly at Santiniketan or in Kolkata. In Santiniketan he was involved in extending social services and associated with the teaching-learning process of school children, primarily of tribes and other weaker sections. During this stage, he was interested and inclined to know the environment, society and culture of *rarah* areas (middle parts) of West Bengal. The most unfortunate part of his life is that he was diagnosed with Alzheimer in 1993 and after prolonged illness he went for heavenly abode on 27 February, 2002 (N.K. Bose Memorial Foundation, 1978).

National to International Linkages and Collaborations

Prof. Sinha had a very wide and deep connections and linkages with reputed academic institutions in India like Indian Institute of Advanced Study (Simla), Indian Institute of Management (Calcutta), Indian Statistic Institute (Calcutta), Cultural Research Institute (Calcutta), Indian Museum, Anthropological Survey of India, Asiatic Society of Calcutta, Bose Institute (Calcutta}, Indian Council of Cultural Relation (ICCR), New Delhi, National Institute of Educational Research and Training (NCERT) New Delhi, Ministry of Tribal Affairs, Ministry of Education and Human Resource Development, Ministry of Science and Technology, and several others. In addition to research institutes and Governmental Bodies, he was well connected with many Universities in India and abroad.

Prof. Sinha was also associated with many Anthropological bodies and associations among them the most important are IUAES, RAI and AAA etc. In India, he was deeply associated with Indian Anthropological Society, Folk Culture Society, and Indian Anthropological Association etc.

Professor Sinha's linkages with foreign Universities were also wide. It is a well-known fact that in addition to his connection with North

Western Universities, Illinois, in USA, he was also linked with Chicago University of USA. Sinha was very fond of Prof. Redfield's ideas on great tradition, little tradition, peasant and civilization. He had several reputed anthropology friends in USA, France, Germany, Great Britain and Japan.

Prof. Sinha was well known for his multi-disciplinary and interdisciplinary academic interactions. As a result, he had varieties of close friends beyond Anthropology among them there were sociologists, Historians, Geographer, Economists, Political Scientists, Geologists, Physicists, Singers, Film Makers and many other professionals. He had several stalwart friends outside of anthropology, a few of them very important are: Prof. Barun Dey, Prof. Hitesh Sanyal, Prof. Sabyosachi Bhattacharya, Prof. Munish Raja and Prof. Sunil Munshi. He had very deep relations with Prof. Nurul Hasan, a famous historian and former Governor of West Bengal. In Judiciary Justice Musud and many others of Calcutta High Court were also very close to him.

Sinha's main areas of research interests were on tribes, particularly the Bhumij of Central India, which he studied both extensively and intensively in the background of peasantry and Indian Civilization. Sinha's original contribution in Indian Anthropology was reflected in some of his important publications. These are: (i) Tribal Culture in Peninsular India (1957), (2) State Formation and Rajput Myth in Tribal Central India (1962) and (3) Tribe-Caste and Tribe-Peasant Continuation in Central India (1965). Through these studies, he had shown that tribes and castes in India are not separate and isolated social and cultural categories, but as parts of greater Indian Societies, cultures and civilization. This he had shown in an evolutionary scheme under which the formation of early states in India took place. In the following section a sketch of his academic contributions are highlighted in brief.

Studies on Tribes, Castes and Peasants

Sinha's focus of study was on tribes later extending to castes and peasants in India. He worked on various categories of tribes at different ecological and social contexts. He studied tribal groups, viz. Hill Marias lived both in isolation as well as in contact zones. He studied Bhumij and examined their social and cultural patterns in relation to environmental, social and cultural contexts. His most popular and unique concept of "tribe-caste-peasant-continuum" is an eye-opening ideas, which he developed through field research. His interests was not simply for ethnography of tribes, castes and peasants, but how those social categories are related and integrated in interlocking system towards forming a complex greater society and civilization of India.

Sinha sincerely worked on tribal transformation, tribal mobilization, tribal movement and finally tribal state formation. His works on tribal social transformation process towards the direction of *varna*, caste and clans was conceptualized by him as "tribe-caste-peasant-continuum". His other concepts like "Bhumij-Rajput continuum" and "Bhumij-Khuspatra continuum" are also the outcome of such transformation process of a tribe who sustained their life through settled cultivation. His model of understanding the relationship between tribe and peasants helps us in understanding the nature of social interaction as well as social transformation at middle and eastern parts of India, where most of the tribal groups living in the social context of regular interaction with the non-trinal groups, i.e. Hindu peasants. Sinha's prime concern was how tribes became integrated with the regional peasant economy and local caste system. He was able to prove how the ascribed primordial tribal identity was fused with the achieved peasant identity through common habitat, economy and social system and ideological beliefs.

Through the studies of tribal transformation and tribal state formation, Sinha has given the importance of theoretical formulation and thereby able to break the conventional (ideal) notion about tribal society as a simple and homogeneous social category, devoid of social stratification system. His unique ideas of tribal state formation and Rajputaization, clearly shows that the sanskritization (a variant form of Brahminization), received less significance, rather "Kshatriyazition" or "Vaishnavization" got much importance among the tribal groups in many parts of India. He held the view that tribes and tribal societies are not static as it is believed to be, but are dynamic like other non-tribal societies around them due to social contacts for functional necessities. His famous concept of "State Formation" among many agricultural tribal groups of India clearly indicates how social complexities have emerged among the simple tribal groups in course of history and gradually imbibed the characters of class stratification, political domination and class consciousness within the traditional egalitarian tribal social system. According to Sinha there has also been a synthesis between tribal and caste world views and that binds them to live together in regional social order. To him the tribal and tribal-peasant cultural attributes what he regarded as little traditions played a very significant role and constituted an important dimension of Indian civilization.

Sinha had the opinion that tribal villages are not simply the isolate localities, but are the functional units and spaces, representing inter-local, inter-regional and even trans-regional connectivity. To him these connectivities do not follow the undimentional pattern, rather multidimensional nature, which sustain the process of acculturation and integration.

Sinha's comprehension of "peasant" as a social category is also very important. He was hesitant to accept "peasant" as simply a economic category living only in relation to land for their sustenance. In his view peasant is a distinct social category based on both economic and socio-cultural attributes. Peasant constituted a highly heterogeneous and diverse social group of people's cuting across ethnic, caste and even religious affiliations. His major focus was to understand the Indian peasantry as inter-connected and inter-locked social groups based on reciprocal roles and relations among and between the various heterogeneous social segments at a local context. He considered peasants who are engaged in intensive agriculture requiring varieties of services to be provided by various groups as a particular ecological and social context. According to him, peasants though form a unique social entity going beyond ethnicity, caste, and religious affiliation, even though there are relative differences among these various groups in terms of their economic position, power and dominance in social functioning.

Sinha explored, discovered, analyzed and interpreted the elements of transition and transformation of tribal cultural elements in the direction of peasant cultural attributes out of interaction and amalgamation between tribes and castes. He had a very clear notion that the social classes in India are very much linked with the ethnic, caste or caste like social groups of a community (1955, 1957, 1962, 1965, 1966a, 1969, 1978).

Sinha's most important contribution to Indian anthropology is his unique approach of examining Indian civilization through a new perspective. In his view, Indian civilization is multi-dimensional having both sacred and secular dimension. According to him civilization in India is a complex and composite whole, which is the synthesis, and amalgamation of many societies, cultures, values and traditions (both great and little) those are interlinked, integrated, synthesized, and syncretized. Indian civilization has historically and functionally grown, contributed by several ethnic, linguistic and socio-religious groups. He boldly stated that India is a vast counting where varieties of peoples with their varied cultures living together since historical times in relation to each other of economic and social necessities. As a result, somewhere their social and cultural elements are converage at the same time diverge to maintaining their distinct identities. Sinha used to believe that Indian civilization does not simply mean what we are but what we have and for this it is distinct from other great civilizations. His approach was to see the processes those relate various social categories of the country, viz. tribe, caste, peasant, urban, etc. those bind them to live together in harmony for their social requirements. Sinha's fundamental concept of "tribe-caste-peasant continuum" is not simply to know the dynamics of tribal, caste and peasant lives in India, but also to consider them as a theoretical and methodological tool for the study of Indian civilization.

Sinha significantly contributed towards evolving a fresh method and technique of doing fieldwork for data collection. His fieldwork legacy is still a source of inspiration to many field researchers. His framework of field research consists of three major vantage points. These are: (i) For a good field research selection of problem and formulation of theoretical and methodological framework of study are very important; (ii) Societies and their cultures (tribal, peasant, urban etc.) to be examined for exploring both missing links and existing links between the members of different social categories. Learning from history is very necessary for understanding the present; and (iii) Anthropological enquiries mostly focus on the problems as well as desires of the people under study, so that research findings to be used for social reconstruction and development.

According to him, fieldwork must be guided by contextual and historical perspectives. The most important lesson he left behind for us is the tridimensional approach of conducting fieldwork. These are temporal and historical, spatial and contextual and ethnic and cultural. His approach of field study is popularly known as spatio-temporal perspective of ethno-analysis. His emphasis was on good and holistic understanding of the research problems and which is only possible if it is backed by very good research design and supported by strong theoretical and methodological foundations. In his view both research design (thinking) and research proposition (acting) are equally important for anthropological field studies.

For fieldwork, Sinha was in favour of both extensive and intensive studies and comparative method, depending on the theme of research problem. He also advocated re-studies for understanding the process of change over times. To him fieldworker must be a good learner, listener and observer. In his view fieldwork is nothing but the recoding of live experience of the people under study. Therefore, a fieldworker should note what the people think? What they say? What they act? and How they perceive the meaning of their acts? He also emphasized the needs of selection of good informants as well as importance of impression management and rapport establishment with the peoples for doing fieldwork. Sinha emphasized the need of both conversational and observation techniques of data collection in field situation and strongly believed the significance of the method of "cultural relativism" in field studies. Repeatedly he pointed out that in anthropological writings the scholar should vividly describe his or her field experiences of conducting fieldwork consisting of field strategies, problems faced and how successfully handled them for data collection. To him maintaining field diary is an essential component for a fieldworker, which he learned from his teachers T.C. Das and N.K. bose.

Sinha himself worked on various ethnic and other social groups at varied contexts and also directed as well as supervised varieties of research problems and subjects. His own academic research was started with tribes of Indian peninsula and them on Bhumij, for which he had undertaken extensive fieldwork at undivided Bihar, Orissa, Bengal and other places. He did intensive field studies among Bhumijs of Barabhum. His field studies continued with dynamics of tribal life, tribal movement, tribal politics, survey of weaker sections, industrial workers, religious centres, rural and urban lives and finally Indian civilization. All these suggest that he had a command on various aspects of anthropological studies in India and those compelled him to understand the Indian civilization (Bose, 1978).

Sinha's contribution not only confined to formulate concepts as well as methods of conducting anthropological fieldwork. In addition to such areas, he was very anxious of colonial legacy and Western domination in Indian anthropology. Even though at the initial phase Sinha himself was, captive of American anthropological tradition, particularly of Chicago school, but at the later phase he initiated an effort to develop the Indian tradition of this discipline and this was continued till he academically active.

His famous writing on "Is there any Indian Tradition in Social/ Cultural Anthropology: Retrospect and Prospect" is still the essential reading for the students and scholars of Anthropology. In this article, he expressed not only the history and development of anthropology in India but also expressed his agony about academic colonialism and Western domination in the disciples of our country. He had the views that we must appreciate whatever best in Western thoughts, ideas and methods in anthropological studies, but at the same time we must be very careful about the use of them in examining the Indian socio-cultural issues, problems and realities. Here again he has not followed the path of other

Indian anthropologists to see India through unidimentionally. His view is unique and different in the sense that India is land of plural and tolerant society. Both diversities and unity are its unique social flavour, composite nationhood with multicultural ethos formulated its traditions. According to him India constituted one grand civilization to which all groups living in this country have made their significant contributions in different ways. For him indigenization of the discipline must require a deeper understanding of Indian history, socio-cultural realities and its social surroundings (1968).

Surajit Chandra Sinha left behind a very rich tradition in Indian anthropology. His contributions are very divergse ranging from theoretical, methodological and empirical dimension, including the future of the discipline in this country. His empirical studies are ranging from tribe, caste, and peasant, urban and industrial-modern societies. All these he has studied and examined from facts based on archival and field sources. All these he examined in historical, structural and organizational frame of Indian societies, cultures and civilization.

His conceptualization of tribe from the perspectives of their world's views and culture patterns is unique. His views on "tribal transformation", "state formation", "Rajputization" and so also the "tribe-caste-peasant continuum" are the clear indication of his civilization model of social-cultural analysis.

Sinha considered that the caste system in India, its essence, stability and even its existence and social influences has been grown historically and changed over times out of emerged circumstances. In his view the system of caste in India to be examined from texts as well as contexts through *Varna-Jati*, model of social analysis. He had the view that the plights of the weaker sections in India should be known meaningfully through the study of caste or caste like systems in this country. He strongly believed that the classes or status groups in India had also a deep relation with caste hierarchy, which is reflected in his visions on *Bhadralok* and *Chhotolok* based social stratification in Bengal. This according to him is the product of the long-range historical stratification of caste hierarchy in changing social context, based on wealth, education and power. He boldly stated that this form of social stratification in Bengal is nothing but a secular adaption of traditional caste hierarchy in this province.

Sinha's anthropological studies were not only confined to tribe, caste, peasant and urban societies but also shifted to science and scientists in Indian socio-cultural milieu. He meticulously noted how traditional idioms played the great role in the pursuit of science and scientists of this country. In his view, science has also acquired some adaptive idioms in India.

The models and methods of field studies that Sinha was formulated in his own field studies is still a strong reference to the fieldworkers. His fieldwork strategy is still a matter of legacy in Indian anthropology. Sinha's thoughts and ideas got the unique shape out of the influences of both anthropologists and social thinkers of India. Ideas of anthropologists like Redfield, Kroeber, Cohn, Singer, Chattopadhyay, Bose, Das and several others in many ways motivated his anthropological visions. Similarly, the ideas of social thinkers of the country like Gandhi, Tagore, Ramkrishna and Vivekananda have also shaped his anthropological visions for India.

In his later phase of professional life, Sinha was very much concerned about the Western apprentiship in Indian Anthropology. His advocacy for an authentic identity of Indian anthropology is still awaited.

Sinha undoubtedly influenced by American cultural anthropological thoughts and ideas .during initial phase of his academic carrier, but at later phase he was successfully able to formulate his own thoughts and ideas to examine the social-cultural reality of Indian societies and civilization of this unique country. His historical and contextual approaches, evolutionary frame and structural-organizational perspectives are still the frame of reference to Indian anthropology.

REFERENCES

Sinha, S.C. 1955, "Evolutionism Reconsidered" in *Man in India*, Vol.35, No.1

Sinha, S.C. 1957, "Tribal cultures in Peninsular India as a Dimension of Little Tradition in the Study of Indian Civilization: A preliminary Statement", in *Man in India,* Vol. 37, pp. 91-118, (Also published in *Journal of American Folklore*, Vol.71, No. 281, 1958).

Sinha, S.C. 1962, "State Formation and Rajput Myth in Tribal Central India" in *Mau in India*, Vol. 42, No.1.

Sinha, S.C. 1965, "Tribe-Caste and Tribe-Peasant continua in Central India", *Man in India*, Vol. 45, No.1, pp. 57-83.

Sinha, S.C. 1966, "Religion in an Affluent Society", *Current Anthropology,* Vol.7, No. 2.

Sinha, S.C. 1966 (a). "Caste in India: Its Essential Pattern of Socio-Cultural integration", Paper contributed to the conference on *Caste and Races,* sponsored by CIBA Foundation, London.

Sinha, S.C. 1967, "Involvement in Social Change", in *Economic and Political Weekly,* September 16, 1707-1710.

Sinha, S.C. 1968, Is there an Indian Tradition in Social/Cultural Anthropology : Retrospect and Prospect" Paper contributed to the conference on the Nature and Function of Anthropological Traditions, Sponsored by Wenner Gren Foundation for Anthropological Research. (Also published by Indian Anthropological Society in an edited volume of S.B. Chakraborty, 2012).

Sinha, S.C. 1969, "Urgent Problems for Research in Social and Cultural Anthropology in India: Perspectives and Suggestions, Indian Institute of Advanced Study, Simla, Transactions No.1, pp.162-169.

Sinha, S.C. 1969, "The concept of Diku among the Tribes of Chotonagpur" in *Man in India*, Vol.49, No.2.

Sinha, S.C. 1969 (a), "Bhadralok and Chhotolok in Rural Area of West Bengal", *Sociological Bulletin*, Vol. 18, No. 1 (in Collaboration with R.K. Bhattacharya).

Sinha, S.C., 1970, "Indian Scientists – The Socio-Cultural context of their professional Environment" in Sinha, S.C. (Edited) *Science, Technology and Culture,* New Delhi.

Sinha, S.C. 1972, "Co-existence of Multiple Scales and Networks of a Civilization: India", paper contributed in Burgwartenstein Symposition (No.55) on Scale and Social organization.

Sinha, S.C. 1974, "Sociology of Religion" in Survey of Research in Sociology and Social Anthropology, Delhi, ICSSR, Vol.II.

Sinha, S.C. 1975, "Expansion of the Social Base of Culture in Modern India", Presidential Address to the Indian Anthropological Society, Calcutta.

Sinha, S.C. 1976, "Rabindranath Tagore's Ideas about Structure and Essence of Indian Civilization", Presidential Address to the Indian Anthropological Society, Calcutta.

Sinha, S.C. 1977, "Structure of Indian Civilization: Continuity and Change", Lecture delivered at the Aurobindo Centre: Calcutta.

Sinha, S.C. 1977(a), "Varna-Jati Model and the rural poor in India today", Presidential Address to the Indian Anthropological Society.

Sinha, S.C. 1978, Re-thinking about Tribes and Indian Civilization", in *Journal of Indian Anthropological Society,* Vol. 8, No. 2.

Sinha, S.C. and B.N. Saraswati, 1978, *The Asitics of Kashi,* Vanaras; N.K. Bose Memorial Foundation, December, 1978.

Sarkar Amitabha and Soumitra Dasgupta (ed.), 2019, *Doyens of Indian Anthropology,* New Delhi: Agamkala Publication.

27
Tarak Chandra Das

Abhijit Guha

Tarak Chandra Das was born in January 1898 in erstwhile undivided Bengal now under Bangladesh. Nothing in detail is known about his family background and school education in the existing literature. He had his early education in Tangail and Rajshahi of present Bangladesh. Das obtained his M.A. degree in 'Ancient Indian History and Culture' from the University of Calcutta. He joined the newly founded Department of Anthropology at Calcutta University in 1921 as a research scholar and then he became lecturer in 1923 and finally retired in the rank of Reader from the Department in 1963.

One comprehensive available account of the list of publications of T.C. Das including a short life-sketch was prepared by the Reference Librarian in the Central Library of the Anthropological Survey of India, Shyamal Kumar Ray, in his invaluable book 'Bibliographies of Eminent Indian Anthropologists (with Life-Sketches)' published by the Anthropological Survey of India and Indian Museum in July 1974. The volume contains the list of publications and short life-sketches of 12 eminent Indian anthropologists including Tarak Chandra Das. It begins with L.K. Ananthakrishna Iyer (1861-1937) and S.S. Sarkar (1908-1969) is the last anthropologist covering a span of more than one hundred years if we take the year of birth of Iyer and the year of death of Sarkar at the two ends of the continuum. T.C. Das falls somewhere in the middle of the continuum.

Bibliographical records of T.C. Das showed that he had altogether 40 publications that are almost one in every year of his academic career. He published 31 full-length articles, 2 books, 6 abstracts, two jointly authored books and one joint article. The national and international journals in which he published were prestigious and they included – Man,

Anthropos, Ethnos, Man in India, Calcutta Review, Modern Review, Sociological Bulletin, Journal of Social Research, Journal of the Department of Letters and Anthropological Papers of the University of Calcutta. Apart from kinship and social organisation, his areas of research interest displayed remarkable diversity which ranged between sun-worship (1924), fish in Bengali culture (1931-32), the disposal of dead among the tribals (1940), improvement of museums (1943), scheme for tribal welfare, impact of industrialization on peasantry (1960) to an anthropological analysis of Bengal dowry restriction bill (1941).

Tarak Chandra Das became internationally famous for his ethnography on the Purum Kukis of North-east India. His brilliant monograph 'The Purums: An Old Kuki tribe of Manipur' published in 1945 by the Calcutta University became one of the major sources of database in the acrimonious debate on descent *versus* alliance theories on kinship in Anglo-American Anthropology which involved mavericks like Claude Levi-Strauss, George Homans, David Schneider, Rodney Needham, Floyd Lounsbury and others. The Indian anthropologists too continued their ethnographic enterprise on the Purum on behalf of the premier governmental institution of the country— the Anthropological Survey of India. A team of anthropologists were sent to the field area where Das conducted his ethnographic observations during 1931-1936 and a book was published entitled Proceedings of the Symposium on Purum (Chote) Revisited in 1985 as an outcome of a symposium in which about 20 anthropologists two educated members of the tribe participated and presented their views/papers on the Purums. L.P. Vidyarthi in the first volume of his book *Rise of Anthropology in India* described in detail about the findings of Das in different chapters of the monograph with much admiration for its meticulousness and penetrating analyses. In the final part of his description, Vidyarthi discussed the suggestions advanced by Das for the betterment of the Purums. According to Vidyarthi, with the publication of the Purum book T.C. Das 'set an example of a systematic presentation of ethnographic data' (*Ibid.,* 1978: 80). He concluded the discussion on Das's monograph with the following comment:

> His monograph, though not well known to Indian scholars, remains a piece of meticulous fieldwork and penetrative analysis. It will continue to serve as a model for ethnographic research in anthropology.

In the concluding chapter of the Purum book Das laid emphasis on the dynamic nature of Purum society which had undergone changes through historical times and also on the different aspects of Purum culture under various kinds of external influences. Secondly, Das was keenly interested to understand the nature of the 'productive system' (he did not use the Marxian term means of production but it was clear that by the term 'productive system' he did not only refer to technology and material culture) in a dynamic rather than in a functional framework. Thirdly, without borrowing terms from the Western Marxist scholars mechanically Das made a very sincere empirical attempt to record the processes by which the new productive system, characterized by plough and plains-land cultivation had begun to influence the different sectors of the Purum society, viz. inheritance, marriage and religion. Apart from looking into the internal socio-cultural changes brought about by the adoption of the plough cultivation among the Purums, Das was also aware of the wider politico-economic forces which were at work in the region where this small tribe inhabited.

Another significant work of Das remained unnoticed by the scholars on Indian Anthropology. This work of Das was published in the prestigious international journal *Anthropos* as early as 1937 under the title "Some notes on the economic and agricultural life of a little known tribe on the eastern frontier of India." In this paper Das dealt with the relationship between the variation in technology of agricultural practices with the natural environment and the socio-economic consequences of this variation within the same tribe. The name of the tribe is Chiru, who like the Purums belonged to the old Kuki group of tribes of the north-east India. A careful reading of the paper reveals that the economic life of the Chirus which Das constructed is not a simple description of the methods of shifting hill cultivation and the associated religious rituals and rites. Neither it is an ethnographic report for the search of borrowed culture traits from the neighbouring tribes and Hinduised populations nor was it an attempt to put the Chirus in the classical scheme of social evolution. The ethnography of Das on the other hand is a penetrating analysis of the various socio-cultural dimensions of shifting hill cultivation in an environmental framework and the slow changes that had been taking place at the time of observation. It is interesting to note that one of the earliest publications of Julian Steward in which he dealt with the relationship between productive technology and the other sectors of culture was published in the same year in *Anthropos* (Steward, 1937: 87-104). If one compares the paper of Steward with that of Das, then certain important similarities become evident. Like T.C. Das, Julian Steward also gave emphasis on the importance of environment and economy in shaping the social organizational features of a culture.

T.C. Das's book on the famine of Bengal which took place in 1943 was a unique and rare first-hand study done by any anthropologist or social scientist on the victims of one of the greatest tragedies of our country under the colonial rule. The book entitled *Bengal Famine* (1943): as revealed in a survey of the destitutes of Calcutta was published by the University of Calcutta in 1949. An earlier version of the book was discussed in the then British Parliament and some of the recommendations advanced by Das were adopted by the Famine Inquiry Commission in 1944 formed by the colonial government for the prevention of future famines in India. Pandit Jawaharlal Nehru in his book The *Discovery of India* also mentioned about the anthropological survey conducted by Das on the famine affected population of Bengal and expressed his confidence on the results of the survey in contrast to the one carried out by the government. The Nobel Laureate economist Amartya Sen has also used Das' original work several times in his famous book *Poverty and Famines*. Of all the works of T.C. Das Bengal Famine can be regarded as the most valuable and unique contribution for the following reasons. The field based study of the Bengal famine of 1943 which was conducted by T.C. Das is not a typical anthropological study of a tribe or a caste village. Let us enumerate the facts. First, this is the only first-hand study done by a team of trained anthropologists under on the Bengal famine. Second, the book which was written by Das has not received any attention by the successive generation of anthropologists and sociologists in India. Third, in this study Das and his co-fieldworkers employed traditional anthropological methods (e.g. genealogy, case history, participant observation) for the collection of data not from a specific tribe or caste in a rural setting, but from a scattered and heterogeneous group of human beings displaced from the different districts of undivided Bengal affected by the acute food shortage. Fourth, the fieldwork and the survey on the famine affected population were carried out mainly in the city of Calcutta. Fifth, the report and the recommendations based on the anthropological study of the famine in Bengal were taken into consideration by the policy makers and administrators at the highest level of governance. Sixth, the explanation provided by Das on the causes of Bengal famine surpassed the prevalent anthropological interpretations of social events. Taken together, the above facts have made Bengal Famine an unorthodox kind of anthropological study even by modern standards.

The anthropological Odyssey of T.C. Das like many of his contemporaries began with observations on tribal social structure, economic organisation, material culture and religion, but he gradually focused his findings towards application and policy oriented arguments in a macro framework. Das was not only a meticulous ethnographer but during the middle part of his journey, he also moved out of tribes and ventured into the territories which did not come under the tradition of anthropology developed in India under the Western influence. The study of the Great Bengal famine is the finest example of this genre. Apart from his success as an ethnographer, Das was also an armchair anthropologist. His studies on culture around fish in Bengal, museums and dowry restriction law provided examples of his keen interest in dealing with archival materials and written texts in social anthropological and sociological studies.

Beside the study of Bengal famine, there were other notable and almost unknown studies made by Das on subjects rarely taken up seriously by the anthropologists. One such study by Das was on Bengal Dowry Restriction Bill and the other was on the Hindu Code Bill. The third paper was on museums. The first two papers were published in *The Modern Review* and *The Calcutta Review* in 1941 and 1944 respectively and the third one was also published in *The Calcutta Review* in the year 1943. In the first and the second papers, Das argued in favour of conducting proper sociological studies before introducing new legislations, which in his opinion might have caused unwanted effects in these intricate and complex social matters. The third article was entitled 'Practical steps towards the improvements of museums in India' (1943) is unique because in this article Das developed the idea of building 'Economic Museums' in which anthropologists and other scientists would work for the economic development of the people.

In the later part of his career Das took up the study of tribal societies in India beyond simple ethnography. His three papers on scheme for tribal welfare (1960), social change in tribal society (1962) and tribal culture under modern impact (1963) are best examples of the aforementioned trend. In all these articles, Das used his massive ethnographic experience to understand the changes that had been taking place among the tribes of eastern India and attempted to formulate general policies towards their development. His ideas about tribal development were pragmatic and he never believed in the policy of isolating the tribals from the mainstream of Indian culture. Das gave top priorities to the spread of primary and vocational education to the tribals and wanted them to be economically self-sufficient. In all these publications, Das strongly advocated the positive role anthropologists in tribal development. But at the same time he was well aware of the limitations of anthropology in this regard. For example, in the article 'A scheme for Tribal Welfare' he cautioned:

> The stock of our knowledge about the tribal peoples of India is very limited. We have about two scores of books on tribal ethnography of India. Many of these books written at a time when the subject itself had not attained its present methodological efficiency are not serviceable to the applied anthropologist. Most of these books do not deal with the economic condition of the tribes in proper detail. As a result the information available from this source are of little value to the State or to the Social worker.

Das envisaged that every state in India having one lakh or more tribal population should set up an independent institution for tribal survey and research for the purpose of the application of anthropological knowledge towards tribal development. These research institutions, according to Das were to be financed by the Government but should be kept outside its control, since these institutions would take up evaluation of various welfare schemes executed by the Government departments. They should be handed over to local universities having anthropology and sociology departments.

In 1941, he delivered the Presidential address in the Anthropology section of the Indian Science Congress. The lecture was a 28-page full-length paper entitled 'Cultural Anthropology in the Service of the Individual and the Nation'. This paper can be regarded as one of the pioneering articles on applied anthropology in India. In the address Das elaborately charted out the future path of Indian anthropology with a rich description of the social dynamics of the tribal and peasant societies in India in the context of the role of anthropologists in nation building.

T.C.Das was a brilliant teacher in the formative years of Indian anthropology at the University of Calcutta and his meticulous training in ethnographic fieldwork was well-known. Famous anthropologists like Ramkrishna Mukherjee, Surajit Sinha, B.K. Roy Burman, Ajit Danda, André Béteille, Probodh Bhowmick and Amal Kumar Das were trained by this unsung hero of Indian anthropology who passed away on 26th July in 1964.

REFERENCES

Das Gupta, B.K., Basu, A., Raychaudhuri, B., Gupta, P. (1985). *Proceedings of the Symposium on Purum (Chote) Revisited*. Anthropological Survey of India. Department of Culture, Government of India. Calcutta.

Das, T.C. (1949). *Bengal Famine (1943)*: *as revealed in a survey of the destitutes of Calcutta*. Calcutta University. Calcutta.

Das, T.C. 1937. Some notes on the economic and agricultural life of a little known tribe on the eastern frontier of India. *Anthropos* 32: 440-449.

Das, T.C. 1941. Cultural Anthropology in the Service of the Individual and the Nation, pp.1-29. *Presidential Address delivered in the Section of Anthropology in the Twenty-eighth Indian Science Congress*. Benares.

Das, T.C. 1943. Practical steps towards the improvement of museums in India. *The Calcutta Review*. November, pp. 97-100.

Das, T.C. 1960. A scheme for tribal welfare. *Journal of Social Research* 3:2, 93-112.

Guha, A. 2011. Tarak Chandra Das: a marginalized anthropologist. *Sociological Bulletin*, vol. 60, no. 2, pp. 245-265.

Guha, A. 2012. Tarak Chandra Das (1898-1964): a forgotten anthropologist. *Science and Culture*, vol. 78, nos. 1-2, pp. 40-46.

Guha, A. 2018. T.C. Das sitting in the armchair: the other side of the fieldworker anthropologist. *South Asian Anthropologist*, vol. 18, no. 1, pp. 109-114.

Nehru, J. (1981). First published in 1946. *The* Discovery *of India*. New Delhi: Oxford University Press.

Ray, S.K. 1974. Tarak Chandra Das (1898-1964), in *Bibliographies of eminent Indian anthropologists (with life-sketches)*, pp. 56-60. Calcutta: Anthropological Survey of India & Indian Museum.

Sen, A. 1999. *Poverty and Famines: An essay on Entitlement and Deprivation*. New Delhi: Oxford University Press.

Steward, J.H. 1937. Ecological aspects of Southwestern society. *Anthropos* 32:87:104.

Vidyarthi, L.P. 1978. *Rise of Anthropology in India: A Social Science Orientation*, Vols. I & II. New Delhi: Concept Publishing Company Pvt. Ltd.

28
T. N. Madan
Integration of Theory and Ethnography

Sukant K. Chaudhury

Professor Triloki Nath Madan, popularly known as Triloki by his seniors and contemporary colleagues, also known as Madan of the Majumdar and Madan fame, was a product of Lucknow School of Sociology.[1] Madan's academic contribution can be divided into four aspects: Kinship Studies, Development Studies, Anthropology of Religion and Secularism including Cognitive Sociology and Historical Sociology and Anthropology.

Madan's life both personal and professional has been very gigantic in the sense that he moved to different places and also moved to study different topics. I am fortunate to have several personal interactions with Professor Madan, particularly when he used to come to chair the Ethnographic and Folk Culture Society's Executive Body meetings and General Body meetings and also to inaugurate the Conferences organised by the Department of Sociology on behalf of the Ethnographic and Folk Culture Society. Majumdar established the Ethnographic and Folk Culture Society in 1945 and started the journal *The Eastern Anthropologist* in 1947 as the main organ of the society.[2] It is worth mentioning here that Professor Madan is one of the eminent life members of the Society. He is the Editorial Adviser of *The Eastern Anthropologist*. He was the President of the Society for six years (2006-2012) and I was the General Secretary. He would ungrudgingly teach all of us in the Society in general and me as General Secretary in particular about ways of functioning of the Society. These personal interactions at Lucknow occurred from 2002 to 2013, notwithstanding the fact that I am still in touch with him. After that Professor Madan almost stopped going outside Delhi and has almost contained himself in Sah Vikas Apartments in East Delhi. A very well dressed, fair complexioned smart and handsome man, Madan has been an influential figure and a referent individual for many. I write this personal note as well as the developments in his career, i.e. professional note both from my interactions with him and his autobiographical note published in 2011 (Madan, 2011: 240-265).

Born and brought up in Srinagar, up to Graduation he lived there and then he moved to Lucknow to pursue M.A. in Economics from the University of Lucknow. But he completed M.A. in 1951 with specialisation in Cultural Anthropology. In fact, the Department of Anthropology, University of Lucknow was established in 1949 by Professor D.N. Majumdar. In 1921 the University of Lucknow was established at Lucknow, and economics and sociology was one of the first departments started in 1921.It was chaired by Professor Radha Kamal Mukherjee. In 1928 D.N.Majumdar joined the department and taught primitive economics. Madan's teachers were luminaries like Radha Kamal Mukherjee, D.P. Mukerji, A.K. Saran and D.N. Majumdar. In 1953, Madan started teaching in the Department of Anthropology, University of Lucknow, where he was simultaneously trying to do Ph.D. on 'Rehabilitation' under Professor Majumdar. In 1956, *An Introduction to Social Anthropology* book came out of mainly Madan's notes which Majumdar probably went through. The book is still reprinted and is in demand from students both for the undergraduate beginners as well as Civil Service Aspirants. Madan says that during his stay at the University of Lucknow, he was fortunate to listen to the lectures of A. Aiyyapan, N.K. Bose, Louis Dumont, Irawati Karve, S.F. Nadel and M.N. Srinivas. S.F Nadel visited University of Lucknow in early 1955 and Madan was greatly influenced by him and had applied to Australian National University for a Ph.D. Eventually he got admission but before his arrival at Canberra, Nadel passed away. He did Ph.D. under Derek Freeman and his Co-supervisor was W.E.H. Stuner. He came back in 1959 and joined the University of Lucknow as a Lecturer. Subsequently he went to the Department of Anthropology, School of Oriental and African Studies, London as a Lecturer in 1963.

Then he came back and joined as a Reader in Social Anthropology in the Department of Anthropology, Karnataka University, Dharwad, where he took interest in study of Urbanisation and Culture of Private Medical Practice near hospitals. He also pursued this research after shifting to Delhi in 1965. He joined the Institute of Economic Growth, Delhi in 1966. There he was the Director for three years (1982-1985) and finally, he retired from there after 31 years in 1997. In between, for about 3 years he was appointed as the Member Secretary of The Indian Council for Social Science Research, New Delhi from 1978 to 1981. Madan enjoyed his teaching career of about ten years, as he says, "Giving up teaching was, therefore, a deeply felt wrench" (Madan, 2011:259). However, he taught intermittently at many Universities afterwards, which include: as a Guest Lecturer he taught kinship theory to M.A. Sociology students at Delhi School of Economics, Delhi University for six years (1972-1977), he was also a Visiting Professor at the University of Illinois, University of Washington, University of Texas, Smith College and Harvard University. He taught Social Theory, Religion and Comparative Ethics in the above five American Institutions. After his retirement, he has been there in the Institute as an Emeritus Professor till today. Besides this he was also associated with the Rajni Kothari fame Centre for the Study of Developing Societies, Delhi where he became Chairman from 2003-2008. He was elected as an Honorary Fellow of The Royal Anthropological Institute, London in 1989 (the other two Indians so far being late Professor M.N. Srinivas and Professor Andre Beteille). He was made a *Docteur Honoris Causa* of University of Paris (Nanterre) in 1994. He received Lifetime Achievement Award of The Indian Sociological Society in 2008.

I very fondly remember the interactions with Professor Madan, mostly it was an interaction with a group of my colleagues and sometimes delegates from different parts of the country who came for a Conference. His sharing of experiences with us about his time spent in Lucknow from 1949 to 1956 and again 1959 to 1962 were truly ethnographic in nature.

His marriage with Mrs. Uma Madan, who was a masters in Anthropology from University of Lucknow, has been influential on his life, particularly in building his personality in the later years of his life. Unfortunately Mrs. Uma Madan passed away in 2013 at the age of 80. His experiences with different Professors who were his contemporaries or juniors have been very rewarding and learning experiences for us. Worth mentioning among them are Professor Andre Beteille, Professor Gopala Sarana, Professor Yogesh Atal, Professor S.C. Dube, Professor M.N. Srinivas and so on.

His numerous publications include:

1. Family and Kinship: A Study of the Pandits of Rural Kashmir (1965)
2. Culture and Development (1983)
3. Non-Renunciation: Themes and Interpretation of Hindu Culture (1987)
4. Pathways: Approaches to the Study of Society in India (1994)

5. Modern Myths, Locked Minds: Secularism and Fundamentalism in India (1997)
6. The Hindu Householder (2010)
7. Sociological Traditions: Methods and Perspectives in the Sociology of India (2011)
8. Sociology at the University of Lucknow: The First Half Century (1921-1975)

His edited books include *Religion in India, India's Religion, Perspectives from Sociology and History* (both are from the series: Oxford in India Readings in Sociology and Social Anthropology) and *A Way of Life: King, Household Renouncer (Essays in the honour of Louis Dumont).* His collected essays have been published by him as *Images of the World: Essays on Religion, Secularism and Culture* (2006). The Oxford University Press published an Omnibus: *The Hindu Householder:* The *T.N. Madan Omnibus* (2010) where it included his book *Family and Kinship* and *Non-Renunciation.* Other books include *Muslim Communities of South Asia: Culture, Society and Power* (2001). One of the important contributions which Madan has made which will be remembered for years to come is that of editing the new series of the premier journal *Contribution to Indian Sociology.* It was established in 1957 by Louis Dumont and David Pocock and they continued to edit it till 1966. Then it stopped for a while. Then the new series was started in 1972, edited by Madan who continued to edit it for 25 years, i.e. up to 1997.He was presented with a Festschrift titled *Tradition, Pluralism and Identity: In Honour of T.N. Madan* edited by Veena Das, Dipankar Gupta and Patricia Uberoi.

Madan has been known as an anthropologist as well as sociologist: he specialized in Cultural Anthropology and worked in anthropology departments at University of Lucknow and Karnatka University, later on he joined as Professor of Sociology at Institute of Economic Growth, New Delhi. According to him "anthropology was best conceived, not as the study of 'other' cultures, but as 'the mutual interpretation of cultures', and that we must adhere firmly to the notion that anthropology resides in the nexus, that it is a kind of knowledge—a form of consciousness-which arises from the encounter of cultures in the mind of anthropologist. What an observer learns about an alien society's observable modes of behaviour will not yield anthropological understanding unless he or she is able to grasp, in the first place, the subjective purposes and meanings that make these modes of behaviour significant to the people concerned. But the knowledge about one's own beliefs and rituals which an informant may impart to the investigator is not anthropological either. In other words, anthropological knowledge is not to be discovered, but generated by confronting, first, what people say with what they do, and, then, confronting the view from within with the view from without" (Madan, 2011: 54).

Madan did fieldwork in Utrassu-Umanagri village in Kashmir for about one year for his Ph.D. work. It has been phenomenal in the sense that the book has been used as a learning material for thousands of students in various universities across the country. It was first published in 1965 by Asia Publishing House and later on the second edition came in 1989 by Oxford University Press. It was reprinted several times. It is a study of Kashmir Pandits from rural Kashmir. Incidentally they have been in news in 2019 after the removal of provisions in Article 370 of the Constitution. In the preface of the fiftieth anniversary Edition Madan said that the book was conceived and written as an ethnographic account of family life on the basis of a yearlong residence in the village of Utrassu-Umanagri in the Kashmir Valley in the mid 1950s. He wrote: "The perspective on everyday life was synchronic, not historical. By what I can only call an irony of history, it has now become a record of the past of a community-history. The secessionist violence that hit the Kashmir valley in the early 1990s led to the migration of almost the whole of the Kashmiri Pandit community to other parts of India and the world; for some families this road led to a final destination through a period of waiting for an unknown future in refugee camps. There is hardly any hope that the exiles will ever return home." The political problems in Kashmir have been going on since long. Aileen D. Ross writing a review of Madan's book in 1967 in *The Journal of Asian Studies* wrote, "The recent political upheavals in Kashmir however, have begun to impinge on the Pandits and, one would suspect, have been as upsetting to their traditional kinship patterns as they have in other parts of the world. It is hoped that Dr. Madan will take advantage of this changing situation to write Volume II" (Ross, 1967: 512).

As said earlier, Madan had joined Australia National University in Canberra in July 1956 then he went to Kashmir to do fieldwork from January 1957 to January 1958. He collected data through interviews, genealogies, family histories and participant observation. Subsequently, Madan visited the village again in 1959 and 1961. The village Utrassu-Umanagri is about 11 miles away from the nearest town Anantnag. There were 87 Brahmin households with 522 people. The two sub-castes of Brahmins are Karkun and Gor Brahmins. In the 1961 Census there were

89,102 Hindus out of 1,899,438 inhabitants. That means 5 per cent population were Hindus. Utrassu-Umanagri is a binucleated village. It is a patrilineal society. The village has many clusters of homesteads known as 'Pur'. Each Pur is named after a family which is predominating. There are 23 Purs in Utrassu whereas Umanagri has 6 Purs with 66 houses. In Utrassu-Umanagri 80 per cent population were Muslims, i.e. consisting of 2,122 persons and only 522 people were Pandits, 214 lived in Utrassu and 308 lived in Umanagri. They were clubbed into 20 'Kotamb' or families. Each family consisted of one or more households of patrilineally related kinsmen, their unmarried female agnates and wives.

Madan used structural theory to analyse the data and had much of Nadel's influence. As said earlier Madan was born and brought up in the city of Srinagar. He joined the University of Lucknow in 1949 as a student and has almost lived out of Kashmir since then. He says that there are only two Brahmin sub-castes in the rural Kashmir and there has been no other Hindu caste there. The Brahmins co-reside with Muslims in most of the villages but do not interdine or intermarry with them. They have economic transactions but they do not combine into a single society.

Madan has dealt with details of birth and adoption rituals, marriage and incorporation rituals, economic aspect of the household, partition of the household etc. He has also analysed the family and the patrilineage, i.e. as said earlier Kashmiri Pandits follow all aspects of patrilineage including patriarchy, patrinymy and patrilocality. There term for a group of households is "Kotamb". For patrilineage they are referred to as "Kol" or "Khandan". Madan says that, "In terms of interkin relationship Kol membership involves the observance of the rules of exogamy and ritual pollution. The fact that agnates usually bear the same Kotamb name, and always the same Gotra name, is enough protection against the unwitting breach of Kol exogamy. And so far as pollution is concerned, the Pandits rationalize that unless one hears of the event (birth or death) there is no pollution."

Further Madan has also analysed the wider kinship structure, i.e. the non-agnatic kin. In fact Madan's Family and Kinship study among Kashmir Pandits has been of great significance and relevance today in the light of political restructuring of Kashmir.

Madan delivered the Prof. D.N. Majumdar memorial lecture on "Culture, Society and Modernization" which was later published as a book: *Culture and Development* (1983). He says that he had developed interest in the broader issues of culture and development and had raised many questions: Were non-Western societies lacking in cultural resources to modernise? Did all cultures have to conform to a single type of development and modernity? Or, should one be exploring the reality, and not merely the idea, of the diversity of cultures of development (see Madan, 2011: 260). He also studied some aspects of profession particularly on education and medical professions. In Dharwar, he had studied the private education institutions and found out co-existence of primordial (caste, religious) identities (representing a tradition that modernists consider a sign of backwardness) and modern technical education provided by caste and community managed educational institutions (see Madan 2011: 258). Further he also studied the pattern of private medical practice among doctors in the city of Ghaziabad.

His ideas on secularism have been expressed several times through his addresses and papers in various fora. He has "emphasized both multivocality of the concept and untenability of a bipolar, scared *versus* secular model of secularization... the Western, secular world view was unlikely to have an easy passage to India in the absence of ideological support from India's three major religious traditions, comparable to Christianity's early distinction between the sacred and secular domains" (see Madan, 2011: 258). Further he said that a re-examination of the concept of the secular state in the Indian context is required. Madan's two edited books on religion have been extremely helpful to the students and researchers in various disciplines and are the best sellers as well.

The Volume on *Sociological Traditions: Methods and Perspectives in the Sociology of India* (2011) is a collection of ten papers, written on both cultural traditions and intellectual traditions in India. On cultural traditions he has included Secularism, Hinduism, Islam, Sikhism, Gandhi and Weber. On intellectual traditions he has included four important Indian Sociologists and Anthropologists: Radha Kamal Mukherjee, D.P. Mukerji, M.N. Srinivas and Louis Dumont. Further he has also written a chapter on Contribution to Indian Sociology which he edited for twenty five years (1972-1997). All these chapters were written between 2005 and 2010 and published in different journals and books.

On Radha Kamal Mukherjee, he says that Mukherjee and Birbal Sahni were the first two professors in the newly established University of Lucknow in 1921. Interestingly had an offer from the University of Bombay (p. 123). He established the Department of Economics and Sociology on the opening day of the University. Madan writes, "In his inaugural address at Lucknow delivered on 8th August, 1921, Mukherjee called for; 'a New School of Economic Thought and Research'; which would be free from 'barren abstractions' through a concentration on the local problems of peasants in the field, the labourers of the factories, the artisans of the cottages."

Madan says that Mukherjee advocated for the use of comparative method based on critique of logical and rational assumptions of classical and neo-classical economics, which marginalised cultural and social institutions. Mukherjee's ideas on Social Ecology and Sociology of Values are two of his most recognised sociological works. According to Madan, notable contemporaries were Benoy Kumar Sarkar (1887-1949) at Calcutta University, G.S. Ghurye (1893-1983) at Bombay University and D.P. Mukerji (1894-1961) at Lucknow University (p. 135).

On D.P. Mukerji, Madan says that he was a great teacher and had "an abiding influence on others through the spoken rather than the written." Further he says that people have two misconceptions about Mukerji: that he was a Marxist and a Hindu intellectual (a conservative who was only superficially modern). Mukerji himself described that he was a Marxologist. His deepest interest was in the Marxian method rather than in any dogmas (Madan, 2011: 153). Further though he was a Brahmin by birth and upbringing, he rejected the religious beliefs and rituals quite early in his own life. Mukerji's main work has been on the Nature of Social Science and Indian Culture.

Regarding D.P. Mukerji's book *Basic Concepts in Sociology* (1932), Madan says that it was "a product of his engagement with the Western Social Thought and it discusses the notion of progress, equality, social forces and social control. His exposition of these concepts is marked by both a positive attitude to the Western Liberal Outlook and also of a lack of ease with the prevailing sociological theories which he considered excessively ethnocentric and mechanistic" (p. 155). Madan goes on to throw light on every volume of D.P. Mukerji including *Modern Indian Culture: A Sociological Study* (1942). Further Madan correctly pointed out that both Radha Kamal Mukherjee's and D.P. Mukerji's published works are not found in the sociological curriculum in most of the Universities. As one of the reasons he points out that most of the Universities in India offering Sociology courses were established after the death of these two scholars.

He also writes in detail regarding Srinivas's contribution and Louis Dumont's contribution. From the write up it seems that Madan was very close to the above two scholars. On Srinivas he gave the title 'Empiricism and Imagination' (p. 174) in which he discussed Srinivas's ethnography and his two short stories. Madan said that the stories provided the idea of a humane personality of Srinivas.

On Louis Dumont, he wrote that he was a towering figure in the world of 20th Century Anthropology and he compared two Civilisations, India and the West (p. 195). Then Madan went on to describe in detail Dumont's work including *Homo Hierarchicus* (1970) and *Homo Aequalis* (1980). Further he discusses Dumont's greatest contribution through the journal '*Contributions to Indian Sociology*' which Dumont established along with D.F. Pocock, which he ultimately closed in 1966.

Another volume of Madan titled *Sociology at the University of Lucknow: The First Half Century (1921-1975)* published in 2013 by Oxford University Press is the eighteenth in the series of Oxford in India Readings in Sociology and Social Anthropology. The General Editor of the series has been Professor T.N. Madan in which he edited volumes on Religion, Village, Methodology and Fieldwork, Politics in India, Family, Kinship and Marriage, Sociology of Law, Historical Anthropology, Economic Life, Social Conflict, Social Stratification, Formal Organisation, Nomadism in South Asia, Social Ecology and the Scheduled Tribes in India. Madan himself edited two volumes: *Religion in India* and *India's Religions.* Definitely this was Madan's seminal contribution for the students of Undergraduate and Postgraduate level in Colleges and Universities in India and abroad. All the volumes were collection of seminal papers already published in journals and books by the authors.

In the above volume Madan edited his own writings on Radha Kamal Mukherjee, Dhurjati Prasad Mukerji, Dhirendra Nath Majumdar and Awadh Kishore Saran. In the end, he also wrote a concluding chapter titled: *Afterward-Looking Over the Shoulder and Ahead.* In this chapter he analysed various aspects of teaching and research in Sociology in the University of Lucknow. He also made some personal remarks on the above stalwarts. The above three gave ideas which ultimately constituted the Lucknow School of Sociology, which many people described and commented upon. However, Madan was surprised to know that students of Lucknow School could not follow or pursue their ideas. Further Madan could not agree to the idea of calling it Lucknow School because there was no unitary concern for some common ideas to be termed as a School. Therefore, he preferred to call it Sociology at Lucknow, where he included D.N. Majumdar as one of the major contributors, who could not find a place in many write ups on Lucknow School. Madan said that he was the first generation of formally trained Indian Anthropologist and was a born fieldworker. Majumdar worked on East Bengal (now Bangladesh), Chota Nagpur in Bihar (now Jharkhand) and then South Eastern and Northern United Provinces (now the states of Uttar Pradesh and Uttarakhand).

Majumdar wrote on many tribes including Hos of Singhbhum, the Korwas of Dudhi, the Tharus of Tarai and the Khasa of Jaunsar Bawar.

Further on Majumdar he said that Majumdar was much concerned about the problem of tribals resulting from disintegrative cultural contact, the presence of exploitative and oppressive outsiders including mining companies, contractors, moneylenders, petty revenue and police officials, politicians and self-serving missionaries. Madan said that Majumdar was very receptive to new ideas. He discussed how Majumdar entered into an agreement with Morris Opler of Cornell University for collaborative village studies in eastern, central and western Uttar Pradesh. However, the collaboration failed due to some administrative and personal reasons. But the project was completed with the support of Planning Commission and the Ford Foundation in India (p. 231). Then Madan goes on to describe how Majumdar highlighted the mutual dependence of Sociology and Anthropology, i.e. theory flowing from Sociology into Anthropology and data flowing back into Sociology as significant feedback. Majumdar stressed the importance of contextualisation of problems and decentralisation of planning. In this context Madan says that Majumdar was ahead of his times (p. 234).

Awadh Kishore Saran, one of Madan's teachers, Madan said that though Saran did not publish much but he was different. He did not follow the pathways of his predecessors at the University of Lucknow, rather he broke away of the pathways laid out by them. Saran acknowledged Ananda Coomaraswamy's work who had said that a true understanding of social life required a 'general theory of symbolism of which the theories of society, art and culture are merely specific aspects' (p. 286).

Madan said, "In Coomaraswamy's writings, Saran found 'a fairly systematic exposition of the traditional theory of man and society'. One has to be cautious for 'tradition' here does not mean 'archaism', which Coomaraswamy considered the 'proof of deficiency'; it rather means 'normal civilisation based on First Principles" (p. 286).

Professor Madan's researches, writings, compilations are unparalleled and will be irreplaceable in the years to come. His ways of teaching, presentations mesmerise the audience and a great learning experience for the students.

NOTES

1. The idea of Lucknow School of Sociology has been very popular, which many do not consider as a School of thought as their stalwarts had different ideas. A School should have some confluence of ideas. Madan himself

preferred terming it as Sociology at University of Lucknow (see for details Madan, 1994, 2011 and 2013).

2. The society functioned from the Department of Anthropology for a long period of time. At present it is functioning from a rented accommodation in Lucknow. Later on the society also started 2 more journals: *The Indian Journal of Physical Anthropology and Human Genetics* and *Manav* (a premier journal of anthropology published in Hindi). Further all the 3 journals are continuing their uninterrupted publication till today.

REFERENCES

Beteille, Andre and T.N.Madan (eds.). 1975. *Encounter and Experience: Personal Accounts of Fieldwork.* New Delhi: Vikas Publishing House.

Madan, T.N. 2016 (1965). *Family and Kinship: A Study of the Pandits of Rural Kashmir*. New Delhi: Oxford University Press.

Madan, T.N. (ed.). 1982.*Way of Life: King, Householder, Renouncer: Essays in Honour of Louis Dumont.* New Delhi: Vikas Publishing House.

Madan, T.N. 1983. *Culture and Development*. Delhi: Oxford University Press.

Madan, T.N. 1987. *Non-Renunciation: Themes and Interpretation of Hindu Culture*. New Delhi: Oxford University Press.

Madan, T.N. (ed.) 1991. *Religion in India.* New Delhi: Oxford University Press

Madan, T.N. 1994. *Pathways: Approaches to the Study of Society in India*. New Delhi: Oxford University Press.

Madan, T.N. 1997. *Modern Myths, Locked Minds: Secularism and Fundamentalism in India.* New Delhi: Oxford University Press.

Madan, T.N. (ed.) (1976, 1995) 2001. *Muslim Communities of South Asia: Culture, Society and Politics.* New Delhi: Manohar.

Madan, T.N. (ed.) 2004. *India's Religions: Perspective from Sociology and History.* New Delhi: Oxford University Press.

Madan, T.N. 2006. *Images of the World: Essays on Religion, Secularism and Culture.* New Delhi: Oxford University Press.

Madan, T.N. 2010. *The T.N. Madan Omnibus: The Hindu Householder.* New Delhi: Oxford University Press.

Madan, T.N. 2011. *Sociological Traditions: Methods and Perspectives in the Sociology of India.* New Delhi: Oxford University Press.

Madan, T.N. 2013. *Sociology at the University of Lucknow: The First Half Century (1921-1975).* New Delhi: Oxford University Press.

29
Professor Uma Charan Mohanty

S. Sumathi

Professor Uma Charan Mohanty (1931-2008) was born to a leading jeweller family at Cuttack, the traditional capital of Orissa. He grew up amidst the charged atmosphere of freedom struggle and associated with some of the top Congress leaders. He evolved as a person of simple living and high thinking. Professor Mohanty's father was Dukhi Shyam Mohanty and mother Pasora Devi and the family had business in Myanmar in the pre-independence period. The family was well connected politically with the then Congress leaders and imbibed the congress ideology and adapted *Khadi. They* embraced nonviolence, national unity, secularism, etc. and practiced these virtues in their everyday life. The great freedom fighters like Naba Krishna Chaudhari, Rama Devi, Surendra Dwivedi were regular visitors to their home and often the children of these families inculcated similar values.

Mohanty completed his school education and took up teaching in his village school founded by his father. Later on, he took up the job of headmaster at his village school soon after his matriculation. He voluntarily took up this job against his father's wishes and looked after the administration diligently. Unfortunately, the school could not get required funding due to the declining family income as Mohanty's father was imprisoned for five years for his freedom struggle activities. After independence when the school got government support Professor Mohanty continued his passion for education. He continued his education and took up a Postgraduate Course in the newly opened Department of Anthropology at Utkal University headed by (Late) Professor A. Aiyappan in 1958. Professor Aiyappan was a committed teacher and mentor for many budding anthropologists and Mohanty was fortunate to be one among them.

Professor A. Aiyappan, the retired Superintendent of Madras Museum, was the first professor and head at the newly opened department at Utkal University in Bhubaneswar. Professor Aiyappan's vast international exposure helped him induct his new students to the emerging field of anthropology—from biological, pre-historic to cultural anthropology. He also initiated the knowledge transfer from Indian and foreign experts in the field by inviting several scholars of repute from different parts of the world (including India) to carry out anthropological research in Orissa. These experts not only gave guest lecturers to the students but also discussed the ground realities of Orissa and other parts of the country. Some of the eminent invited scholars with whom Professor Mohanty interacted were Professor F.G. Bailey from London School of Economics, Professor Cora Du Bois from Chicago University, and Professor N.K. Bose the former director of Anthropological Survey of India who in particular practiced Gandhian ideology and provided Professor Mohanty intellectual opportunities. Such exposure has been reflected in all his academic work and gave profound contribution to anthropological literature.

Professor Mohanty's ethnographic writing on a coastal village in Odisha elucidates the then political system and was greatly appreciated by Professor F.G. Bailey. Similarly, his discussions with eminent scholars like Professor N.K. Bose resulted in the publication of an article that critically justified the argument posed by Professor Freeman and substantiated it, eliminating the theory of Buddha's birth in Bhubaneswar. Professor Cora Du Bois offered Mohanty an invitation to Chicago for his doctoral work. Unfortunately, his parochial values and his son's illness compelled him to stay behind. His Ph.D. at Utkal University without a guide and his work among the *Saora tribe* of Odisha are monumental works. Similarly, his Masters dissertation on *Kela*, a community professing snake charming, was selected by the external experts for publication as a unique monograph and was posthumously published.

During 1961-1964, he worked with Tribal Research Bureau, Government of Orissa. This research experience of four years gave him an empirical anthropological understanding of matters relating to his State. In 1964, Mohanty moved to the Department of Anthropology, Utkal University as a Lecturer and then to the Anthropology Department, University of Madras as a Reader in 1976. He later became the Professor and Head in the same Department. In 1990, he was offered Fulbright Scholar-in-Residence and visited several universities in USA and Canada.

In 1991, he retired from the University of Madras and took up a prestigious project from Smithsonian Foundation, USA to study senior citizens of Tamil Nadu. His work on comparative study of socio-political changes, dance forms of selected *tribal* groups, ethnographic profile and the impact of *development* planning among *Saora* villages are considered landmark research till date in anthropological studies.

30
Verrier Elwin

P. C. Joshi

Verrier Elwin whose full name was Harry Verrier Holman Elwin was born in England at a place called Dover, Kent in the year 1902. His father was Edmund Harry Elwin, a Bishop in Sierra Leone of West Africa who died a tragic death due to yellow fever at a young age of 38 years. Verrier Elwin was the second child of his parents, the eldest being a sister named Eldyth and the youngest being a brother named Basil. Eldyth was two year senior to Elwin while Basil was five years junior to him. His childhood was a period of intense hardship as they were reared by their mother yet, they were able to live in dignity and maternal affection with indigence. He was more than average student of his time. He was enrolled in Dean Close School, Cheltenham which was religious in nature and therefore, it offered continuity in terms of religious upbringing that was but natural to Elwin being from the family of a Bishop. According to Elwin, the headmaster of the school was father of a contemporary poet which had great influence on the young mind of Elwin.

According to Elwin, the seeds of an anthropologist were already sown in the school itself. He tells that he used to classify his classmates with respect to personality characteristics that they possessed such as morality, intelligence, attractiveness and so on thereby exhibiting the trait of being a systematic data collector. He pursued his career in study of English literature. He won Charles Olkham scholarship and Mathew Arnold Union Prize. He took English final in 1924 and was awarded the First – Alpha plus for 3 papers and Alpha for remaining papers. After doing English, he enrolled himself to do Theology. He was indeed doing very well and he became Vice Principal of Wycliffe Hall. In all these years, his tutor named Green has been advising him to leave the luxurious life of Oxford and served the poor and impoverished instead. At the same time, he was developing deep interest in mysticism and spiritualism, coming in close contact with Indian like Sadhu Sunder Singh. He was full of some kind of guilt for what the Britishers had done to India, taking away its wealth. He had a deep desire to somehow return to India whatever was taken by his countrymen by his relentless service to the poor in India.

Elwin had degree in English and Theology and no degree in anthropology, though; he later received a D.Sc. on his work among the Indian tribal communities from Oxford University. While he was deciding to take interest in India he came in contact with a Ceylonese (Sri Lankan) named Bernard Aluvihare who actually kindled his interest on Indian in the real sense. Elwin read about Indian freedom struggle and the radical views of Tagore and Gandhi. He became deeply interested in coming to India and serve the poor and untouchables there. He got to know of one organization named Christa Seva Sangh run by Father Jack Winslow. In the company of Oliver from Oxford and Robertson from Cambridge, he decided to visit Christa Seva Sangh in Poona. At the Christa Seva Sangh, he started living the life of a poor Ashramite sleeping on the floor and eating simple food. He then visited Gandhi who was in Sabarmati Ashram at that time. He got the taste of the simple yet eventful life at the Ashram. In Gandhi's Ashram, he came in contact with people like Meerabain, Jamnalal Bajaj, Sardar Patel, Acharya Kripalani, Khan Abdul Gaffar Khan and Thakkar Bapa. Once while he was discussing with Sardar Patel, his plan to work among poor untouchables, he was advised that there are plenty of social workers and volunteers ready to work among the untouchables as Gandhi himself was involved in ameliorating their lots, but, there were really very few people to serve the tribal people who live in remote areas deprived of education, scientific knowledge and health care. Jamnalal Bajaj also advised him to work in the then Central Province (today's Madhya Pradesh) among the tribal community of Gonds, about whom he had never heard of but was now going to devote his life working for their cause.

Elwin along with his close associate Shamrao Hivale started to look for a suitable place to work among the Gond tribals. Elwin initially looked for a place near Betul but could not locate a site suitable for their kind of work. He then sought advice from a Bishop in Nagpur, who suggested that he should start working for the welfare of the Gond tribals in a place called Karanjia in the Mandala district. With the help of his close associate Shamrao Hivale and merely 200 rupees in his pocket, he started with his luggage on a bullock cart and moved towards Karanjia. Elwin had a very equivocal position while he was choosing to work among the Gonds. His links with the Christa Seva Sangh and family background in missionary associations made him a natural allay of the Indian missionaries but, his close association with Gandhi and Congress made him support anti-imperialistic ideology. He was not only close to Congress leaders but was openly supporting their cause making him a sore in the eyes of British bureaucracy of that time. In fact, while he was working in Karanjia, his house was raided many times for anti-government incriminating material. He was quite often supported by people from Bombay, like J.R.D. Tata and other philanthropists. Verrier Elwin did not established his residence in the heart of Gond tribes for anthropological fieldwork but he started by establishing an ashram to serve the people living in this remote part of India. Since he had an interest for writing, being a scholar at the Oxford, it was but natural that he would write. His initial writings were not monographic but small expositions like "Truth about India – Can we get it?"; "Dawn of Indian Freedom"; "Christ and Satyagraha"; "Religious and Cultural Aspects of Khadi" and "Mahatma Gandhi's Philosophy of Truth".

Verrier Elwin had a checkered career in the sense that he changed his goals and interests as he went along. He started with a dream to spread the message of Jesus Christ for which he enrolled himself in a school and studied Theology in Oxford. He was a true pragmatic scholar who was always open to new ideas, provided the ideas appeal him. Verrier Elwin was a great writer and one of the probable reasons why he was able to come close to Congress leaders was his writing skills in favour of Gandhi's ideas. His early writings in India were not liked by the British administrators and the missionaries. He was often labelled as an Englishman with evil ideas. His early writings were semi-political but became poetic, philanthropological and analytical in subsequent years. One can see a distinct growth in his writings with time. Elwin was not a typical anthropologists, interested in doing fieldwork and write about people in scientific terms. He, in fact has compared his style which he liked to call as humanist with the other style in vogue those days, the scientific. He wanted to serve the tribals and feel the hardships and then write about them in humanistic terms. In his endeavours, he was helped by the friends and well wishers in England, but, he would also pay a visit to Bombay and give lectures to receive financial support. The Tatas were one of the strongest supporters of Elwin besides Jamnalal Bajaj. Bombay in the beginning of 20th century was a hub of anthropological activities and the local Parsies were quite active in pursuit of anthropological themes. His first monographic book on the tribals titled "The Baigas" was published with a generous financial support from DorabJi Tata Trust which incorporated his seven years of experience among these tribals. He had also written the Jubilee volume titled "*The Story of Tata Steel*" for the Tata Iron and Steel Company which according to him gave him the maximum amount, Rupees ten thousands, for any of his writing so far. He started writing on the central Indian tribals in the company of Shamrao starting with a book tilted "Songs of the Forest". Its sequel titled "*Folk Songs of the Maikal Hills*" was published in 1944 with Shamrao as co-author.

His ethnographic monographs, besides on the Baigas, were on Agaria, Maria, Muria and Bondo highlanders. He was deeply moved by the interaction of the simple tribals with the Indian penal system. He studied the prisoners and ex-convicts among the Muria and the Bondo highlanders.

Before we take up his contribution to anthropology proper, it is worth mentioning that he was a vociferous writer who had written for a variety of readers. We would like to start with two of his fictional novels, namely "*Phulmat of the Hills*" and "*A Cloud that's Dragonish*", both published by Murray in the years 1937 and 1938, respectively. The first novel was a tragic story of a beautiful tribal girl getting leprosy while the second novel was about tribal youth playing the role of detectives, a possible inspiration from Sir Arthur Conan Doyle.

He was among the very few anthropologists to have written on the homicide and suicide among the tribals. He did many case studies to ascertain that the motive and intend of the tribals accused of committing crime are not the same as of the civilized society. More often then not, the tribal convicts were a victim of circumstances. He, therefore, had a sympathetic view on the murder accused among the tribals. Besides writing on the crime scene among the tribals, he would also wrote petitions to decrease the sentence of the convicts. In one case, he was able to prevent capital punishment for a female tribals convict.

He had a special interest at appreciating the cultural heritage and he wrote a total of six books on the art, myths, folk-tales and folk songs of the tribes in Central and North-east India. Two of his books titled "*The Aboriginals*" and "*A Philosophy for NEFA*" published by the Oxford University Press and NEFA administration, respectively were extremely valuable contributions in enhancing our understanding of the problems of the tribals and suggesting policy guidelines for their welfare. It was in his book "*A Philosophy for NEFA*" that India's Prime Minister Pt. Jawaharlal Nehru revealed his Panchsheel which has relevance even today in the absence of any worthwhile official policy on the scheduled Tribes of India.

While Elwin was a great scholar, he was also quite simple human being. In his autobiography, he makes an observation that he used to be troubled by malaria quite often but once he started smoking cigar, he never got malaria. At another occasion, while he was on a visit to Delhi with his family to attend Republic Day Parade, his son Wasan was separated from them which made his and his wife Lila very worried. An astrologer was consulted who told them that their son would be back after five and an half hours. Elwin reluctantly agreed but was astonished to found that exactly after five and a half hours, Wasan was with them.

Elwin was a freelance anthropologist who occasionally received recognition and official designation. Once while he was finding it difficult to work in Bastar, he was made Official Ethnographer by the administration which was published by the local newspapers as Official Stenographer. He had joined Anthropological Survey of India as Deputy Director when its office was located at Benaras Cantonment but he did not like the restricted environment of the An.S.I. He has shared his experience when he was not accorded with the Indian citizenship and he met Nari Rustomji with a desire to visit NEFA (the erstwhile North Eastern Frontier Agency) and the present dayArunachal Pradesh. Nari told him that the land of NEFA is out of bound for him as he is a foreigner. But as the destiny had it, he got the Indian citizenship and was called by none other than Pt. Jawaharlal Nehru, the Prime Minister of India to be the Adviser NEFA administration and train a cadre of administrators to serve the Northeast India. His contribution to create a generation of sensitive and humane workers to serve the tribal areas of Northeastern India would be considered as his seminal contribution to tribal welfare. Not only that he trained people, he also taught them the art of research and administration. He penned down his observations and views in large number of books and monographs that he wrote while serving the tribals. He had many positions such as Anthropological Consultant, Adviser on tribal affairs for Tripura and Assam. His style of doing anthropology was distinct as he would learn while serve. He started by opening an ashram catering to various needs of the tribals named Gond Seva Mandal which in 1949 reorganized into Tribal Welfare and Research Unit (TWARU). He was crystal clear in his view regarding the objectives of the Seva Mandal, which were primarily educational and health development and strictly not missionary and political.

In his autobiography Elwin has coined a term "Philoanthropology" and it amply summarizes his brand of anthropology. It was not anthropology for the sake of anthropology but it was human service with anthropology – a humane anthropology which not only tries to understand tribal cultures but also feel and empathize with their cause, pain, suffering, struggles and hardships. In marrying a (two) tribal woman, his idea was not to indulge in worldly pleasures but to understand the tribal life from inside thereby to experience the 'emic' view of the tribal life. His monographs were less 'scientific' but more humane giving preference to true feelings and emotions at the cost of dry facts. His writings were not only full of anthropological details but also literary creations and he was the first anthropologist to receive a literary award "Sahitya Academy" from Sarvapalli Radha Krishnan posthumously. The only other anthropologist getting such literary honour was Irawati Karve. Among his contemporaries, he stood apart since he created a dedicated team of compassionate officers to serve the Northeastern tribal areas.

31
Ajit K. Danda

Dipak K. Midya

Ajit K. Danda, a man with professional integrity and extraordinary intellectuality, is considered to be one of the ground-breaking Anthropologists in India. Professor Danda was born at his maternal grandparents' home at Noagaon in Dacca district of undivided India (now in Bangladseh). He was born of late Dr. Sachindra Nath Danda and late Smt. Snehalata Danda. At his very early age, when he was only a few months old, his family moved to Perua Kachhari Bari campus at the then Sylhet district (now Sunamganj district), where his father was posted as the in-charge of a Health Centre run by the Gouripur Estate of Zamindar Birendra Kishore Roy Chowdhury. Parts of Bengal and Assam were then included in the said estate. Danda's early rearing up, along with his three elder sisters and an elder brother, was in the Perua Kachhari Bari campus, located on the brink of a tributary of the Surma river. Serenity of the river, greeneries around the campus, and the warmth of parents and elder siblings provided an extraordinarily permissive background for socialization of a tender mind. These got further reinforced through humming a Bhojpuri folk tune, tutored by the Kachhari Bari Darwan, locally called Panre. Life was full of beauty and excitements. They together helped him in crystallization of thoughts and that had deep-rooted influence on his personality formation, that often got reflected on his later decision-making processes. But, life has its own dynamics and often pulls up a man into new venture. When he was only about five years old, his father got a transfer as in-charge of the hospital of Baromasia Tea Estate in Chittagong district, belonging to the estate of the same zamindar. This horse-shoe shaped valley on the hills, overlooking Bay of Bengal and Chittagong Port, and the famous Hindu shrine Chandranath Dham on the mountain top made it a delightful sight. Here he attended the local pre-primary school for just a day. This enjoyment of the bounties of nature was rather short-lived.

When everything looked fine, his family life, like millions of others, was facing a great uncertainty with the beginning of the World War- II. At a very tender age, he could, from his hill top residence, watch the bombarded Chittagong Port. That jeopardised the rhythm of life altogether. To avoid the stress of war, soon, along with his mother, grand-mother, and siblings he moved to an interior village, Gadadhardi, in Dacca district, their native place. His father had to stay on there, till he resigned from the job. The escapade was a nightmarish experience, since in order to avoid attack from the "enemies", they had to drive down through the hills in total darkness without using headlights of the car they were travelling. The journey from Chittagong to Dacca by train was also in enforced 'Black Out' condition of total darkness.

The World War II was followed by a famine that affected mostly the working class. Distressed scenarios of tormented humanity made him cry along with his mother and grand-mother. Nevertheless, here too, he attended a primary school, again only just for a day. Since he did not like the ambience of the school, the seniors in the family never pressurised him. Instead, after a gap of a year, he was admitted directly to Class-III in Baradi High English School, located on the bank of the mighty Meghna river.

It may be of interest to note that this was the school where once his grandfather Rajani Nath Danda, a man with double honours, served as the headmaster. In all probability, one of the students of the latter was Jyoti Basu—the longest served Chief Minister of West Bengal – whose maternal uncle's home was at Baradi. Here Danda was greatly influenced by his Mathematics teacher and Assistant Headmaster Barada Kanta Chakrabarty, a man of extraordinary discipline and English teacher Subed Ali Khan.

But when he was studying in class VII he faced the greatest challenge of his life. The famine followed by the partition of the country. The partition of Bengal, in particular, came into force in 1947 with the Independence of India. This was the second time that Bengal was divided, after the first one caused by the British in 1905. As his father firmly believed that the division of the country was the result of a British ploy to divide the people of the country just to continue with the power and would not last long, he opted to stay in but shifted along with the family to another place, Jagannathpur, again in Sylhet district. At this time a paramilitary force was being created in the then East Pakistan. Danda wanted to join the regiment but refused on count of his subscription to Hinduism. Because of the socio-political turmoil in East Pakistan at that time, he and his elder brother were sent to his elder sister's home where her father-in-law was an employee of Calcutta Tramways Company.

The extreme uncertainty and threat to life during post-partition days forced his father ultimately to decide to leave East Pakistan and to come to India in search of a new destiny. But where to go? As it happened so, the then Deputy High Commissioner of India at Dacca, Mr. Niranjan Bardhan, who was a distant cousin of his father, came forward to help Sachindra Nath and was successful to arrange for him an assignment at Silda Auxiliary Hospital – a military hospital - in the erstwhile Medinipur (now Jhargram) district of West Bengal.

Sachindra Nath with his family settled at Silda. Ajit K. Danda was admitted to Silda Radha Charan Institution, that was named after the father of a great social reformer Sital Prasad Laha and grandfather of Anadi Charan Laha, who later became a teacher in anthropology and served Sitananda College, Nandigram and Seva Bharati Mahavidyalaya, Kapgari, both in West Bengal. Danda was in this school till his School Final examination in 1953. He did his intermediate study during 1953-55 from the Jhargram Agricultural College that was later renamed as Jhargram Government College and then again renamed as Jhargram Raj College.

Professor Danda did his graduation with Anthropology in 1957 from Bangabasi College, Calcutta, where Prabodh K. Bhowmick, Manish Ranjan Chakraborty, and Satkari Mitra were his teachers in Anthropology. He got a chance for admission into Masters in Anthropology in Calcutta University by virtue of having distinction in his graduation. Here he learned anthropology under the illustrious anthropologists like K.P. Chattopadhyay, T.C. Das, T.C. Roy Chowdhury, D. Sen, A.N. Chatterjee, M.L. Roy Chaudhuri, G.S. Roy, S.S. Sarkar and M.N. Basu, and belonged to the first batch to have a specialization at the Masters level. This was in 1957. He did specialization in Advanced Social and Cultural Anthropology with dissertation on the slums of Calcutta under the guidance of K.P. Chattopadhyay.

Before completing his Masters course, because of circumstantial reasons, he was forced to search for a job to meet expenses of his studies. He appeared in West Bengal Public Service Commission Clerkship examination and, five months before his final examination, joined Public Works Department and was posted at the Writers' Building, the then State Secretariat of West Bengal. But, he was trying for a better job and hardly after five months he left this job and joined the post of Senior Research

Assistant at the Cultural Research Institute (CRI), Calcutta. The then Deputy Director Amal Kumar Das was his senior there, who happened to go to Pittsburg University for his Ph.D. but came back without finishing his assignment. Here, on counts of some ethical reasons, he found it impossible to continue there without making certain compromises, therefore, he decided to leave the job. While leaving CRI, Amal Kumar Das advised Danda to try his luck in the U.S. and supplied three addresses, where he could apply.

Life came to him literally with its glorious uncertainty and, at the same time, with 'miracle' of opportunity. At this juncture, he approached B.K. Roy Burman for a new job and the latter advised him to register his name in the Employment Exchange Office at Calcutta. He did accordingly, and quite interestingly had a call for an interview from the office of Registrar General of India. By the way, he joined the post of Senior Technical Assistant there in 1961. As he did not find the new assignment academically very challenging, he applied to the universities suggested by Amal Kumar Das for his Ph.D. programme. Soon he got an offer from Cornell University Anthropology Department as a Teaching Assistant.

Ajit K. Danda did his Ph.D. in Cultural Anthropology from the Cornell University on 'Community Development and Leadership in Rural India' in 1966. He did his major in anthropology under Morris E. Opler and minors in Asian Studies under Robert Smith and in Sociology under Gordon Stribe. Cornell University provided him with a scope to teach a course along with Victor Turner. He also taught another course along with Joan Mencher. On completion of his Ph.D. programme, Prof. Opler desired that he gained some further teaching experience in the U.S. that could help him to find a job when back in India and fixed an assignment. Danda preferred to return to home first and try his luck over here.

He started his career as a professional anthropologist in 1966 as a Senior Research Fellow and Deputy Director at the National Institute of Community Development, Hyderabad. While in Hyderabad, he married Dipali Danda, a Ph.D. from University of Calcutta. who was already working for the Anthropological Survey of India (AnSI). He carried out his first major fieldwork with his wife at Noada, Burdwan, West Bengal (the work was known as Basudha study). Development and Change in Basudha was published and circulated by the National Institute of Community Development. That had drawn attention of Prof. M.N. Srinivas and Andre Beteille who desired that Danda should be in teaching. In fact, M.N. Srinivas took him to Pantnagar University to gain some experience and the University offered him the position of Reader (now designated as Associate Professor). Danda was also made Senior Research Officer and in-charge of a collaborative project with the Rockefeller Foundation. The Foundation was represented by Professor Gilpatrick, who was with the Delhi University as a Visiting Professor. Here, again, on ethical ground, he decided to disassociate himself from the project and left this job.

Soon, thereafter, he joined Anthropological Survey of India as the Superintending Anthropologist in 1969. He was the third incumbent to the position, after Verrier Elwin and S.C. Dube in order. He was initially posted at Nagpur Regional Centre of the Survey, where he became the Deputy Director in 1973. Soon he was recommended by the Union Public Service Commission for the position of Joint Director of the Survey. But this promotion was stayed for five years by a Court's Order obtained by a Deputy Director.

While in the Survey, Danda tried to bring about a change in the overall functioning of the research faculty, as he felt that the junior partners of a research team have been exploited by the seniors. He insisted that one who does the fieldwork and drafts the research report, would be the senior author when the report is published. As a result, quite a few Senior Technical Assistants of the Survey became senior authors of the joint publications even along with the Deputy Directors. He also insisted that fieldwork should be mandatory for all researchers. Priorities in publication of reports should be strictly on the basis of merit, not official seniority of the authors. Such reforms were not liked by many.

In 1976 Ajit Danda came to Calcutta. Within a few months he had to move out to Udaipur in Rajasthan and continue there till 1978. The following year he, along with Shri Benoy Sarkar, the then Secretary of Central Excise Club, earned the Runners Up Trophy as Veterans Doubles partners in lawn tennis. The Champions were the Sports Star brothers; Chuni Goswami and Manik Goswami. Danda was also the President of the Central Services Club, Calcutta for five years.

By 1990, he sought voluntary retirement from the Anthropological Survey of India to join the post of Professor and Head of Department in the erstwhile Department of Social Anthropology and Sociology, North Bengal University which was initially offered to him in 1975. He was in this university till he accepted the offer of the Asiatic Society in 1995 as Professor and Research Director. He was in-charge of the project, Encyclopaedia Asiatica. He served the institution until his retirement in 1998. Thus ended the official career of a born fighter, who dedicated himself to the cause of Anthropology.

Seminal Contribution

Ajit Danda's major contribution to anthropology includes: (i) idea about multiplicity of identity and ethnicity, (ii) study on weaker sections in Indian villages and tea plantations, (iii) area studies in Chhattisgarh and North-East India, (iv) tribal studies, (v) village studies, and (vi) introduction of the Indian Anthropology Congress under the aegis of Indian National Confederation and Academy and Anthropologists (INCAA).

Danda proposed an idea of pluralism in ethnic identity in the International Congress of Anthropology in 1978. The IUAES Congress at Chicago organized by Sol Tax 1974 discussed the issue extensively, primarily around the 'melting pot' theory of ethnicity. In 1978 IUAES Congress in New Delhi, Danda was asked to co-chair a two-day long symposium, along with Yu Bromley of the then Soviet Union on "Theoretical and Methodological Issues in Ethnicity". There were as many as 18 papers from Soviet Union, all of whom had highlighted the character of singularity of identity. Danda, by citing several illustrations from Indian situations, stressed upon the plural nature of identity. In 1982 IUAES Congress in Mexico City, a five member study group, including Danda, was formed for the purpose of further examining the issues related to ethnicity and identity. His major publications on ethnicity includes *Ethnicity in India* (1991) besides a number of edited volumes (e.g., *Ethnicity, Nationalism and Integration*, 1999; *Identities, Ethnic Boundaries, and the State*, 2017) and articles in different journals. He came out with two-fold perceptions of ethnicity: (i) adoption of the system of categorization that lays emphasis on the condition of belonging to a particular ethnic group with its own set of cultural characteristics; and (ii) emphasis on the dynamic character of ethnicity in order to appreciate the inherent processes of ever-changing alliances based on specific and defined interests (Danda, 1971: 73). On the processes of ethnic integration, he observed that at the cross-national perspective "cultural system unites whereas the political system divides" as the "nature of cultural boundary is relatively more stable than the nature of political boundary". He further detected the 'discontinuous' as well as 'inter-penetrating' nature of ethnic boundary management and 'fluid' nature of identity formation.

Weaker Sections in Indian Villages (1993, in 2 vols.), Social and Economic Processes in Tea Plantations with special reference to Tribal Labourers (1968) and numerous articles reflect Danda's understanding about the problems of the weaker sections in Indian population. His significant contribution to tribal study includes Tribal Economy in India

(1991), Tribal Ethnography (1996), Tribes and Economic Transformations: India (2017), The Nagesia of Chhattisgarh (1984), The Kodaku of Surguja (1986) etc. His significant contribution in the field of research methodology is Research Methodology in Anthropology (1992), in addition to a number of journal articles on the domain.

He has about 50 books (including edited volumes) and more than 230 research articles and critical writings to his credit. His latest contribution is One Hundred Years of Anthropology in India (2019) which is a rare compilation of, among other valuable materials, B. S. Guha's assessment of Anthropology in India after its 25 years of existence, N.K. Bose's assessment of anthropology in India after its 50 years of existence and the assessments of anthropology in India after its 75 years and 100 years by Danda himself. On the growth of anthropology in India after its one hundred years, Danda identified two divergent tendencies: (i) as an academic discipline, anthropology in India is 'heavily inclined' towards the Western tradition; and (ii) as a body of knowledge, anthropology in India is very distinct having scarcely any influence from elsewhere. He argued that anthropology in India needed to be redefined and remodelled by making the tendencies complementary to make the discipline socially more relevant since "an academic discipline always receives its sustenance from the body of knowledge that emerged out of local experiences and experiments" (Danda, 1991: 294). On the whole anthropologists in India, he observed, appear to be on the threshold of a major breakthrough to demonstrate how this specific branch of science could meaningfully serve any society and humanity, by suggesting innumerable alternatives of life-styles that in turn are likely to transform the entire world (*Ibid.*, pp. 294-95).

The Indian National Confederation and Academy of Anthropologists (INCAA), the largest platform of professional anthropologists in India with 991 founder members and life members till 2019, is the brainchild of Ajit Danda. The root of formation of INCAA can be traced back to the event of election of the Sectional President in Anthropology and Archaeology to the Indian Science Congress of 1975, which Professor B.M. Das had contested but just because of unethical behaviour of a couple of senior members of the profession had to accept humiliation. Beside, since Anthropology never gets its due importance in Indian Science Congress Association meetings, anthropologists felt formation of its own platform as the need of the time. After various informal discussions over decades, ultimately in 2004 in a symposium at IGRMS, Bhopal, INCAA emerged as an apex body of the profession in India with

B.M. Das as its founder President and Ajit Danda as the Member-Secretary. Credit for its formation also goes to the notable participants of the symposium such as Sujit Som, the then Joint Director, IGRMS, Bhopal, P.K. Misra, A.C. Bhagabati, B.M. Das, T.B. Subba and N. Subba Reddy, among others. The first INCAA Congress was held in NEHU, Shillong in 2004. Since then INCAA has been organizing Indian Anthropology Congress/Inter-Congress every year in different universities and/or research organizations across India.

Danda was the President of Anthropology and Archaeology section of the Indian Science Congress Association in 1975-76. He was the Editor of the *Journal of Indian Anthropological Society* for the longest time (1989-2014) in its history so far during which the journal achieved its true international standard. During this period he was also the President of the Indian Anthropological Society. He was also the Editor of the Human Science. He has been serving as the founder Editor of the *Indian Journal of Anthropology*.

Danda was a member of the National Selection Committee in Anthropology and Sociology of the Ministry of Culture, Government of India, National Advisory Committee of the Anthropological Survey of India, Ministry of Culture, and member of the Executive Committee and the Academic Advisory Committee of IGRMS, Ministry of Culture, Government of India. He also served as a member of two Expert Committees of ICSSR: one on Development of Scheduled Castes and Scheduled Tribes, under the chairmanship of S.C. Dube, and the other on Educational Problems of SCs and STs, under the chairmanship of I.P. Desai. He, along with M.N. Srinivas, Lila Dube, B.K. Roy Burman, Lakshman Mahapatra served as the member of the Research Team of the B.P. Mandal Commission. Here again, on counts of ethical issues the entire team, except B.K. Roy Burman and Lakshman Mahapatra prematurely resigned.

Ajit Danda has a number of awards and medals to his credit. He was awarded with the Cornell University Teaching Assistantship during his Ph.D. work (1963-1966). He was the recipient of Prof. R.P. Chanda Birth Centenary Medal in 1972 from the Asiatic Society, Kolkata, Prof. L.K. Anantha Krishna Iyer Momorial Medal in 2016 from the Anthropological Association, Mysore and Prof. M.N. Basu Memorial Plaque from Calcutta University in 1997. His one of the best achievements was to become the Fellow of the National Academy of Science, India [commonly referred to as FNA (Sc)] in 1975. He was also the youngest Sectional President (below 40 years of age) in Anthropology and Archaeology of the Indian Science

Congress Association. His academic excellence and outstanding contributions were recognized with the grant of Lifetime Achievement Award in Anthropology and Museum by the Ministry of Culture, Government of India in 2015-16. He has the distinction of being the first recipient of the award introduced by the Government of India and given through the Indira Gandhi Rashtriya Manav Sangrahalaya (IGRMS), Bhopal. He was also given the Lifetime Achievement Award by the Department of Anthropology, University of Delhi.

Ajit Danda is one of the Founder Members of the World Council of Anthropological Association (WCAA), the 1st meeting of which was held in Brazil in 2004. He was also the member of the Commission for Review of Environmental & Social Sector Policies, Plans and Programmes (CRESP), Government of Sikkim, with Professor B.K. Roy Burman as the Chairman and C.V. Tripathi as the other member. The members of this Commission were given the status of the Minister of State.

As Director of AnSI, Danda envisaged that there should be at least one Field Camp with a minimum of one officer and six supporting co-workers in each and every State/Union Territory of India. The proposal was sanctioned though, could not be implemented, as the budgetary provisions got diverted for the People of India project.

He had accomplished a number of international collaborations. As a Distinguished Scholar he was in Australia for three months in 1975 and visited the University of Western Australia, Melbourne University, Sydney University and Adelaide University. He visited University of Berlin, Germany as a Guest faculty perhaps in 1978. He had also been in France for three months under the cultural exchange programme between the two nations. He was offered a Fellowship to work in France for two years, which he could not accept.

After retirement, Danda and his wife are busy with a Play School for children, the moto of which is learning with pleasure. He is also acting as the Chairman of INCAA and the founder editor of the *Indian Journal of Anthropology*.

Danda has the credit of having supervised 17 Ph.D. scholars of different universities, including Satyabrata Chakrabarty (CU), B.R. Rizvi (Nagpur), Saran Singh, Masahiko Togawa (Hirosima University), Sibir Ranjan Das, and several others. Justice Bijitendra Mohan Mitra of Calcutta High Court also registered himself for Ph.D. under his guidance but passed away just after submitting the first draft of the dissertation. Danda arranged to get the draft published.

REFERENCES

Danda, A.K. 1968. *Social and Economic Processes in Tea Plantations with special reference to Tribal Labourers*. New Delhi: Office of the Registrar General of India (with co-authors).

Danda. A.K. 1984. *The Kodaku of Surgujia*. Calcutta: Anthropological Survey of India.

Danda, A.K. 1991. *Ethnicity in India*.New Delhi: Inter-India Publications.

Danda, A.K. 1992. *Research Methodology in Anthropology*. New Delhi: Inter-India Publications.

Danda, A.K. 1993. *Weaker Sections in Indian Villages*, Vols. I, II. New Delhi: Inter-India Publications.

Danda, A.K. 1996. *Tribal Ethnography*. New Delhi: ICSSR.

Danda, A.K. (ed.) 1999. *Ethnicity, Nationalism, and Integration*. Kolkata: The Asiatic Society.

Danda, A.K. 2019. *One Hundred Years of Anthropology in India*. Jhargram: INCAA. Jhargram.

Danda, A.K. and D. Danda. 1971. *Development and Change in Basudha: A West Bengal Village*. Hyderabad: National Institute of Community Development.

Ekka, W. and A.K. Danda. 1984. *The Nagesia of Chhattisgarh*. Calcutta: Anthropological Survey of India.

http://www.incaa.net

32

Asok Kumar Ghosh

A Distinguished Anthropologist of the Twentieth Century

Ranjana Ray

It is an honour to write about Professor Asok K. Ghosh, who was one of my revered teachers. He had made important contributions to several subfields of anthropology, namely, prehistory, human biology and social anthropology. Professor Ghosh was born in Calcutta in 1934. His family hailed from Jessore, eastern part of Bengal of undivided British India. His father moved to Calcutta because he was a Government service holder. He was the eldest child of his parents. He had two brothers and two sisters. His schooling was in Calcutta. He graduated from Bangabasi College in Kolkata and took admission in Anthropology for post-graduate courses in Calcutta University in 1957. He had an ambition to study medicine but this ambition was not fulfilled under unavoidable circumstances. Although he took up anthropology for his post-graduate studies, it is said that he had no idea about what is the subject matter of the discipline (Bellwood, 1988: xiii-xv). He passed M.Sc. in Anthropology in 1959 and scored first class first marks. He chose to specialise in Prehistory because Advanced Prehistory as a specialisation was offered in the final year of his M.Sc. class. Since it was a new subject he got interested in it and took up the specialisation. It may be mentioned here that from that year specialization in physical, social anthropology and prehistory started for the first time in the Department of Anthropology, Calcutta University. Earlier to this, anthropology was not divided into specialised branches. Soon after completion of Masters Degree in Anthropology, Ghosh began research in advanced prehistory under the guidance of Professor Dharani Sen, a famous anthropologist. In 1964 he was awarded Ph.D. Degree for his work on Palaeolithic Culture of Singhbhum district. Meanwhile in 1963 he joined as a faculty in the

Department of Anthropology, Calcutta University. In addition to Ph.D. He got Prem Chand Raichand Scholarship and was awarded D.Sc. Degree for his work in prehistory of Eastern India in 1975. He continued with his teaching and research and was promoted as a Reader then as a Professor until he died suddenly in April 1997 at the age of 63 years. Professor Ghosh was an anthropologist not only in degree but in his devotion to the subject.

Professor Ghosh always mentioned that he was fortunate to be student of some distinguished teachers in anthropology in Calcutta University. Professor Dharani Sen was his mentor in Indian Prehistory. He got special attention from Professor Dharani Sen. Afterwards he got Fulbright Fellowship and went to Harvard to work under Professor Hallam L. Movius and other stalwarts in Prehistory, such as, G.H.R. Von Koenigswald and Francois Bordes. Professor Ghosh considered them as his teachers. Asok Ghosh had great reverence for Professor H.D. Sankalia. Professor Sankalia who embraced all serious scholars, had also admired Professor Ghosh and may be considered as one of his mentors after Dharani Sen. He had very cordial relationship with his peers Professor G.C. Mohapatra of Punjab University; Professor V.N. Misra, Professor S.N. Rajaguru, G.L. Badam of Deccan College, Pune; D.P. Agrawal of Tata Institute of Fundamental Research, Navrangpura, Ahmedabad; Professor K.C. Tripathy of Utkal University, Bhubaneswar. These are a few of his colleagues but there are a large number of other dignitaries who were quite close to Professor Ghosh.

He travelled a lot at various places both India and abroad. He had been member of a number of societies both in India and abroad. He held executive position for International Union for Prehistoric and Protohistoric Sciences (UISPP), International Geographical Union (IGU), International Association for Quaternary Studies (INQUA) and Indo-Pacific Society for Prehistory (IPPA). He was elected Sectional President for 62nd Indian Science Congress in the Anthropology and Archaeology section in the year 1975. The presidential address entitled "Man Evolving in India" was highly acclaimed by anthropologists and archaeologists. The copy of the Presidential address shows that he was F.A.A. (USA), F.R.A.I. (London), M.I.I.P.P. (Fierenze). Ghosh's interest was not limited to prehistory alone but he was an anthropologist in proper sense. His interest and research covered all the main branches of anthropology, namely the physical, socio-cultural and prehistoric archaeology. He had supervised doctoral thesis on prehistory, human evolution, domestication of plants, education, communication, tribal studies and women studies.

He had done fieldwork in Punjab, Narmada valley and in Kotallyar valley in the Southern part of India.

Professor Asok Kumar Ghosh has carried out research in various fields of human science but the work that he had carried out for his doctoral thesis stands out as a very important contribution in anthropology, especially in the field of Indian prehistory. The thesis was published in the form of a paper, entitled 'The Palaeolithic Cultures of Singhbhum' in the Transactions of the American Philosophical Society with the enthusiasm of Professor Movius in 1970. The thesis was supervised by Professor Dharani Sen, himself an eminent prehistorian and his teacher in the Department of Anthropology, Calcutta University. Professor Sen had qualified both in geology and archaeology. This had a profound impact on the researches of Prof. Ghosh. Though he himself was not a geologist but he always accompanied any geological expedition that took place in the eastern plateau region. That way he acquired profound knowledge in geology and could put the cultural remains in their proper geo-chronological and environmental perspective. His research reflected man, culture and environment of the palaeolithic period in its proper sense.

Professor Ghosh started the work in Singhbhum going through the past reports on finding of palaeolithic tools from Singhbhum district in the erstwhile state of Bihar, which is now in the Jharkhand state. He had thoroughly explored the district covering Saraikella, Kharswan, Dhalbhum, Kolhan, Porhat and Saranda; tracking the river valleys of Subarnarekha, its tributaries, Koel and Baitarani valley. When his students went to field with him they found that he knew the district as the back of his palm. He has gone through the topography, fauna-flora and climate of the region. For the first time he has put forward a clear geo-stratigraphy of the district and had placed the palaeolithic cultures in its meaningful sequence. He also had reconstructed the palaeo-climate from the stratigraphic study to understand the man, environment and subsequent adaptation of man with his culture to the contemporary environment. Going through the prevalent terms of the cultural sequence in Europe and Asia he coined his own terminology for the cultural phases of Singhbhum. This had scientific basis. He had firmly defended his terminologies with stratigraphic sequence, technology, typology and chronology. The terms coined were on the basis of tool making raw material, rather the blank, the form of the material. In the sequence of ordering of palaeolithic culture of Singhbhum, earliest was the pebble-core element, then flake element, flake-blade element and finally blade-blade-bladelet. This meant that the tools of the successive stages were made predominantly on the specific blanks. He emphasised that palaeolithic cultures evolved through the choice of technology from core to flake and blade. In India, both pebbles and core were used for making tools at the lower palaeolithic level. With the discovery of prepared core technique, flakes became the main blank for making tools. A refinement of technique and gradual size diminution took place in subsequent evolution of the culture. He felt that the terminology will be India's own without compromising European or African cultural terminologies. It is clear that early cultures developed in response to respective environmental condition and of course, with development of biological characteristic features.

Geological formation of Singhbhum was meticulously studied by Ghosh. He compared findings from each of the forty palaeolithic sites he discovered in Singhbhum district. On the basis of such research, he had established the composite stratigraphy of the region belonging to Quaternary time period and cultural sequence of palaeolithic was firmly established.

This is a prestigious scholarship and is considered as an award based on original research by the University of Calcutta. Asok Ghosh had prepared thesis for this award. Work was mainly done in the state of West Bengal. Major part of the state of West Bengal is in the Gengetic alluvial plain. The western part is an extension of eastern plateau. The Gangetic basin was not suitable for human habitation during Pleistocene period. Ghosh's work was carried out in Bankura and Medinipur districts. His exploration work in West Bengal began in 1961 and he discovered a few new sites in Bankura district and for the first time he found evidence of presence of Palaeolithic tools from Medinipur district (Ghosh, 1961). After conducting exploration and in some cases trial trenching for assessing stratigraphy for the contextual analysis of tools, Asok Ghosh presented his findings in the form of a thesis entitled 'The Stone Age Cultures of West Bengal", in the year 1965.

Ghosh wrote in the introduction of his thesis for D.Sc. degree that he felt for an analysis of pan-Indian situation of Palaeolithic culture and its relation with the contemporary cultures of South East Asia. He started his research accordingly. In fact the thesis was an accumulation of his research both in India and abroad carried out between 1969 and 1975. The synthesis emerged from two points. First, out of his fieldwork and data collected through exploration and excavation. Second, building up of hypothesis from the data collected so far. Information on South and South East Asian Palaeolithic culture was also collected from museums and institutions in India and abroad. He followed conjunctive approach for his study by using methodologies from disciplines other than anthropology. He laid emphasis on bio-cultural dimensions. He studied regional patterns of Palaeolithic cultures of India and made a comparison with the cultures of South-East Asia. For understanding emergence of man in India he extended time dimension of his study beyond Quaternary into late Tertiary. Starting with the humanoid creature, Ramapithecus, the only fossil remain from India of the time of his writing up the thesis. He had deliberated on the terminology of palaeoanthropology, which he considered better alternate for prehistory. In the perspective of lower Palaeolithic cultures of South and South-East Asia he had discussed what he meant by pebble, pebble-core and chopper. He had taken into consideration handaxe and pointed out its presence in the lower Palaeolithic tool kit of India (Ghosh, !973). He had shown the development of Palaeolithic culture in India in the chronological sequence. He had given much attention to terminologies for cultural stages. Type concept according to him was a major issue. In his quest for Mousterian element in India he conceded that there is a stage, which may be considered as Mousteroid because he found that not only all the types of Mousterian are not found in India and the flakes were quite distinctly different in nature in India (Ghosh,1974). While ordering the Palaeolithic culture of India into Pebble core element the earliest, then flake and finally flake blade. His argument was that unlike Upper Palaeolithic culture of Europe, flakes dominated over blades in India in the terminal Palaeolithic culture at the end of Pleistocene.

Comparing Lower Plaeolithic cultures of South Asia and Southeast Asia, he concluded that both the regions had a single generic culture but in time with the adaptation to respective environment variation took place. This happened through an immense time range. He had explained evolution of man in India through cultural evidences in climatic background (Ghosh, 1975).

The identification of geo-stratigraphy, chronology for the deposits and reconstruction of past environment from the nature of the deposits and its composition together with cultural remains from the stratigraphic sequence and ordering of Palaeolithic culture in Eastern India may be considered as seminal contribution to the discipline.

Professor Ghosh had done some work on prehistoric and ethnologic religion. This was an emerging issue in the Vulcamonica Congress in Italy (Vulcamonica Symposium 72- Actes Du Symposium International sur les Religions de la Prehistoire, capo de Pomte Ed Del Centro, 1975). He deliberated on Megalithic burial system of prehistoric and present day context and explained the religious aspect of the ritual (Ghosh, 1975).

Professor Asok Ghosh believed in multidisciplinary approaches for anthropological researches. Culture change in Stone Age India was a major concern of his research (Ghosh, 1973-74) . With the help of geology, geography, botany and zoology he had reconstructed the environmental condition and change of the same and had pointed out the change due to adaptive mechanism.

During his fieldwork in eastern India he had come across secondary laterite, which he called implementiferous laterite because it had yielded Palaeolithic cultural evidences and had given evidence for evolution of Palaeolithic culture deposited in the detrital or secondary laterite. With the same zeal he had located the exact characteristic of the deposit in respect to its position in quaternary sedimentation and had established the cultural evolution (Ghosh, 1967).

Since he had started his research on Man evolving in India – a bio-cultural process, he had undertaken research on the fossil remains of hominoids found in the Siwalik region. He had taken remains of Dryopithecus, Sugrivapithecus, and Sivapithecus. Attribute analysis of molars of the fossils were made (Ghosh and Sen, 1981). At the same time he had also studied the land use pattern of the said hominoids (Sen and Ghosh,1982).

Asok Ghosh had done research on man and plant relationship, especially in the tribal area. His purpose was to find out balance between ecosystem in the form of utilisation of plant resources by man. In this connection he had taken data from the Birhor, Kharia and Santal tribes. The first is hunter-gatherer, second is primitive cultivator and the third is settled agriculturist, respectively. All are from Eastern India. Utilization of plants was considered from the view point of utilization for medicine, food, socio-religious purpose, for construction of structure and for making tools. Types of plants were also taken in the data for research.

Department of Anthropology has got good museums of Physical Anthropology, Ethnology and Prehistory. Professor Ghosh was very keen on the display and arrangement of the same. He also wrote articles on Ethnographic Museum – a design to human integration.

Professor Ghosh has supervised a number of dotoral researches. There were works done on Flake-blade elements of India, Mesolithic culture and adaptation with the tool kits to the contemporary environment. Both the thesis was in the line of Bordes and Binford school with attribute analysis. In the same method he supervised a work on

Siwalik hominoids. As mentioned earlier he had guided scholars from disciplines other than Anthropology. He had taken up supervising a work on cultivated variety of rice. This was to unveil the mystery of the domestication of rice by the Neolithic people in eastern India. He had discovered some rock art from Ghatshila region and had guided a thesis on prehistoric rock art. One of his scholars came from Santal community. Perhaps he was the first tribal to get a Ph.D. Degree in Anthropology in the Calcutta University. Study was mainly on the Santal culture and language. This work had revealed clue to many of the early cultural status of the Santals of Eastern India. He guided a thesis on early technology of iron smelting to a scholar who came from the background of metallurgy. Media and communication were his favourite topic and guided media persons on theatre and communication and audience survey. Persons with economy, history and education background also had done socio-economic studies chosen from their respective areas of expertise under the guidance of Asok Ghosh. He not only guided scholars in his own University but also had taken scholars under his supervision from S.V. University, Tirupati, Hyderabad University and Jadavpur University.

Asok K. Ghosh had good number of friends in the fraternity of anthropology and archaeology both in India and abroad. It is much apparent in the volume called Man and His Culture (1988). The book was compiled to felicitate Professor Ghosh and was edited by Peter S. Bellwood of Australian National University. Subeditors were Amiya K. Sen, P. G. Chatterjee and Asok Datta. Contributors were thirty four foreign scholars from all over the world. Each of them was renowned in their own field. There were also seven famous Indian anthropologists who enriched the volume. Professor Ghosh had undertaken a few international collaborations, though they did not end in full scale, perhaps due to problem of getting permission from Indian Government for such collaboration during his time. He had worked with Professor Per Sorensen on Lower Palaeolithic culture of Eastern India and South-East Asia with special focus on Thailand. Work was carried out with Professor Peter S. Bellwood of Australian National University for which a number of seasons of fieldwork was carried out in the Eastern Plateau region. An extensive exploration of Sanjay River Valley, a tributary of River Subarnarekha was done. A large number of prehistoric sites were discovered. These were of Palaeolithic, Mesolithic, Neolithic and Chalcolithic cultural sites. (Ghosh *et al.,* 1984). However, this also did not see its completion perhaps due to some problem with permission of such collaboration.

Professor Asok Ghosh was very helpful towards all his students. He even had helped a few foreign scholars at their initial stage of work in

India. All of them are famous now in their own right. Mention may be made of J.R. Lukacs, a student of late Professor Kenneth A.R. Kennedy, Jonathan Mark Kenoyer, who worked among the conch shell workers of Bengal and is now famous for his work on Indus Valley Civilization. Both Lukacs and Kenoyer were from United States of America. Peter B. Anderson of Copenhagen, had worked on the Santal religion and now is famous for his contribution towards tribal religion. Professor Ghosh had helped in carrying out his fieldwork in the Santal villages.

Professor Ghosh did not find time to author a book by himself but he had edited a few volumes. First was the book edited on the occasion of hundred years of discovery of first prehistoric tools, rather the first hand axe by Robert Bruce Foote, a geologist of British India. This was done in 1863 and to commemorate the great occasion, Ghosh jointly with Professor Dharani Sen edited a book entitled, *Studies in Prehistory* (1966). The other book that he edited was in felicitation of his Teacher, Professor Dharani Sen (1974). There are a few more edited volumes edited jointly with other anthropologists. These are: *India at the dawn of history: Essays in memory of Sh. V.D. Krishnaswami* (1995); *People of India : Bio-cultural dimensions : K.S. Singh festschrift* (1993); *Sociology in the rubric social science: Ramkrishna Mukherjee felicitation volume* (1995).

It is recorded in the year 1988 that he wrote about 300 articles on various subjects of his research findings (Bellwood, 1988: xii-xv). Unfortunately those are not at hand at the moment; therefore, some very important ones are given in this write up. Perhaps he would have contributed more to the knowledge of prehistory but for his death prior to his final retirement from the University.

REFERENCES

Ghosh, Asok K., 1961. *Prehistoric Studies in Eastern India, Science and culture*, vol. 27, pp. 369-375.

Ghosh,.Asok K, (jointly with Dharani Sen), 1966. *Studies in Prehistory: Bruce Foote Memorial Volume*. Calcutta, Firma K.L. Mukhopadhyay.

Ghosh, Asok K., 1967. Laterite and associated artefact bearing strata in Eastern India. Quaternary Soils: Proceedings of the VII congress of International Association for Quaternary Research. (ed) R.B. Harrison and H.E. Wright. Reno Nevada: Centre for Water Resources Research, Desert Research Institute. University of Nevada., pp. 146-155.

Ghosh, Asok K., 1970. *The Palaeolithic Cultures in Singhbhum*. Transactions of the American Philosophical Socity. N. S. 60: 1- 68.

Ghosh, Asok K., 1973. *Handadzes in the Palaeolithic Culture of India*. Asian Perspective, 15: 156-66.

Ghosh, Asok K., 1973. Chronocultural perspective on the Palaeolithic culture in *India in Radio carbon and Indian Archaeology*. (ed) D.P. Agrawal and A. Ghosh. Bombay, Tata Institute of Fundamental Research; pp. 23-51.

Ghosh, Asok K., 1973-1974. Culture change in stone age India and its bearing on environmental adaptation. *Anthropological Forum*. 3(3-4): 325-330.

Ghosh, Asok K., 1974. Denticulates in India: Examination of a type concept. *Journal of the Hong Kong Archaeological Society*. 5: 47-56.

Ghosh, Asok K., 1974. *Perspectives in Palaeoanthropology: Professor D. Sen Festscrift*. Calcutta: Firma K.L. Mukhopadhyay.

Ghosh, Asok K., 1975. Reconstruction of prehistoric religion from megaliths in India, *Proceeding of the 1st symposium of the international Association Prehistoric and Ethnographic Religion*. (Ed) E. Anati, Vulcamonica: Centro Camuni di Studi Prehistorichi, pp. 1-16.

Ghosh, Asok K. 1978. Further note on Sangiran flake industry, *Proceedings of the Konoklijlke Academie von Wetenschappen,* Amsterdam, series B. Vol. 81(2): 211-214.

Ghosh, Asok K., and Amiya K. Sen, 1981. *Fresh light on Phylo-taxonomy of Siwalik Hominoids, Proccedings of the Field Confernce Neogene Quaternary Boundary*, 1979, pp. 55-61.

Ghosh, Asok K., (jointly with Amiya Kumar Sen), 1982. Land use and early hominoid in India: A critical Review. *Journal of Indian Anthropological Society*, pp. 39-46.

Ghosh, Asok K., Ranjana Ray, P.G. Chatterjee, Poresh Nanda and Peter S. Bellwood. !984. *Archaeological reconnaissance in the Sanjay Valley*, Singhbhum district, Bjhar. Indo-Pacific Prehistory Association. Vol. 5: 29 -38.

.Ghosh, Asok K. (jointly with S.B. Roy). 1993. *People of India : bio-cultural dimensions : K.S. Singh festschrift*. New Delhi, India : Inter-India Publications.

Ghosh Asok K. (Jointly with Asok Datta and C. Margabandhu) 1995. *India at the Dawn of History : Essays in Memory of Sh. V.D. Krishnaswami*. Delhi : Agam Kala Prakashan

Ghosh Asok K. (jointly with Ranjit Bhattachary) 1995. *Sociology in the rubric social science : Professor Ramkrishna Mukherjee felicitation volume*. Calcutta: Anthropological Survey of India : Ministry of Human Resource Development, Department of Culture, Government of India,

Peter S. Bellwood (ed). !988. *Man and His Culture: A resurgence*. New Delhi. Book and Books.

33
Dr. Binod C. Agrawal

A Multi-facet Anthropologist

Arbind Sinha

Today if anybody talks of an anthropologist who ventured out of basic discipline to enter into other fields and linked with anthropology, if someone refers to communication research in India, one name that comes to mind is Dr. Binod Chand Agrawal. To me, after Dr. L.P. Vidyarthi, the legendary anthropologist of India, I do not know anyone else who left his footprint in other disciplines. Dr. Agrawal is widely travelled, extensively written, and has contributed a lot in bringing anthropological perspective in communication teaching and research. He scaled all continents of the world and there is hardly any state in India where he did not conduct or coordinated field research.

He started his journey from a district town of Ballia in Uttar Pradesh of eastern India where he was born in a business family on the last day of 1942. Although he was part of a large joint family with his siblings and many cousins, he spent most of his time in loneliness. Apart from his study in a local school; he also used to spend some time in the evening with his grandfather at his business centre and help him in counting and calculating the money, for which he was given a token amount as an appreciation of his work.

He did his schooling upto class 10 from Government High School Ballia and against wishes of his parents, he went to study at Lucknow where his uncle was working who was also a role model for him. Here he completed his Intermediate education (class 11 and 12) from K.K. Intermediate College and graduation from Shia College of Lucknow. Although he wanted to study physics in his graduation, he could not get a seat in physics stream and compromised to study Geology. His score in Geology was also not very high and those days getting admission for a masters seat in Geology was no easy, so finally, he enrolled himself to do Anthropology from Lucknow University. He did well here and his Masters' thesis on 'Doctor-patient relationship' RELATIONSHIP got him a gold medal.

In Lucknow he stayed in college and university hostel and could make a lot of friends. His loneliness during childhood was counterbalanced here onwards. He spent his quality time with his uncle who was a faculty member at King George Medical College. Once I met his uncle and was asking about Dr. Agrawal's early life. He said that when he came from Ballia, he was not very clear about what he wanted to do. But as time passed, and he observed the respectful life of his uncle as an educationist and he interacted with others in their circle, he was more inclined to get into academic life. Still he was not a very serious student.

He has an amazing capability to impress upon people, often with his hard work. After his Masters in Social Anthropology in 1963 from the University of Lucknow, he helped Prof. J.W. Elder of the Department of Sociology, University of Wisconsin, Madison, USA by coordinating his fieldwork carried out in Uttar Pradesh and Tamil Nadu (India). Prof. Elder was impressed with his work and invited him to join the Ph.D. programme at the University of Wisconsin (USA). Dr. Agrawal was in Wisconsin from 1964 to 1971 and completed his M.S. in Cultural Anthropology in 1969 and Ph.D. in 1970 with Anthropology as a major, from the University of Wisconsin. Thereafter he worked as Assistant Professor with the Department of Anthropology and Sociology at Iowa State University, Ames, Iowa, besides working on some research projects.

In 1971 he decided to come back to India and joined Indian Agriculture Research Institute, New Delhi as Associate Professor till he moved out of Delhi to join Space Applications Centre, Ahmedabad by the second half of 1973. It was a major turning point in Dr. Agrawal's career – from Teaching to Research.

He joined Space Applications Centre (SAC), Ahmedabad, one of the major Centres of the Indian Space Research Organisation (ISRO)[1] to head its Research and Evaluation Cell. They had to launch the Satellite Instructional Television Experiment (SITE[2]) covering six states of India. The one year experiment of using satellite to take development communication messages directly to the villages of six states was to be evaluated in terms of its social impact and this was his major responsibility. The project engaged almost sixty social scientists to work on the research and evaluation part.

He introduced the new components in evaluation research – 'holistic study' where the trained anthropologists were engaged to study the whole process of impact brought out by one year of SITE. The anthropologists stayed in one/two of the SITE villages in each state.There were nine such villages identified and the anthropologists used ethnography as a tool to study by staying in a single village for 18 months. I was one of them studying in Bihar. Other social scientists were working on survey and feedback research.This was a landmark innovation in Indian social science research where large scale projects had used ethnography method and it established the anthropological method of communication research in the context where mostly quantitative survey methods were used across.

SITE evaluation study gave worldwide recognition to Dr. Agrawal and he travelled across the world to share this experience. Although he was also part of the large scale survey that evaluated SITE and the survey report that came out of it, his compilation of SITE evaluation studies titled as '*SITE Social Evaluation*' (Agrawal, 1981[3]), edited book '*Anthropological Method of Communication Research*' (Agrawal, Verma, and Doshi, 1986[4]) and another established him as a guru of communication research. Even today people ask him to share his SITE experiences and he cherishes sharing anecdotes from all the states under study. He worked with SAC and DECU for two decades holding different positions. When he left DECU-ISRO, he was the Group Director of Social Research in DECU. While in SAC and DECU (Development and Educational Communication Unit), he undertook various nationwide projects related to applications of space technology. It needs special mention that for acquiring Sriharikota Island to establish a satellite launch centre, a small tribal community – Yanadis were displaced to another corner of the Island. Professor Satish Dhawan, the then Chairman of ISRO wanted to rehabilitate them in a very planned way and SAC appointed and deploying two anthropologists who stayed among the Yanadis for five years and helped to implement culturally compatible develop plans (Agrawal, Rao, and Reddi, 1985[5]). This was a perfect example in Action Anthropology.

Television as a new communication technology and its use for the national development as well as for providing healthy entertainment to the mass was talk of the day and in 1982 Dr. Agrawal was nominated as a member of PC Joshi committee[6] an honour to himself as well as to the organization. He contributed to augmenting research in the system.

Since ISRO's mandate is to work for the national development using space science and technology, the organization encouraged him and his team to work on science-technology-society related projects. Fund was never a problem for this resource-rich organization, so the team worked on many applications area including video revolution, rural telegraphy, use of communication terminals for transmission, tele teaching experiments in different extension areas, and applications of remote sensing for fisheries development in coastal states of India, under different collaborations. He converted all the project reports into publication and it enriched his profile. Since all these studies were carried out in collaboration with different government departments and education and research organizations, he came in contact with various organizations that helped to increase his network.

In 1984, the software system group was reconstituted as Development and Educational Communication Unit (DECU) as an independent unit of ISRO, located within the campus of Space Applications Centre, reporting to ISRO through Director, DECU. The erstwhile REC became Social Research Cell of DECU, headed by Mr. Kiran Karnik. There was a time when Dr. Agrawal was almost sure of taking over from Mr. Karnik when the later left ISRO in 1991, but it did not happen. It was temporarily headed by the then Director of SAC and then another colleague of him became the Director, DECU leaving no scope for him to head DECU. Although he never expressed it, he was disappointed with this decision and had decided to leave the organization. In April 1993, he joined Mudra Institute of Communications, Ahmedabad (MICA), a private management institute as its founder Director. But he could not adjust to the environment of the private educational institution and returned to DECU after 15 months. Back home, he was given the position of Adviser, SAC. He kept looking for other avenues and finally took voluntary retirement from ISRO and had set up a private non-profit organization – TALEEM Research Foundation, located in Ahmedabad under the banner of Zee Network. Here onwards it will be referred to as Taleem.

These 22 years of his career with ISRO were the best phase when he conducted a large number of researches, mostly on the intersection of society and communication. More of his known publications came out of this researches. He visited and lectured or chaired sessions in lots of the Institutions dealing with social sciences or communication in India. He served on numerous committees in India and abroad that he continued doing even when he was with Taleem.

He established Taleem with financial support from Zee Network[7]. Mr. Subhash Chandra, Chairman of Zee Network is the Chairman of Taleem. He headed this organization as Director, and later as Director-General from 1996 to the middle of 2015. He was the chief and was given free hand to set up the Foundation. He invited a couple of his old friends and associates who helped him set up the Foundation. The foundation worked in media communication and health communication. It was almost his pocket organization and he decided on everything. The foundation was operating from a small place, very close to his residence. This place never changed, even today after 25 years of its existence. I remember, once Dr. Agrawal went to USA for more than a month. During this time, Mr. Subhash Chandra, the Chairman visited Ahmedabad for his other business and I had time to interact with him. In our two meetings in 2001, I impressed upon him to look for some good office campus for Taleem and I appreciate that SubhashJi took cognizance of this and he did talk to two important people of Ahmedabad to see if Taleem gets a proper place. Whatever could be the reason, it did not happen and I saw Dr. Agrawal not very keen on changing the space. Very recently, I attended a meeting at Taleem where a very senior bureaucrat also came and he commented to the present Director – 'Please change the place, it is not a proper place for Taleem'.

Under neoliberal policies in the early 1990s, to sustain the quality of education and to produce responsible citizens, the education sector was opened to private players. It became another vertical for many of the business houses who entered into education (Sinha, 2020). The promotors of Taleem also used Taleem as a platform to run educational institutions and had set up a university – Himgiri Zee University at Dehradun in Uttarakhand, India, and Dr. Agrawal was given additional responsibility to run it as its Vice-Chancellor from 2005 to 2012.

During his second-largest tenure of almost two decades, he mostly struggled to run this private institution as he had to sustain the institution and its human power. The major focus was on sponsored research and often there is a clause in the contract of commissioned study that the funding agency will have a proprietary right on its publication. So, very few original research publications were credited to him during this time frame. However, he aggressively pursued his academic interest by publishing old kinds of stuff and writing with other scholars on various issues. We have a long list of his authored, co-authored, edited, and co-coedited volumes[8]. Here we find diversification of his interest and some dilution of scholarly rigor in the output, which is mainly because of the quality of work carried out by the younger scholars collaborating with him. He also consolidated his position in an international network and travelled a lot to attend meetings, seminars, and conferences. Wherever he actively participated in any international forum, he made it that he becomes a nodal person for organizing their academic activities in India.

Dr. Agrawal is an avid traveller and most of his travels were for attending national and international seminars/conference, meeting, sometimes relevant and sometimes not so relevant. I coined a word – Seminarian – for those who will be there for most of the national and international colloquiums and he fits very well in this frame. Being so prominent personality both in anthropology as well as in communication, he would receive invitations now and then, and attended most of them and contributed in different roles. These conventions were both – sponsored by the organisers and also for which he paid from his resources, depending on the role he was invited for. He was fortunate to have worked with resource-rich organisations like ISRO, MICA, and Taleem and in all these organisations, he was in a leading role so he had organisation's resources at his command. I remember one of his seniors in SAC-ISRO telling him – "Binod ! at your position you will get all types of invitations, but you have to be choosy in deciding which one you want to attend.

By mid-2015, finally the curtain was down and now Dr. Agrawal is a retired person with countless ideas but a lot of restrictions. After his leaving Taleem, he continued travelling and attending all possible meetings and conferences. He became an Academic adviser for institutions such as Manipal Institute of Communication, Manipal; and LJ Institute of Management, and Gujarat Vidyapeeth, Ahmedabad. Recently, by the end of 2018, because of his age, he developed some health complications and has been advised by the doctors not to travel alone. This is the biggest repentance anybody like Dr. Agrawal can feel. Now he only visits local institutions with some other person by him.

Dr. Agrawal may not be highly rated, but he is popular. In his class also he starts with examples of culture and how communication is culture-bound. He tries to correlate the subject/topic with a particular example from Indian settings that make the students excited to know more about it. There were occasions when I also sat for the class and did not find anything amazing or even new in his discussion, but he was highly appreciated for his delivery. He involves the audience with his simplicity and his simple examples keep them engaged. I learned from him that you may not give more information, but whatever you talk; explain it with several examples, preferably from the background the students come from. It reminds me of Prof. Yash Pal[9] who told that when he talks to the group of scientists, he talks more about social science, and when he talks to the social scientists, he correlates it with science. He explained that scientists know about science and they can explore more about it, but when they start thinking about the application of science for society, it interests them more and *vice versa*. Dr. Agrawal also applies the same method and with knowledge of satellite imageries to ground truth, he has been managing it well. Moreover, he worked on varied projects and situations that he can place the ball in any corner. However, lately with his age, he may not be preparing well for his speeches/lectures so the people, who worked with him and those who attended earlier lectures, find it repetitive and old stuff, but for those who listen to him the first time, it is a treasure of information. As a teacher he tried to integrate anthropology with communication, with design and planning, with development, and with education.

Dr. Agrawal is an excellent guide and he piloted a large number of masters and doctoral students. I was his first official doctoral student to get a degree. Although SAC-ISRO had quite a few competent Ph.D. degree holders with lots of experience who could have guided the Ph.D. students, the Gujarat University did not accept ISRO scientists, engineers, and others as an approved guide. Most of the Indian Universities have such stringent rule. I remember when I decided to do a Ph.D. under his supervision; I had to go to a University in Madhya Pradesh who allowed outside guide and outside students to enroll as their doctoral students. It took quite some time before deemed to be universities, private universities and other universities opened the window for outsiders to be approved guides and some students did Ph.D. under his supervision. I can say with a high level of appreciation that there will not be very many supervisors like him who puts that much effort in preparing the students for writing a quality thesis and for defending the viva exams. Our sitting for my Ph.D. project was regularly starting in the morning from 8.00. During the discussion, he would be so tough and often makes the student lose hope. His philosophy is clear – if you convince me what you want to write, you write, else, I will tell you what you should write. This makes you so confident that when I presented for the defense in an open viva (where the thesis date and topic is announced in university bulletin and any of the faculty of the university can come and ask a question), faculty present there were asking questions and I was just smiling and answering to their queries because those questions were asked several times by Dr. Agrawal during our discussion on the thesis.

Post the 1980s, he became an official doctoral adviser for quite a few scholars and the topic varied from anthropology, sociology, religion, communication, language, and planning. Anyone who approached him, sometimes not very capable scholars, he found it difficult to say 'NO', because he did not want to spoil personal relation with her or him. Lately, maybe because of his age, I found that some of his students were not as well prepared as he prepared us and it did not reflect well on him.

Dr. Agrawal is remembered as an outstanding organizer and he did not only impress upon Dr. Elders who took him to Wisconsin, he impressed Dr. L.P. Vidyarthi and many others. Dr. Vidyarthi, in the capacity of President, X International Congress of Anthropological and Ethnological Sciences nominated him as the Executive Secretary of the International Conference, New Delhi. Later they appointed me as Assistant Secretary. The Delhi Congress was a great success. He also steered the 1986 International Conference of the International Association for Media and Communication Research (IAMCR) in Delhi, another feather in his cap. We all were deputed by ISRO to work for these international conferences and it was great learning for us.

In August 2019, two of his close students – Dr. N. Sudhakar Rao[10] and Arbind Sinha organized a national conference on Culture, Communication and National Development to honour Dr. Agrawal and to count his contribution on the theme of the Seminar. A good number of eminent scholars from Anthropology, Communication and allied sciences – his friends, associates, and students from across the country came together to felicitate him. It was a great event but unfortunately he fell sick and could not physically attend the Seminar and participated through video conferencing only.

Dr. Agrawal has a peculiar quality to impress the person he talks to. As Anthony Wallace (Wallace, 1970[11]) said that one's personality has a bearing of the cultures/he comes from, it is very true in his case – the true reflection of his background of anthropology. When he meets people, he starts investigating, in a very friendly manner and with a stylist American accent, about the whole background (sometimes genealogy also) of the individual. His training of researching about the cultural context and anthropological knowledge of different Indian cultures, in terms of race, dress, nomenclature, language, and terminology, accent, the way they write their name including surname, and characteristics of the places/he comes to help him connect with the person in their cultural context. He has learned a few sentences/words of a few Indian languages and does not mind using it when he meets someone from that language group. His excellent memory of remembering the individual when he meets the second time makes an impact on the people. Even if his guesswork does not work, he efficiently manoeuvers and engages the person in the conversation. If some woman he sees with vermilion and a shell bangle, he will immediately welcome saying "Nomoskar, Aapni Bengali" and the person is truly impressed. It is another thing that he may not continue with this language for more than a few sentences or words, but that's enough. Once he sees a man with *tilak* (a sacred mark on forehead) – horizontal or vertical, he tells which sect he comes from and also explains the value of vertical or horizontal *tilak*. He goes deep into understanding the genealogy of the person and once they talk at length and in detail, he gets a welcome gesture. I met several people who met him and fondly remember him with great respect and affection and say he knows so much about Indian culture that he immediately fixes you in your cultural context.

His talent has been recognized well and he is conferred with several awards, significant among them are AMIC Asian Communication Award 2009 for outstanding contribution and leadership in Asian Communication Research, Emerald/AIMS Research Fund Award 2007 by the University of Wisconsin, Distinguished ISRO Service Award in 1976, Graduate School Fellowships 1968-69 by the University of Wisconsin, and Inderjit Singh Gold Medal for the best thesis in Anthropology in 1963 by Lucknow University.

A great tribute to Dr. Binod Agrawal from all of us.

NOTES

1. Later in 1974 ISRO became part of the Department of Space, Government of India.
2. SITE was an experiment that used a satellite to take development information directly to selected villages of underdeveloped districts of six States of India for one year from August 1, 1975 to July 31, 1976.
3. Agrawal, Binod C. (1981). SITE Social Evaluation Results, Experiences, and Implications. Ahmedabad: Space Applications Centre.
4. Agrawal, Binod C., Verma, K.K., and Doshi, J.K. (Eds.) (1986). Anthropological Methods for Communication Research: Experiences and Encounters During SITE. New Delhi: Concept Publishing Company Pvt. Ltd.
5. Agrawal, Binod C., Rao, N. Sudhakar, and Reddi, Gurivi (1985). *Yanadi Response to Change: An Attempt in Action Anthropology*. New Delhi: Concept Publishing Company Pvt. Ltd.
6. Government of India had set up a committee known as PC Joshi Committee to guide on the Software for Doordarshan (Television Authority of India).
7. Zee Network, now known as Zee Entertainment Enterprises Ltd. owned by the Essel Group that consists of a number of TV channels, including Zee TV, launched in 1992.
8. The list of his publications and association with academic institutions is long and is placed on Google.

9. Professor Yash Pal, a highly decorated scientist was Director of Space Applications Centre, Ahmedabad from 1973 to 1980. He later worked as Secretary, Department of Science and Technology, Government of India and was Chairman of University Grants Commission of India.
10. Retired Head, Department of Anthropology, Central University of Hyderabad.
11. Wallace, Anthony F.C. (1970). *Culture and Personality*. New York: Random House.

34
Dibyendu Kanti Bhattacharya

M.K. Singh

Late Professor Dibyendu Kanti Bhattacharya was born on June 28, 1938 in Old Delhi. He was the son of Mr. Jitendra Mohan Bhattacharya and Mrs. Manorama Bhattacharya. He was in a family of five brothers and two sisters. Ever since the age of five, Prof. Bhattacharya suffered from a poor health, so much so that his parents thought that he might not survive for long. However, his will to strive and survive was such that not only he excelled as an academician but also kept inspiring everybody throughout his life. He was married to Ms. Prathibha Savarkar (grand-niece of Mr. Veer Savarkar) and had a daughter named Deepra.

Prof. Bhattacharya completed his formal education from Bengali Boys Senior Higher Secondary School in Delhi and graduated from Hindu College, University of Delhi in 1958. He was a polylingual and could speak in languages like Hindi, English, Marathi, German and Bengali.

Aspiring to dedicate his life for people's welfare, he decided to leave home and joined the Bhoodan movement under Acharya Vinoba Bhave in the year 1958. Due to his involvement in the movement, after much struggle, he was able to complete his post-graduation in the discipline of Anthropology from University of Delhi in 1960. Later, under the supervision of Late Prof. P.C. Biswas, he was awarded Ph.D. in the year 1965. His doctoral thesis was titled, "A Study of ABO, Rh-HR, MN Blood Groups among the Anglo-Indians of India with a Note on Some Other Morphological Traits".

Soon after receiving his doctorate degree, Prof. Bhattacharya joined the Department of Anthropology at Lucknow University as a lecturer for the academic sessions of 1965 to 1966. In 1966, he joined as a lecturer at the Department of Anthropology, University of Delhi. Prof. Bhattacharya was a physical anthropologist but had started developing interest in

Archaeology. During his brief teaching involvement at Lucknow University, a very interesting event led him to develop interest in the field of Archaeology. Looking at the bones which he had discovered lying unacknowledged in his assigned cupboard at the university, he was informed that these bones were collected from a place called Roopkund in Uttarakhand. A curious personality, Prof. Bhattacharya thoroughly explored the terrains in front of him and read about the mysteries of the place. He decided to work upon other materials found from the region. Consequently, Prof. Bhattacharya along with some of his colleagues were able to present a summary of their findings on the Roopkund Mystery to National Geographic Society in 2001 which was greatly appreciated.

Prof. Bhattacharya was a physical anthropologist but his interest in archaeology encouraged him to undergo an advanced training programme in archaeology at Deccan College, Pune where he learnt Pre-history with Late Prof. H.D. Sankalia. Courtesy his passion towards archaeology, he used to teach topics related to archaeological anthropology, paleo-anthropology and ethnology.

In December 1971, Prof. Bhattacharya went to Germany with DAAD Postdoctoral Fellowship for 3 years. He also had the privilege of working with Late Prof. Francois Bordes (1919-1981) of the Bordeaux University in France, an internationally known French archaeologist who was an authority on the culture of Neanderthal man. During his fellowship in Germany, he visited various archeological centres of Great Britain, Denmark, Norway, Sweden, Austria, Norway and Switzerland. He also did some extensive fieldwork in India. His interests were concentrated in regions of Bihar, Jharkhand, West Bengal, Andhra Pradesh, Rajasthan, Orissa, Gujarat and Maharashtra.

His most acknowledged contribution to archaeology was his book titled *Paleolithic Europe: A Summary of Some Important Finds with Special Reference to Central Europe*, which was published in 1977 by the Humanities Press of Netherland. It is referred to as a text book all over the world. In the year 1983, he was awarded a degree of doctorate in literature from Ranchi University for his work on Paleolithic Europe. In 1985, Prof. Bhattacharya was appointed as a Reader and then promoted to Professorship in 1991 in the Department of Anthropology, University of Delhi. He retired from the university service in the year 2004.

Professor Bhattacharya spanned a career in Indian Archaeology for almost 40 years. He authored articles and books on various topics of anthropological and archaeological relevance. In 1972, he authored the first of his textbooks referring to Indian Archaeology. After his visit to

Europe, Prof. Bhattacharya wrote a one of its kind book entitled "*Stone tool typo-technology*". His books are considered marvelous sources of information especially for undergraduate and post graduate students since they provide information on the archaeological material cumulatively. He also worked upon the 'palmar dermatoglyphics' of the Anglo-Indians of India during initial phase of his career (1964, 1972), and also wrote articles on folklore and social health. Some of his notable works are mentioned below:

- 1972: *Prehistoric Archaeology: A Comparative Study of Human Succession*. Hindustan Publishing Corporation, Delhi.
- 1977: *Paleolithic Europe: A summary of some important finds with special reference to central Europe*. Atlantic highlands, The Humanities Press and Oosterhaut, Netherlands: Anthropological publications.
- 1978: *The Emergence of Culture in Europe*. B.R. Publishing Corporation, Delhi.
- 1979: *Old Stone Age Tools: A manual of Laboratory Techniques of Analysis*, K.P. Bagchi and Co., Kolkata.
- 1986: *Aspects of Human Ecology: A Dynamic Inter-Relation between Man and Environment* (Co-Author: S.L. Malik), Northern Book Centre, Delhi.
- 1987: *Prehistoric Archaeology: A Comparative Study of Human Succession*. Hindustan Publishing Corporation, Delhi.
- 1989, 1999, 2003: *An Outline of Indian Prehistory*, Palka Parkashan, Delhi.
- 1990: *Ecology and Social Formation in Ancient Indian History*, K.P. Bagchi and Co., Kolkata.
- 1994: *Steps to Indian Prehistory*, Step 1, Arvind Publications, Delhi.
- 2010: *Catalogue of Prehistoric Tools: Indraprastha Museum of Art and Archaeology*. (Co-author Sudipa Saha). Kaveri Book Service, New Delhi.

In his book *The Emergence of Culture in Europe* (1978), Prof. Bhattacharya mastered the art of maintaining the balance between oversimplification and incorporation of the latest empirical details on the other hand while detailing the concepts of prehistoric literature. As Sachchidanad said in his foreword to this book, Prof. Bhattacharya brought first hand study of the material collected in various countries of Europe and brought the information together in this volume. Prof.

Bhattacharya was trained in India, and was well acquainted with the problems of the Indians. This made him capable to catch the 'wavelength' of the Indian students in much better way than any European author of a similar book could have achieved, such that the students could be exposed to the rapid and multi-disciplinary development in the field of archaeology. He regionalised Palaeolithic traditions and made sure that 'culture' was never caught up in the technical and over specialized details. He shared his knowledge on the various European archaeological sites he had visited including Bilzingsleben in east Germany, Sesselfelsgrotte in West Germany, Tata in Hungary and others.

In his book *Catalogue of Prehistoric Tools: Indraprastha Museum of Art and Archaeology* (2010), he elaborated upon the entire collection comprising thousands of prehistoric tools from different parts of the world including rich river (Narmada, Godavari etc.) valley collection from India. A selection of the representative types has been made from most of the sites distributed in four continents of the world, namely Europe, Africa, Asia and America.

Prof. Bhattacharya's contribution to the discipline of Anthropology has been tremendous, not only in the field of Physical Anthropology but also to other sub-disciplines of Palaeo-Anthropology, Prehistoric Archaeology, and Human Ecology. He has over 200 research publications in different national and international journals of anthropology which is reflective of his research interests in different concepts of anthropology and archaeology. He also contributed 20 chapters as an online teaching/ learning material for students under the UGC e-Pathshala programme and recorded 35 chapters of Archaeological Anthropology in 2016. All these chapters and videos are available on the website of the University Grants Commission. These videos are explicit and wholesome packages of information not only for students but research scholars as well. Prof. Bhattacharya had the art of making the learning process easier. He exemplified knowledge by relating them to the everyday mundane life situations. His ability to think anthropologically was remarkable. He saw the world through the lens of anthropology and applied his anthropological knowledge to solve different problems.

In his career, he was awarded with many distinctions and honors. He was awarded the Panchanan Mitra Lecture award (1993) by the Asiatic Society, Calcutta; Dharani Sen Memorial Lecture award (1997) by the Department of Anthropology, University of Calcutta; D.N. Majumdar Memorial Lecture award at Lucknow (2003); and J. S. Bhandari Memorial Lecture award (2015) by the Indian Anthropological Association, Delhi.

Prof. Bhattacharya was also associated as a subject expert with a Rock Art exhibition titled 'Adi Drishya—A Primeval Vision of Man', a one month long mega event to showcase several aspects of Indian and Global Rock Art, organized by the Indira Gandhi National Centre for the Art (IGNCA), New Delhi in collaboration with the Indian Archaeological Society, New Delhi, at Matighar and Twin Art Gallery of IGNCA during 6th-26th December, 2012. His scholarly aptitude shines through the 'Introduction' part of the catalogue written by him where he presented a survey of Rock Art of India as well as in the global context.

Prof. Bhattacharya headed the Department of Anthropology, Delhi University during the period 1993 -1996. He served as a visiting professor for universities like Lucknow University, Dharwad University (Karnataka), S.V. University (Tirupati), Amity University (Noida) and the Institute of Archaeology, Archaeological Survey of India. He was also one of the members of the UGC's visiting team to evaluate the Tenth Plan of Vidyasagar University (Midnapur) in November 2002. He was a life member of the Indian Science Congress Association (Kolkata); the Indian Anthropological Association (Delhi)—of which he was one of the founders; the Ethnographic and Folk Culture Society (Lucknow); the Indian Society for Prehistory and Quaternary Studies (Pune); the Indian Archaeological Society (New Delhi); and the S.C. Roy Institute of Anthropological Studies (Ranchi). He became the President of the Anthropology and Archaeology Section of the 86th Indian Science Congress (1999) held in Chennai. He acted as an adviser to UGC, Anthropological Survey of India and UPSC on several occasions. He was felicitated with the "Best Teacher Award" on the Foundation day of University of Delhi on May 1, 2016.

Prof. Bhattacharya played a very important role in re-establishing the Indraprastha Museum of Art and Archaeology (first established under the auspices of the Indian Archaeological Society, New Delhi, in 1997), inaugurated by Shri Tejendra Khanna, the Hon'ble Lt. Governor of Delhi on 29th October, 2010. The museum has been re-organized with a central theme 'The Ascent of Man', possessing a rich repertoire of art and archaeological materials of various categories representing different periods. He wrote a monograph as the principal author titled, 'A Catalogue of Prehistoric Tool', which is a unique demonstration of a rare collection donated by Late Dr. A.P. Khatri to the Indraprastha Museum of Art and Archaeology. He also served as member of the Editorial Board of a catalogue of the Rock Art published by IGNCA and Indian Archaeological Society, New Delhi in December 2012.

He served as an Associate Editor of the journal '*Current Anthropology*' published by the Wenner-Gren Foundation (USA). He was a member of the Anthropological Society of Nippon (Japan). Prof. Bhattacharya was also the coordinating author for the Chapter on "Cultural Services" sponsored by the Millennium Ecosystem Assessment, for which he visited Indiana University, Bloomington and Indianapolis in USA (in January 2003); Frankfurt in Germany (in May 2003); and Czech Republic (in October 2003).

Prof. Bhattacharya served the Department of Anthropology, University of Delhi from 1966 until his retirement in 2004. His sensitivity and concern for others earned him admiration not only from his colleagues but his students as well. He established the importance of developing respectful relationships with students. He dispersed his knowledge to a large number of students at the University of Delhi and others. He supervised eight doctorate students. Many of whom became scholars, professors and some others who established their careers in archaeology.

His empathetic understanding of human behaviour made him a person who could relate to the problems of the others. His love for anthropology was contagious enough to encourage the people around him to perceive life through an anthropological perspective. An excellent teacher and a wonderful human being, Prof. Bhattacharya left for his heavenly abode on December 25, 2017 after a brief illness. The contributions of Prof. D.K. Bhattacharya to Indian Anthropology and Archaeology will never be forgotten.

35

Professor N.K. Behura

Passionate Teacher and a Strict Disciplinarian

Prasanna K.Nayak

Professor N.K. Behura was my teacher. I owe a lot to many of my teachers starting from my primary school to college days to university career. They have left a deep imprint on my mind and on my personality. They have shaped my academic outlook. Professor Behura was one of them. He taught us social anthropology at the post-graduate level. He was a strict teacher and a hard taskmaster. He had earned a reputation as a stern disciplinarian. He loved teaching. He didn't just teach; like all great teachers, he changed lives.

Professor Behura was a maverick. He was critical of his colleagues who did not do their jobs properly. He decried mediocrity wherever he came across it—in schools, colleges and universities. In the class, he mesmerized students with his teaching style and deep understanding of social anthropology, both theory and ethnography. He contributed immensely to promoting the discipline of anthropology in undergraduate colleges of Odisha. He passionately believed that all students, when properly prepared and motivated, could succeed at academically demanding course work, no matter what their social or economic background. He pushed for tougher standards and accountability for students and junior lecturers, often irritating colleagues along the way with his brusque manner and uncompromising stand.

I remember the day Professor Behura entered the class room of Part II Post-Graduate class in Anthropology and delivered his lecture on 'Need Theory of Malinowski'. This was nearly 45 years ago. We listened to him spell-bound. It seemed to me as if Malinowski, the British anthropologist himself, had descended on our Department and explained to us his theory. The portrait of Malinowski flashed across my mind, and for a moment it appeared to me as if Professor Behura resembled Malinowski, dressed spotlessly and brilliantly engaging the attention of the audience. The first impression stayed with me.

Generations of students who have been taught by Professor Behura will no doubt share my feelings about him. He never ever came to a class unprepared. He was determined to give his best to his students. Suspending a class was unthinkable on his part, for teaching for him was a sacred duty. We do not remember his turning up for a class even five minutes' late. If anything, he arrived a few minutes before our class was to begin. He was interested not only in imparting knowledge to his students; he was also keen to instill a sense of punctuality in future citizens of the country.

Professor Behura looked upon himself as a teacher or a scholar but primarily as a senior student ceaselessly striving to acquire more and more knowledge. For this reason, he was extremely fond of students who were diligent, and frowned upon sloth and negligence. However, there is no mistaking his boundless love for his students. He remembered most of them by name and followed their careers with deep paternal pride and anxiety. The achievement of any student of brings tears of joy to his eyes. His happiness is centred in his students. In this aspect, reverentially he was an exception. Every time I have visited him in his house he offered me tea along with thin Arrowroot biscuits. I developed so much likingness for the biscuit brand that every morning while taking tea I opt for having that brand of biscuits only. Madam Mrs. Behura was so much affectionate that she would not leave you without offering you some or other home-made snacks. With Prof. Behura's blessings and moral support I was enabled to begin my career at Utkal University.

During lunch hour in the Department we, his choicest colleagues and fellows, used to go to his office chamber daily, sit there and he ordered tea for all of us. There, matters ranging from academic topics to personal problems are raised and discussed amiably and quite often some jokes come up in the process of discussion and we all enjoy bursting into laughter.

Unlike many of his colleagues, and teachers of the present generation, Professor Behura brought to his profession a tremendous sense of dedication and commitment. In his private as well as public life, he remained every inch a teacher. He believed in the crucial roles teachers play in society. He had little patience with colleagues who did not value their profession. Like Greek sophists, Professor Behura was engaged in the lonely but heroic endeavour of raising the level of consciousness in his students. His view of life may be summed up as follows: man is man, the sophisticated being, and nothing else.

Professor Behura served the Post Graduate Department of Anthropology, Utkal University with distinction for about twenty years. He succeeded Professor Mahapatra as the Head of the Department in 1989. Professor Behura's contribution to research in social anthropology deserves special mention. His pioneering study of Peasant Potters of Orissa has been widely acclaimed as a first-rate ethnographic study. He has published a dozen books and more than hundred research papers in India and abroad. He wrote a series of books in Odia for the beginners in Anthropology and general readers.

He is one of the few teachers of anthropology who could interest students in difficult and challenging subjects like kinship and linguistics. He played a key role in training students of anthropology in doing meaningful fieldwork. Way back in 1973, under the field training programme he took us, the final year students of social anthropology to Jeypore, Koraput a well known tribal districts of Odisha for undertaking one-month fieldwork among the Gadaba tribe. We were to put up in a long row of vacated horse-shade in close proximity to the King's palace. He selected specific Gadaba villages and allotted these as base villages to our batch-mates suiting to the respective topics of study. He prescribed a strict daily routine to us to wake up early in the morning and leave for the field soon after finishing breakfast at 6.30 and return from the field not before 1.30 p.m. lunch hour. In the afternoon we were asked to process the data, write down the daily diary and submit it to Prof. Behura for his suggestions and comments. Very meticulously, he reads our daily diary notes line by line and writes his comments. Every evening he holds a discussion session where he assesses the progress of work of individual students. And, programmatically he makes surprise visits to the base villages allotted to students to check whether they were enthusiastically pursuing their fieldwork or not. At Utkal University, he devoted his entire energies in doing what he always wanted to do: teach.

To say that Professor Behura's teaching and research achieved a national and international reputation is an understatement. He was a vital force in the field of authentic and original anthropological research. He understood how important fieldwork was for students of anthropology. He impressed everyone with his integrity, incredible vitality, and insatiable scientific curiosity. He made his presence felt at seminars, scientific meetings, where everyone admired his energy, his straight-forward, and engaging presentation style, and the precision with which he made his points during discussions. He recognized no boundaries and was never afraid to take sides in a debate on scientific matters and was indifferent to fashion and conventional wisdom. If a scientific concept was shaky, he was the first to declare that the 'the emperor wore no clothes.'

During his tenure at Utkal University he was well conversant with his teaching of social anthropology, ethnography, theory and anthropological thought and linguistic and psychological anthropology. He used to studiously pursue reading higher level and original text books at home and prepare class notes and come fully prepared to deliver the best to his students in the classroom. His classroom teaching was so very absorbing that all students listen to his lectures in a balanced state of mind. Indeed, a brilliant classroom teacher! As a teacher, the other attribute he possessed was, besides having acquired a full grasp of all topics relating social anthropology and showing curious and keen interest in this sub-discipline, his acquisition of professional knowledge in biological as well as archaeological anthropology which he had acquired during his teaching career in undergraduate colleges. His mastery over biological and archaeological anthropology was truly impressive. One would say, he was 'what not an anthropologist'!

Professor Behura mentored over 100 young anthropologists; those who listened attentively to his lectures and avidly learnt from him were the ones who later succeeded in establishing independent scientific careers. He possessed an encyclopedic knowledge not only of social and cultural anthropology but of the history of his discipline. Success never made him lose his endearingly human qualities: he was generous with his time; he was ready to discuss key concepts and latest theories with anybody in the department. His comprehensive understanding of his subject enabled him to effortlessly reach the heart of the matter. His inquisitiveness and his love for knowledge remained strong until the last hours of his life. His death has left a void which no one can fill. However, the ideals he stood for and strove to realize as a teacher and a researcher will continue to inspire his former students.

Prof. N.K. Behura, born in 1933 in a rural coastal village of Kendrapara district, Odisha, was brought up in a large-size Indian family that was economically less secured. Due to financial constraints he had to pass through many hurdles in pursuing higher education, but struggled hard to achieve his goal. While pursuing Post Graduation in Economics in Ravenshaw College, Cuttack, as an ardent student he got an opportunity to interact with Professor N.K. Bose, the then Director of Anthropological Survey of India (ASI), and with whose support he eventually moved to

Ranchi to pursue Anthropology and succeeded in securing University Gold Medal in Anthropology in 1959 from the then Bihar University and later joined ASI, Calcutta also. While serving there (1959-1965) he started his doctoral research under the guidance of N.K.Bose, but after Prof. Bose's sad demise he completed his Ph.D. degree in Social Anthropology in 1973 under the guidance of Prof. L.K. Mahapatra, Utkal University. However, in 1966 he left ASI and came to join the Department of Anthropology, Utkal University as Museum Curator for about a year-and-half. And, after getting qualified in Orissa Education Service (OES) in 1968 he joined the Orissa Government as a lecturer and continued till 1973, and finally in the later part of 1973, he achieved his goal of serving a University Post Graduate Department and joined the Anthropology Department, Utkal University as a lecturer in Social Anthropology. In 1976, he was promoted to the substantive post of Reader in Social Anthropology and became Professor in 1985 and continued till his retirement in 1993. A self-made man indeed! That Professor Behura had a checkered career, is quite evident from this. Post-retirement, he was awarded UGC Emeritus Fellowship in Anthropology (1995-97) and earned the distinction of becoming an Honorary Fellow (1997-2008) of the NKCD Centre for Development Studies, Bhubaneswar, an ICSSR sponsored research institute and, at the same time continued from 1999 to 2002 as a Member of Orissa State Commission for OBCs.

Professor Behura became President of Anthropology and Archaeology Section of the 80th Indian Science Congress Association held in Goa in 1993 and second time, also elected as President of the same that was held in Madurai in 1998. He was recipient of Raisaheb P.R. Chanda Medal from the Asiatic Society of India in 1992 and was conferred Nandighosh award for the year 1995 by the Nandighosh Institute, Bolagada, Odisha, and Professor Khageswar Mahapatra award in 2007. He was felicitated by the Department of Anthropology, University of Calcutta in 1996 under the auspices of its Platinum Jubilee Celebrations and also by the Department of Special Assistance in Anthropology, Utkal University in 2010.

Professor Behura has produced 24 doctoral students, 16 are in social anthropology and the rest belong to other social sciences like Sociology, Social Work and Home science and Performing Art.

Professor Behura has altogether published 23 books, out of which sixteen are based on empirical research and the rest seven are text books meant for students at the graduation level. Of the sixteen research based books, he authored thirteen books either as sole author or as the main author. Of the other three books one has been solely edited by him and the other two jointly edited by him and his colleagues. Besides his well know book on Peasant Potters of Orissa, the other outstanding books are such as, Pottery Techniques in Peasant India, Structure and Change in a Sakti Temple in India: The Mangala of Kakatpur; Anthropological Thought and Theories; Science Culture and Development; A Man Without a mask; Anthropological Econnomics: Substantivism *versus* Formalism; Bio-cultural Frontiers of Man; Urbanization, Street Children and Their Problems; Aged in Changing Social System: Their Problems; Status and Empowerment of the Girl Child: Aspects in Cross-Cultural Context; Family Welfare in India – A Cross-Cultural Study; Tribes and the Indian Constitution: Functioning of the Fifth Schedule in the State of Orissa; Tribal Orissa – Readings in Social Anthropology; Self-Image and Development Perspective; Anthropological Economics – Tribal Development and Globalization; Indian Society and Culture; and 6 other text books in Oriya for Graduate level students.

Out of a total number of 122 research articles covering several branches of social anthropology and development anthropology published by Professor Behura in various books and journals quite a good number of them deal with various dimensions of methodology and theoretical aspects and issues in social anthropology; problems of development of weaker sections; contemporary socio-cultural problems and issues in Indian society; and several special ethnographic accounts on various aspects of tribes of Orissa. Some of his seminal contributions are on topics like: "Social Stratification and Discrimination among three Harijan Castes in a coastal village in Orissa", "Structural Analysis of Juang Myths: A Critique", "Caste and Class in Rural Orissa", "Linguistic Paradigms and Anthropology", "Dynamics of Cultural Assimilation among the tribes of Orissa", "Structuralism and Anthropology", "Ecology and Development: The Dongria Kondh of Orissa", "Problems of Conceptualization and Operationalization in Cross-cultural Studies", "Future of Social Sciences in India", "Indian Social Structure and Democratic Socialism", "Aspects of Dongria Kinship", "Involuntary Displacement and Changing Frontiers of Kinship", "Caste Hierarchy, Status and Power: A Critique", "Tribes, their Development and Quality of Life: A Critique", "Concept of Indian Identity – Reflections on Society", "Vulnerable Ethno-cultural Groups", "Shifting Cultivation: Cause of Environmental Degradation", "Crisis Management: Lessons from the past: A case study of Drought Situation", "Concept of Self in Indian Culture", "Bose on the Unity of Indian Society and Culture", 'Tribe, Caste and

Kinship in Orissa", "Conflict, Politics and Harmony: A case Study", "Componential Analysis of Meta-Koya Kinship", "Child Labour in Orissa: Its Socio-economic magnitude", "Education and Economic Development: The Orissa Context", "The Paradigm of Koya Concept of Human Diseases", "Protective Discrimination and National Integration in India", "Indebtedness and Tribal Development", "Constrains in Tribal Culture for Formal Education", "Environmental Changes Affecting Tribal Women: Problems and Solutions", "Socio-economic Problems and Social Change among the Relocatees of Rengali Dam: A Case Study", "Impact of Evolving Forest Policy and Planned Development on the Indigenous People of Orissa", "Problems in Tribal Education with special reference to Orissa", "Environment, Displacement and Development: Case Study from Orissa", "Gender Issues in Tribal Societies", "Gandhiji's Vision of Education for India", "Functional Dimensions of Weekly Markets in Tribal Areas", "The Scheduled Castes and their Problems", "Development of Primitive Tribal Groups and the Role of Government in Orissa", "Sociology of Pottery among certain groups of Potters in South India", " The Potter Servants of Jagannath of Puri", "Santal Sub-nationalism and New Identity: The Orissa Situation", "Forest and Tribal Worldview", "Position and Problems of Working Class Tribal Women in Urban and Industrial Setting", "Tribal Development in India", "Panchayatiraj and Education in the State of Orissa", "Planned Development and Quality of Life among Indian Tribes", "Cultural Dimensions of Diseases and their Treatment: Case studies from Tribal Orissa", "Social Situation of Aged in Urbal Fringes of Bhubaneswar City", "Sex Preference and Educational Facilities in Urban Fringes", "Socialization and Grassroots level Leaders from Development Perspective", "Structural Continuity of Tribal Culture and Indian Civilization: An Analysis of Orissan Situation", "Dandakaranya Rehabilitation Project and the Koyas of Malkangiri: An Impact Study", "E.E.Evans-Pritchard: The Heretic in British Anthropology", "Art, Symbolism, and Ritual in a Non-literate Society: A Study of Social Context and Modern Relevance of Saora Icon", "Transformation of Human Sacrifice among the Konds of Orissa", "Raja Parba: The Festival of Fertility Cult in Orissa", "Jagannath of Puri and His Pilgrimage", "Religious Rites and Festivals of Tribes of Orissa", 'Effect of Drought on Health and Nutritional Status of People", "Social Dimensions of Family in Rural India: An Analysis", " Saora Guar Parba".

At the same time, during his stint in academic and research institutes in Orissa Professor Behura has carried out a good number of research projects sponsored by Government of Orissa as well as India and produced the reports during tenure as a Fellow of NKCDS, Bhubaneswar. They are, such as, Seventy-Third Constitutional Amendment and Primary Education – Prospects and Problems (sponsored by ICSSR); Redefinition of Ethnic Identities among the Tribes of Odisha (sponsored by UGC); Rehabilitation Action Plan for Project Affected Persons (PAPS) of Mahanadi Chitrotpala Island Irrigation Project (sponsored by World Bank); Functioning of the Fifth Schedule of the Constitution in the State of Orissa (sponsored by ICSSR).

Professor Behura has participated in a number of national and international conferences, seminars and symposia and presented talks which have been published in various issues. As Sectional President of the 80th Indian Science Congress Association his address was on 'Tribes, Their Dvelopment and Quality of Life – A Critique' which had drawn the attention of the Union Government.

Professor Behura passed away on 6 February, 2013 after a year-long illness. News of his death saddened students and friends in India and abroad. Professor Behura leaves a daughter, Archana and her family, and a large extended family consisting of former students. We will all miss him sorely. And his student army will soldier on.

36
Prasanna Kumar Nayak and His Journey as an Anthropologist

Manas Ranjan Kar and *Rajkishor Mahana*

Professor Prasanna Kumar Nayak is revered as an erudite scholar not only in India, but also abroad. Having been awarded the prestigious Alexander-von-Humboldt Fellowship early in his university career, he has brought glory to the discipline of anthropology in India and his first visit to Freie University, Berlin boosted up his scholarly career and he continued his interaction, association and close collaboration with many internationally reputed social science scholars in a number of well-known universities in Europe. Even after his superannuation, a host of Euro-American scholars continue to remain in touch with him and he is accompanied for his contribution to interdisciplinary research. Throughout his career at Utkal University, he concentrated on teaching anthropological 'theory', 'thought' and 'methodology' and promoted teaching a special course on 'development anthropology'. The long years he spent doing fieldwork among several Adivasi societies of Odisha equipped him to inspire students to pursue anthropology as a field science, and as a hard empirical discipline.

Prof. Nayak is also well-known as an institution builder, and an able and astute administrator. As a researcher he is an independent thinker. As a teacher he is affable and inspirational. As a research guide he is open-minded, responsive and helpful. As an administrator he is resolute and a strict disciplinarian, yet humane and compassionate.

Prof. Nayak was born in 1951 in Barihapur in Dhenkanal district of Odisha, a very big rural village inhabited by as many as 19 occupational groups, Jatis. He was brought up in a very big joint family of 24 members (two of his grandfathers and their children and grand-children over three generations were living together in the same joint estate until 1968). He had four brothers and two sisters. He belonged to a family the head of which was called Dalei, a title which the then king of Dhenkanal bestowed on his grandfather's grandfather who was reputed in the sub-region as a very caring and benevolent village headman. The villagers were so familiar with the Dalei title than the Nayak title that up to his generation he was referred to as Prasanna Dalei. In keeping with the family status and tradition, for the last several generations his family used to establish marriage ties only with village headmen's families in the sub-region. After the death of his father's great grandfather his father dropped out of high school and returned to village to look after the landed property and cultivation of crops. The family was getting a lot of the land produce but had no money. Although his mother did not study in a school, she was privately taught by the family Brahman priest. She was instrumental in many ways in providing higher education to all her children by putting pressure on his father to sell huge quantities paddy every month. In the entire village, his elder brother was the first person to acquire a graduate degree and he himself the first post-graduate degree. Following the ideals of Dalei family, other well to do people of the village were prompted to provide higher education to their children.

After the completion of upper primary course at his village school Prasanna Kumar Nayak had to move out of his village to pursue Middle English school education and later high school and college education by staying in hostels all through. He passed his high school examination securing good marks and pursued science studies. After completing a Bachelor of Science degree from SCS College, Puri he studied Anthropology at Utkal University and completed Master of Science (M.Sc.) degree in Anthropology. In M.Sc. he secured first position in the University in 1974 and was awarded University Gold Medal for this.

Six months before the M.Sc. examination result was declared, Prof. Nayak got the opportunity to join the Tribal Research Bureau (TRB), Bhubaneswar as a Research Scholar in November 1974, courtesy a special recommendation of Prof. L.K. Mahapatra, the then Head of the Department of Anthropology. He was assigned the task of undertaking fieldwork among the Bonda and the Dongria Kondh, two hill tribes of Odisha and prepare ethnographic reports by conducting socio-economic surveys. The first draft of the monograph on the Dongria Kondh prepared by him was later published by TRB, Government of Orissa. In August 1975, he joined the Post Graduate Department of Anthropology, Utkal University as a Research Assistant and was associated with the regular research activities of the Department and began taking regular classes.

After a year, he was appointed as a Lecturer in Social Anthropology in the Post Graduate Department of Anthropology at Utkal University in November 1976.

Before entering the Niamgiri hills, the Dongria land in February 1975, Nayak for the first time witnessed a Dongria Kondhs' congregation in Chatikona, a foothill rural town. Shivaratri festival was being observed there. In the festival ground he saw the Dongrias merrymaking, singing and dancing in separate groups. To his utter astonishment, all of a sudden he observed how group fights broke out among the Dongria Kondhs and the festival ground turned into a battle field. All celebrations came to an abrupt end. Nayak wanted to investigate the incident and the very next day he climbed the hills and reached Khambesi, a Dongria Kondh village where he stayed for five months. Gradually he came to know about the clan feuds among the Dongria Kondhs. This goaded Prof. Nayak to zero in on clan feuds, a challenging topic, for his doctoral research. R.K. Merton labels it as serendipitous pattern of research.

In the meantime, in December 1981, he was awarded the University Grants Commission (UGC) Fellowship for undertaking doctoral research under the guidance of Prof. L.K. Mahapatra, one of the eminent Indian anthropologists. With a prolonged stay among the Dongria Kondhs of Rayagada district in Odisha, he learnt their language (Kui) and carried out intensive fieldwork for one and half years by putting up in the Dongria village, Khambesi. In subsequent years, he utilized vacations and holidays to make field visits in several spells to as many as 18 Dongria Kondh villages for preparation of his doctoral thesis. He was awarded the doctoral degree (Ph.D.) in Anthropology for his thesis titled "Structure and Function of Clan Feud among the Dongria Kondh" in 1985. In the same year, he became a Reader in Social Anthropology in the Post Graduate Department of Anthropology, Utkal University.

In early 1987 Prof. Nayak was awarded the prestigious Alexander von Humboldt (AvH) Fellowship to carry out post-doctoral research in Freie University, Berlin, Germany for two years. Back in the department, he became Professor in 1990 at a very young age of 38. To his credit, he was one of the few youngest professors in the history of Utkal University. This may be considered as one of the important milestones in an illustrious academic career spanning over three and a half decades. During this period, between 1976 and 2011, he has received many awards and reached some important milestones while holding key administrative positions and continued his teaching and research till his superannuation in 2011.

He always expressed admiration for all his teachers who taught him during his student career. As a student he was a favourite of all his teachers. He had the blessings of all in the Department of Anthropology, Utkal University and everybody knew how close he was to L.K. Mahapatra, N.K. Behura and B.K. Behera, his revered mentors. Professors of Universities of Delhi, JNU, Kolkata, Chennai, Karnatak (Dhharward), Andhra (Visakhapatnam), Ranchi, Patna and Lucknow knew him personally and cherished him as a budding academic scholar in social anthropology. His personal interaction with Professor F. G. Bailey inspired him to complete his Ph.D. thesis concentrating on case studies of feuds and making institutional analysis of them. Professor Mario D. Zamora, University of Virginia, was the external examiner of his Ph.D. thesis and in appreciation of his work wrote the foreword to his book *Blood, Women and Territory*, and invited him to contribute an article to his edited volume The Anthropology of Peace in honour of E. Adamson Hoebel. Prof. Zamora even offered him to visit Department of Anthropology, Virginia, U.S.A.

Besides being a bright student and a disciplined scholar, Prof. Nayak had been a passionate and sincere teacher all through his academic career. All his endeavours were concentrated on bringing holistic development to the subject as well as to the students of anthropology. Despite being a social anthropologist he believed in the integration of the discipline of the anthropology and so promoted specialization in biological anthropology. Soon after assuming the headship of the department he persuaded the university to reserve eight seats for students of biological sciences to get admitted to Anthropology and always wanted students of biological anthropology to accompany students of social anthropology under the field training programme of the department. Realizing the importance of ethnographic fieldwork, he very often says, "fieldwork is the backbone of anthropology and field settings are the laboratories for the anthropologists". He was instrumental in organizing celebration of the J.B.S. Haldane birth centenary and inviting Honourable Biju Patnaik, former Chief Minister of Odisha to inaugurate the function and it was with his blessings and support the Haldane Chair was founded in the Anthropology Department. In order to enthuse his colleagues and students he wrote a critical article, "Biocultural Anthropology: Limitations of Physico-chemical Research" which was published under the Special Assistance Programme of the Department in 2007.

Prof. Nayak's scholastic and teaching achievements can be judged from the fact that he has published as many as five books and a number of journal articles and has prepared 16 project reports. Besides, he had participated in nearly 18 national and 22 international seminars and presented papers there. As a research supervisor, he had guided 37 M.Phil. students and 15 Ph.D. scholars during his academic career.

Prof. Nayak is regarded as a storehouse of knowledge on tribals and tribal societies belonging to Odisha. He had intensively studied the Dongria Kondhs, the Gadabas, the Bondo Highlanders, the Koyas, the Kolhas, the Kutia Kondhs, the Hos, the Saoras and the Pauri Bhuiyans. He focuses on the study of tribes, their social structure and culture and examines them in historical perspective seeing their connections and interactions with the ruling kings and vassal kings in the past. He considers tribes as kingly people. He admires Evan-Pritchard's view that 'they are different but not primitive'. He lays emphasis on emic conceptualization in social anthropological studies. His research interests included kinship and conflict, socio-political structure of tribes, ethnography of tribes, tribal rites, rituals and arts, tribal and rural development, involuntary resettlement and development, and theories and methodology in social anthropology.

Prof. Nayak has contributed immensely to the understanding of Indian society, particularly tribal societies and cultures and the anthropology of development by contributing research articles to national and international journals, and edited volumes. Most of his early writings, which date back to 1974, were primarily on tribal economy. For instance, some of his research papers were on gift exchange among the Gadabas, "Transformation of Barter to Peasant Economy among the Gadaba of Jeypore", "Market and Money in Contemporary Tribal Economy of Orissa" and "Shifting Cultivation among the Koya Tribes". Later, he wrote extensively on problems of planned tribal development, issue of displacement and rehabilitation, ecology and development, tribal education, tribal art, craft and aesthetics, role of anthropology in natural calamity, tribal forest economy, and gender and development under the broad theme of anthropology of development. Some of his papers on the anthropology of development that need special mention are "Tradition and Development in Tribal Orissa", "Tribal Development: From Sport to Sonata to Science", "Revisiting Tribes and Reconsidering Tribal Development", "New Paradigm of Tribal Development", "Reconsidering Tribal Development in India", "The Rise and Fall of 'Tribal' Development in Orissa" and "What Tribal Development is Not!".

Having immense knowledge on anthropological theories, he had special interest in applying anthropological thoughts and theories to social problems and realities of Indian society. In this regard, it is worth mentioning that he wrote some seminal research papers like "Levi-Strauss Anthropology: An Appraisal", "Beginning at the Beginning of Anthropological Theory", "Elementary Structure of Beauty and Love", "Appraising Development Anthropology", "Appraising Methodology in Development Anthropology" and "New Role of Home-Country Anthropologists of the Developing World". Besides, some of his scholarly writings that help one to understand the dynamics of tribal social institutions and their ramifications are: "They are Different, but not Primitive", "Inheritance of Kingly Citizenship: Tribals at Cross-Roads in Modern State of Orissa, India", "Kingly Rites in Tribal Religions: Some Reflections from Middle India", and "Owning the King: Ethno-Cultural Politics in Bhuiyan Pirha".

Prof. Nayak, as the Coordinator of UGC-sponsored Department of Special Assistance (DSA) programme in Anthropology, was instrumental in bringing out a volume titled Human Encounter with Drought, the inaugural volume of the DSA in Anthropology. While this was one of the most important anthropological publications on a development theme, it was the first of its kind on urgent anthropological issues. Being the first editor of the volume, in his introductory article on "Anthropology and Natural Calamities" he has spelt out the anthropological perspectives and approaches towards the study of calamitous situations and has stressed the need for holistic understanding of the problems of the affected community to effectively curb and solve them. Outlining the empirical situation of drought in Kalahandi, Prof. Nayak says, "The socio-cultural sphere of operation and management of the micro-cultural level might appear mysterious to a Western Man, but it works and does solve the problems to a great extent. Under the circumstances what causes anxiety and concern among such humanity is not so much the natural hazard and hence the deprivation but protracted machination of man against man, the greater man against the lesser man, a sinister design of man against man." In other words, he suggested that disasters like drought could be overcome by analyzing the socio-cultural and institutional matrices of the people and putting them in practice keeping the peoples' agenda in view.

One of his most scholarly and cited book *Blood, Women and Territory* (1989) makes an analysis of clan feuds among the Dongria Kondhs of Odisha. It documents various definitions, approaches and explanations of feud; delineates inter-clan and intra-clan feuds with extended case studies and comparison of these two types of feud; analyses feud as culturally derived form of societal conflict in relation to economic, political, kinship and magico-religious domains; and discusses the trends of transformation in this feuding society. The book is of immense interest to anthropologists, ethnologists, political scientists, social philosophers, development sociologists and social workers. Besides, his edited book Tribes of Orissa (1995) presents brief sketches of all the 62 tribes of Odisha. His ILO-INDISCO study was published by ILO and Ministry of Tribal Affairs under the title "From Bondage to Rural Enterprise: A situational Analysis and Participatory Strategies with the Bondo Highlanders" (2005).

Throughout his academic career Prof. Nayak has been awarded for his hard work, dedication and knowledge. Besides being awarded the AvH Fellowship to pursue post-doctoral research, he got opportunity under the Europe Fellowship programme of the AvH-Stiftung to undertake research and orientation programmes and library work on anthropology of development at Institute of Social and Cultural Anthropology, Oxford University; London School of Economics and School of Oriental and African Studies, University of London; and Institute of Development Studies, University of Sussex. In 1997 he was awarded the Baden-Wuertemberg Fellowship, Germany under the auspices of German Research Council (DFG), Bonn for participating in joint teaching and research programme of the South Asia Institute, University of Heidelberg. There, as a Visiting Professor, he taught a full semester course on Tribes and castes in India today. In 2012 he was awarded the Indian Council of Cultural Relations (ICCR) Visiting Professorship under the Ministry of External Affairs, Government of India to visit Institute of South Asian-Tibetan and Buddhist Studies, University of Vienna, Austria where he delivered semester lectures on: "Scheduled Tribes in India: Changing Perspectives" and semester seminars on "Marginalization, Maoism and the State in Central India".

Professor Nayak earned the distinctions of attending and participating in a number of national and international conferences/ Symposia/Seminars/Workshops in India and abroad. They are as follows: (1976) Zonal workshop on "Problems of Pre-farming & Marginal Tribal communities of East-Central India" held at Ranchi University, Ranchi; (1978) National level Interdisciplinary workshop-cum-symposium on "The methodology of Social Sciences with Special emphasis on Anthropological Procedures" held at Karnatak University, Dharwad; (1979) National Seminar on "Ecology, Population Policy and Population Research", Utkal University; (1981) National Seminar on "Forest Ecosystem", Utkal University; (1982) National Seminar on "Development

Aspects of the Tribal Areas of Orissa",THRTI, Bhubaneswar; (1983) National workshop-cum-symposium on "Modernization of Courses in Anthropology", New Delhi; (1985) National Seminar on "Monitoring and Evaluation of Development in Tribal Areas", THRTI, Bhubaneswar; (1985) National Seminar on "Tradition and Development in India with special reference to Eastern India", A.N.Sinha Institute of Social Studies, Patna, Bihar; (1986) State level Workshop on "Environment and Resource Management in Dongria Kondh Area", Chatikona, Odisha; (1986) National Seminar on "Anthropology in the service of the Nation", Department of Anthropology, University of Delhi; (1987) UNESCO sponsored Indo-American Students exchange Orientation Progamme, OUAT, Bhubaneswar; (1989) National Seminar on "Poverty Alleviation Programme of cysd: The Role the NGOs", Bubaneswar; (1989) National Seminar on "Tribal Unrest, Tribal Movement and Tribal Development", BIDISA, West Bengal; (1989) National Seminar on "Problems of the Aged and their Development", OVHA, Bhubaneswar; (1992) National Seminar on "Changing Tribal Societies", Department of Anthropology, University of Delhi; (2010) National Seminar on "Biocultural Anthropology: Prospects and Challenges" held at NKCDS, Bhubaneswar and as the Director and Convenor of the conference delivered the inaugural address; (2016) National Seminar on "Celebrating Anthropology: The Human Science" held at Department of Anthropology, University of Delhi; (2019) National Conference on "Livelihood of Vulnerable Groups: Empirical and Theoretical Dimensions" held at the Department of Anthropology, University of Hyderabad.

(1978) International Congress of Anthropological and Ethnological Sciences, New Delhi; (1978) International Seminar on Anthropology of Shifting Cultivation, Utkal University; (1987) International seminar on Asian and African Studies in Anthropology, Institute of Volkerkunde, Koeln, West Germany; (1988) XII International Congress of Anthropological and Ethnological Sciences, Zagreb Yugoslavia; (1994) 3rd Conference of European Association of Social Anthropologists, Oslo, Norway; (1994) 13th European Conference on Modern South Asian Studies, Toulouse, France; (1997) International Conference on Jagannath Revisited organized by Prof. Hermann Kulke and Prof.Burkhard Schnepel, Heidelberg, Germany; (1998) As Director, organized International Conference on Rethinking Orissa Society, Culture and History, Bhubaneswar; (1999) International Symposium on Various Identities: Orissa, Salzau, Germany; (2005) International conference on Worte: Konflictfuehrung in Suedasien, Max-Planck Institute, Halle, Germany;

(2007) on the occasion of the Golden Jubilee of Department of Anthropology, Utkal Unversity, as Director organized International Conference on Anthropology in India Today: Postmodernism and Globalism in Perspective, Bhubaneswar; (2008) International Conference on Citizenship and Modernity Reconsidered, SAI, Heidelberg, Germany; (2008) International Conference on State and Tribal Development, IIAS, Leiden, Amsterdam; (2008) awarded travel grant by the Organizers of ECMSA, Manchester to attend the 20th European Conference on Modern South Asian Studies held in Manchester from 8 to 11 July, 2008; (2009) International Conference on Citizenship and Modernity Reconsidered: Flow of Ideas between Europe and Asia, held at Seoul National University, Seoul, South Korea; (2009) DGV (German Anthropological Society) International conference on Cultural Appropriation: Assimilation-Adaptation-Camouflage, held at University of Frankfurt, Germany; (2009) International Colloquia on Myth, Rite and Symbol: Aspects of Indian Religious Experience held at faculty of Fine Arts & Humanities, SAPIENZA, University of Rome; (2009) Chaired the first session and delivered an invited talk on "Society, Religion and Politics in Contemporary India" at the Institute of African and Oriental Studies, Rome; (2010) International Conference on Citizenship and Modernity Reconsidered: Flow of Ideas between Europe and Asia, held at Xavier Institute, Bhubaneswar; (2011) International Conference on "Wa(h)re "Kultur": Kulturelles Erbe, Revitalisierung und die Renaissance der Idee von Kultur" organized by German Ethnological Society (DGV) in Vienna; (2012) Colloquium on Indigenous People in India: Changing Perspectives, organized by Froebenius Institute, University of Frankurt ; (2017) DGV conference, Freie University, Berlin.

As a distinguished anthropologist he had the privilege of becoming Expert Member (Steering Committee, Consultative Committee, Working Group and Sub-Group committees on ST & SC Development, Revamping TRIs), Ministry of Tribal Affairs and Planning Commission (NITI AAYOG), Government of India, New Delhi (from 2000 to 2008 & from 2011-continuing); Subject Expert Member, UPSC Selection Committees, Government of India since 2009 continuing; UGC Subject Expert to review the progress of work of Research Scientists, UGC Special Assistance Programmes (SAP) since 1990 and continuing; Member, Court, Central University Ranchi, Jharkhand (2010-2015); Chairman of all Academic and Research Committees (Anthropology), Utkal University (from 1995 to 2009); Expert Member, Cultural Policy, Government of Orissa, 2003; Member, Advisory Committee, DSA/DRS, Department of Anthropology,

Andhra University (2007-2010) and Department of Anthropology, Central University of Hyderabad (2018-continuing).

Apart from being the recipient of several awards and fellowships, Prof. Nayak visited many European institutes and delivered lectures on core anthropological topics. Prof. Nayak was awarded the Alexander von Humboldt Fellowship, Germany, for Post-Doctoral research and joined the Institute of Ethnologie, Freie University, Berlin; worked on the research topic "Kinship and Clanship in Tribal Orissa : An Empirico-Theoretical Analysis" at the Institute of Ethnologie, Freie University, Berlin (West) from 1.9.1987 to 31.5.1989. Prior to that he joined the Goethe Institute, Berlin for undertaking a 4-month German Language Course from 4 May to 31 August, 1987 sponsored by the AvH-Stiftung, Germany. Under the Europe Fellowship Programme of the AvH-Stiftung he undertook research and library work on "Anthropology of Development" at Universities of Oxford – Institute of Social and Cultural Anthropology; London – LSE & SOAS; and Sussex – (IDS) Institute of Development Studies (from 1.12.1988 to 30.2.1989). As Visiting Fellow of Wolfson College, University of Oxford he attended the seminar lectures and guest lectures at the Institute of Social Anthropology and participated in the regular deliberations and discussions held at the Centre for Asian and African Development Studies, Queen Elizabeth House, Oxford. He attended a three-week orientation course on "Rapid Rural Development Strategies and Methods" at the Institute of Development Studies (IDS), Sussex, University of Sussex commissioned by Prof. Dr. Robert Chambers. Under the Revisit Programme of the Alexander von Humboldt Foundation got invited to the Institute of Ethnologie, Freie University, Berlin for 5 months, from June to October 1994 and participated in the academic programme, teaching a semester course jointly with Prof. G. Pfeffer, and conducted higher level researches on "Comparative Kinship" getting orientation in modern and post-modern theories in Social Anthropology in collaboration with Professor Dr. G. Pfeffer, Chairman of the Institute. He was invited to the Department of Ethnologie, South Asia Institute, University of Heidelberg, Germany from 10 to 30 July, 1994 as a Visiting Fellow. He visited the Institute of Social Anthropology, University of Oslo, Norway in August 1994. He visited the institute of Social Anthropology, University of Toulouse, France in September 1994. He was invited to South Asia Institute, University of Heidelberg as a Visiting Professor on the award of Baden-Wuertemberg Fellowship, Government of Germany for 6 months from January 1997 to June 1997 and taught a full semester course there on "Tribes and Castes in India Today". He was a visiting fellow at the

Department of Ethnologie, South Asia Institute, Heidelberg, Germany from July 1998 to September 1998 and worked jointly with Professor Dr.Burkard Schnepel, University of Heidelberg. He was invited to the Department of Indology, University of Potenza, Italy as Visiting Professor in October 1998 and delivered 18 special lectures as part of the Post-Graduate course in collaboration with Professor Fabio Scialpi under the broad theme, "Indian society, economy, culture and politics: Challenges of the 21st Century". On invitation, visited the famous Institute of African and Oriental Studies, University of Rome and delivered a guest lecture on "Women in Modern India" on 15th October, 1998. As Visiting Professor visited the Institute of Historical Anthropology, University of Frankfurt, Germany, June-July 2000 for six weeks. As Visiting Professor visited the Institute of Historical Anthropology, University of Frankfurt, Germany, May-June 2001for 6 weeks; October 2005 for four weeks and July-August 2008 for four weeks. As Visiting Professor he visited the South Asia Institute, Heidelberg (August-September 2009) and (September-October 2011). As Visiting professor on the award of ICCR visited Institute of South Asian-Tibetan and Buddhist Studies, University of Vienna for a period of one Semester (September 2012 - February 2013); (i) delivered lectures on "Culture History: STs in India: Changing Perspectives" to 28 Graduate and Post-Graduate students, (ii) organized and conducted Seminars on "Regional History: Marginalization, Maoism and State in Central India" in which 9 students participated regularly and evaluated their Semester examination papers, (iii) delivered two public lectures, and (iv) attended 3 guest lectures, one-day workshop on Tibetan studies and cultural programme organized by students of the Institute. 2012 December7, as Guest lecturer he visited Institute of Religion, Culture and Modernity, University of Lausanne and Frobenius Institute of Ethnologie, University of Frankfurt during the 2nd week of December 2012 to deliver special lectures. 2017 taught a semester course on "Indian Anthropological Studies", Froebenius Institute, Goethe University, Frankfurt.

In the introductory section it has already been mentioned that Prof. Nayak was an able and astute administrator. He was resolute and a strict disciplinarian. He possessed the rare ability to take administrative matters to their logical conclusions without compromising his honesty and integrity. He had earned both wrath and accolades for this attitude, and had accepted both gleefully. In the present section, some of his notable administrative achievements have been listed. He took charge as Coordinator of UGC sponsored Department of Special Assistance (DSA)

Programme in Anthropology in 1990. He served as Coordinator of DSA Programme till 1997, UGC-sponsored ASIHSS programme (2005-2007), and UGC-sponsored CAS in Anthropology (2008- 2011). Under the UGC sponsored special assistance programme of the Department he had invited distinguished anthropologists, namely, Nick Allen and Robert Parkin from Oxford University, Burkhard Schnepel from University of Frankfurt and Frank Heideman from University of Muinch, Germany to deliver a series of seminar lectures in the Department. While he got Nick Allen's lectures published under the Occasional paper series 2 & 3, 1993; Robert Parkin's lectures were published as a book on social anthropology in 2001 under the title *Perilous Transactions*. It may be mentioned that Prof. Nayak being influenced by publications of IDS, University of Sussex, England ventured to introduce special publications of Occasional papers, Discussion papers and Seminal papers under the Special Assistance Programme of the Department.

Having awarded the prestigious AvH Fellowship and being conferred Professorship at a very young age, by 1990 Prof. Nayak had established himself as a researcher par excellence. However, his administrative acumen caught the eye of the State Government and in 2000 and he was appointed as the Director of Scheduled Caste and Scheduled Tribe Research and Training Institute (SCSTRTI), Bhubaneswar. His notable achievements as its Director include the establishment of the first of its kind ethnographic tribal museum. During this period he also held the position of Director, Academy of Tribal Languages and Cultures, a Government of Odisha institution. As the Director of the SCSTRTI, he revamped the institute, renovated the office building including its old library building, computer room, seminar room, rooms of the institute's guest house as well as the tribal house structures on the campus. Prof. Nayak initiated setting up of the new library building, the conference hall, organized 12 national and state level seminars/symposia/workshops on various issues of tribal development and 48 training programmes for skill development of tribal participants and orientation of government officials. The innovative research and training activities of SCSTRTI, Bhubaneswar were warmly appreciated by Government of India and it created avenues for regular flow of funds for its further development and it emerged as one of the most reputed and attractive tribal research institutes in India.

Upon his return to the University in 2004, Prof. Nayak served as the Chairman, PG Council, Utkal University. During his tenure he also held the position of acting Vice Chancellor of the University on several occasions. Being a strict disciplinarian he, as PG Council Chairman, ensured that all teachers must come to their departments on time.

In addition, Prof. Nayak has also served as Head of the Department of Anthropology for two terms, Coordinator for the UGC sponsored Assistance for Infrastructural Development of Humanities and Social Sciences (AIHSS) Programme in Anthropology, Coordinator for UGC sponsored Centre for Advanced Study (CAS) Programme in Anthropology, Syndicate Member of Utkal University and Dean of Faculty of Sciences.

Prof. Nayak enjoys the reputation of being a teacher par excellence among the students. He resorted to unique method of teaching whereby he ensured that all students in his class attain the same level of understanding. He always advised his students to follow original authors to understand their thoughts. As a human being he was revered and loved by the students and colleagues of his Department. He earned the appreciation of the faculty of other Departments, the office staff, and above all, of the higher authorities in the State Government.

As a nature lover, he tried his best to create an urban forest inside the SCSTRTI campus and also in the Utkal University campus by planting exotic species (Sorea robusta). Even today his love for nature remains undiminished. His house in Bhubaneswar has a beautiful garden with a mix of big fruit-bearing trees like mango, jackfruit, lemon, lichi, bel and varieties of ornamental plants.

His unique research work has led many a foreign academicians to collaborate with him to carry out interdisciplinary research. His research collaborations with foreign universities from Berlin, Frankfurt, Heidelberg, Halle, Munich, Bonn, Oslo, Paris, Rome, Oxford, London, Manchester, Leiden, Seoul and Lausanne have strengthened his credentials as a reputed anthropologist. He was Member, Steering Committee and Field Director of German-Orissa research project on Orissa Revisited, sponsored by German Research Council (DFG) from 1999 to 2006. Similarly, he was Member, Steering Committee of Excellence Cluster Project on Citizenship as conceptual flow executed by South Asia Institute, University of Heidelberg from 2007 to 2010. Prof. Nayak is so popular in Europe that any European scholar would consult him before embarking on a study in Odisha. In the field of interdisciplinary collaborative research programmes he has interacted with a good number of India-area Euro-American researchers in economics, history, political science, sociology and Indology and shared his views with all of them individually. Besides, he has also served as Member, Task Force on Resettlement and Development, Washington DC between 1992 and 1995.

Post retirement, from 2012 to 2015, Prof. Nayak assumed the office of the Chairman of Nabakrushna Chaudhury Centre for Development Studies (NCDS), Bhubaneswar, an ICSSR institute. Currently, he heads a registered trust named Labanya Institute of Indian Studies (LIIS) functioning in his residential premises. As Chairman of the Trust, he focuses on organizing lectures on various topics of anthropological and Indological interest by inviting distinguished scholars from India and abroad. He finds pleasure in inviting his intimate friends, scholars and students to participate in such academic deliberations.

Finally, to conclude, it is evident from the account presented above that Prof. Nayak's academic credentials are his pride and others' envy. His anthropological thought on citizenship has huge ramifications in the current development scenario, particularly when the stakes and concerns of Adivasis are taken into account.

37
Surinder Nath

Ravinder Singh

Dr. Surinder Nath, born on 13 September, 1945 in Lahore, now in Pakistan, was youngest child among the siblings in the family. His parents were constraint to move to India after independence. His parents settled in Kamla Nagar, well known area near University of Delhi. Here he completed Higher Secondary School in 1962. In 1962 he took admission in B.Sc. (Hons) Anthropology in University of Delhi, a new course then began in that current session July, 1962. So he became the student of first batch of B.Sc. (Hons) Anthropology. He had been hard working, obedient and sincere student of his time and completed his honors graduation in Anthropology in 1965, and further continued to earn M.Sc. Anthropology in 1967.

Prof. Nath began his Ph.D. work under the supervision of Dr. Abhimanyu Sharma, Reader in the department. He received Ph.D. in 1971. Meanwhile he was part of the department as post doctoral fellow. In 1975, he joined Department of Anthropology as Lecturer in Forensic Anthropology. Besides he received special training in Forensic Science and Serological Investigations at crime sites in Central Forensic Science Laboratory of CBI, New Delhi. Gradually he focused and specialized in Forensic Sciences, Finger printings, Somatometery and Somatoscopy, identification of skeletal remains, Optometry, sport anthropometry; biological anthropology and human growth and development.

Prof. Nath had created an indispensable space for himself in his chosen field in the country. He developed curriculum for M.Sc. Forensic Science, Optional paper of Forensic Science for the post graduation programme in Anthropology or Human Biology. He had joined Certificate Course in Forensic Science and remained several years as main Coordinator in the Department of Anthropology, Delhi University. He also developed the syllabus for Compulsory paper of Human Growth and development in M.Sc. Anthropology in Delhi University. He had been invited for developing the Syllabus for post-graduate programme in Forensic Science in NFSC, New Delhi and of Bundelkhand University, Jhansi. He had been member of the modernization of Forensic Science in NFSC, New Delhi syllabus. Further he also developed the Post-graduate diploma in Forensic Science for Amity Institute of Behavioural and Allied Sciences, Amity University.

He was an eminent teacher and was in demand for the guest speaker in Police Training Academy or such training colleges. He was faculty in LNJN National Institute of Forensic Sciences and Criminology, New Delhi. Besides he used to visit often to lecture in Academic Staff College of various Universities in Delhi, Gorakhpur, Chandigarh, Amristar, Jodhpur, Patiala, and Manipur. Further he had been faculty of Life Sciences and Forensic Sciences, Panjab University, Patiala. He had been the Member of various committees such as Departmental Research Committee, Institute of Forensic Science, BU, Jhansi and Members of Board of Studies, Amity Institute of Biotechnology AU, UP.

Prof. Nath has published more than hundred research papers, written ten books (10) on different areas of anthropology, mainly concerned to finger identifications, forensic science, anthropometry, food and nutrition. Some of these books are Fingerprint Identification (1984); An Introduction to Forensic Anthropology (1989); Fingerprint Identification in Crime Detection (1991); Forensic Anthropology (1995); Nutritional Anthropology (1997); Anthropometry (2005); Encyclopaedic Dictionary of Food and Nutrition Volume-I (2006); Personal Identification through Fingerprints (2006); Vayaktigat Pehchan Mein Ungaliyon Ke Nishaan (Hindi) (2009) and Fingerprint Identification (2010).

He has edited books on different areas of his interest. Some of them are Application Areas of Anthropology (1992); Criminology: A Psychological and Anthropological Analysis (1992); Issues and Trends in Rehabilitation Research (1993); Advances in Forensic Science (2001); Role of Forensic Science in the new Millennium (2002); Society, Crime and Prosecution (2005); Forensic Anthropology Science and Medicine (2005); Forensic Science and Crime Investigation (2005); Modern Trends in Forensic Science (2006); Human Blood Analysis (2007) and Forensic Science and its Related Issues (2012).

In early 1994 Prof N.K. Chaddha, President, Aastha, organized a Seminar on Health in collaboration with Department of Anthropology, HNB University, Srinagar, Garwhal which Dr. P.C. Joshi, Head of the Department coordinated this Seminar. We, most of the research scholars—Abhik Ghose, Satish Kedia, Ms. Bharati, etc. with Prof. Nath and Dr. Chadha participated in Seminar and enjoyed most. He asked me to prepare an abstract and write full paper for this seminar. I was first person to read the paper and it was my first experience to participate and present the paper. He keenly listened to my deliberation among the audiences, which I still recall. He appreciated my oratory presentation skills. It was a big achievement for me to receive such compliments from him.

Prof. Nath guided more than 25 students, mostly girls, for Ph.D. in Forensic Sciences, Finger printings, Somatometery and Somatoscopy, identification of skeletal remains, Optometry, sport anthropometry; biological anthropology and human growth and development. It was his tender love and care for his students. Most of the girls of the time have attracted to work with him. Some of his senior women students worked for Ph.D. were Prabha Badkur (1985) and Reita Jain (1989). Some of my contemporary Ph.D. girls were-Kavita Jain (1993), Shivani Aggarwal (1997), Sunita Roy (1997), Shivani Chhibber (1998); Sumider Kaur (1998); Preeti Jain (1999); ten girls between 2008 and 2012 have earned their Ph.D. under his supervision. Three boys only who received Ph.D. under his supervision were: N. Satish Chandra (1989) and Swetansu Shekhar Rath (1994) and I was, as boy, his last student worked with him for Ph.D. (1995).

Prof. Nath had been an ideal person, full of moral values and integrity. He held several key positions in the Delhi University, such as he had been the Provost of Gywar Hall for two years, a student Hostel in Delhi University. He was the longest serving Coordinator for Certificate Course in Forensic Science, a programme runs in the evening in the Department of Anthropology. Besides being Head, Department of Anthropology (2004-2007) he was also the Dean of Science Faculty, University of Delhi during 2005-2007.

He had been member of various Research Panels of various research Organizations: University Grant Commission, Council of Industrial Research, DMRC Jodhpur, Sport Authority of India; Ministry of Tribal Affair, Government of India; National Institute of Fashion Technology (NIFT), Delhi and Bureau of Police Research and Development (BPRD), New Delhi. He had been the expert member in M.Phil. Advisory committee for Clinical Psychology, a residential training programme, in IHBAS since 2004.

Further he has been active member of various Academic bodies and other organizations. Life member of Indian Academy of Forensic Science; Forensic Science Society of India; Ethnographic and Folk Culture Society of India, Lucknow; Indian Anthropological Association, Delhi; Vice-President and Founding Member of Aastha, a voluntary Organization working for elderly people in Delhi.

His long time friend Dr. G.D. Gupta, Central Forensic Science Laboratory (FSL), of CBI, CGO Complex, New Delhi shared his professional contribution in crime investigation, particularly skull bone, long bone identification of human remains etc. Dr. Gupta also shared a case, Tandoor Kaand or Naina Sahani murder case, where Dr. Nath, as leading Forensic Anthropologist, Central Forensic Science Laboratory of CBI, New Delhi sought his opinions on the partially burned Skull cap for aging and sexing of the victim. "CBI, New Delhi consulted Delhi University Professor" was the news title in National leading daily in Delhi during mid 1995 then I was writing thesis. Tandoor Kaand was national limelight news where burned Skull cap of victim was under question. Dr. Gupta added his Superimposition Technique and its history of proceeding in investigations in this murder. Further he briefed some more cases where Dr. Nath was asked to share his opinion in identifying the human long bone or skull bone.

Professor Nath initiated short term courses—Finger printing, Forensic sciences, research methodology, psychotherapy and counselling, etc. in collaboration with Dr. N.K. Chaddha, Professor of Psychology and Former Head, Department of Adult Education, University of Delhi. These courses were very popular among the students and the classes of these courses used to be held in different colleges—Deen Dayal Upadhaya, Ramjas and Rajdhani Colleges. He also developed a novel method of Finger Printing with Prof. S.S. Sodhi of Department of Chemistry, G.T.B. Khalsa College.

After retirement, Professor Nath had been very busy in giving guest lecturers in the institution as mentioned earlier. He often used to visit to lecture in Academic Staff College of various Universities in Delhi, Gorakhpur, Chandigarh, Amristar, Jodhpur, Patiala, and Manipur. Further he had been faculty of Life Sciences and Forensic Sciences, Panjab University, Patiala. He was also faculty in LNJN National Institute of Forensic Sciences and Criminology, New Delhi. Besides he had been Member of various committees such as Departmental Research Committee, Institute of Forensic Science, BU, Jhansi and Members of Board of Studies, Amity Institute of Biotechnology (AUUP). He had been enjoying life with family and extended family members. He also used to travel, often with family members to other places as experts member of the committee. I used to go with him too, to attend seminar in different places like Chandigarh and Patiala.

Some of his notable students are Prabha Badkur (1985) Scientist in Bhopal, M.P.; Reita Jain (1989) Senior Associate Professor in Indira Gandhi Institute of Physical Education and Sports Sciences, Vikaspuri, Delhi. Late N. Satish Chandra (1989) used to work independently and was running a voluntary organization working for health and development. He died in outside India while working for an international project. Swetansu Shekhar Rath (1994) is senior Associate Professor of Anthropology in Government College, Pulbhani, Orissa; Sumider Kaur (1998) is working as Assistant Director in Forensic Science Laboratory, Government of Delhi. Piyusha Majumdar (2007) is Assistant Professor in IIMHR, Jaipur. She expressed about Professor Nath, as her mentor:

> We all need a little inspiration every now and then. One such person with whom I got the inspiration was Dr. Surinder Nath. He was my mentor, Ph.D. guide when I was doing my higher studies in Anthropology way back in the year 2004. His extraordinary ability to explain generated our interest in complex subjects like osteology, osteometry and finger printing. He was incredibly open minded and sensitive to students who came from different backgrounds. The best quality is his guardianship for his students. He revealed to me my real potential and helped me realize that I can excel in research. In fact, he only facilitated in getting my first assignment with ICMR's task force project. What made him a great professor was his dedication to educating in the subject matter, helping students and encouraging persistence towards student's learning.

He suffered of stroke in late 2012. He was admitted to Sunder Lal Jain Hospital, Ashok Vihar, Delhi. I was out of Delhi, as usual on the weekend, when it happened. Next morning I rushed to Delhi and by noon I was in the Hospital. He was in ICU being treated for the Stroke, right side full arm and leg paralyzed, slurring in speech, writing skills and memories affected drastically. I also took independently opinion from Dr. V.K.S. Gautam, Neurosurgeon, my colleague in IHBAS Hospital also came to visit him in ICU and also discussed concerning issues about post stroke life. It was a hard time for him as well as to his family. While consoling, I briefed Mrs. Nath about its time in recovery, post stroke life and skills. He came home and remained on physiotherapy of right hand and foot, both were affected mainly. His speech came back but writing and reading skills could not, a permanent neurological deficit and irreparable loss.

Further his walking also took more than six months for being visibly normal. As I observed him, he was living with neurological deficit, as his writing and reading skills were difficult to acquire back normal. He became dependent upon the family for outdoor activities as well as fine indoor activities- eating, bathing, etc., dexterity of his right hand was still poor. Then often I, while returning home from office, used to spend evening with him in family and used to discuss his feeling about his sufferings and other intra-family members dynamics which has also affected him more. I, being in neuropsychiatric clinical setting, could better understand him about the under-expressed or unexpressed feelings. Then I often made suggestions to family members to address his needs or minimize his sufferings.

Last days, though I had been meeting him regularly till mid of 2015 as well as had telephonic conversation. But on 4th November, 2016, I received a call from his home I was told that he was admitted in the same hospital for his uncontrollable anxious behaviour. When I met him next day, 5th November, 2016, then he was in ICU in conscious state and there were no family members around. I saw in his eyes and touched his feet; he too recognized me and greeted me with his both folded hands…as if it is final goodbye! I sat near his feet on his bed and remained staring in his eyes. Meanwhile he was shifted to Neurosurgery ICU, Max Hospital Shalimar Bagh, Delhi and since then he never returned home after one month of technocratic and ventilator suffering in ICU he breathed last on 16th December, 2016.

38
Vinay Kumar Srivastava

R.P. Mitra

There are teachers who redefine their discipline through their teaching and research and give a new direction to it. Professor Vinay Kumar Srivastava is one such teacher who through his contributions influenced the teaching and learning of social anthropology in India. He is undoubtedly one of the best teachers of anthropology and spent more than forty years in the University of Delhi. His classes in the Department of Anthropology, University of Delhi, were often quite lengthy but mesmerizing and left students spell bound and in awe of him. It was often a common saying even among those students who disparaged social anthropology as a soft subject that it appears meaningful only in his classes. Such was his appeal as a teacher and a researcher in anthropology.

Anthropology is not a very popular subject in University of Delhi, and not the first choice for those who opt for it. Students take up anthropology often for non-academic reasons, like admissions being over in other courses, or they are cases of gap year or they just want to study in a campus college, but do not have the requisite marks. Many enroll just to prepare for medical entrance examinations or to appear in the civil services examination. But once they join the department and read the subject, they just get so hooked to it that they often go on to make a career in anthropology. Vinay Srivastava also had a similar beginning to his anthropological journey in 1969, when he joined as a bachelor's student. Things were quite challenging in the beginning, as he came from one of those English-medium schools of Delhi where Hindi was the medium of teaching. Even the prescribed books and compositions in the paper on English were taught through Hindi medium.

Initially he was not at ease with the department's culture but by the end of first year, he had settled down and had stated enjoying anthropology. He was outstanding as a student and topped his class and decided to pursue further studies in the department itself. He completed his master's in 1974, again getting a first division and topping his class. In Anthropology Department of Delhi University, a student had to opt for a specialization in the final year of their master's degree. Surprisingly Vinay Srivastava decided to opt for physical anthropology, which was quite at odd to his later career interest. Perhaps he was influenced by the fact that the department being in the science faculty was well known for physical anthropology and also students in physical anthropology often outscored their social anthropology counterparts. Both during his graduation and post-graduation he was the recipient of the Delhi University medal for academic achievements.

Although it is difficult to get a Ph.D. seat in the department, but Vinay Srivastava was offered seats by the then three senior faculty members to take up doctoral research. One of them wanted him to work on sex chromatin bodies, and another advised him to work on human dentition. He was quite influenced by Dr. Abhimanyu Sharma, who asked him to do his research on the growth of human pelvis using radiological methods. But at that point of time, Professor Srivastava was interested in joining civil services rather than taking up academics. In order to further this goal he decided to pursue an M.A. in Sociology from the Delhi School of Economics, University of Delhi. Going for a second master's was not an easy choice considering the fact that he came from a middle-class and a large family. His father was in a government job and there were his three younger siblings who were all studying. In the entrance test for admission to master's in sociology, he wrote an essay on 'Unity in Diversity', which was well-liked by his examiners, and he easily cleared the written examination. Before appearing for an interview test before admission to sociology, he met Professor André Béteille, who advised him to continue his research interest in Anthropology, rather than joining sociology, because this would be spending another two years as a master's student, with admission to the doctorate programme being delayed. He explained to Srivastava the value of time, but Professor Srivastava, instead of telling him his true motive of joining sociology, tried to convince him that since he was greatly interested in sociology, and was keen on joining the Delhi School of Economics.

After joining sociology department in 1974, he was awarded a university scholarship of rupees one hundred and fifty per month, for his academic excellence and that provided him with some monetary relief, which took care of his immediate expenses and he did not have to ask money from father. The master's programme in sociology was quite rigorous and it was period of real hardwork for him. Not only was he reading for his master's, but he was also preparing for the civil services examination. He did very well in sociology and was awarded the Kunda Datar Gold Medal and Dr. R.D. Sanwal Memorial Prize in recognition of his academic brilliance and getting a first class first in the M.A. Programme.

Four months after the declaration of his master's result, in September 1976, he got a job offer and joined as a lecturer in Sociology in the prestigious Hindu College of University of Delhi. He was in his early twenties and the first year of teaching was very challenging. Along with teaching in the college, he was also extending academic help to Professor M.S.A. Rao in conducting a course on urban sociology in the university department. The first year of teaching proved to be a turning point of his life. It was a job which helped him, as he puts it, to discover himself and realize where his true calling lay. He proved to be a very popular teacher and in his fascination for teaching, he gave up his earlier yearning for civil services and he was now fully devoted to academics with teaching, writing and research as his only priorities. He was greatly influenced by Professor André Béteille and initially wanted to join him for a Ph.D. student to study social change among the Oraon.

However, a UGC rule that year made M.Phil. compulsory before admission to Ph.D. The then head of the Department of Sociology did not allow him to enroll as an M.Phil. student because he was employed in Hindu College as a lecturer; and there was no provision of being a part-time student. He had no option but to join an M.Phil.at the Department of Chinese and Japanese Studies, where under the able supervision of Prof. Krishna Prakash Gupta, in 1983, he completed his M.Phil. securing an O-grade (the highest grade). His dissertation on the process of charisma-building that took place in China after the death of Chairman Mao Zedong in September 1976 was an important contribution to the political sociology of post-Mao China. It was a critical appraisal of Max Weber's understanding of power, authority, and imperative control. This research work yielded several articles that were published in reputed journals. The examiner liked the thesis so much that he commented that it was worthy of a Ph.D. degree. In 1987, he was awarded the prestigious Commonwealth Fellowship to pursue a Ph.D. in Social Anthropology from the Cambridge University. By that time he had joined the Department of

Anthropology as a lecturer in social anthropology. The movement from sociology to anthropology was home coming for Vinay Srivastava. He had left the department as a budding physical anthropologist in 1974, but after eleven years, he returned as a master social anthropologist. His long association with sociology greatly influenced how he approached social anthropology. In 1988, he went to King's College, Cambridge University, for a Ph. D. in social anthropology under the supervision of the Professor Caroline Humphrey, on religion among the community of Raika/Rabari, a pastoral, camel herdering people of Rajasthan. Family commitment and his nationalist leaning and his association with anthropology department brought him back to University of Delhi in 1993. He often says that whenever he left the department or had plans to leave the department, the department brought him back.

Professor Srivastava has been a very prolific contributor with more than twenty books authored or edited by him along with hundreds of articles in both national and international journals. His writing has touched upon social anthropology of religion, development, ecology, health, caste and tribe systems, anthropological theory and methods. His contributions have been in topics ranging from museum, death, mental health, sanitation, family dynamics, old age and ageism, pastoralism, tribal situation, social tension, methodological issues, national integration, Nehru and tribal anthropology, women-headed households, urbanization, teaching of anthropology, tribes in cities, children as individuals, writing up qualitative research, future of anthropology etc. The list is endless and one is left agape with the span and range of issues Professor Srivastava has contributed to. His first book, *Essays in Social Anthropology*, was compilation of four articles dealing with past and present of social anthropology, a review of Malinowski's work on civilization and freedom, anthropology of development and issues of national integration. His approach to social anthropology is best represented in his three works, viz. *Religious Renunciation of a Pastoral People* (1997, Oxford University Press), *Methodology and Fieldwork* (Oxford University Press, 2004) and *Contribution to Sociological Theory* (Sage, 2014). The trilogy brings together important issues of theory, method of fieldwork and how it all can be combined together in an ethnographical study of a community. To start with the third book, which is part of the series, *Readings in Indian Sociology*, is an edited work by Professor Srivastava which looks at the contributions in the journal titled *Sociological Bulletin* by Indian authors on *Western Social Thoughts*.The introduction written by Vinay Srivastava itself runs into fifty-four pages. It is a comprehensive overview of the emergence and development of sociological theories. Beginning with August Comte, it gives an outline of work of all major sociologists and anthropologists including Max Weber, Émile Durkheim, Karl Marx, Talcott Parsons, Claude Lévi-Strauss, Bronislaw Malinowski, A.R. Radcliffe-Brown and the other post-modernist and structuralist thinkers. If this work was more inclined towards sociology, his second book was purely social anthropological, dealing with qualitative research method with special reference to fieldwork and ethnography. In this edited book, he examines the theory and practice of fieldwork and how they come together to produce ethnography. The book brings together the best of articles on ontology and epistemology of social research and the introduction of the book, which runs into fifty-six pages, authored by him, is an excellent account of how researches are to be carried out in the fieldwork tradition. It deals with elementary but significant problems not addressed in other texts, like how to select a research problem, the suitable methods to collect data, the actual act of doing fieldwork, using observation and interviews and how to take notes in the field. It is a must reading for all those who are interested in undertaking fieldwork based researches. The third work in the trilogy which was in fact the earliest was on the anthropology of religion. The work is an exemplification of how sociological and social anthropological theories are to be combined and weaved into an empirical study. The work examines the religious practices and ascetic ideology of pastoral Raikas of Rajasthan. It was significant as it highlights a non-Jain/Brahmanical perspective on renunciation. It shows how empirical facts are to be linked with theory and methodology. In the other articles authored by him, like the ethnography of Baigas, a central Indian tribal community, published in the *Economic and Political Weekly*, he tried to demystify how fieldwork is done by anthropologists using his own example how he carried out his fieldwork.

Professor Srivastava brought a new approach to the practice of social anthropology in India. Anthropology in India in many important centres like Delhi, Calcutta and Punjab is part of the Faculty of Science and a student is awarded a degree of master's in science. Apart from learning social anthropology, the students have to study physical and archaeological anthropology also. As a result in most departments theoretical social anthropology does not get the kind of attention it deserves. They have an empirical orientation where collection of facts and their description takes primacy over theorization. Professor Srivastava through his teachings and writings tried to redress this imbalance by emphasizing theory and methodology in social anthropology. With reference to topics there are often many commonalities between allied subjects like social work, sociology, education or cultural studies. But what makes a work anthropological according to Vinay Srivastava 'lies in the domain of anthropological theory'. There are two other recurring domains one finds in Srivastava's writings. One relate to tribes, its conceptualization and its many characteristics. His many important articles in reputed national and international journals like *Economic and Political Weekly*, Seminar, and Anthropos examine this in detail. One oft-quoted article by Vinay Srivastava is on the concept on tribe in the Draft National Tribal Policy, 2006. The second topic which has been explored extensively in his writings is the discipline of anthropology itself, its present status, its teachings and research being done in the discipline and the future of anthropology in India. Other than writings he is the Chief Editor of Journal of the Anthropological Survey of India, a Sage Publication; and one of the two Editors of Social Change, a journal of Council of Social Development, published by Sage. For fifteen years (from 2001 to 2016), he was one of the three Editors of *The Eastern Anthropologist*, a Journal published by the Ethnographic and Folk-Culture Society.

Of all his academic achievements what Professor Srivastava is known above all is as a great teacher. Students just love his classes. He transformed the learning of anthropology through his inspiring class room lectures. As a teacher he was like a Piped Piper, students would like to write down each word he spoke in the class. Even those who had no interest in the discipline would flock to his classes and listen to him in rapt attention for hours. He motivated many students, including me to take up a career in academics. He has guided twenty-four doctoral theses and twenty-nine M.Phil. dissertations. One unique distinction of Vinay Srivastava has been that he has written most number of obituaries of his teachers and 'peers who are no more'.

Administrative and Institutional Building

All through his career in teaching, Professor Srivastava has held many distinguished administrative positions. He was the Principal of Hindu College for two years, from 10 March, 2010 to 7 March, 2012. Hindu College is one of the most renowned and important undergraduate colleges of Delhi University to many renowned alumni who are occupying important position in all fields of life. As a principal of this prestigious College he brought a new energy to the institution by filling up the vacant positions and streamlining its activities. He ensured that all functionaries should perform their assigned duty.Under his leadership the College once again became a lively and dynamic place. In the process it unruffled many people with vested interest but he managed them very well using his charm and being firm and stern when required to be. He brought the same vigour to the Department of Anthropology when he took over as its head on 9 January, 2014. During his three years tenure he made the department a very vibrant place brimming with regular lectures, seminars and other academic activities. He ensured that classes happened on regular basis and no teacher was missing. It was during his tenure, the department introduced a new postgraduate programme in Forensic Science.

The most important feature of his administration was participatory and democratic functioning. All decisions were taken in consultation with colleagues and once he delegated a responsibility he would not interfere with it. His model of administration and bureaucracy was anti-Weberian in the sense that hierarchy, authority, control of information and power was replaced by access, collapsing of rigid hierarchy and decentralization as his operating style. He brought in the same philosophy when he took over as the Director of the Anthropological Survey of India on 1 August, 2017, just five months prior to his superannuation from the Department of Anthropology, University of Delhi. He brought in the same enthusiasm, vigour and dynamism to his new positions. In all these positions he has served his approach has been not to go in for an overhaul but rather gradually building up by consolidating what has already been achieved. As the Director of the Anthropological Survey, his first priority was to complete the ongoing projects and fill up the existing vacancies and reshuffle and deploy the existing human resources in the best possible way. He gave a new life to the prestigious official journal of the Anthropological Survey by getting the Sage India on board to publish and distribute the journal and taking over the overall management of the journal himself. He was the Director-in-Charge of the Maulana Abul Kalam Azad Institute of Asian Studies and is currently the holding charge of the Raja Rammohun Roy Library Foundation, Kolkata, both very prestigious institutes under the Ministry of Culture, Government of India.

Professor Srivastava is the brand ambassador of anthropology for the outsiders. He in one of the most well-known anthropologists outside the discipline of anthropology and he is the most sought after speaker by other departments. He has made anthropology popular to the outside world, thereby bringing great admiration and respect for the discipline. He has also contributed to the formulation of many policies, For example he was member for the formulation of the Mining Policy for the Government of India. Presently, he is a member of National Commission that Ministry of Social Justice and Empowerment, Government of India, has set up for the Sub-categorization of the Other Backward Classes. He was also a member of the Second Commission that Government of India set up for De-notified, Nomadic, and Semi-nomadic Communities (2015-2018). Recently, he has been made a member of the Committee that Government of India has set up for the inclusion of some more communities in the list of De-notified, Nomadic and Semi-nomadic Communities. In all these high level committees, he has changed the prevailing stereotype of anthropologists as past-oriented and no changers to a specialist who can propose change with minimum of disruption to vulnerable communities. He has also been associated with doctors especially those working on mental health issues and has published articles in the prestigious medical journals, like the *International Psychiatric Review*. He has contributed to the popularity of anthropology by contributing many articles to the well known national newspapers, like *The Times of India*, *The Hindustan Times, The Statesman* etc. In a nutshell he has proved to outside world why anthropology matters (which in fact is title of one of his articles).

He has also been involved with many international contributors in their writing and other projects. In 1993 he contributed to the text of L'Inde des Tribus Oubliees (1993), a French work, which was later published under the title *Tribes of India* by Bookwise (India) Pvt. Ltd. In 2008 he collaborated with Professor Umberto Mondini, a well-known Italian anthropologist, on his project on Raika, Allevatori di Cammelli del Rajasthan ('The Raika, the Camel-breeders of Rajasthan'), which was published later on by the Roma: Edizioni Progetto Cultura. Again 2005, he was part of an international authors group who looked at the concept of nature in different national traditions and cultural contexts. The work was edited by the famous philosopher Nadia Tazi and published under the title *Keynotes: Nature* by Sage Publications, New York.

It is quite natural that such a distinguished anthropologist would leave his imprints on his students. It was said about Professor Srivastava that he had the largest number of students who are posted as District Collectors and District Police chiefs. His students are occupying important administrative and academic positions. Some are of the rank of Secretary and Joint Secretaries to Government of India. Many of them are professors and mid-level academicians in many renowned universities and colleges in anthropology, public policy and sociology. All those whom he taught he touched them personally by changing their perspectives of the world and by broadening their outlooks. His humility, his non-assuming nature, his strength of conviction, his infectious positivity and above all his humanness has some form or the other has shaped the outlook of all his students. They have carried his teachings forward and are trying to make a better world wherever they are placed.

39

Nadeem Hasnain[*]

Virendra Pratap Yadav

Nadeem Hasnain may be counted among only a few anthropologists who popularized anthropology among the administrators and civil servants besides introducing it, through popular lecturers, to the lay educated persons and masses. Through this endeavour he contributed meaningfully to raise the awareness level of people about the discipline of anthropology.

Born on 20 March, 1952 in Ghazipur located in Eastern Uttar Pradesh, he is the youngest among his brothers and sisters, being older only to a younger sister living in USA. Thus, as per order of the day, it was a big family. Prof. Nadeem Hasnain's father was a police officer who spent most part of his career under British rule. When he retired, he had to choose between Lucknow and Allahabad, the two best centres of education in Uttar Pradesh during those times. He found close proximity to Lucknow because of its culture. That is how Nadeem Hasnain's life journey began in Lucknow. Hasnain had his earliest schooling in a Christian missionary school and then moved to the Government Husainabad Inter College and finally had his undergraduate and post-graduate education from University of Lucknow. He obtained his Ph.D. degree from the same university under the supervision of the internationally renowned anthropologist K S Mathur. He admits that Lucknow played the most important role in the formation of his personality. He always says that if he is uncompromisingly secular and tolerant, it is because of Lucknow's composite culture popularly known as Ganga-Jamuni Tehzeeb. This love for Lucknow may be seen in his much acclaimed book. *The other Lucknow: An Ethnographic Portrait of a City of Undying Memories and Nostalgia* published in 2016.

Hasnain's coming to anthropology is an interesting story. Like many parents of those times his parents too wanted him to become an engineer or doctor but his heart wanted something else. He dropped out from B.Sc. first year and decided to move to humanities and social sciences. When he was filling up the admission form his immediate neighbour, a professor of economics, happened to visit his house to see his elder brother. Seeing him filling up the form he suggested anthropology as one of the three subjects to be chosen. Till that point of time he never heard of anthropology yet he opted for it under the advice of this gentleman. Thus, it was by sheer accident that he entered into anthropology. He says that he would always be indebted to the professor (who is no more in this world) for dropping in at that moment and suggesting to take anthropology.

Besides academics, he is fascinated by literature especially Urdu and Hindi poetry. In the world literature, Russian and French fiction and among the Indian languages besides Urdu and Hindi he is most interested in Bengali and Marathi literature. He has a rich collection of books one-fourth of which consisted of literature. The legendry Urdu-Hindi writer and poet Rahi Masoom Raza was his maternal uncle whose influence in his interests is obvious. Besides literature he maintains a deep interest in sports and games especially cricket. He has strong social concerns because of which he is also a social activist.

Dr. K.S. Mathur was his teacher and mentor and he regrets that he left the world suddenly before he was awarded Ph.D. He obtained his doctorate in 1978 and his dissertation was examined by Scarlet Epstein of London University and L.P. Vidyarthi from Ranchi. Immediately after getting his masters degree he got appointment as a lecturer in the local Shia Degree College, an associate college of Lucknow University, before being appointed as a full professor in Lucknow University. While teaching at the college he continued his Ph.D. research. Initially he wanted to work on the socio-economic status of North Indian Muslims after the partition of the country and Dr. Mathur agreed with this topic. Like his coming into anthropology, finalization of his topic of Ph.D. dissertation was also a sheer accident. While Hasnain was preparing synopsis, one of the two American anthropologists doing their field work in Lucknow for their Ph.D. work suggested to him to work on 'Culture of Poverty', propounded by Oscar Lewis, in a rural-tribal setting. This was the time when there was no access to internet to consult the relevant literature and the university's library did not offer anything on this topic. Steve Gariguess, one of the two American scholars, arranged the xerox of the special number of

Current Anthropology devoted to 'culture of Poverty' and the second Keith Hjorshoj, now at Cornell, arranged two books from US which gave him substantive ideas to formulate his synopsis.

Just after completing his Masters Hasnain got an opportunity to work as research assistant for three months in a research project investigating the socio-economic condition of Koltas and other Scheduled Castes of Jaunsar bawar (Dehradun), Jounpur (Tehri Garhwal) and Rawain (Uttar Kashi), the three contagious areas in the Himalyan region (now in Uttarakhand). The plight of the Koltas, an untouchable caste living as bonded labour, moved him immensely and he decided to change his topic. His supervisor Dr. Mathur was a bit reluctant as it was not his area of interest and specialization but sensing his students' devotion and commitment, was kind enough to accept this change. Thus the topic now decided was "Socio-Cultural Factors in the Meaning of Poverty among the Koltas." Hasnain still fondly remembers the two American anthropologists who played an important role for him adopting a field which is now his lifelong interest.

Bonded for ever, based on his Ph.D. thesis was published in 1982 and was well received by the reviewers but the publication could not receive the attention it deserved till Mahasheweta Devi, the legendary Bangla writer, wrote a note in a newspaper. When Hasnain was serving as Pro-Vice Chancellor of Mahatma Gandhi International Hindi University, she visited the University to be the chief guest for the Foundation Day of the University, invited him to the guesthouse and talked about at length about the problem Hasnain probed. She asked him to visit the field again, see the changes and publish the revised edition with a new introduction. Hasnain immediately agreed extracting promise from her that she would be writing preface of the book. To the pleasant surprise of Hasnain she not only agreed but offered to help him publish its Hindi translation for a wider readership. The revised edition with its Hindi translation both were published in 2012 by Prakashan Sansthan, Delhi a reputed publisher of Hindi books. The title of the Hindi translation is 'Bandhua Jeewan Hamara.'

The fieldwork for his Ph.D. thesis was eventful. During the first phase of fieldwork his key informant, Sri Ratan Singh Chauhan, asked him to change his Muslim sounding name for smooth data collection. A new similar sounding name 'Naveen Hansnayan' was decided and the entire fieldwork was conducted with this new name. Once, when Hasnain returned after four days to the road side shop to collect some items brought from Dehradun, the shop owner enquired about his absence for those days and when Hasnain told him that he stayed in a nearby Kolta village for data collection, the second question was fired about the source food. He was shocked to know that Hasnain had food in a Kolta household and tersely commented that if he could eat from a Kolta's kitchen then he could also eat in a Muslims home. A number of such anecdotes may be narrated by him. A close relationship with Ratan Singh Chauhan continued till his death and now the relationship continues with his family.

Hasnain regards K.S. Mathur as his mentor. Besides him B.R.K Shukla and U.S. Misra had also influenced him. Misra was also his close associate and co-author of a book. He imbibed a number of academic traits from Verier Elwin and is highly impressed by his lofty humanism and his approach to anthropology which reflects in one of his quotes – "The essence and art of anthropology is love without which nothing is fertile and nothing is true." Some other Indian anthropologists admired by him are M.N. Srinivas, S.C. Dube, T.N. Madan and D.K. Bhattacharya while from outside India Margaret Mead and Oscar Lewis are his favourites. B.D. Sharma occupies a special place in the academic pursuits of Hasnain because of his great concern and commitment for our Adivasi citizens.

Three of Hasnain's works may be counted as pioneering in respective fields. His book *Shias and Shia Islam in India: A Study in Society and Culture* (1988), *Bonded For Ever* (1982) and *The Other Lucknow: An Ethnographic Portrait of a City of Nostalgia and Undying Memories* (2016) are considered as first works in their respective fields. While the book on Indian Shias and on Lucknow are the first ethnographic studies in these fields, the concept of 'culture of poverty' was applied for the first time in a rural/tribal setting in India.

Hasnain's areas of interest and specialization are largely focused on marginalised and deprived sections of Indian society. His book Tribal India, first published in 1986, continues to be the most popular and largest selling book on Indians tribal citizens. Now available in Hindi and Telugu, it is very popular among the university students as well as those appearing for civil services examination. Along with Indian Anthropology it makes a twin set of most widely read books of anthropology in India. He has also co-edited with H.S. Verma, a pionering work on OBCs with the title 'OBCs' in the Process of *Change in India* (2005). He has also co-edited with H.S. Verma and R.B.S. Verma a set of 3 volumes on the *status of Indian Women – The Indian State and Women's Problematics* (2007), *Towards Empowering Indian Women* (2007) and *Study of Women's Problematic* (2009). He has edited four books on *South Asian Islam and*

Indian Muslims. His latest book *Muslims on Crossroads: Changing Face of 'Lived Islam' in India* (2018) is considered as the first ethnographic study of the growing trend of orthodoxy and radicalization of Indian Muslims and how the 'moderate' Muslims are resisting this trend.

Besides promoting anthropology in the academic circles he has facilitated the entry of hundreds of persons into civil services and state's services by writing relevant books for the aspirants as well as taking classes for them in Delhi, Patna, Hyderabad, Lucknow and Bangalore.

Prof. Hasanain was selected as Fulbright 'Scholar in Residence' and he spent 2006-07 at St. Lawrence University, New York State. Later he was again invited to serve as visiting professor in the same university for 2007-08. During this period he delivered lectures in the department of global studies, department of anthropology and department of religious studies where he was extremely popular among the students and faculty. After returning from United States he was invited to serve as Pro Vice-Chancellor of Mahatma Gandhi International Hindi University (a Central University). He did not complete his 5-year tenure and stayed there for only two years yet during this brief period, he established an independent department of anthropology, the second in western India. This department is now making rapid progress and emerging as one of the most vibrant departments of anthropology in the country.

Hasnain strongly believes that one must have at least some interest in literature to be a good and sensitive anthropologist. In fact he looks at the literature from the lens of ethnography. He exhorts his students to read Mahashweta Devi's novels to understand tribal society, its problems and culture and for understanding caste system one must read such Hindi novels as *Nacheo Bahul Gopal* by Amrit Lal Nagar, *Tamas* by Bhisham Sahni and *Aadha Gaon* by Rahi Masoom Raza. He has been keenly interested in promoting anthropology through Hindi medium and hence he has been insisting to his publishers also to publish the Hindi translations of his books and hence most of his books are also available in Hindi.

After he retired from Lucknow University in 2014, he became more productive and academically active. After his retirement he was awarded senior fellowship by ICSSR and he wrote the path breaking book on Indian Muslims based on this research project. Almost simultaneously he wrote another path breaking book on Lucknow sponsored and founded by Ayodhya Research Centre. Presently, he is editing two research journals – *Manav* (the only research journal of anthropology in Hindi and *Islam and Muslim Societies: A Social Science Journal* (www.muslim societies.org) now being published online and one of the few journals on

Islam and Muslims providing forum for all the scholars of social sciences working in this field. Besides these activities, he is guiding hundreds of civil services aspirants in Hyderabad and Bangalore.

Among those obtaining Ph.D. degree under his guidance, Virendra Pratap Yadav, Munna Lal Gupta, Shailendra Kumar Verma, Maushri Shukla and some others are occupying positions in academic institutions. The respect Prof. Hasnain commands among his students working in different spheres may be the envy of many.

40
Charting an Anthropological Montage
Pooran Chand Joshi and His Works

Prashant Khattri

Biographical sketch of an academician may take at least two forms. First, it can be written in the form of an academic CV, which is usually done, that includes mostly his academic and administrative achievements and the second is a more embedded understanding of a person, both as an academician and as a personality sharing academic and personal relations with his colleagues, students and the discipline. This biographical article is more of the second type. Ontologically speaking, relationality and interactionism are at the core of understanding the persona. Although it is quite difficult and nearly impossible to create a complete picture, but still an attempt is made at understanding multiple facets of Professor Pooran Chand Joshi's (hereafter PCJ) life and works. My positionality as his research student has a profound influence on what follows hereafter. At one level it gives me immense pleasure and a sense of honour and belongingness in writing about my mentor and at another level an extreme sense of responsibility. This entails a kind of uncomfortable role reversal wherein a mentor and a teacher par excellence will be in a sense 'limited' by whatever is written about him by his student. Therefore, at the outset I must admit that my understanding of the subject and social relationships at this time might not be able to fathom the depth of the achievements made by PCJ. But still it gives me immense satisfaction and joy in writing and knowing about anthropology through the biographical route.

Biographies are one of the most challenging forms of writings. This challenge comes from at least two sources, viz. locating biography within the disciplinary methodology and practice and personal influence on the selection of material and coterie of ideas that shape the practice of writing itself. Biography as a legitimate anthropological method gained prominence when the anthropological focus shifted from 'gaze' to 'voices'. Anthropologists influenced by the positivist epistemology and law generating agenda were antithetical to the biographical method. However, the larger anthropological agenda always envisaged a dichotomy of the local and the global or of the general and the specific. The aim to study the specific is to illuminate the general understanding about society and culture or any phenomenon under study. Biographical studies fit into this agenda. It is for this reason that while writing a biographic article it is taken into consideration that how the 'general' is reflected in the 'specific' and also on the contrary, how the 'specific' has influenced the 'general'. This biographic sketch is no exception to this spontaneous and continuous shift between the general and the specific. In a more concrete sense it can be understood as both life and works of PCJ that are shaped by the larger context of society, profession and institutions and in turn shapes and builds institutions, professions and society at large.

The resources or the data that is used to pen-down this biographical sketch can be categorized into three types— (a) academic writings in the form of books, research articles, popular articles in press, national and international project reports, reports submitted to the Government of India, sections and chapters in books and national and international conference proceedings, (b) personal communication with PCJ, and (c) lived experiences as a master's student and research scholar. The methodology followed for this sketch subscribes to 'primary characterization'. A more detailed and complete biography could have emerged through the portrayal of secondary characterization that means illuminating the life of PCJ through his friends, family, and professional companions.

For students in the Department of Anthropology, University of Delhi (DU), PCJ as a teacher is known for his punctuality and regularity in taking classes. When I was a master's student in the department (2004-05), the general perception about PCJ among the students was that he is a kind of professional who is always completely engrossed in his work, a no non-sense guy who is kind at heart and always ready to help students. Beyond this, his contribution to the field of anthropological knowledge lies not only in explaining and making students understand what anthropology is but it lies in making students understand that how it is done? He was in-charge of the social anthropology practical that required students to go out in the field and collect first-hand data. I still remember taking lots of interviews in the campus, collecting life histories of local vendors outside the university campus, doing an un-structured observation of a shoe shop at Kamla Nagar market, and filling a structured observational schedule of traffic rules violation at the Law Campus crossing. Every year PCJ engaged his master's students in a compulsory project titled 'Human Behaviour in Public Places' that students undertake normally in their Dushera breaks. This project required students to make observations under the headings like littering behaviour, spitting behaviour etc. It also included photographic, tabular, ethnographic and narrative documentation of events. Students normally used to do this project in their respective hometowns so by the end of the project we had human behaviours on diverse dimensions from different parts of the country. I also remember doing a project on representation of violence in Hollywood and Bollywood movies as a part of a special paper on Communication Anthropology that was co-ordinated by PCJ.

Such diverse ways and locations of doing anthropology helped in putting across a very powerful message – that anthropology is not limited to the 'tribal lands' or the so-called 'other.' To a great extent it helped in bridging the gap between the self and other that was created by the colonial anthropology. Such projects under the supervision of PCJ prompted students to look at the 'self' as the 'other'. This led to the emergence of a critical thinking and questioning long-held and cherished ideas about the self and the practice of 'othering' those that were located far away from Delhi in the 'tribal' heartlands in India. This also helped in questioning the entire notion of civilization and 'civilized' ways of living. It is for this reason that when our batch went to the field in Jhabua district in Madhya Pradesh among the Bhils in 2005, the practical and 'local' anthropological training helped in seeing 'us' in 'them' and *vice-versa*.

At an elemental level, this can be explained as an idea of 'relational ontology' as opposed to an 'occupying ontology' that is based on demarcation and exclusion. The relational ontology is more inclusive and is marked with a sense of mixed-ness and syncretism. To me PCJ exemplifies the relational dimension in his ontological understanding of the anthropological data and universe. There is a dimension of empathic understanding in his way of doing anthropology. This can also be seen as an effort towards collective existentialism that supports and celebrates human cultural and biological diversities and capabilities. The construction of such an outlook cannot only be attributed to anthropological training but also to his immediate familial and personal environment that helped shaping his thoughts and practices.

Pooran Chand Joshi was born on June 1, 1956 in the Uttarakhand hills in a village called Kherakot. He spent his early childhood in the village. He was educated mostly in government schools and did his higher secondary from Gandhi Memorial Government Boys School, Delhi. His father Pandit Prem Ballabh Joshi worked with the electricity department and his mother Smt. Rewati Devi was a home maker. He is from a very humble economic background. His grandfather and generations above him were engaged in agriculture in Uttarakhand. His father's job in the electricity department located the family within the lower middle class economic bracket. He had, therefore, all the aspirations linked with the middle class Indian family in which education and gaining formal knowledge becomes an important tool that helps in social mobility. The imagination of the future in the post-independent India is intricately linked to the ideas of development, liberal, rational and scientific thinking and quality higher education. This larger futuristic imagination was complemented well within PCJ's family as his father and mother instilled in him the values of rationality, honesty and truthfulness. PCJ points to the fact that although he was born in a conservative hill Brahmin family but his parents were quite liberal in their thinking (personal communication).

The scientific and rational values in the family and the larger society directed towards development and rationality prompted PCJ to take-up Physics, Chemistry, Mathematics, English and Biology at the higher secondary level. He wanted to do graduation in medicine after this. In those days it was a trend that everyone taking biology was aspiring to go for medical and everyone taking mechanical drawing in higher secondary would go for engineering. However, due to his less percentage at the higher secondary PCJ could not enroll himself into an M.B.B.S. course and came to Delhi University (DU) to pursue a Bachelor of Science degree in 1972. He was not sure that what courses he will opt for in DU science faculty. He visited the science faculty office which was at that time located in a building where the present day three storied administrative building is constructed. He met a science faculty clerk outside the building and enquired about the courses that were available there. The clerk told him that he can opt for anthropology that he will easily get with the kind of percentage in Physics, Chemistry, Biology (PCB). PCJ asked the clerk about the prospects of anthropology in the job market to which he replied that although jobs are limited in anthropology but still one can manage in getting a job as the competition is also less as compared to other science subjects. He also told PCJ that he can visit the department that was located in the science faculty itself and inquire more about the prospects.

PCJ went to the department where he met Mr. Kamlesh Guha who was the museum curator of the department at that time and enquired about the subject and its prospects. Mr. Guha in his typical Bengali accented English, told him about the subject. He decided to take anthropology and got enrolled in Hans Raj College. PCJ did his B.Sc. honours course, M.Sc., M.Phil. and Ph.D. all from the DU Department of Anthropology. He specialized in the field of Medical Anthropology which to some extent I suppose emerged from his desire to join the field of medicine after his higher secondary.

His interest towards Medical Anthropology was also shaped by his teachers and mentors in the department. For the first time Prof. D.K. Bhattacharya (DKB) gave PCJ the idea to take-up a topic related to Medical Anthropology for his Master's fieldwork and dissertation. For his master's fieldwork he conducted a study of 'ethno-medicine' in the village Khanpora, located in the Badgam tehsil in Kashmir valley. He was fascinated by shamanism that he witnessed in Uttarakhand and therefore, became interested in knowing the 'local' ways of healing. It is worth mentioning that Medical Anthropology was not offered as a specialized paper in masters when PCJ was a student. It was only when the syllabus of anthropology was revised in the year 1984 that PCJ was asked by the then Head of the Department Prof. I.P. Singh to prepare a syllabus of Medical Anthropology that was supposed to be offered at the masters level. PCJ was a research scholar at this time. Although it was DKB who motivated PCJ to take-up Medical Anthropology topic but PCJ was supervised for his M.Sc., M.Phil. and Ph.D. by Prof. J.D. Mehra (JDM). The paper on Medical Anthropology was initially taught by JDM and he also guided Masters and M.Phil. students on topics like 'Disease and Cure', 'Ethno-medicine' etc.

Prof. Mehra had an interest in medical anthropology but he was particularly interested in the personalistic dimension of medical anthropology that includes topics like supernaturalism, mysticism, shamanism etc. Although Prof. Mehra had not done any work in the field of medical anthropology but according to PCJ he was a brilliant and original thinker, qualities that helped PCJ to move ahead in his doctoral journey. PCJ's Ph.D. thesis was titled "*Illness, Health and Culture: Dynamics of Therapy in a Central Himalayan Tribe*" and was based on one year fieldwork in a village Silgaon (pseudonym) of Jaunsar Bawar region of Uttarakhand. His M.Phil. thesis was titled "Ethnomedicine in

Jaunsar Bawar."As a researcher he also came in touch with leading medical anthropologists like Charles Leslie, Arthur Klienman, Ronald Frakenberg and George Foster. In fact according to him, when he seriously started doing medical anthropology, he wrote a letter to Charles Leslie and showed his interest in medical anthropology. Leslie wrote back and informed him about H.K. Bhatt and Rishikesh Maru as two Indian scholars working in the field of medical anthropology. PCJ considers himself to be quite lucky to have got in touch with great medical anthropologist who not only advised him on the subject but were quite liberal in sharing their research work and research papers with him.

As a research scholar PCJ was not only limited to his topic of research but as a young man was also influenced and affected by his immediate political environment. The 1984 anti-Sikh riots in Delhi is one such incident that is worth mentioning for revealing this dimension of his personality. After the riots, PCJ became actively involved in helping the victims. On October 31, 1984, Indira Gandhi was assassinated and shortly thereafter the riots began. PCJ became very disturbed by the killings and from 2nd November onwards he became a very active member of a DU research team. He visited a place called Nathupura in order to help the victims of the riots. Initially they worked as members of Mother Teresa's organization 'Sisters of Charity' and later as DU team.

After completing his Ph.D. from DU in 1985, he left Delhi as he was appointed as Lecturer in the Department of Anthropology, H.N.B. Garhwal University, Srinagar, Uttar Pradesh. He started his teaching career from Garhwal University as he joined the Department on May 5, 1985. At that time there were no students enrolled in the department of anthropology. He started as the only lecture in the department as there was no other teaching staff to support him. This also implied that he was the head of the department. In the first session beginning July, only two students got enrolled in the department, however, later on masters course and fieldwork was also started in the department. He had a multi-task staff to support him and after that he also hired a lab assistant who was a Ph.D. in anthropology. In the very first year of joining the department he organized the Ethnographic and Folk Culture Society's annual conference to make his presence felt among the anthropology community. It was quite a difficult task to mobilize resources and make arrangements for scholars as many people were coming from outside. However, with limited human and economic resources the conference was successfully organized.

A small museum was also established in the department for which he personally collected specimen from his visit to Shillong. He also requested his Ao Naga friend Mr. Apok Zamir, son of erstwhile Governer of Maharashtra and Odhisa, to gift him a Naga artifact and he provided him his family *dao* which became a prized possession of the department museum. Subsequently the department started progressing and during his tenure Prof. R.S. Negi, Dr. Har Bhajan Singh Chauhan, Dr. Vidya Singh Chauhan and Dr. Bina Saklani were appointed in the department as Professor, and Lecturers, respectively. Within four years and four months of his joining the department at Garhwal, he became a Reader.

Within the holistic frame of anthropology we can locate PCJ's contribution in the fields of social, biological and archaeological anthropology. Epistemologically his orientation is both positivistic and interpretive. He is an ardent believer in the method of triangulation in research. The concept of holism when applied to the methods of data collection, give us a battery of methods that try to investigate social phenomenon from every possible angle.

His academic writings include ten books, around ninety research articles, more than fifty chapters in edited books, around fourteen project reports and six reports submitted to the Government of India. Besides this he has also written newspaper articles and editorials. His writings can be categorized into four broad themes, viz. Health, Religion, Disasters and Environment. His writings also include reflexive accounts of the growth and status of the discipline of social anthropology in general and medical anthropology in particular.

His most important contribution is in the field of medical anthropology. Academic interests in other sub-fields of anthropology are an obvious extension of his dedication towards medical anthropology. He has extensively written and is still engaged in writing on the issues of tribal health and medicine, an area very close to and also very important for the realization of his academic, professional and personal self. His focus had been on the issues of health seeking behaviour, alternative and traditional forms of healing and their contemporary relevance and interaction with the state, democratic polities and global forces, etiologies of disease causation, epidemiology, drug use and mental health. Doing justice to the bio-social nature of medical anthropology, he has also extensively written on biological dimensions, indicators and factors that are influenced by and in turn influences the social realm of human existence. Such studies focused on, for example the assessment of cardiovascular risk factors among Sunni Muslims in Delhi, prescriber and dispenser's perception about antibiotic use in the case of childhood diarrhoea. Another contribution of his is in the form of relocating concepts, and disciplinary ideologies to inhabit new areas like inquiring the status of health in general and child health in particular in a disaster context. Such studies not only create new knowledge but also give new life to earlier concepts in disciplinary history.

If one wants to locate his works within a paradigmatic category then his works can be best described as subscribing to the 'cognitive justice' paradigm. Within this understanding, it is believed that the ideas of justice and equality will not be fully realized if we compartmentalize knowledge into 'scientific' and 'non-scientific' just for the sake of symbolism in order to promote a particular kind of knowledge at the expense of 'other', 'indigenous' categories of knowing and knowledge formations. Indigenous ways of knowing are equally experiential and empirical and should be given due recognition. However, within the dominant Western idea of knowledge formation, oriental ways of knowing and knowledge has always been looked down upon.

While writing on the issue of environmental sustainability and human-wild life conflict he argues that sustainability is seen as a technological and scientific intervention whose contours are drawn within the scientific knowledge and jargons. The local community is seen as more a barrier in the implementation of this scientific knowledge rather than a facilitator with indigenous knowledge. This amounts to completely overlooking the alternative discourses on sustainability and being guided by a singular hegemonic discourse. Such an assumption also undermines the agency of the people in being partners in sustainability intervention and is always seen as a unit that needs to be governed along with the environment. This argument is empirically supported by his ethnographic work in the Nanda Devi Biosphere Reserve (NDBR) in the Himalayas and the Human-Wild animal conflict in the Jaunsar Bawar region of Dehradun district inhabited by the Khos Scheduled Tribes (ST).

The paradigm of cognitive justice within the discourse on medical knowledge entails that due recognition needs to be given to the psycho-social dimensions of therapeutic value of the indigenous systems of medicine. This becomes more important in the light of new evidence that suggest the important role of faith and belief in healing. The social and cultural contours of the ethnomedicine make it more embedded and inclusive system than the hierarchized and hegemonized modern system of medicine.

The paradigms of justice and equality are closely linked and inform the issues of advocacy, public policy and human rights. A great deal of his writings subscribes to and is directed towards the advocacy for the rights and improvement in the overall condition and quality of life of the most marginalized sections of the society. His relational understanding of the reality is an offshoot of his anthropological training and worldview which is also reflected in his approach towards advocacy and public policy. He contends that in order to undertake advocacy efforts, an integrated and interdisciplinary approach is needed where anthropologists, biotechnologists, pharmacologists, social activists come together to uphold the intellectual property rights of the tribals on their indigenous knowledge. Within this paradigm of advocacy and within the larger anthropological discourse on post-colonial studies, PCJ strongly believes that agency of the 'tribes' is of utmost importance to realize such goals. In this entire process of claiming and re-claiming rights, tribes should be alert and aware. In this context he calls for a political consciousness among the tribes that should be the basic driver behind any such effort towards policy, advocacy or human rights. In a true anthropological sense, he calls for a change from within. This has important bearing on the relational dimension of the tribes with the state and other philanthropic agencies. According to PCJ the entire process of claiming rights and advocacy should not look like a give-and-take exercise where a hierarchy is set from the very beginning and the agencies responsible for the 'development' act as benevolent 'sahebs' and the tribals as illiterate and un-interested 'beneficiaries'. He calls for role reversals and de-centering of the entire processes linked to policy and advocacy.

The Oriental ways of knowing and knowledge formation were based on difference and hierarchy. In contrast to this, French Structuralism, Interactionism, Linguistics and studies on Human Communication in Anthropology has largely focused on the issues of commonness. This was largely responsible to bring about an 'empathic turn' in anthropology in which cultural sameness, existence as human beings, capacity of myth creation by Homo sapiens-whether it is shamanism or capitalism or socialism becomes central themes for explorations. Within this paradigm, knowledge systems of the world are seen not in terms of their superficial differences but in terms of their underlying similarities. It is the job of the anthropologists according to PCJ to bring this cultural 'essence' or '*taaseer*' to the forefront and show that belief systems are not anti-existential. PCJ writes: "Should we act as social reformers and teach them that their beliefs and practices are all hocus-pocus and they should stop believing in them...We will also have to know the clinical and social importance of the tribal magico-religious practices. The psychotherapeutic significance of magico-religious practices, that have been so much talked about needs to be contextualized...One of the great strength of tribal systems of medicine is the involvement of group in therapy."

In one of his path-breaking work on the issue of entitlement in the context of flood disasters that was done in collaboration with Supriya Akerkar and Maureen Fordham, it is argued that mere extension of the Amartya Sen's entitlement approach assuming that people and the government are bounded in a citizen-state dichotomous relation is actually at the cost of other non-formal, cultural and social ties that are informed by patron-client relationships. This study based on empirical research and findings challenges Sen's entitlement thesis. It calls for a critical evaluation of Sen's entitlement approach that overlooks the important dimension of 'culture of entitlements' that are embedded in the moral economies informed by structures of power, wealth and prestige that are grounded in more traditional ties rather than secular and modern notions of state-citizen relations.

Anthropology within the contemporary critical discourses on post-modernism, post-colonialism and feminism has undertaken an 'engaged turn.' This engagement is of the anthropologists with his discipline and the subject of study. Anthropology has come of age from a period where research topics, areas and people were chosen on the basis of their 'exotic value' to a phase where anthropological researches are grounded in global and local problems of the people concerned. The location and topics are such that they resonate with the immediate needs and understanding of the current socio-political and cultural issues. PCJ's attempt in doing anthropology can be located within this broad turn. The engagement of the anthropologist can be located at various levels. To begin with, the choice of doing research on one's area of interest is guided by one's experience of the 'everyday'. This choice is guided not by locating an event to start exploring but is more inclined towards exploring the non-event, mundane and the everyday as an important part of shared experiences. Within such locations anthropologist himself is a part of the field that he wishes to explore. In one such study PCJ tries to understand the "awareness of antibiotic resistance and antibiotic prescription for treatment of acute upper respiratory tract infection and marginal in children: a qualitative study among primary care doctors and community pharmacists in NCT, Delhi." In another study he explored the health, social and economic impacts of extreme weather events, especially floods in Eastern Uttar Pradesh. In yet another study he was engaged in understanding the social and cultural issues leading to affect, morbidity and mortality associated with the 2004 Indian Ocean Tsunami in

Nagapattinam district of Tamil Nadu.

At a more methodological level, the idea of engagement entails a non-hierarchical relation between the researcher and the researched. Within the objective and scientific paradigm, a researcher is supposed to be detached with the people on which research is conducted. This ontological understanding was considered important to generate objective data. However, within the interpretive paradigm, inter-subjectivity becomes the aim of the researcher. The role of the researcher and that of the researched within this paradigm gets transformed from mere collector and provider of the data respectively to a more active participation of both and engagement in collective knowledge generation. The researched remains not only the tool or the source of the research but also becomes a partner in knowledge creation. This entails certain rights of the researched. One of the rights is knowing the outcome of the research conducted in his/her area. I still remember working with PCJ on the MICRODIS project that was in collaboration with the European Union where one of the important task assigned to the fieldworkers was to go back to the community on which we conducted research and share the outcomes of the research. This was done through publishing booklets in vernacular containing bullet information and findings on the topic and discussing results with the people. PCJ himself was part of this activity.

At an organizational level, engagement means an interaction with different stake holders engaged with people directly or indirectly. This level of engagement is realized through collaborative research projects and partnerships. PCJ had been interacting with various government and non-government organizations to work on various issues of public importance. Various reports submitted to the Government of India and other international agencies is testimony to this dimension of his engagement. PCJ has collaborated with the European Union, SAARC Disaster Management Centre, New Delhi, Asian Disaster Reduction Centre, Kobe, Japan, World Health Organization, NGOs like the Global Forum for Disaster Reduction, Mumbai and Voluntary Health Association of India, New Delhi. One of the methodological outcomes of this kind of collaborative research for anthropology is the development and enhancement in doing team ethnographies that are informed by inter-disciplinary theories and methods. One of the advantages of this kind of ethnography is that in a relatively short period of time researchers are able to explore more areas of ethnographic universe. Team work also leads to debates and discussions that lead to a more nuanced understanding of the issue at hand.

At yet another level, engaged anthropology entails imparting anthropological knowledge with a sense of engagement and participation. At this level engagement means engaging with students in the class and outside during fieldworks. PCJ accomplishes this task through various micro-projects that he gives to his students that help them to understand the practical dimensions of doing anthropology. Right from the time of deciding on a topic to data gathering, interpreting and analysis, PCJ is engaged with his students on various topics during field expeditions. One may say that fieldwork is his passion and this becomes obvious with the kind of enthusiasm with which he approaches the field. This enthusiasm is actually infectious that instills a sense of active involvement among his students and key informants.

As an individual we are influenced by one or the other dimension of disciplinary practice. In this context PCJ seems to have been influenced by photographic and video graphic documentation of the field and in effect influenced the way in which anthropology is done in India. One of his original contributions to anthropology is in the form of documentary films that he makes during his fieldworks. Besides being a record and evidence of the events that took place in the field and a rich document capturing the unfolding of cultures, these video files are an important and effective source of imparting education to young anthropologists.

One of his first documentaries was on the mask dances of the inner Himalayas. He also submitted this documentary film to the Indira Gandhi National Centre for Arts (IGNCA), New Delhi. He has to his credit three documentary films, namely Inundated Lives, made on recurrent annual flooding in Bahraich district of Eastern Uttar Pradesh, Safe School, Safe Community, made for the MICRODIS project funded by the European Union and Cyclone Aila: The Cycle of Misery, made on the 2009 cyclone and captures death and destruction caused in the Sundarban Delta. These documentaries are made on the issue of disaster induced hardships among the people and the emerging state-citizen relationships. People's narratives about the disasters form the main focus the documentaries. The idea is to understand how people make sense of death and destruction caused by natural and human-made events and how public policy in this context facilitates or hinders people resilience and vulnerability reduction. Besides these he made seven more documentary films on disasters during the course of the MICRODIS project for which he was the Asia coordinator.

While on a field trip one can always find PCJ with his camera clicking photos of various events and frames. He has a great 'photographic sense' and will tell you in definite terms how to use the lens, from what distance to take the picture and which angle and brightness will be best suited to a particular situation. He is an ardent believer that photographic and video-graphic documentations are as important as other forms of data collection. Besides telling much about the culture under the lens, it also tells a great deal about the perspective and focus of the anthropologist filming or capturing the events. Such photographs also become a great tool for illustrating various cultural phenomenons in a classroom interaction. PCJ uses these techniques of illustration in his classrooms.

Visual techniques also become important in order to illustrate some intangible dimensions of culture. For example in one of the videos made on Oraons of Chotanagpur, PCJ tried to capture some rituals with all their elaborate practices. Words alone were not sufficient to bring home the point or to understand the significance of these rituals. Similarly, mundane looking events like children playing on the embankments or children socializing with their peers and parents when filmed can be later on analyzed for their significance.

Another dimension to his contribution to anthropology is in the form of his reflexive accounts of the disciplinary history in India and in the Department of Anthropology at DU. These reflexive accounts relate to emergence and consolidation of social anthropology in the DU Anthropology Department and the emergence of medical anthropology in India. It helps in locating the discipline, its emergence and ideological trajectories within the boundaries of a national tradition of practicing the discipline. It also shows a concern on the part of the author of such a form of writing about the disciplinary history, its achievements, limitations and one's own location within the entire matrix. For young anthropologists, such texts provide a source of attachment and at the same time give room for critical thinking on the disciplinary projects.

While writing on the emergence of anthropology and social anthropology in DU, PCJ argues that the department was formed only in 1947, much later than it was established in Bombay, Madras and Calcutta. The reason for such a delay is accorded to the fact that these were much important economic and political centres than Delhi during the British period. Interestingly he writes that behind the establishment of the department in DU it was non-other than the legendry B.S. Guha who played a key role in convincing the then Vice-Chancellor of the University. It is also interesting to note, writes PCJ, that in the post-independent period the department in DU collaborated more with American Anthropologists as many of them like Morris Opler, Robert Redfield, David Mandelbaum etc. visited the department but at a more ideological level it carries the legacy of British social anthropology. He attributes this influence to one of the founding figures in social anthropology in DU department, Mrs. Hilda Raj who was trained in anthropology from Cambridge University.

Similarly, tracing the advent of Medical Anthropology in India he goes back to one of the first articles on the subject published in 1923 by S.C. Mitra, a Social Anthropologist from Calcutta University. Such historical researches are important addition to the existing body of knowledge in the Indian context. He then turns towards historically tracing the teaching of medical anthropology in India. In this context he writes that as a separate discipline or paper Medical Anthropology started in mid 1970s for the first time in Poona University. He also recognized that India owing to its diversity of people and their philosophies is a rich ground for the development and practice of Medical Anthropology.

More recently, PCJ has shifted his focus towards creating an Indigenous anthropology informed more by the realities and theoretical paradigms relevant to the specific socio-political scenario in India. Anthropology has been criticized for being a Western discipline governed largely by the theories developed by Western scholars that are only applied in the South Asian and African contexts. Theories that looked more liberal of their times later came to be seen as being promoting the colonial agenda. Colonialism was not only an enterprise interested in lands but it was more interested in people. Western theories have produced a sort of 'academic colonization' where the mind is held captive by ideas generated in the West. Critical Anthropology, however, brings such issues to the discussion floor and tries to give ample space to the alternative ways of knowing realities. This alterity is actually based on the demolition of the establishment and has its own value system that resonates with the outliers, marginal, protesters and revolutionaries. Upholding such values in illuminating contemporary realities then becomes a new epistemology within a disciplinary practice. Within this context one can locate PCJ's interest in Gandhian values and ideas. Although Gandhian ideas are influenced by Western thoughts but still the kind of churning that those ideas went through in the specific socio-political and cultural landscape of India is something unique and worth noting. Relevance of Gandhi's ideas to illuminate Anthropological methodology and concept building then becomes an important disciplinary practice in itself.

Taking his cue from such an ideological and conceptual background,

PCJ is more recently writing on Gandhian notions of health and well-being and how these notions inform the theoretical paradigms of Critical Medical Anthropology. It was PCJ who came-up with the idea of doing a fieldwork at the Sewagram Ashram exploring the changing notions of Gandhian values on health as they are being practiced at the Ashram. I was then working at the Mahatma Gandhi Antarrashtriya Hindi Vishvavidyalaya, Wardha. He shared this idea with me. Thereafter, we jointly came up with a paper exploring the post-modern critique of modern medicine as envisaged within the Gandhian thoughts and other post-modern scholars like Foucault. He then moved on towards exploring the Gandhian notions about Sanitation and how they can be located within the discourses on colonialism, post-colonialism, nationalism and social structures of caste in the Indian context. In continuation to this, PCJ being the Head of the Anthropology Department at DU, organized a one day seminar on "Gandhi and Anthropology" on 150th birth anniversary of the Mahatma on October 2, 2019.

At a more practical level, anthropological interest in Gandhi can be seen as an effort towards doing 'Public Anthropology'. Ideas and icons that resonate at the national and international level becomes a rallying point for re-defining and re-formulating some fundamental questions within a discipline. Besides this, anthropological knowledge and essence is used to illuminate understanding of such ideas and icons. By doing this, anthropological framework shifts more towards the domain of the public discourse. Gandhi is more relevant in questioning basic anthropological ideal of 'otherness'. It is an attempt towards being 'emic' at the level of thoughts and paradigms.

Owing to his contributions in the field of Anthropology, PCJ has also been awarded with several honors and recognitions. He is the recipient of the Indira Priyadarshini Vriksha Mitra National Award for the year 1987. This award was conferred upon him or founder member of organization called 'The Friends of Trees' in recognition of his environment related work. In the year 2007, he received the Certificate of Honour conferred upon him jointly by the Delhi Psychiatry Society and Psychiatres—Du Monde, France. A plaque of appreciation was awarded to him by the Department of Sociology and Anthropology, Xavier University – Ateneo de Cagayan, Cagayan de Oro City, Philippines in 2008. Again in the year 2009, he was awarded with Certificate of Appreciation in the III National PG Convention of the Indian Association of Public Health Dentistry, K.D. Dental College and Hospital, Mathura. He also received a certificate of appreciation for his research on disaster impacts in Asia and Europe by the Faculty of Public Health, University of Indonesia in 2009. Besides these awards and appreciations, PCJ also has the honour of being a visiting faculty to some of the world's renowned universities like the University of Heidelberg, Germany, Global Forum for Health, Geneva, University of Hyderabad, India etc.

He has also contributed by submitting various research reports to the Ministry of Home Affairs, Government of India on the issues related to state's response and people's perception of relief during and after flood disasters, mainstreaming disaster risk reduction in corporate entities, mental health issues among women in post-disaster context, impacts of cyclone Aila on livelihoods of people in West Bengal and issues of long-term recovery after Gujarat earthquake. He also submitted a report to the Indian Council of Medical Research (ICMR) on the issue of Mental Health Service Needs in the context of earthquakes. Besides these he has also written several reports for the UGC-SAP (University Grants Commission, Special Assistance Programe), ICSSR (Indian Council for Social Science Research), ICMR, UGC etc.

Besides contributing on the academic front, he has immensely contributed towards administration and institution building. He has worked in the capacity of an adviser to many Government, Semi-Government, Non-Government and International Organizations. This includes organizations like the ICSSR, Ministry of Health and Family Welfare, Ministry of Tribal Affairs, State Mental Health Authority, Delhi, Apollo Hospital, Education and Research Foundation, World Health Organization Multi-centric anti-microbial use and resistance project etc. He was also the Asia coordinator of a European Union funded 6th Framework MICRODIS project. He has also worked in the capacity of expert member to various Board of Studies (BoS) in different Universities across India. As a member of the BoS, he has helped in formulating syllabus, reading material and reference material in Anthropology at various Central and State funded Universities.

PCJ at present is the President of the Society for Indian Medical Anthropology (SIMA). This is one of its kind organization working in the field of medical anthropology in India. PCJ while talking about the germination of idea to form SIMA says that the idea to form SIMA was germinated in Pune in 1978 when PCJ and Prof. H.K. Bhat were participating in post plenary session on medical anthropology at the X International Conference of Anthropological and Ethnological Sciences. Both of them were sharing a room in the conference so they had a chance to indulge in a lot of intense discussion. In fact, PCJ had a tape recorder with him and the whole conversation was tape recorded. In India, in 1978, tape recorders were not a very commonly used devise. The society was not registered until 1985. Initially it was started from Jawahar Lal Nehru University, New Delhi (JNU) with Dr. S.K. Sahu from Centre for Social Medicine and Community Health being the first General Secretary, PCJ being the President and Prof. Bhat being the executive member. SIMA Bulletin was also printed and released that was edited by PCJ. An account in the name of SIMA was opened in the JNU bank. Dr. Sahu had also organized a one day seminar in his centre under the aegis of SIMA. However, Dr. Sahu died very early in a train accident while he was coming from Odhisa by Purushottam Express and SIMA could not be formally registered. PCJ was in Garhwal, and therefore, was unable to get SIMA registered and so the idea of continuing with SIMA was dropped. It was later in 1993 that Prof. Bhat had established himself in Mysore after teaching in NEHU Shillong and having a dynamic team of students that the SIMA was registered in Mysore. SIMA is the only registered body of medical anthropologists in India.

It can be said that PCJ's contribution to the discipline is not only within the boundaries of the university lectures and academic publications but it extends to his entire approach towards the knowledge cosmology. Casual conversations with him can give you a very deep insight into the issue under discussion. A very mundane looking event can turn out to be an event of great anthropological importance. His biggest contribution to the discipline besides generating academic knowledge is in the form of generating human resources who get ample training under him to develop and practice an anthropological vision.

As an extension of his academic commitment to bring about a change in the society, he has been associated with various organizations working in the field of environment and health. He works as an adviser to the Himalayan Environmental Society and Conservation Organization, Dehradun and to Sri Bhuvaneshwari Mahila Ashram, Tehri. He is the founder member of the organization Friends of Trees in Garhwal. As already mentioned he also received awards for his contribution towards social service and promoting the cause of human and environmental dignity. As an educationist and an experienced practitioner of anthropology, he is also associated with the Kendriya Vidyalaya Sangathan (Central School Organization) as its nominated chairperson. He is extensively and intensively engaged in social work and welfare activities for the subaltern.

PCJ's work and contribution in the field of anthropology is

internationally recognized. His international collaborations are a testimonial to this fact. He has been engaged in research activities with the Catholic University of Louvain, Belgium and University of Heidelberg, Germany. He worked as a Co-Principal Investigator and India Team Leader on an international project mapping the mortality and injury risk factor in Tsunami in Tamil Nadu, India. This was a collaborative work with the United Nations and the Centre for Research in Epidemiology of Disasters (CRED), Belgium. He worked in collaboration with the Asian Disaster Reduction Centre, Kobe Japan funded research project on Indigenous Knowledge in Disaster Management, Lead Institution, SAARC Disaster Management Centre, New Delhi and with Global Forum for Disaster Reduction, Mumbai in International Platform for Recovery, Kobe Japan funded research project on Status of Recovery in Gujarat Earthquake.

Besides collaborating in international research projects, PCJ has also contributed and is still contributing towards shared knowledge generation at the international level by sharing his expertise and research with some leading universities in the world as visiting faculty to these institutions. He was a visiting lecturer at the Department of Tropical Hygiene and Public Health, University of Heidelberg, Germany. He visited Hanoi, Vietnam to deliver lectures in Hanoi School of Public Health on participatory and Qualitative Research Methods. He represented India at the Asian Youth Leader Forum Pyeongtaek, Korea. He participated in United Nations framework Climate Change Conference (COP 14) as a delegate of European Union at Poznan, Poland.

PCJ has heading the Department of Anthropology, University of Delhi. Under his headship, the Department engaged in academic activities like seminars, conferences, academic discussions, talks, and workshops. He promoted new dimensions in anthropological research like visual anthropology, anthropological visions of Mahatma Gandhi, and mapping the cultural montage of the Indian subcontinent. Very recently, the Department organized a training workshop on 'Child Rights'. This was organized in commemoration of the 30th anniversary of the adoption of the Convention on the Rights of the Child by the United Nations. Under his headship, the Department also organized brainstorming sessions on Draft National Education Policy, and a course on Ethnographic Film Making. He also organized various special lectures in the Department on topics, like Water and Land in North Bihar: An Ontology delivered by Dr. Louisa Cortesi, Cornell University, Is it God Speaking? Identity and Agency of Deities in the Western Himalayas by Dr. Asaf Sharabi from

School of Behavioural Sciences, Peres Academic Centre, Israel and Relational Perceptions of the Psyche: Psychology, History, Anthropology by Prof. Youval Rotman of the Department of Jewish History, Tel Aviv University. He was also actively engaged with the activities of the SIMA and promoting research and teaching of Medical Anthropology in India and abroad.

Students who did Ph.D. under him are now placed in various fields ranging from academics to administration. Dr. Beena Saklani is working as a Professor of Medical Anthropology at the HNB University, Garhwal, Uttarakhand. Dr. Urfat Anjem Mir and Dr. Oinam Hemlata are employed as Assistant Professors in the Ambedkar University, Delhi. Dr. Sonia Kaushal and B.S. Aribam are working as Assistant Professor at H.S. Gaur University, Sagar, Madhya Pradesh. Dr. Kalindi Sharma is working as Assistant Professor at the Amity University, Delhi and Dr. Sandeep Kumar is working as a Rural Development Officer with the Bihar Government.

He superannarated from University of Delhi as its Pro Vice-Chancellor and Acting Vice-Chancellor between 2020-21. Post-retirement PCJ is continuing his present works related to research, teaching and learning. He is engaged in writing books and publishing in various journals and propagating the ideas that he holds close to his heart.

41

The Inner and Outer Selves

A Bio Sketch of an Anthropologist Subhadra Mitra Channa

Rukshana Zaman

Subhadra Mitra Channa, an anthropologist is known for her unsurpassable spirit and a humane nature. She served as a Professor of Anthropology, in the Department of Anthropology, at the University of Delhi till the year 2016. Born on 6th October, 1951, Subhadra's role model in the formative years was her mother Basanti Mitra, a graduate from St. Stephen's College. Her mother's graduation warrants a reference, as she was one among the three girls who graduated that year, a time when educating the girl child was not in vogue. She recalled her mother narrating that the Principal of Queen Mary's School had gone door to door appealing parents to enroll their daughters in the school. Basanti Mitra was one of the first students of the school. Walking in her mother's footsteps Subhadra completed her eleventh from Queen Mary's school and joined B.Sc. Honours in Physics at Hindu College. While pursuing her B.Sc. Honours in Physics, Subhadra realized that the theories of quantum was not her cup of tea. She found it very dry as she was more interested in literature and writing. At this critical juncture when she was at the crossroads, her father Biswanath Mitra, a professor of English Literature in Hindu College, renowned for his teaching of Shakespeare, initiated her to the anthropological works. Borrowing from her father's personal collection she read Frazer's *Golden Bough*, Tylor's *Anthropology* in two volumes and Hoebel's *Anthropology: The Study of Man*. Some of these books are still her prized possession. These readings were a turning point in her life and thus, began her love and journey in anthropology.

In the year 1970 Subhadra joined the Department of Anthropology as a masters student. She had an aptitude for physical anthropology.

Having topped the first semester her teachers Dr. Abhimanyu Sharma and Professor Indera P. Singh encouraged her to pursue a career in physical anthropology. However, she was drawn towards Professor Jai Dayal Mehra's teachings. Speaking about Mehra's classes she had once stated that during the course of the lectures he used to take the students to another realm. She was attracted to social anthropology because it provided engrossing reading material and was close to literature and satisfied her love for writing. Drawn towards social and environmental causes from an early age, she was convinced that it was the knowledge of social anthropology that would help her take forward the cause of mobilizing human beings towards co-existing in harmony with nature. Her first interest was in economic anthropology as it was structured and well suited her science background. Later, along with Prof. Vardesh Channa, she worked towards introducing ecological anthropology in the Department of Anthropology at Delhi University. This was among the first Universities to have a paper on Ecology. Later this interest in ecology developed into a passion for environmental issues and she also taught for many years in the School for Environmental Studies in Delhi University. In later years many of her students too followed in her footsteps and worked on environmental issues. Her interest in economic anthropology and in-depth readings of Raymond Firth, Maurice Godelier, Karl Polanyi and others were reflected in her seminal doctoral work on the *Dhobi* (washerman) community of Delhi who belong to the Old city of Delhi, traditionally washing clothes on the banks of the river Yamuna.

Professor Vardesh Chander Channa, her husband, introduced her to the *Dhobi* community. For a young mother with a one-year old child and a family to look after, it was challenging to conduct fieldwork. At times for documentation of rituals and ceremonies like marriage, *jagaran* (religious functions where people sing *bhajans* till early morning), etc. she had to spend the entire night in the field. Her husband accompanied her on such occasions. He was her pillar of strength during the tenure of her fieldwork from 1974-1978. The *katras* (cluster of dhobi houses) became her second home during her fieldwork days. The grit determination she showed to finish her doctoral work amidst hurdles became inspiration for many. Juthika Sen was one such student of hers. A contemporary of Subhadra, Sen completed her Ph.D. under Subhadra's supervision after a long hiatus from academics, owing to personnel reasons. One of her Ph.D. scholar's son's addresses Subhadra as "Nani Ma'am", (grand-mother) as she become a support and created a bond with her students, who were trying to juggle work and family.

Reminiscing about her days as a student of Professor Jai Dayal

Mehra she had stated that working under him was nothing short of trying to conquer Mount Everest. Drafts of the research work would fly out to the corridor once submitted with the words "utter rotten nonsense". A fate that was meted out to each of his students' manuscript that they had meticulously worked on. Subhadra had stated that Mehra's critical sagacity had given her the incitement to look at things from different perspectives. Her first article was published in *Man in India*. The article having met with the same fate of being reduced to scrap by her supervisor, it would have never seen the light of the day had her husband not encouraged her to send it to the publishers for a feedback.

Subhadra fondly recalls that the teachers at the Department were devoted teachers, spending little time on getting accolades for themselves, but were rigorous in taking classes and teaching the students. A quality that she imbibed from her teachers, yet at the same time worked on publishing papers, chapters in books, articles in journals, along with attending seminars and conferences. Teaching as an *ad hoc* lecturer in the department from 1978-79 she worked on writing, analyzing and interpreting her thesis. The thesis was submitted to the department in 1980. The doctorate degree, however, was conferred in 1982, owing to a delay from one of the external examiners from US. "I went to collect my degree with a baby bum, as I was expecting my second child", she had laughingly shared once during a conversation.

Subhadra had once stated that her academic life has been shaped by the international community. Recipient of numerous international fellowships and awards she had subsumed the international standards. During her days as a Charles Wallace Visiting Fellow in Anthropology for three months to Queens' University, U.K. from February–May 2000 she had stated that it was her first experience of working on a computer. This statement was utterly unbelievable for me, as during my student years' I had seen her fingers flying on the computer keyboard while typing our progress reports. Her zeal and jest to learn and acquaint herself to new ideas, technologies have been the mantra to her success. Even as a teacher she never gave up on opportunities to learn from her senior teachers. Many a times she had reflected on Professor Bhandari and his fieldwork techniques. She would quote him as a fine example of a fieldworker whose favourite haunt would be the local tea shop in the field. As a student I remember her class on Kinship, while teaching us the web of kinship relations she would create patterns with her hands, and this remained with me and my classmates for ever. The web of kinship relations became easier for us to comprehend, as we would relate it to her hand gestures and patterns. We could feel her heart and soul in her lectures, that it was always mesmerising us.

The traits of being meticulous and perfectionist she had incorporated from the British scholars she met during her stay in Queen's University Belfast. Subhadra had also spent a great amount of time in the United States of America at various points of time. As a Fulbright Lecturer to U.S.A. for one teaching semester, August –December, 2003 she taught one semester of Women's Studies and also Anthropological Theory at Auburn University, Alabama. She was a Fulbright Scholar-in-Residence (Visiting Professor) to University of South Carolina, U.S.A from 15th August, 2008 to 15th May, 2009. A visiting scholar to the University of Kentucky, Lexington, U.S.A. from August –November 2012. She was a nominated Fellow of the Society for Applied Anthropology, U.S.A. Besides the fellowships and the Visiting Professorships, she presented papers and participated in discussions based on invitations from foreign countries. On the invitation of the French Government she was a visiting Professor to *Maison Des Sciences De L'Homme*, Paris from March- April 2004. She was invited by the Japanese Government in September 2002 as a visiting scholar to Kyoto University for presenting a paper at the symposium, "Is Race an Universal Idea?"

These fellowships had nurtured the academician in her and inspired her in critical thinking that has been reflected in her writings. She states that she owes these levels of seriousness towards her work to all her interactions with the international academic community. Introduction to critical thinking and being attuned to current trends came from her US scholarships. Joan Mencher's work on looking at caste from bottom up, inspired her even during the course of thesis work. Critical approach, critical historiography were some of the areas that she came face to face during her scholarships. Her interaction with African American scholars and those from the marginalized regions of the world, stirred her attention towards marginalization and gender issues. Such inspiration allowed her to revisit her own fieldwork data on the *Dhobis.* Subhadra analyzed and reanalyzed much of her data that had not been presented in the thesis. She offered critical insights from gender perspectives on the life of the *dhobis* in her future works.

In the years to come she was reckoned as one of the leading figures in the study of marginalization and gender issues. Her seminal writings like *Inner and Outer Selves: A Study of Gender, Cosmology and Ecology on the Himalayan Borders*, *Gender, Livelihood and Environment*, *Gender in South Asia: Social Imagination and Constructed Realities*, *Gendering Material Culture* (co-edited), *Life as a Dalit: Discrimination in Everyday Life in India* (co-edited), *Tribes and Government Policies* (co-edited), *Understanding Society, Culture and Change, Nagaland: A Contemporary Ethnography* (edited) were works that involved not only fieldwork but also a critical thinking and understanding of society being looked at from the perspective of those on the margins, including the lower castes, tribes and women.

For Subhadra attending her first International Union of Anthropological and Ethnological Sciences (IUAES) conference in USA at Virginia, William and Mary College, in 1998 was a memorable event as she met Faye V. Harrison, who is now her lifelong friend.The year 2001 Subhadra reckons as a turning point in her academic life. With Ford Foundation sponsorship to read a paper on "Metaphors of Race and Caste based Discriminations against Dalits and Dalit women in India" she went to Durban to attend the 'World Conference Against Racism held in Durban Conference. This was one platform where she met other feminist scholars and Dalit activists including Faye and Helen Safa. Recognition of her work in the area of marginalized groups and gender issues was reflected when she was elected the Co-Chair of the Commission on the Anthropology of Women of the IUAES, from 2003 -2008. She became the elected Chair of this honoured body in the Congress in Kunming, China in 2009 and continued till 2013. She delivered a Key Note Address at the Major Congress of the IUAES in Kunming China, representing entire South Asia, which was one of the largest anthropological conferences with more than 5000 delegates. Subhadra was elected Vice-President of the International Union of Anthropological and Ethnological Sciences (IUAES) in July 2013. Presently she is serving as elected Senior Vice-President of the International Union of Anthropological and Ethnological Sciences (IUAES) since July 2018. She is also a member of the Steering Committee of the World Anthropological Union (WAU).

At present, along with her lifetime friend and colleague, Faye V. Harrison, she chairs the Commission on Marginalization and Global Apartheid, that both of them founded. Through this Commission, a large number of similar minded scholars are coming together on a platform to discuss and carry on debates on issues of gender, feminism, global racism, populism and issues that people all across the globe are facing.

Today Subhadra, is known for her works on Feminism and Identities and more specifically of Selves and Bodies; and has been published in many anthologies and Encyclopaedias including the Encyclopaedia of Anthropology edited by Helen Calan that came out in 2018, and carries the writings of most well known anthropologists of the world, and she is one of them. Her paper on Selves and Codified bodies appears in the Companion to Contemporary Anthropology published by Routledge. Her works have been translated into Polish, Japanese, French, Portuguese, Spanish and other languages and she is one of the most recognised names in international anthropology from India.

The list would go on and on if I start writing about each and every contribution of Subhadra. Herein, am presenting a brief sketch. She was the President of the Indian Anthropological Association from 1997-2000. She has been visiting professors to many Indian Universities, to some of them for several times. She has been an active presence at many conferences and evaluated numerous Ph.D. theses, and been associated with several universities in variety of ways. At Calcutta University she took a course on Human Rights from 2001 onwards for many years. In the year 2011, the Asiatic Society of India conferred her with the Sarat Chandra Roy Gold Medal for life time contribution to Cultural Anthropology.

She has been actively serving on many governing bodies and school boards and contributed to the growth and development of many national level institutions, such as the Indira Gandhi Rashtriya Manav Sanghrahalaya, where she has been associated in various capacities and also contributed towards writing a catalogue.

During the year 2000 when I joined M.Sc. in the Anthropology Department at the University of Delhi I first heard about Subhadra Mitra Channa from my seniors. That was the era when internet was just coming of age and our seniors tended to be the most reliable source for information. Subhadra had just completed her tenure as a Charles Wallace Fellow in Queen's University Belfast and returned to the department. At that juncture she was the most talked about eminent anthropologists and her scholars who were working under her supervision proudly spoke about her achievements. My seniors had described her as a well acclaimed and celebrated anthropologists, with a sweet smile,.but as a tough nut to crack. The later part of the statement I could relate to in the years to come, during my own research work, under her supervision and numerous interactions we had in the Expert Committee meetings for Indira Gandhi National Open University while designing the curriculum. However, I have also felt her warmth every time she calls me up, if we are not in touch for a few days, or updates me about her travel plans so that I can plan Expert Committee Meetings or other academic work accordingly, that it doesn't hamper my work or whenever I visit her she prepares meals for me especially fish.

For a career spanning from 1992 when she joined as an associate professor in the department till her retirement in 2016 as a Professor, Subhadra had supervised numerous M.Phil. and doctoral works. Students under her supervision had worked on all imaginable dimensions of social anthropology. Keeping with the trends and change that mars the everchanging societies, her foresight, impeccable understanding, critical thinking and perfectionism is reflected in the topics that her students had worked on. Her first research scholar was Mamta Misra from Odisa, her work presented an interesting insight into the lives of the Langia Sauras. Achan Mulung working on her own community had been able to provide an insight to the struggle of her people, trying to get recognition as a Tribe under her supervision. Achan's home town in the Manipur-Nagaland Border is a place that takes almost three days to reach her village from Kohima. In her work Achan, had mapped the entire genealogy of her Tribe. Subhadra, inspired her to continue her work under all adverse conditions and remains one of her best friends and supporters. Achan's dedicated work under the supervision of Subhadra was rewarded when the tribe was recognized as a separate entity in the year 2000. Achan is now working for the cause of the Burmese refugees and remains in constant touch with her supervisor. Anung Lima Longkumer had also worked on Naga identity. Meenakshi Munda, now better known as a tribal activist is another of her student who is globally recognized for her work on the welfare of tribes. Her work on Religion and Identity of the Sarna Oraons of Jharkhand looked at the issues faced by the Sarna Oraons. Subhadra remains involved with the work that is being done by her students and is always in support of the persons like Meenakshi Munda and others. Mary Panmei worked on "Customary Law and Gender Relations among the Rongmei Tribe of Manipur". Sudeep Ghosh had worked on Women in Panchayati Raj. I write this with a sad note as he passed away, while I was working on this write-up. Antu Saha, one of her international student's worked on Indo-Bangla border and migration. Aiman under Subhadra's guidance worked among the Kinnaurese of Mohrang Tehsil in Himachal Pradesh. Subhadra in many of her conversations likes to cite Aiman's example as a fieldworker, a person hailing from Lucknow carrying out his fieldwork in Himachal Pradesh. Aiman is now engaged in teaching anthropology in Shia College, Lucknow. Ujjal Sarma another of her student from Assam had worked on bio diversity and the Kaziranga National Park in Assam. Ujjal now teaches in the National Institute of Forest Management in Bhopal. While I worked on, Odissi Dance and the construction of the Oriya identity. Nutan Maurya had looked at the environmental impact of the Kumbh Mela. Taking the concerns of environment and health forward one of her students have also worked on the farmers of Punjab who were using genetically engineered seeds.

Saakshi Joshi critically looked at the aftermath of the Tehri dam in her work *Belonging to New Tehri: An anthropological study of the oustees of the Tehri dam*. While her student Kalyani Sahal looked at *Water and Mining: An Anthropological Study of Khetri Copper mine in Jhunjhunu district, Rajasthan*. Pushpendra looked at the Hanji community of Kashmir in his work the *An Anthropological study of the Social Structure in Kashmir with a focus on the Houseboat- Hanji community*.

Subhadra's passion and commitment towards gender issues was taken forward by her student Gunjan Arora who worked on *Body, Gender and Social Space: An Anthropological Study of Working Women's Health and Social Adaptation in Delhi*. Priyanka Adhikary focused on understanding the role of NGOs and how they interact with women victims of gender-based violence in her work *Beneath the Surface: An Anthropological Study of Interactions between NGO Professionals and Women Victims of Gender-Based Violence in Delhi*. While, Anu Bhawana worked on the *Approaches to the health seeking behaviour of Bihari Migrant Labourers in Delhi*. Anupama AR's work on performance and protest *The People's Art as a Means of Protest and Discourse on the Political Theatre in Kerala* leaves a mark on the wide range of topics that Subhadra had guided her students to research on.

Her commitment towards her students is not only acknowledged by her students when they describe her as a mother 'she is my eternal mother who has given me the unconditional love in every possible way' by Anu Bhawana, Anupama A.R prefers to describe her mentor through a quote: *'A great man shows his greatness by the way he treats little men'*, Pushpendra enthused that 'Channa Ma'am had been the most kind, empathetic and helpful teacher throughout my academic career'.From being a friend to her students, with whom she would go for the occasional movie during her early days to the time her students reckon her as a mother Prof. Channa has come a long way. Recognition of her aptitude and attitude towards teaching and learning came when the University of Delhi conferred on her *The Distinguished Teacher Award of Delhi University* as the best serving teacher in 2016 taking into account the years she dedicated to teaching, the quality of her publications and the numerous accolades she has won on behalf of Delhi University.

Subhadra is committed wholeheartedly to academic theories and is at the same time a staunch advocate of critical thinking. Her knowledge and scholarship finds reflection in her numerous works. An activist in her own right, her unconditional support to the cause of women rights, Dalits and the marginalized section of the society is unparallel. Subhadra had taken up these causes at all platforms available to her, through her lectures and writings.

Index